Realism

Realism

Aesthetics, Experiments, Politics

Edited by
Jens Elze

BLOOMSBURY ACADEMIC
NEW YORK • LONDON • OXFORD • NEW DELHI • SYDNEY

BLOOMSBURY ACADEMIC
Bloomsbury Publishing Inc
1385 Broadway, New York, NY 10018, USA
50 Bedford Square, London, WC1B 3DP, UK
29 Earlsfort Terrace, Dublin 2, Ireland

BLOOMSBURY, BLOOMSBURY ACADEMIC and the Diana logo are trademarks of
Bloomsbury Publishing Plc

First published in the United States of America 2022
This paperback edition published 2023

Copyright © Jens Elze, 2022

Each chapter © of Contributors

For legal purposes the Acknowledgments on p. viii constitute an extension of this copyright page.

Cover design: Eleanor Rose
Cover image: Stuart Mayo / 500px / Getty Images

All rights reserved. No part of this publication may be reproduced or transmitted in any form or by any means, electronic or mechanical, including photocopying, recording, or any information storage or retrieval system, without prior permission in writing from the publishers.

Bloomsbury Publishing Inc does not have any control over, or responsibility for, any third-party websites referred to or in this book. All internet addresses given in this book were correct at the time of going to press. The author and publisher regret any inconvenience caused if addresses have changed or sites have ceased to exist, but can accept no responsibility for any such changes.

Library of Congress Cataloging-in-Publication Data

Names: Elze, Jens, editor.
Title: Realism : aesthetics, experiments, politics / edited by Jens Elze.
Description: New York : Bloomsbury Academic, 2022. | Includes bibliographical references and index.
Identifiers: LCCN 2021052937 (print) | LCCN 2021052938 (ebook) | ISBN 9781501385483 (hardback) | ISBN 9781501385520 (paperback) | ISBN 9781501385490 (epub) | ISBN 9781501385506 (pdf) | ISBN 9781501385513
Subjects: LCSH: Realism in literature. | Political realism.
Classification: LCC PN56.R3 R355 2022 (print) | LCC PN56.R3 (ebook) | DDC 809/.912–dc23/eng/20220113
LC record available at https://lccn.loc.gov/2021052937
LC ebook record available at https://lccn.loc.gov/2021052938

ISBN: HB: 978-1-5013-8548-3
PB: 978-1-5013-8552-0
ePDF: 978-1-5013-8550-6
eBook: 978-1-5013-8549-0

Typeset by Deanta Global Publishing Services, Chennai, India

To find out more about our authors and books visit www.bloomsbury.com and sign up for our newsletters.

CONTENTS

List of Figures vii
Acknowledgments viii

Introduction: Realism, Political Aesthetics, and (New) Materialism   *Jens Elze*   1

PART I Aesthetics 27

1. Uses of "Realism": A Term in History and the History of a Term   *Andreas Mahler*   29

2. George Eliot's Realisms   *Nadine Böhm-Schnitker*   41

3. Medical Realisms and the Magic of Reality: Art and Insight in Thomas Hardy's *The Woodlanders* and Émile Zola's *Le docteur Pascal*   *Maren Scheurer*   60

4. Conrad on Epidemics: From *The Shadow-Line* to Covid-19 (and Back)   *Nidesh Lawtoo*   81

PART II Experiments 105

5. "Should I Call It Horror?": Reflecting Realism by Exploring Contingency in Ror Wolf's Adventure Series *Pilzer und Pelzer*   *Barbara Bausch*   107

6. Trawling Truth: B. S. Johnson's Evacuation of Realist Epistemology   *André Otto*   132

7. Cultural Realism: Reconsidering Magical Realism in Louise Erdrich's *Love Medicine*   *Nasrin Babakhani*   153

8. Narrative as Realistic Thinking   *Kai Wiegandt*   169

PART III Politics 189

9   Realism for Sustainability   *Caroline Levine*   191

10   Network Realism/Capitalist Realism   *Dirk Wiemann*   209

11   Postcolonial Realism and Rohinton Mistry's *Family Matters*   *Eli Park Sorensen*   228

12   Settler-Colonial Realism: Naturalizing and Denaturalizing the Frontier   *Hamish Dalley*   248

Notes on Contributors 269
Index 273

FIGURES

1.1 La rencontre ou "Bonjour, Monsieur Courbet" (The Meeting or "Bonjour, Monsieur Courbet") by Gustave Courbet, 1854 30
6.1 Typeset as it appears on the opening page of *Trawl* 140

ACKNOWLEDGMENTS

This volume has been developed out of the "Realisms" workshop, which was held at Georg-August-Universität, Göttingen in July 2018. I would like to thank the people involved in making this conference a success, above all my co-organizer Nasrin Babakhani and our student assistant Avrina Jos. A generous funding from the *Universitätsbund Göttingen* made this conference possible. The Graduate School for the Humanities, Göttingen, generously provided the rooms and technology for this workshop. Many of the ideas collected in the chapters of this volume would not have been possible without the intense discussions at that workshop. Therefore, I must also express my indebtedness to those participants of the workshops, who have not contributed to this volume, but whose ideas and thoughts reverberate on many of its pages: Maggie Ann Bowers, Thomas Clavier, Jan Lietz, and Pam Morris.

For the production of this volume I would like to thank the editors and assistants at Bloomsbury, most notably Amy Martin, who promptly and patiently responded to my many inquiries and who was a constant source of support throughout. I'd also like to acknowledge Catherine Cocks at Michigan State University Press who generously agreed to let us reuse sections from Nidesh Lawtoo's book *Conrad's Shadow: Catastrophe, Mimesis, Theory* for this volume. Regarding my own writing and editing process, I am very indebted to Eike Kronshage for his critical reading of the introduction that greatly helped me with polishing the text. Finally, I wish to acknowledge the three anonymous readers that offered valuable perspectives on the project during the proposal stage, which helped to steer the book into the more concise and fruitful direction that it has hopefully taken.

Chapter 4, "Conrad on Epidemics: From *The Shadow-Line* to Covid-19 (and Back)" by Nidesh Lawtoo: This project has received funding from the European Research Council (ERC) under the European Union's Horizon 2020 research and innovation programme (grant agreement n°716181; HOM: Theory and Criticism).

Introduction

Realism, Political Aesthetics, and (New) Materialism

Jens Elze

After a few decades in which New Criticism, postmodernism, and postcolonialism in different ways fostered an "impatient and apathetic attitude to realism,"[1] since the mid-2000s realism has made a spectacular comeback that brought it renewed attention and legitimacy in the wider field of literary and cultural studies.[2] Broadly speaking, this realist turn has been driven by an impulse to complicate widely circulating denigrations of realism that have depicted it as a naively representational "formal underachiever" or even as a deceptive "concoction programme"[3] for bourgeois norms and modern power.[4] Challenging such negative and monolithic assumptions, scholars ventured beyond the corpus of the nineteenth century to highlight "realism's centuries-long plurality and vitality."[5] These recent attempts to restore realism to aesthetic and political relevance, find their precursors, among others, in Roman Jakobson, who had long ago argued that realism's vitality relied on continuous innovation, because it needed permanently to renew the formulas that will otherwise quickly blunt art's access to reality.[6] Similarly, George Levine had conceived of realism as a permanent escape from the conventions of language and literary form to enable new expressions and perceptions of reality.[7] Levine and Jakobson—among others—had already prepared realism studies for the relative "loosening of formal requirements" that now helps scholars to account for "new realisms" and to draw texts into the realism debate that would so far have been outside of it, sometimes at the risk of blurring realism as a mode of writing and realism as a method of "reading for reality."[8] Insofar, the realist turn not only meant that "realism is back on the critical agenda" as a literary mode to be analyzed. It also coincided with a broader reorientation for literary and cultural studies who after years of critically foregrounding literature's resistance to reality—and the postmodern world's general unreality—no longer assumed that "nothing was real," but that "Now—everything is."[9] In this climate, Jed Esty felt confident that it "no longer goes without saying that a realist text written in the twenty-first century is somehow vestigial with regard to the dominant strains of late modernist or magical realist aesthetics."[10] Nonetheless, realism's critical revaluation is still often enough paralleled by invidious comparisons that oppose "realism" to more experimental forms of literature and that focus on realism's representational, ideological, and epistemological limitations, like Pieter Vermeulen's recent claim that the realist novel cannot tackle the realities of climate change:[11] a questionable charge that I will get back to later and that will be strongly contradicted by two of the contributions to this volume (Lawtoo and Levine).

Three main concerns underlie the organization of this volume: A first set of chapters questions the widespread assumption of a simplistic and consensual representationalism of nineteenth-century realism in favor of more worldly and dissensual accounts of realism's *aesthetics* that will help to complicate the "familiar narrative of realism as a subordination to convention."[12] Secondly, some contributions to this volume discuss how realism not only is challenged but also remains a central reference point for more evidently *experimental* literatures of the twentieth century. Looking at such ostensibly non-realistic texts from the perspective of realism—assuming "realism" as a method of "reading for reality"[13]—can help to question the problematic distinction between (servile) realism and (heroic) literary experiment: a distinction that for decades has fostered pervasive anti-realist academic ideologies that have prevented more complex engagements with realism and its aesthetic and political possibilities. Thirdly, the volume looks at the *politics* that realism has to offer especially in response to the contemporary world of capitalist globalization and climate emergency. While the chapters and the works treated in them follow a rough chronology, this is not an argument about literary evolution—or about the "rise and fall" and return of realism—in the first place. Rather, it is to reorient our assumptions about realism and the debates it has inspired across the board.

Before going into more detail concerning the arc of the volume, the introduction will lay the groundwork for a more dissensual understanding of realism that holds the chapters together. Afterward, I will link such a revamped notion of realism and the contemporary valorization of realism to the recent prominence of new materialism and actor-network theory (ANT) and to some of the theoretical reorientations that these methods have inspired in literary studies. I will conclude these reflections by thinking about how realism in various ways can be central to political conceptions of world literature.

Realism's Political Aesthetics

An indispensable reference point for any account of realism remains Erich Auerbach's *Mimesis*. Quite famously, Auerbach finds in the nineteenth-century novel a perfection of mimesis, because it begins to treat even the most squalid forms of existence—previously at best confined to comedy and satire—in detail and with seriousness and even considered them as possible sources of knowledge.[14] In this vertical extension of the purview of serious mimesis, begun with the bourgeois novel and bourgeois tragedy in the eighteenth century, nineteenth-century realism also crucially embedded mundane objects and people into the "general course of contemporary history."[15] As important as Auerbach's work is, however, I suggest that it is best to understand realism not primarily as a gradual perfection and extension of mimesis and representation, but as a more radical departure from previous regimes of literature and their vertical and hierarchical modes of integrating (conceptions of) reality into literature toward a more horizontal vision of literature, reality, and politics.

To grasp how nineteenth-century realism can be understood to inaugurate a radical project of literary and political aesthetics, I turn to the work of Jacques Rancière. For Rancière, the nineteenth century witnessed not a perfection of the process of representation, but a complete transformation of the role of art and its relation to reality and to politics; one that he explicitly frames in distinction to the task of "representation," as he understands it. Prior to the nineteenth century, according to Rancière, art was committed to what he calls the "representative regime."[16] In this regime, art was defined as a specific form of activity and its foremost task was to represent "an orderly world governed by a hierarchy of subject matter and the adaptation of situations and manners of speaking to this hierarchy."[17] Representative arts were central to the political task of a "distribution of the sensible" and thereby re-articulated and artistically strengthened the dominant classifications and stratifications of society: "The representative primacy of action over characters, of narration over description, the hierarchy of genres according to the dignity of their subject matter . . . figure into an analogy with a fully hierarchical vision of the community."[18] Following the political revolutions of the eighteenth century—though not simply embracing their republican politics—the nineteenth century also saw the emergence of a perpetually revolutionary and democratic regime of art, which Rancière calls the "aesthetic regime." Whereas the representative regime of literature was geared toward fabricating "consensus" with existing norms through the ways in which its *aestheticization of politics* legitimated and distributed what was visible and invisible, proper and improper, and ordered the multiplicities of reality into narrative patterns, the aesthetic regime of literature was geared toward creating "dissensus."[19] It inaugurated a resistant *political aesthetics* attuned to a permanent "redistribution of the sensible"[20] that sought to render visible what had been deemed improper and invisible in previous forms of mimesis. In order to achieve that, the aesthetic regime of literature thrived on and strongly relied on the *autonomy of art* from dominant conceptions and representations of reality. But Rancière makes clear that this autonomy of art is not to be confused with an "anti-communicational use of language,"[21] "the refusal of figurative representation,"[22] or with "arts concentration . . . on its own materiality"[23]—in short: with anti-realism. Positing the aesthetic regime against representation does not mean for Rancière to posit it against an interest in reality or against realism. Quite the contrary, he confirms that the aesthetic regime's "inaugural moment has often been called *realism*."[24] By tying realism's emergence to the "redistribution of the sensible,"—to the "causing something to be seen and heard"[25]—Rancière suggests that the "representations" of reality that realism is interested in must always exceed what has been consensual about reality: the political aesthetics of realism always question the vertical hierarchies that restrict what counts as reality in favor of more inclusive, egalitarian, and horizontal versions of reality that include subjects, relations, and things hitherto excluded from the realm of representation and visibility. This view of realism is radically different from routine caricatures of realism that accuse it at best of epistemological and aesthetic naivety because it allegedly "assumes a fundamentally unproblematic relationship between reality and its representations,"[26] and at worst oppose it as an irredeemably ideological "tool for naturalizing a particular worldview"[27] that was "plausible not because it reflects the world, but because it is constructed out of what is (discursively) familiar."[28] Quite the opposite, Rancière argues that rather than relying on and reproducing familiar representations of reality, realism has inaugurated an aesthetic regime of literature that "does not in any way mean the valorization of resemblance but rather the destruction of the structures within which it functioned."[29] By sensitizing readers for the mundane, by emphasizing the devastated lifeworlds of the marginal, and by showing "the breathing of things freed from the empire of meanings,"[30] realism was not a "strategy to keep under control . . . disruptive possibilities,"[31] but rather initiated a permanent questioning of regimes of classification and representation: "novelistic realism is first of all the reversal of the hierarchies of representation . . . or the hierarchy of subject matter."[32] Whether in Balzac's complex relations of production or Dickens's abject social worlds, in Eliot's unexplored mundane emotions and routines or Flaubert's superfluous objects, realism has often focused on the *in*credible and the *im*proper realms of reality that have been excluded from prior representation and whose literary life helps to aesthetically shift our perception toward the margins of what has been deemed meaningful, legible, and legitimate in society and art. While realism is thus deeply committed to reality, it cannot from this perspective be charged—as will be clear by now through its problematic relation to "representation" and "resemblance"— as operating with a simplistic and ideologically dubious reflectionism.

Rather, realism as a political aesthetics, only makes visible and sensible as if for the first time—and insofar only projects and constructs—relations, thoughts, people, or things that have not existed in prior versions of reality. This notion of realism clearly unsettles the polarity between representation and invention, reflection and construction, or poeisis and mimesis, in which realism is often logged in as the lesser term of these hierarchical binaries.

Realism, then, is absolutely about making reality readable and sensible, but not in the tired sense of "reproducing facts,"[33] transparency, consensus, resemblance, or easy readability that representational understandings of realism—especially as formulated by its detractors—often assume, that equal all realism to the easy pleasures of plot driven and "life-like" airport literature and the ideological work they perform in naturalizing familiar visions of reality.[34] The problem with such assumptions is not only that transparency is dependent on conventions and codes as Barthes has famously observed in *S/Z*;[35] codes that will change over time and with cultures, as Ulka Anjaria has demonstrated in her *Realism in the 20th Century Indian Novel* and Nasrin Babakhani will make clear in her conception of magical realism as cultural realism in this volume. Rather, realism *is not even about* projecting an easily readable and consensual notion of reality. First of all, while it is true, as Andreas Mahler argues in the first chapter of this volume, that realism often effaces the process of its making in order to simulate the illusion of an unmediated access to reality, many realist texts also betray an astute awareness of the difficulty of constructing reality in the codes of language and literature. Even—perhaps especially—in its canonical origins, as in George Eliot's *Adam Bede* (1859), realist novels are often surprisingly open about their own constructedness and perspective and about literature's limitations at capturing reality, as in Eliot's narrator's acknowledgment that "the mirror" of the world that is his writing "is always defective; the outlines will sometimes be disturbed; the reflection faint or confused."[36]

Secondly, and more importantly, realism is not about affirming one consensual image of the world, but about challenging and redistributing existing notions of the sensible and the visible. Realism, thus, is not only devoted to polyphony, which has been important to nuanced discussions of realism since Bakhtin coined the term in the context of Dostoyevsky to denote the modern novel's aesthetic commitment to ambiguity and multi-perspectivity. It is also fundamentally about *defamiliarization* (an often forgotten element of realism that Caroline Levine will also return to in the present volume): about introducing practices, people, relations, and objects into our perception of reality that have previously eluded it. Realism, then, is not only an epistemological mode or style—alternatively marked by empiricism or synthesis, narration or description, by pseudoethnographic observation or totalization—but also works with changing political and even ontological assumptions about the contours of reality, confirming George Levine's claim that "realism exists as a process, responsive to the changing nature of reality."[37] The style and the politics of realism, then, may differ dramatically with what is counted in a work as vital for a particular vision of reality: from global relations of capital to the life of social classes and cultural groups to psychological states and physical sensations, a realist prism can range all the way to molecules, affects, and viruses—in its history turning (for better or worse) from the dialectics of historical materialism to the contingencies of "new materialisms."

Realism between Dialectics and Assemblage

Drawing heavily on Rancière, Pam Morris in her book *Jane Austen, Virginia Woolf and Worldly Realism* further complicates realism, via her epithet "worldly." For Morris, "worldly" denotes a plethora of previously unacknowledged social relations and lifeworlds, but also very crucially the material reliance of realist stories and characters on a world of things, matters, and the ecologies that connect them. Beginning with Jane Austen's rejection of both detached rationalism and formulaic melodrama as unsuitable modes of conveying the material turmoil of reality, Morris emphasizes realism's "inclusive horizontality" that "convey(s) a materialist, non-hierarchical and encompassing perception of existence, a horizontal continuity of self, social world and physical universe."[38] Realism, then, is not only allied to historical materialism and an emphasis on the previously unacknowledged human forces of history. It is also relatable to new materialisms that focus on affect and on posthumanist conceptions of society as actor-networks and the human as "anthropotechnical" creature.[39] Being "worldly," realism, therefore, has not only *humanistically* eradicated the hierarchy that condemned different social and human groups to invisibility and silence, but also—*anti-anthropocentrically*—unsettled the threshold between the human and the nonhuman. According to Morris, then, realism initiated an "egalitarian tide of materiality . . . and the concomitant dethroning of human exceptionalism. . . . In a new regime of the perceptible, subjects and things and molecules are all equally noteworthy."[40] Realism's "egalitarian tide of materiality" resonates with what political philosopher Jane Bennett has proposed as the "method" for new materialists, which should aspire to "linger in those moments during which they find themselves fascinated by objects, taking them as clues to the material vitality that they share with them."[41] A focus on the movements of affect is central for Bennett and others in achieving such an attentive reorientation toward the forces and things that continuously assemble reality and to overcome anthropocentric notions of agency, politics, and society that largely credit human intention and political ideologies with the shaping of society and that privilege literary and critical strategies that expose and demystify these agencies.[42] In his work on Joseph Conrad—often considered a border figure between realism and modernism—Nidesh Lawtoo has developed a mimetic theory that accounts for the horizontal relations, environmental influences, and physical affects that shape human and more-than-human communities and that modernist literature especially began to be interested in.[43] For him, this ontological form of affective and horizontal mimesis stands in stark contrast to the vertical representational mimesis of Western aesthetics that also—in his estimation, at least—pervades realism. If, however, we conceive of realism in terms of a "worldly realism" and as implicated in an aesthetic regime of literature this distinction begins to blur and realism—with its interest in totalization, but also in objects, in affect, in states of emotional intensities, in superfluous bodies—becomes opened toward modernist mimesis.

Fredric Jameson in *Antinomies of Realism* has also turned our attention to how affect may be central to realism: for Jameson realism is fundamentally torn between a "storytelling impulse" that orders reality into relatable temporal, narrative, and ideological patterns and an "affective impulse," that is interested in conveying the scenic, the experiential, and an unassimilated present that cannot be absorbed by the narrative momentum of traditional literary forms or political ideologies. Realism cannot be defined as the one or the other of these tendencies, but "lies at their intersection."[44] Therefore, many concerns that we often associate with challenges to realism have, in fact, always defined realism at heart and have turned it into a notoriously unstable entity that is often approached from its margins. As Jameson states, "this is why it is also justified to find oneself always talking about the breakdown of realism and never about the thing itself, since we will always find ourselves describing a potential emergence or a potential breakdown."[45] In the second section of this volume "Experiments," the contributions by Bausch and Otto will indeed explicitly approach realism from the perspective of its breakdown by focusing on late modernist and postmodernist experimental writers who ponder over and play with this difficult relation between contingent and affective reality and narrative form. By inserting affect *into* realism Jameson acknowledges that realist authors are also always already in the business of working on the "resistance of affect"—and by extension reality—"to language," trying to find different stylistic solutions to "seize its fleeting essence and to force its recognition."[46] Lawtoo's chapter, for example, discusses Conrad's impressionistic aesthetics and complex narrative patterns as such an attempt to produce a literary "glow" of the fleeting and unexplored realities that shape our lives. This is a long way off from accounts that view realism as a stable assortment of forms and techniques or that emphasize its exclusive identification with totalization and rationality and with a naïve reflection of what is known to exist in favor of an "insatiable colonization of the as yet unexplored and unexpressed."[47]

New materialist approaches to literature and culture, however, are not only helpful to theorize an expanded notion of realism toward protomodernist affect and its complicated relation to narrative form. The critical advent of new materialisms and of ANT may also push us toward the re-appreciation of qualities that are more traditionally associated with realism, like description and accumulation, an attention to long temporalities, or an emphasis on exteriority. Jed Esty has suggested that the theoretical shift from post-structuralism and deconstruction to new materialism and ANT perhaps not incidentally coincides with a renewed appreciation for realism in the contemporary era.[48] In a gross generalization, we could say that new materialisms and ANT urge us to be attentive to the manifold activities and permanent associations of human and nonhuman forces—*actants* as Latour calls them[49]—that make up social reality; a process that new materialism privileges as *assemblage*.[50] Critics of society, according to ANT, should not study the human agency or the abstract social ideas that lie "behind" activities and social constellations—an anthropocentric activity of *critique* that Latour derides as "anti-fetishism" and Bennet problematizes as "demystification." Rather, we should pay close attention to the distributed agencies and the multiple activities that constantly shape reality, while assuming that there "exists *nothing* behind those activities even though they might be linked in a way that does produce a society."[51] New materialisms, it seems, have a strong affinity with a notion of literature and criticism that privileges rather than belittles realism's powers of description, accumulation, and registration. "Today's realisms," Esty spells out, "appeal to those new literary methodologies, because they appear to satisfy a posthumanist demand to move beyond both depth psychology (from emotion to affect) and depth hermeneutics (from suspicious to surface readings)."[52] The opening toward other matter, other scales, and other temporalities highlighted by newer materialisms is, therefore, one of the central aspects that new realisms and new theories of realism have to approach, without, however, sacrificing entirely—or "uncritically" to turn around new materialism's rejection of "critique"—the dialectical and totalizing powers of realism.

New materialism's emphasis on surface readings and on worldly assemblage stands in stark opposition to Lukács's influential conception of realism as being able to render legible a "complete human personality" as the total expression of the movement of history.[53] In fact, Lukács rejected naturalism for a similar tendency to register society's multiplicity—"showing merely one or the other of their aspects"—rather than to totalize and synthesize, and he would reject the non-dialectical temporality that underlies the process of assemblage that realism is interested in vis-à-vis new materialism.[54] Jameson has long ago tried to tackle such a tension between multiplicity and totalization in *The Political Unconscious*. In a very nuanced discussion of Marxist conceptions of literature as "expressive totality" (Lukács) or homology (Lucien Goldmann) that have been rejected for their "obliteration of difference,"[55] Jameson suggests that texts, like historical systems of production, should be understood as being made up of "semi-autonomous" social and literary forms.[56] Jameson, however, also defends the literary and critical method of totality and suggests that critics and writers cannot simply stop at being fascinated by the heterogeneous assemblages—by the "rich and random multiple realties"—that make up society.⁵⁷ Literature and Marxist literary criticism, instead, should piece together these different elements into a mode of production. The totality that they project, however, should not unduly homogenize all elements of a mode of production but pay attention to the "discontinuities, rifts, action at distance, within a merely apparently unified cultural text."⁵⁸ Jameson does not quite say as much, but arguably it is realism (not only as a specific mode but also as the reality construction of texts) that registers this multiple overlapping of entities and social forms and that urges us to piece them together in an interpretation (akin to what Jameson later famously called "cognitive mapping").⁵⁹ This realist "hermeneutic model" should, however, be "antitranscendent": it should not paranoiacally demystify the origin and shape of the capitalist system, but must remain attentive to the contradicting and moving reality that the texts aesthetically try to imagine. Eli Park Sorensen in a frustrated response to anti-realist postcolonial orthodoxies has similarly suggested in recourse to Lukács that the "utopian-interpretative . . . *ideal*" of realism is that it "consists of a sequence of events or parts that are always already interpreted as being *in relation* to each other . . . and which in sum form a narrative totality."⁶⁰ This totality, however, is always an "*ironic* totality": it might offer a "glimpse of epic truth" but is also aware of the constructive work of interpretation—the strategic paranoia, as it were—that is involved in constructing such totalities. Sorensen's notion of an "ironic totality" may be particularly suitable in the context of new materialisms, in order to conceive of realism's attempts to connect the different human and nonhuman *actants* and the processes of assemblage that it is interested in into momentary glances of wholeness and—quasi-dialectical—accountability.⁶¹

In recent literary practice, this realist tendency to map complex agencies is foregrounded especially in the long and extremely interlaced spatiotemporal structures of the "global novel" or the "world novel," (which Wiemann theorizes in this volume) like David Mitchell's *Cloud Atlas* (2004). The aesthetic strategies of such "multi-site historical fictions" tend to invite their readers to map across space and/or time the "vast networks that now constitute lived experience and which can only be observed through their epiphenomenal effects,"⁶² that remain unpredictable and difficult to totalize. Multi-plotted and temporally complex novels have of course always been a staple of realism—especially in Balzac, Dickens, or Flaubert—but these newer novels add to that, by often inserting long temporalities and nonlinear causalities, and by extending their attention more insistently onto the nonhuman. They also tend to leave more gaps between the different narrative strands, events, and agents, which allows for a more active and speculative forging of connections, rather than a totalization of social structures into relations of direct cause and effect (as Balzac and especially Dickens often tended to do). Through their distributed agencies and skewed causalities, newer realist world novels defy simplistic notions of human intention and social totality but can still remain committed to inspiring the mapping of accountability, agency, and possibility.

The distributed agencies and long temporalities of the world novel lead to a last intersection of new materialism and realism that needs to be shortly addressed: the importance of ecology and climate change. The editors of a recently published volume on *Climate Realism* have also commented on the simultaneous proliferation of realism and the emergence of new materialisms, and linked this constellation to an awareness for climate change and its representational challenges.[63] Because of the complexity of climate data, they argue, it is "obvious that the focalization of environmental detail cannot be reduced to the view of a single type of observer," often cherished by realism, both in its omniscient and its subjective mode.[64] Instead, they link climate realism to a proto-modernist attunedness to affect and a softening of the ontological division that has long separated observer from observed environment (discussed in this volume by Lawtoo). In its new materialist and post-anthropocentric emphasis on the complex assemblages and the (very) long and skewed temporalities that underlie climate change, *Climate Realism* also performs a "weirding of the coherence of the world"[65] that challenges the causalities, temporalities, and modes of perception that realism has privileged historically. At the same time, climate realism must also take as one of its main tasks the historicization of anthropogenic climate change, which means the scaling of literature to a strategic anthropocentrism that foregrounds the importance of human actions to the strangely delayed and displaced effects of climate change, which Robert Nixon so memorably had termed "slow violence."[66] This task links climate realism to one of the flourishing sub-genres of realism today: the historical novel (discussed in this volume by Dalley in the context of settler colonialism) with its interest in the long and complex prehistories that have shaped the present. Realism, then, when tackling climate change not only is interested in posthuman assemblages but often strives to combine the work of new materialism with the more dialectical and genealogical work of historical materialism and the historical novel. After all, the editors of *Climate Realism* astutely state, "the earth did not warm itself."[67]

Pieter Vermeulen in his—otherwise brilliant and timely—recent volume *Literature and the Anthropocene* takes a narrower and less generous view of realism and takes aim at realism's incapacity to deal with the emergencies of the climate catastrophe: "novelistic realism constrains the imagination of *the probable* and the credible; the mundane lives of novel characters cannot be disturbed by freak weather events.... Realism remains blind to the frankly improbable ways in which the Anthropocene derangement of Holocene conditions proliferates uncertainty and risk."[68] This is a contestable assumption: Vermeulen's rejection of realism does not consider how the dense description of lifeworlds destroyed and threatened by climate change and ecological catastrophe that realism—even in a traditional understanding—can provide may very well tackle the realities of climate change. Amitav

Ghosh in his landmark collection of lectures *The Great Derangement* was also among the strongest critics of realism's incapacity to depict the skewed temporalities and spatialities of climate change and almost programmatically expanded—or abandoned, depending on perspective—realism towards the realm of the improbable in his fantasy-cum-thriller-cum-romance *Gun Island* (2019). But Ghosh's own earlier—and by most accounts: realist—novels actually do a formidable work of realistically depicting the seeping work of ecological undoing and the subaltern practices of surviving it; everyday practices that sometimes—as in *The Hungry Tide* (2004)—conflict with top-down Eurocentric environmentalist strategies for ecosystem preservation. In this volume, Caroline Levine will also discuss how realism may even be particularly suited for addressing the reality of climate change by emphasizing the sustainable tasks that we must become more attuned to in order to tackle the temporalities and devastations of climate catastrophe.

Furthermore, Vermeulen's claim that realism fails to "factor in the agency of nonhuman forces" can simply not be upheld, even historically.[69] Nineteenth-century realism has been very attentive to and very much shaped by the nonhuman—technical and environmental—elements that impact social assemblages: *Bleak House*'s (1853) infamous fog and mud with which the novel opens may largely be symbolic, but it also points to the actual pollution of London's air and water that culminated in London's "Great Stink" of 1848 that had severe effects on the living conditions and health of the population and eventually impacted urban planning and sanitary reform. Furthermore, in *Our Mutual Friend* (1865), the Thames is a veritable plot-making protagonist—or *actant*—that is sustaining, transforming, and killing numerous of the novel's characters. The same can be said of the sickness—probably smallpox—of Jo, the street sweeper in *Bleak House*, which spreads horizontally across vast parts of the novelistic population regardless of social stratification and has severe consequences for the novel's plot and social constellations. These arbitrary examples attest to the multiple ways in which the realist novel has always managed—even relied on—the inclusion of nonhuman forces into its vision of social life in modernity.[70]

Literatures from the postcolonial world have been at the core of many recent reconsiderations of realism as well as to debates surrounding the literary representations of climate change. I would also like to close my remarks with a more explicit consideration of realism in the context of postcolonial world literature, especially because such an engagement can help us to pick up the question of realism's torn commitment between totalization and local difference and how this feeds into a tension between realism's dialectical notion of history and a new materialist and transcultural dynamics of assemblage. Lukács famously demanded that great realism should let its plots and characters articulate and embody "periods of transition" and the movement of history,[71] or even to depict "an entire society in movement."[72] In postcolonial studies, such realism was often met with rejection, because it was related to the failed nationalisms of the decolonization period and because historical dialectics was linked to a developmentalism that was seen to downplay the agency, heterogeneity, and creativity of the local.[73] The issue of realism's political temporality remains, however, an urgent one, because it begs the question of how it can locate the dynamics of change and futurity; both to identify political (options for) resistance and to better project a world that is—for better or worse—constantly in motion. Lauren Goodlad has debated this question under the rubric of "worlding realisms" and argued that in the contemporary world of globalization and financialization, realism's ultimate vocation is to detect and map those elements across the world that are not yet fully homogenized by capital: "there are things that financialization has not yet managed to abstract. It follows that registering these things and—one hopes—mobilizing them over and across multiple temporalities is a task that worlding realism may help us to achieve."[74]

I want to pick up on Goodlad's concerns by focusing more explicitly on the concept of *worlding* as introduced into postcolonial studies by Pheng Cheah. Cheah's theory can help us get a sense of where a temporal notion of realism in postcolonial world literature might be located, without resorting to simplistic ideas of local resistance on the one hand or overdetermining notions of structure and abstraction on the other hand. In *What Is a World?* Cheah turns to Heidegger's notion that the world is held together by the time in which it unfolds: "The world is neither objectively present nor at hand, but temporalizes itself in temporality."[75] By virtue of this linear temporalization the world is fundamentally a process of constant change and newness: a temporal process that Heidegger refers to as "worlding" in the elusive passage "world never is, it worlds."[76] Cheah, in a more dialectical application of Heidegger, considers this temporal shape of the world as the "gift of time," because it includes the ineradicable "messianic" possibility for an opening of the world toward different futures. From this conception of worlding, he programmatically assumes that "world literature has the normative vocation of opening new worlds."[77] Cheah's postcolonial interest is with worlds that are threatened and destroyed by the forces of global capitalism, but that nonetheless persistently "traffic with the opening of worlds," even in the "most devastating scenarios."[78] This (re)worlding can happen against the destructive forces of capitalist globalization as a bringing the "attention of the wider world to the plight of peoples impacted by global forces and their struggles to safeguard a future for their worlds."[79] World literature, in this scenario can project the "persistence of revolutionary time in neo-colonial conditions" or can sensitize readers toward "worldly ethics or practices of inhabiting the world where the teleological time of revolution no longer seems feasible."[80] Cheah does not exclusively credit realism with the task of worlding, and he does not develop a theory of literary realism. His emphasis on worlding, nonetheless, shatters some of the anti-realist orthodoxies of postcolonialism; he privileges a "critical mimesis that deploys various forms of realism, allegory, and symbolism" and at least implicitly shares Coleen Lye's and Esty's critique of a "prevailing critical habit of reading against realism,"[81] insofar as he argues that we should be interested in more than a work's formally disruptive features if we want to attend to the specific worlds it projects and how they may generate the opening of new worlds.

Despite the attention to local detail and subalternity, the temporality of worlding cannot be understood in the sense of a local that is insulated from globalization. Cheah argues that "there are no already-existing transcendent worlds from which to resist and counter globalization," but that "worlding is immanent to and ... part of the circuits of globalization ... exceed[ing] them from within by drawing on what constitutes them as an effective resource for opening new worlds."[82] This means that postcolonial world literature also offers counter-worlds to globalization that deform globalization's original intentions by incalculably responding to and working with the technologies, materials, and ideas circulated by globalization. Capitalist globalization is reliant on temporality in that it constantly seeks to expand and self-transform through time. Because of the incalculability of "the gift of time" and because of the new relations that globalization constantly establishes in the world, processes of renewal and reworlding are permanently taking place through globalization. In distinction to much globalization theory, however, Cheah is adamant to insist that world literature has the task not only to depict local "disjunctures" within global capitalism or the "cultural heterogenization," "indigenization,"[83] or "alternative modernities"[84] that it allows—which can all too easily be commodified and used for an expansion or reinvention of capital—but to use literary form and the messianic and incalculable time of literary worlding to "poin[t] to something that will exceed and disrupt capital."[85]

Cheah's notion of world literature, then, shares an interest in the material and cultural dynamics of globalization and a readiness to depart from "accepted measures of properly historical motion" with anthropologists of globalization like Arjun Appadurai and with ideas of postcolonial hybridization. Cheah, however, is insistent not to understand worlding only through the often too uncritical prism of hybridization—which in some respects resembles new materialist assemblage in their shared rejection of social or colonial intentionality in favor of local dynamics. His problem is that such perspectives tend to inspire temporalities of cultural difference or postcolonial material assemblage that are too intrinsic to capitalist globalization. These temporalities of hybridity and assemblage, according to Cheah, remain "within the order of presence" and lack the normative and/or dialectical perspective that postcolonial world literature must also provide—or at least provoke.[86]

Cheah's reservations about hybridization, assemblage, and alternative modernization can also help us to assume a more "critical" reading perspective—one more attuned to realism's tendency to totalization—that may read realistic depictions of postcolonial assemblage as heterogeneous temporalities of the specific and the local, without, however, falling for what Colleen Lye has called an "implicit optimism about marketization."[87] Especially from the perspective of a Western readership, the culturally dynamic worlds registered by world literature should not only be considered a celebration of cultural difference in globalization and as—potentially depoliticized and non-dialectical—evidence of the temporality and the material dynamics of local assemblage. Anthropologist Brian Larkin has recently analyzed images of infrastructural life in Lagos. He argues that images of over-crowded streets in Lagos should be viewed for the new social dynamics that they convey, as people in Lagos' infamous traffic jams have created new economies and new social practices on the back of these seeming infrastructural failures. At the same time, he argues that these images should also be scrutinized for the political aesthetics that are inscribed into them. They are not only a testament to the new materialist life of infrastructure and the social but also an indictment of the "failed ... promises" of globalization and development. As such they can also provoke a "social hermeneutics" that urges us to engage with these assemblages in a more dialectical manner interested in inquiring who or what may be responsible.[88] This, I think, can be transferred to realist literature, where the same realist depiction can acknowledge the concrete temporality of assemblage and resilience, while also provoking realist totalization and dialectical engagement. In the very same narrative world or image, then, the realism of postcolonial world literature can track globalization's production of precarity *and* depict practices of resilience and processes of assemblage with and against globalization. This can unsettle the paralyzing antithesis between the potentially unpolitical assemblages privileged by new materialisms and an allegedly too Eurocentric and anthropocentric dialectical temporality of historical materialism—sparked for example by images of postcolonial precarity that urge a reconstruction of the relations that produce it. It is this dual political-aesthetic work of mapping the effects of global capital and of showing the concrete lifeworlds that are continuously assembled by and in response to its abstractions that mark a central task of realism in world literature today.

Arc of the Volume

Part I of the volume, "Aesthetics," consists of four chapters that attest to the contested and dissensual origins of realism in the nineteenth and early twentieth centuries. Together, they challenge the idea of realism as a homogenous formation and reject caricaturing assumptions about realism's relation to common sense, its simplistic belief in representation, or its inability and ideological unwillingness to engage with contradictions.[89] Andreas Mahler begins with the origin of realism in Gustave Courbet's unsentimental painting and in his goatishly anti-academic and anti-conventional exhibition "Du Réalisme" of 1855. From there the chapter offers a thorough contextualization of the term "realism" in the French and English debates of the early to mid-nineteenth century. The contribution embeds the term in specific historical discourses about art and clarifies the marginal and worldly position from which realism originally articulated its subject matter against the dominating formal and thematic conventions, both in painting and in literature. The essay also covers the later "history of the term" in the twentieth century and argues against a predominantly modal and typological usage of the term. Mahler's preference for a historical use of "realism" is a challenge to some of the essays that follow in this volume and deal with later realist practices that highlight realism's historical mutability and adaptability. But his historicization also supports the volume's revaluation of realism in that it problematizes those modal approaches to realism that fail to understand it from its original radical impulse, and instead define it as a fixed typological mode defined by readability, transparency, and common sense.

Nadine Böhm-Schnitker turns to *the* realist author of mid-Victorianism: George Eliot. Rather than being a detached "moral" or "ethical" realism, Böhm-Schnitker argues that Eliot's realism is aisth-ethic, in that it reveals the importance of individual sense-perceptions of characters—and by extensions readers—to aesthetically establish the "worlds" they live in and the ways that they act in them. The extremely perspectival nature of Eliot's fiction is also metaleptically underlined by the famous self-reflexive narrative interruptions of *Adam Bede* that perform the difficult transition from reality over individual perception to linguistic representation. With *Middlemarch* (1871) Eliot begins to emphasize how perceptions of reality are also conditioned by the specific social embeddedness of characters and the historically specific symbolic forms that determine their perception of and action in the world. Characters in Eliot are not preexisting entities but emerge only through their physical and psychological interactions—also called "intra-actions" because the participants do not precede these encounters, but are formed in them—which means they become the subjects of realism only by means of their embedded agency in the world. Böhm-Schnitker analyzes how these inherent "enmeshments" of characters and readers into sensescapes, lifeworlds, and networks of responsibilities relate to what philosopher Karen Barad described as "agential realism." The notion of agential realism complicates our understanding of Eliot's realism away from an individualist or moralist metaphysical project toward a quasi-new-materialist awareness of the affective relations between subjects and material world that co-constitute one another and that perform the inextricable entanglement between matter and meaning.

Maren Scheurer's chapter moves to the later nineteenth century to analyze the prominent role of medicine in Thomas Hardy's *Woodlanders* (1887) and Émile Zola's *Le docteur Pascal* (1893). This interest, she argues, is not only part of realism's and naturalism's alleged focus on science. Rather, literature and medicine are also intricately related, because medicine occupies an intermediate perspective between strict scientific rigor and artistic form. By virtue of being a profession of caring and healing, medicine always needed to abet its experimental rigor with sympathy and speculation and be able to connect different social and physiological contexts. Similar to medicine's reliance on imagination, speculation, and sympathy, realist literature should not be mistaken for the unadulterated registration and collection of surface realities. Hardy's and Zola's naturalist interest in experiment may (in)famously borrow from scientific method, but they are too often reduced to a scientific determinism, which ignores how their realism also resonates with natural sciences on other levels: Scheurer observes how, similar to good scientific method, their texts also know that they can never conclusively define and arrest the world. Life and reality can be approximated, but remain ultimately unknowable, because they cannot be brought to a standstill. This provisionality, however, does not mean frustration, but pleasure in reality and in the ever-evolving artistic and scientific attempts to grasp it. Scientific observer and literary artist are thus entangled with the living world they seek to penetrate and represent realistically: a world that despite these attempts always remains magically vibrant and alive.

Nidesh Lawtoo looks at Conrad's *The Shadow-Line* (1917) in order to theorize forms of community that exceed the collection of individual subjects that literary realism is often said to privilege. Analogous to the context of the epidemic that the story treats, Conrad's notion of community is one that is dominated by affect and by forms of physical and social contagion. In order to survive, Conrad's cooperative community must be made up of subjectivities that are not self-contained and sovereign, but responsive to the bodies, the activities, the risks, and the environmental forces that shape humans into (more-than-human) communities. Conrad's main poetic project famously and elusively was "before all, to make you see."[90] Conrad's "modernist mimesis" achieves this visibility by paying particular attention to the nonhuman elements that infect human relations, by highlighting the contingency of forms of civilization, and by aborting narrative patterns of individual progress in favor of impressionistic and narratologically distorted glimpses of a (horrible) truth of reality: a truth that lies beyond hubristic ideas of human authority and (self-)deceptive representations of enlightenment civilization. Conrad pushes realism from its nineteenth-century origins toward other contexts (empire), genres (romance), and styles (modernism) in which literature may be changed, but in which realism's aesthetic principle of getting in as much world as possible remains a central ambition.

Continuing the work in Lawtoo's chapter on Conrad, Part II of the volume, "Experiments," consists of four chapters that engage with the question of realism from outside of the modes and canons that realism has traditionally been related to. The experimental texts discussed in this part work more strongly than those discussed in other sections to "avoid the inevitable conventionality of language," which includes challenging and rejecting some realist conventions, like point of view, plotting, description, and verisimilitude.[91] On the one hand, according to George Levine, such a struggle to shed linguistic and literary convention is a central effort of realism in its pursuit of "unmediated reality" and puts these texts into continuity with a realist project. On the other hand, these works were all written after what Zadie Smith has called "the wound" that had been afflicted by Joyce on any project of pursuing an unmediated reality through language.[92] Therefore, the texts discussed in this section are much more suspicious than their nineteenth-century predecessors (who were by no means unaware of the difficult relation between representation and reality) of *any* narrative conventions, cultural codes, and epistemological assumptions and how they perpetually govern and restrict literature's access to reality. Therefore, they reflect both literature's limitations to ever fully grasp the contingencies of reality and the powerful construction of possible worlds that realist literatures nonetheless can afford. The challenges posed to realism that are discussed in this section, then, are not simple rejections of realism but help us to reflect on realism and can in many respects be understood as a textual radicalization and cultural recontextualization of realism's own original aesthetic vocation to create dissensus.

Barbara Bausch's chapter introduces the experimental prose of Ror Wolf into the debates on realism. Wolf's playful and self-reflexive texts are little known in the English-speaking world. They clearly fall outside the modalities of realism, especially if realism is seen as a mode of plotting that seeks to offer a stable and transparent literary representation of reality. At the same time, Wolf's texts are not simply performances of self-reflexive artistic autonomy. Rather, they offer a playful exploration of the contingency—as in incalculability and indeterminacy—of reality and of the contingent—as in path dependent and culture specific—forms that literature applies to frame it. Wolf's prose is, therefore, not a critique of an outmoded reference to reality, but an attempt to perform the multiplicity and contingency of reality through literary texts that play with uncertainties and multiple possibilities. In doing so, his texts expose the overbearance of textual patterns and conventions in literature's attempt to register the world. When Wolf takes up elements of the adventure tale in his prose, for example, this may be understood as a hyperbole of the "narrative impulse" that pulls realism into the direction of literary convention and away from contingent reality.[93] Wolf's experimental prose instead, emphasizes the aesthetic creation of multiple possible worlds over the representational attempt to fix the world within narrative patterns and chronotopes. His "realism of the possible" can enhance our understanding of realism's aesthetic vocation and of the reflexivity that literature must maintain in facing and exploring the contingency of reality.

André Otto's contribution tackles the relation between realism and the experimental writings of B. S. Johnson. Otto, of course, does not simply try to reclaim Johnson for an extended realist project but points out some striking resonances of realist epistemologies in Johnson's work. Reading Johnson's novel *Trawl* (1966), Otto shows how Johnson does not reject reality and experience as ontological categories, but that he problematizes the narrative codes that shape the proliferation of worldly and experiential details into coherent plots and forms. Johnson's protagonist and orienting consciousness uses the eponymous practice of "trawling," which is a radical form of memory through which—like a fishing net that trawls the sea—he tries to accumulate random bits of reality and experience. Eventually, this process of radical memory is geared toward a process of "evacuation" that seeks to expulse the abject materials and realities that disturb the narrator's psyche. By showing how even this evacuation of memory is governed by tropes, by conventions, by frames of psychic wholesomeness, and by modes of representation the novel gestures toward the unavoidable textual and perceptual tendencies to put heterogeneous experience into meaningful form. While we may not be able to do without such mechanisms of coping, mapping, and ordering, realist literary art should also be committed to perpetually developing new textual strategies that prevent textual and worldly accumulation and progression from corroding into overdetermining form.

Nasrin Babakhani's contribution looks at magical realism from a sustained perspective on realism, an element that is often neglected in discussions of the genre in favor of foregrounding its disruptive magicality. Babakhani argues that if realism is the representation of a culturally mediated reality then magical realism must be understood as yet another cultural version of realism. The alleged magicality that magical realist texts are routinely identified with is from this perspective more of an exotic projection than an actual anti-realist device. Babakhani looks specifically at Louise Erdrich's novel *Love Medicine* (1984) to analyze how some of the allegedly magical devices in it—like trickster figures, non-scientific forms of healing, communion with the dead—are deeply rooted in the everyday life of the community. If realism's task was to get previously marginalized aspects of social reality into the purview of serious literature, this inclusion of "magical" customs and beliefs is a consistent cultural extension of realism. Through its inclusion of communal beliefs and rituals into the sphere of realism, Babakhani estimates that Erdrich's cultural realism also gestures toward alternative forms of collectives that extend beyond the communities of individuals that most versions of Western realism were operating with originally.

Kai Wiegandt's chapter opens with an analysis of J. M. Coetzee's *Elizabeth Costello* (2003); a text that itself explicates a conception of realism through lectures delivered by its eponymous protagonist. Costello and Coetzee argue for, and perform, a notion of realism as embodied and embedded thinking, which assumes that ideas are best processed in narrative, because it embodies them in living, breathing characters and experientially embeds them in social situations. Wiegandt discusses how this tendency toward realistic embodiment is recalibrated in the recent works of Rachel Cusk, notably in her trilogy *Outline* (2014), *Transit* (2017), *Kudos* (2018). Cusk also offers a form of narrative as embodied thinking by consisting entirely of the testimonies of individuals. On a first level this is a reality effect associated with pseudo-orality and with the reduction of narrative voice in favor of character. This embodied dimension of Cusk's realism, however, does not primarily serve the purpose of depicting individual character. Increasingly, throughout Cusk's trilogy the characters and their speeches become less distinguishable and their voices and opinions become repetitive. These similarities and overlaps between the different voices perform the fact of a shared reality, in which ideas and speech are always social and mimetic, rather than (only) individually expressive. Whereas Coetzee focuses on the corporeal embodiedness and embeddedness of ideas, Cusk reorients realism by increasingly performing the social embeddedness and mimeticism of ideas, character, and speech as a signature of social reality and of realistic narrative.

Part III, "Politics," highlights the Politics of realism. What the chapters assume, however, is not a simple return of realism that turns back the challenges of modernism and metafiction in order to resurrect an engaged literature that presents an easily represented world with easy to delineate political responsibilities and clearly demarcated subjectivities. Quite the contrary, the chapters in this section attest to the "waning power of the modernism/realism dyad" for the multiscalar mappings of political subjectivities, agencies, and relations under neoliberal globalization and anthropogenic climate change.[94] In some instances, the contributions emphasize the importance of realism as a commitment to attend carefully to the mundane workings of daily life in and against capitalism and ecological crisis. But they also discuss newer realisms that privilege "relatedness over representativity as a way to write across the globe"[95] and even attest to critical methods and literary styles that assume that the reality of global capitalism and the improbable transformations that it engenders are best explored by a more gappy and metafictional—hence, ostensibly "irrealist form" of—realism: one, however, that perhaps better "retains the originality of the concept of realism."[96]

Caroline Levine's chapter urges us to think about the importance of realism for the imagination of ecological and social sustainability. In order to put these concerns and the literary strategies that benefit them center stage, Levine argues that literature and literary studies should focus some of their attention away from an obsession with the aesthetics of rupture toward an ethics of maintaining life. While eco-critical perspectives have thrived on experimental poetry and dystopian fiction as modes that are trying to wrestle us from complacency, Levine argues that realism is actually the most suitable mode of envisioning sustainability. This nexus between realism and sustainability does not assume a simplistic representational understanding of realism or the perpetuation of the belief that realism naturalizes social forms and relations. Quite the opposite, Levine draws on a quality of realism that is often muted by its detractors and that becomes even more vital to realism's politics in the Anthropocene: defamiliarization. Levine looks at a range of historical and contemporary texts and TV series, from Dickens's *Bleak House* over the BBC's *Call the Midwife* (2012-) to Chimamanda Ngozi Adichie's *Americanah* (2013) to explore how they deploy a realist aesthetics of defamiliarization in order to restore to our awareness those social tasks, infrastructures, and routines that are vital to maintain and imagine socially and ecologically sustainable forms of communal life.

Dirk Wiemann's contribution theorizes realism's ambiguous relation to politics in the context of globalization, by attending to the relation between network realism, capitalist realism, and the "world novel." Global capitalism is often understood as a mode of production that generates a networked world, in which the most distant locations and live-worlds are connected through the abstract workings of capital. In this vein, Wiemann reads the fragmented and loosely entangled form of recent "world novels," like David Mitchell's *Cloud Atlas*, as symptoms of a world networked by capital, as a form of network/capitalist realism. At the same time, he maintains that these network-realist novels only construct the very networks and relations that they purport merely to register, because their loose juxtapositions of distinct locations, characters, and events and the skewed temporalities and causalities that connect them are what draw readers into the process of creating and imagining capitalist networks across space and time. Wiemann argues that we need to be aware that realism's historical vocation to map the systemic connections between different spaces and across different times always bears the risk of reification, mystification, and overdetermination at the expense of difference, agency, and possible resistance; at the same time, such a "gappy" network realism is the only possible mode of making tangible the abstractions produced by global network capitalism.

Eli Park Sorensen's chapter takes a closer look at the problematic relationship between postcolonial studies and literary realism. For the most part, postcolonial studies at least since the 1990s either ignored realism or criticized it as being naïve, anachronistic, deceptive, or complicit with colonial discourse. Sorensen mourns that despite postcolonial studies being centered in and around literature departments, no general theory of postcolonial realism exists, even though many postcolonial literary texts are realist by most definitions. Sorensen's text speculates what lies behind postcolonial studies' general reluctance to engage with literary realism and discusses recent attempts to think beyond this reluctance. He reads the works of Rohinton Mistry and looks particularly at his novel *Family Matters* (2002) to discuss the various ways in which realism continues to occupy a crucial role within postcolonial thought. In the past, if postcolonial realism was acknowledged to have a function at all, it was usually tasked with the representation of concrete and spectacular political and historical crises in the postcolonial world. In opposition to such an exoticizing and narrow notion of postcolonial politics,

Sorensen's reading of *Family Matters* is especially interested in the political dimension of realism as an engagement with questions of postcolonial community, collectivity, economics, and everyday life.

Hamish Dalley's chapter analyzes how settler-colonialism twists realism for its particular problems of imagining cultural encounter and forging settler-colonial identity. Crucially, settler-colonial realism from South Africa and Australia complicates Lukács's historical-dialectical conception of realism and the historical novel in favor of what Dalley terms "metamorphosis" and "revelation." Settler-colonial identity is predicated on metamorphosis and revelation because the process of becoming native to the settled territory requires the settler to have the revelation that he must self-transform into an indigenous subject through an open engagement with the land. On the one hand, this non-dialectical process of metamorphosis generates more uncertain, open-ended, and contingent transformations than the (allegedly) closed mechanism of historical dialectics. On the other hand, Dalley makes clear how the emphasis on metamorphosis and revelation in settler-colonial realism is a critical reminder that settler ideology has violently rejected a dialectical engagement with the indigenous (as) other. Metamorphosis is, therefore, not only the more uncertain and horizontal replacement of dialectics but also underpinned by a historical process of elimination that has ontologically and epistemologically purged the human antithesis from a dialectical equation in favor of settler self-transformation.

Ranging from Courbet to Rachel Cusk, from close reading to theory, from social classes to viruses, and from the psyche to the mappings of global capitalism, the contributions to this volume collectively demonstrate realism's—and realism studies'—ongoing capacity to engage with the aesthetic and political questions that continue to beset modernity. Realism can only do that, the chapters in this volume cumulatively demonstrate, because it is not—and never has been—a fixed style based in ideological and epistemological consensus, but a dissensual aesthetic and political strategy that brings to our attention reality as it is constantly made and unmade.

Notes

1 Matthew Beaumont, "Introduction: Reclaiming Realism," in *Adventures in Realism*, ed. Matthew Beaumont (Malden, MA: Blackwell, 2007), 2.

2 See among many others monographs and edited volumes Richard Menke, *Telegraphic Realism: Victorian Fiction and Other Information Systems* (Palo Alto, CA: Stanford University Press, 2008); Ulka Anjaria, *Realism in the Twentieth Century Indian Novel: Colonial Difference and Literary Form* (Cambridge: Cambridge University Press, 2011); Elaine Shonkwiler and Leigh Claire La Berge, *Reading Capitalist Realism* (Iowa City: University of Iowa Press, 2014); Lauren Goodlad, *The Victorian Geopolitical Aesthetic: Realism,*

Sovereignty, and Transnational Experience (Oxford: Oxford University Press, 2016); Pam Morris, *Jane Austen, Virginia Woolf, and Worldly Realism* (Edinburgh: Edinburgh University Press, 2017); Eike Kronshage, *Vision and Character: Physiognomics and the English Realist Novel* (Abingdon: Routledge, 2018); Charlotte Jones, *Synthetic Realism: Realism, Form and Representation in the Edwardian Novel* (Oxford: Oxford University Press, 2021). Many journals have also run special issues to survey realism's extended scope. See *Worlding Realism*, ed. Lauren Goodlad, special issue of *NOVEL: A Forum on Fiction* 49, no. 2 (2016); *Peripheral Realisms*, ed. Jed Esty and Colleen Lye, special issue of *Modern Language Quarterly* 73, no. 3 (2012); *Genres of Neoliberalism*, ed. Jane Elliot and Gillian Harkins, special issue of *Social Text*, no. 115 (2013).

3 Lauren Goodlad, "Introduction: *Worlding Realisms Now*," in *Worlding Realism*, ed. Lauren Goodlad, special issue of *NOVEL: A Forum on Fiction* 49, no. 2 (2016): 183.

4 See Beaumont's "Introduction" (3) for a concise analysis of the rejection of realism by postmodernist scholars and the "institutional entrenchment" of anti-realist ideologies. For a critique of postcolonialism's problematic relation to realism, see Neil Lazarus, "The Politics of Postcolonial Modernism," *The European Legacy* 7, no. 6 (2010): 771–782.

5 Goodlad, "Introduction," 183.

6 See Roman Jakobson, "On Realism in Art," in *Language in Literature*, ed. Krystyna Pomorska and Stephen Rudy (Cambridge: Belknap, 1987), esp. 22, 24.

7 See George Levine, *The Realistic Imagination: English Fiction from Frankenstein to Lady Chatterly* (Chicago: University of Chicago Press, 1981), esp. 8.

8 Goodlad, "Introduction,"183; Colleen Lye, "Afterword: Realism's Future," in *Worlding Realism*, ed. Lauren Goodlad, special issue of *NOVEL: A Forum on Fiction* 49, no. 2 (2016): 346.

9 Jones, *Synthetic Realism*, 1; Lye, "Afterword," 343.

10 Jed Esty, "Realism Wars," in *Worlding Realisms*, ed. Lauren Goodlad, special issue of *NOVEL: A Forum on Fiction* 49, no. 2 (2016): 319.

11 See Pieter Vermeulen, *Literature and the Anthropocene* (Abingdon: Routledge, 2020), 60–65.

12 Devin Ford, *Realism after Modernism: The Rehumanization of Art and Literature* (Cambridge, MA: MIT Press, 2012), 8.

13 Esty, "Realism Wars," 339.

14 See Erich Auerbach, *Mimesis: The Representation of Reality in Western Literature*, trans. Willard R. Trask (Princeton, NJ: Princeton University Press, 2003), 491–492.

15 Ibid., 491.

16 Jacques Rancière, *The Politics of Aesthetics*, ed. and trans. Gabriel Rockhill (London: Bloomsbury, 2004), 16.

17 Ibid., 13.
18 Ibid., 17.
19 Jacques Rancière, *Dissensus: On Politics and Aesthetics*, trans. Steven Corcoran (London: Continuum, 2010), 115ff.
20 Rancière, *Politics of Aesthetics*, 40.
21 Jacques Rancière, *The Politics of Literature*, trans. Julie Rose (Cambridge: Polity Press, 2011), 7.
22 Rancière, *Politics of Aesthetics*, 19.
23 Ibid., 5.
24 Ibid., 19.
25 Rancière, *Politics of Literature*, 7.
26 Beaumont, "Introduction," 2.
27 Vermeulen, *Literature and the Anthropocene*, 60.
28 Catherine Belsey, *Critical Practice* (London: Methuen, 1980), 47.
29 Rancière, *Politics of Aesthetics*, 19.
30 Rancière, *Politics of Literature*, 25.
31 George Levine, "Literary Realism Reconsidered: 'The World in its Length and Breadth,'" in *Adventures in Realism*, ed. Matthew Beaumont (Malden, MA: Blackwell, 2007), 13–14.
32 Rancière, *Politics of Aesthetics*, 17.
33 Rancière, *Politics of Literature*, 15.
34 On the realist repertory of popular fiction and its differences from nineteenth-century realism, see Peter Brooks, *Realist Vision* (New Haven, CT: Yale University Press, 2008), 5–6.
35 Beaumont mourns that Barthes's important diagnosis has primarily fuelled a rejection and ignorance toward realism rather than a rethinking of realism on more complex and historical terms. See "Introduction," 2.
36 George Eliot, *Adam Bede* (Oxford: Oxford World's Classics, 2008), 159.
37 Levine, *Realistic Imagination*, 22.
38 Morris, *Jane Austen, Virginia Woolf, and Worldly Realism*, 5.
39 For an analysis especially of German inter-war realism and its commitment to restore from the abstraction of modernism a quasi-post-human figure whose body was marked by technology, prosthetics, and standardization and whose mind and speech was "prefabricated" by media circulation, see Devin Fore, *Modernism after Realism: The Rehumanization of Art and Literature* (Cambridge, MA: MIT Press, 2012).
40 Morris, *Jane Austen, Virginia Woolf, and Worldly Realism*, 7.
41 Jane Bennett, *Vibrant Matter: A Political Ecology of Things* (Durham, NC: Duke University Press, 2010), 17.
42 Not a new materialist by any measure, even Lukács was skeptical about certain trends of demystification. For him, the dialectical potential of Balzac's

and Tolstoy's novels lies not in how the novelists inscribe them with their world views (*Weltanschauung*)—which in both cases were quite reactionary—but in how their art was attentive and sympathetic toward the people, to material life, and to the forces of history. This equipped their novels with their own particular expression of reality—its own complex *Weltanschauung*—that was quite independent of the authorial intention that some critics want to reconstruct behind them. See George Lukács, *Studies in European Realism* (New York: Grosset & Dunlap, 1964), 10–16.

43 See Nidesh Lawtoo, *Conrad's Shadow: Catastrophe, Mimesis, Theory* (East Lansing: Michigan State University Press, 2016).

44 Fredric Jameson, *The Antinomies of Realism* (London: Verso, 2013), 26.

45 Ibid.

46 Ibid., 31.

47 Ibid., 30.

48 See Esty, "Realism Wars," 324.

49 On "actants," see Bruno Latour, "On Technical Mediation: Philosophy, Sociology, Genealogy," *Common Knowledge* 3, no. 2 (1994): 29–64.

50 See Bruno Latour, *Reassembling the Social: An Introduction to Actor-Network-Theory* (Oxford: Oxford University Press, 2007). The idea of assemblage has gained prominence in cultural studies and philosophy through Gilles Deleuze and Felix Guattari, *A Thousand Plateaus*, trans. Brian Massumi (Minneapolis: University of Minnesota Press, 1987). It is also intensely discussed in the context of new materialism in Jane Bennett's chapter "The Agency of Assemblages." See Bennett, *Vibrant Matter*, 20–38.

51 Latour, *Reassembling the Social*, 8.

52 See Latour, "On Technical Mediation," 45.

53 Lukács, *Studies in European Realism*, 5.

54 Ibid., 6.

55 Fredric Jameson, *The Political Unconscious: Narrative as a Socially Symbolic Act* (Abingdon: Routledge, 1983), 35.

56 Ibid., 15–22.

57 Ibid., 5.

58 Ibid., 41.

59 Ibid., 6.

60 Eli Park Sorensen, *Postcolonial Studies and the Literary: Theory, Interpretation, and the Novel* (Basingstoke: Palgrave Macmillan, 2011), xii.

61 Akin to such ironic totalizing, even Bennett in *Vibrant Matter* acknowledges that there are constellations when it may be politically salient to strategically understate "material agency in the hope of enhancing accountability" (38).

62 Treasa De Loughry, *The Global Novel and Capitalism in Crisis: Contemporary Literary Narratives* (Basingstoke: Palgrave Macmillan, 2020), 8.

63 See Lynn Badia, Marija Cetinic, and Jeff Diamanti, "Introduction," in *Climate Realism: The Atmospherics of Weather and Atmosphere in the Anthropocene*, ed. Lynn Badia, Marija Cetinic, and Jeff Diamanti (Abingdon: Routledge, 2021), 4.
64 Ibid., 8.
65 Ibid., 6.
66 See Robert Nixon, *Slow Violence and the Environmentalism of the Poor* (Cambridge, MA: Harvard University Press, 2011).
67 Badia et al., "Introduction," 14.
68 Vermeulen, *Literature and the Anthropocene*, 61.
69 Ibid., 61.
70 For a longer view on environmental issues in Victorian Literature, see for example Jesse Oak Taylor, *The Sky of Our Manufacture: The London Fog in British Fiction from Dickens to Woolf* (Charlottesville, VI: University of Virginia Press, 2016).
71 Lukács, *Studies in European Realism*, 10.
72 Georg Lukács, *The Historical Novel*, trans. Hannah Mitchell and Stanley Mitchell (London: Merlin Press, 1962), 139.
73 For a critique of anti-developmental and anti-realist tendencies in postcolonial and globalization studies, see Timothy Brennan, "From Development to Globalization: Postcolonial Studies and Globalization Theory," in *The Cambridge Companion to Postcolonial Literary Studies*, ed. Neil Lazarus (Cambridge: Cambridge University Press, 2004), 120–138 and Lazarus, "The Politics of Postcolonial Modernism." See Kwame Anthony Appiah, "Is the Post- in Postmodernism the Post- in Postcolonial?" *Critical Inquiry* 17, no. 2 (1991), 336–357, for the most canonical account of the relation between realism and experimental forms in postcolonial literatures.
74 Goodlad, "Introduction," 198.
75 Martin Heidegger, *Being and Time*, trans. Joan Stambaugh (Albany, NY: State University of New York Press, 1996), 334. Original: "Die Welt ist weder vorhanden noch zuhanden, sondern zeitigt sich in der Zeitlichkeit." Martin Heidegger, *Sein und Zeit* (Tübingen: Niemeyer, 1967), 365.
76 Translation in Pheng Cheah, *What is a World? On Postcolonial Literature as World Literature* (Durham, NC: Duke University Press, 2016), 117. Original: "Welt ist nie, sondern weltet." Martin Heidegger, "Vom Wesen des Grundes," in *Wegmarken*, ed. Friedrich Wilhelm von Herrmann (Frankfurt: Klostermann, 1976), 164.
77 Cheah, *What Is a World?*, 16.
78 Ibid.
79 Ibid., 17.
80 Ibid., 214.
81 Jed Esty and Colleen Lye, "Peripheral Realisms Now," in *Peripheral Realisms*, edited by Esty and Lye, special issue of *Modern Language Quarterly* 73, no. 3 (2012): 280.

82 Cheah, *What Is a World?*, 17.
83 Arjun Appadiraj, "Disjuncture and Difference in the Global Cultural Economy," *Theory, Culture & Society*, 7 (1990): 295.
84 For a critique of "heterotemporality" and the notion of "alternative modernities," see Cheah, *What Is a World?*, 98–110.
85 Ibid., 11.
86 Ibid., 208.
87 Lye, "Afterword," 351.
88 Brian Larkin, "Promising Forms: The Political Aesthetics of Infrastructure," in *The Promise of Infrastructure*, ed. Nikhil Anand, Akhil Gupta, and Hannah Appel (Durham, NC: Duke University Press, 2018), 196.
89 See Belsey, *Critical Practice*, 60.
90 Joseph Conrad, "'Preface' to *The Nigger of the Narcissus*," in *Heart of Darkness*, ed. Paul B. Armstrong (New York: Norton, 2017), 259.
91 Levine, *The Realistic Imagination*, 8.
92 Zadie Smith, "Two Directions for the Novel," in *Changing My Mind: Occasional Essays* (London: Penguin, 2009), 79.
93 See Jameson, *Antinomies of Realism*, 15–26.
94 Esty, "Realism Wars," 337.
95 Ibid.
96 Lye, "Afterword," 345.

PART I

Aesthetics

1

Uses of "Realism"

A Term in History and the History of a Term

Andreas Mahler

"Realism": A Term in History

In the Musée Fabre at Montpellier, France, visitors can see exhibited a rather sober-looking painting made by nineteenth-century French painter Gustave Courbet, entitled *La Rencontre*, "The Meeting" (Figure 1.1).[1] The painting shows three men and a dog against a cloudy sky, meeting on a sandy road in a somewhat nondescript drab Mediterranean landscape, with a coach in the background happily scurrying off to other places. The three men are the painter himself, who seems to have just arrived, and his longstanding patron Bruyas together with his servant, who have come out with the already panting dog into the midday heat to greet him and take him to their place. The scene is situated somewhere near Montpellier where Bruyas lived and collected art. While Bruyas and his servant look properly dressed, Courbet the artist, with his wild and untrimmed beard and a somewhat overenthusiastic joviality, is depicted in a rather casual white shirt and ordinary gilet, which, according to the dress code of the time, makes him appear frivolously "naked," or at least uncouth, rough, and uncivilized, in comparison to the other two welcoming him.

The painting was made, and shows an event taking place, in 1854. A year later, Courbet was striving to become part of the *Exposition Universelle*

FIGURE 1.1 *La rencontre ou "Bonjour, Monsieur Courbet"* (*The Meeting or "Bonjour, Monsieur Courbet"*) *by Gustave Courbet, 1854. Reproduced with the permission of Musée Fabre, Montpellier, France.*

in Paris, but was dismayed to hear that on May 15, 1855, the jury of the exposition had decided to turn his contribution down on the grounds of finding his art "destructive." In his disappointment, he stubbornly and provocatively reacted by opening, on June 28 of the same year, a counter-exposition in some barracks nearby (which he self-confidently called a "pavilion"), using for it the programmatic—and at the time still rather innovative—title "Du réalisme," a term that had been prompted to him by a friend who, as one of the most influential art critics of the time, was publishing under the name of Champfleury. This can be seen as the birth of "realism."[2]

Among the paintings incriminated by the jury may have been the one originally entitled *La Rencontre*, which very soon came to be also known as *Bonjour Monsieur Courbet*. The change in title may be due to the fact that the painting triggered, as early as in October 1855, a parodistic "ode funambulesque" by the French poet Théodore de Banville, up and on a friend of Courbet's, who wrote a poem in thirteen stanzas precisely called

"Bonjour, Monsieur Courbet," in which he took up Courbet's painting and formulated a literary reaction to it.³ The poem is what has been termed a *"transposition d'art,"* a transposition from one art medium to another, based on the visual painting and "altermedially" turning it into a textual poem by pretending to make the words of the text perform what the painting technique did for the picture. As Klaus Hempfer has shown, this means that the enterprise is not so much mimetic in the sense that the poet depictingly tries to create a second copy—the poem—of a first copy—the painting—but that it is rather performative in the sense that the media change from image to text tries to show that the poet can "perform"—in the sense of "make" (*"poein"*)—through his use of words even a "picture" much better than the painter can do with his brush.⁴

The point of the poem, however, is not so much that it transposes visuality into textuality but that it simultaneously undertakes a caustic critique of the new movement of "realism" in its very *status nascendi*. The Parnassian poem transposes not only Courbet's painting into a seemingly descriptive ode but also the presentation of Courbet's arrival in May into an imagination of his departure, or perhaps flight, in October by (narratively, or even metaleptically) placing a slightly disoriented fictitious observer-speaker in the poem's landscape ("En octobre dernier j'errais dans la champagne"$_1$ [Last October, as I was wandering about through the countryside]), which, as the text makes clear, the poet is actually on the brink of leaving with the help of the coach ("Courbet qui remontait dans une diligence"$_{47}$ [Courbet who was getting back onto the coach]). In doing so, Banville seems to imply that the real painter, after creating his (arguably) "ugly"—and to a certain degree unartistically "photographic"—work of art (with its "Nature . . . horrible à voir"$_4$ [Nature horrible to see] and a direct reference to Nadar in line 20) is able, and only too willing, to escape from his own painting, whereas the fictitious homodiegetic speaker, according to the logic of diegetic levels, unfortunately, and of necessity, forever remains trapped in the artifact.⁵ In other words, what the speaker of the poem obliquely, and polemically, tries to suggest is that "realism," and realistic art, condemns one to eternal, trivial ugliness, while its "destructive" creators are always already moving on toward new horizons, potentially spoiling other things.

Despite everything, Courbet's painting does seem to fulfill all the relevant criteria of "realism." In showing a contemporary everyday event in a non-comic manner, it seems to tally perfectly with one of the most powerful definitions of "realism," or rather "classical realism," which is Erich Auerbach's view of it as a "representation of reality" that follows the two criteria: (1) "the serious treatment of everyday reality" and (2) "the embedding of random persons and events in the general course of contemporary history."⁶ According to Auerbach, taking the humdrum everyday banality of life seriously and linking the fiction to contemporary references are the two historical features that precisely distinguish nineteenth-century "realism" from its preceding ("non-realist") epochs, which, as in the classicist or even pre-classicist—for example the "picaresque"—tradition, could treat the "low" and the "ugly" in the "comic mode" only, or which, as for the romanticism of a Sir Walter Scott, embedded its stories in contexts long past, as did the early-nineteenth-century historical novel.

In the course of the nineteenth century, this continually leads, as is well known, to narratives explicitly referring to the (then) present moment, simultaneously formulating some kind of accusatory critique of what, according to the author, is going wrong—especially with a view to the poor, the exploited, the outsiders—in the society at stake. On the level of contents, this entails a continuous widening of objects to be treated without any bias as to the mode of their representation. If on the level of *histoire*—on the diegetic level—there is a continuous extension of what can aesthetically be addressed (an extension that is arguably still going on today), this is extradiegetically—on the level of narration—increasingly accompanied by a self-eclipsing technique of presentation that tries to make the effect of (transparent) immediacy, and hence illusion, greater and greater.[7]

This can be seen as part of what the art historian Ernst Gombrich has described as the very specific Western development in art that leads, as his phrase is, "from making to matching."[8] According to Gombrich, it is possible to determine two important phases in Western art history which are characterized by the fact that they push the aesthetic idea of creating a kind of "life-like" art—the first period attempting this being the fifth and fourth centuries BC in ancient Greece; and the second period then starts (again) with what we, precisely for that reason, have come to call the "Renaissance," leading to what is, in the large sense of the word, considered to be the period of "Modernity." "The Greek revolution," Gombrich states with regard to the first period, "is unique in the annals of mankind. . . . What makes it unique is precisely the directed efforts, the continued and systematic modifications of the schemata of conceptual art, till making was replaced by the matching of reality through the new skill of mimesis."[9] It is this "new skill of mimesis" which in the course of the nineteenth century finds itself more and more perfected in the attempt to create in art a (textual, artistic) "world" that is almost exclusively defined by its veri/similitude, plausibility, and "truth" in relation to what at the same time is perceived as the "real world," which means that the textual techniques for "matching" are increasingly forged toward a faithful "reproduction" of what is supposed to be a recognizable, familiar "fact"—as can be seen in Stendhal's notorious "mirror" metaphor from as early as 1830[10]—along with a concerted effort to simultaneously hide the processes of artistic "making" so as to be able to foreground the result of the illusion.[11]

As a skill, the idea of mimesis reaches its highest degree of perfection in photography, which, as can be seen in Banville's rather malicious reference to Nadar ("Et l'on eût dit les rocs esquissés par Nadar!")[20] [And one might almost have said that the rocks were sketched by Nadar]), by the mid-nineteenth century seems to have become the central paradigm for this project of transparent matching in giving its beholders a particularly faithful reproduction of an object while at the same time concealing its very own mediality. The "reality effect" achieved by a photograph is, however, as has been shown, in itself the resultant only of different strategies of make-believe, such as framing, point of view, contrast, and the like.[12] This means that the seeming perfectibility of the "skill of mimesis" through the new medium of the photograph, which somehow came as a shock to the other mimetic arts, is in itself heavily indebted to representational techniques, to "continued and systematic modifications of the schemata of conceptual art," which make the artifact only appear "as if" it were a "match" to the world outside (whether it is assumed to exist or not); it is a question of "illusion" and its strategies to instill in us, as the saying is, a "willing suspension of disbelief" that makes us read as if the text were the world.[13]

This reshuffling of the media system has had a strong impact on the novel.[14] On the level of story, the novel under "realism" begins to programmatically suggest a recognizable contemporaneous world (augmented at times by seemingly superfluous minor details such as Barthes's/Flaubert's notorious barometer[15]); on the level of narration, it strives to try its best to adapt its techniques of transmission to the conventions that are least obtrusive in their own foregrounding, eventually leading to something like the Flaubertian narrator, who, in Flaubert's own terms, is supposed to be present everywhere but visible nowhere ("présent partout, visible nulle part"), or the Joycean (or rather Stephen Dedalus's) narrator-God seemingly disinterestedly "paring his fingernails" instead of explicitly telling his story.[16] Historically speaking, then, "realism" seems to be the epoch in which the (narrative) skill of mimesis reaches one of its utmost representational perfections, along with a highest degree of illusionistic believability.

"Realisms": The History of a Term

The *Robert*, authoritative dictionary in all matters concerning the French language, dates the first use of the term "*réalisme*" in the sense of referring to an art concept, or a concept of literature, to the year 1833, three years after Stendhal's programmatic comparison of his novelistic endeavors with an all-reflecting mirror.[17] The English language seems to have been rather slow, or even reluctant, in taking this up.[18] The *Oxford English Dictionary* notes a literary or art-bound use of the term—in addition to the philosophical denotations of "realism" as opposed to "nominalism" on the one hand and "idealism" on the other hand—for as late as 1856 only. Its third entry specifies the phenomenon as "3. Close resemblance to what is real; representation, rendering the precise details of the real thing or scene," and adds as connotational value: "In reference to art and literature, sometimes used as a term of commendation, when precision and vividness of detail are regarded as a merit, and sometimes unfavorably contrasted with idealized description or representation. In recent use it has often been used with implication that the details are of unpleasant or sordid character."[19] The dictionary then proceeds to differentiate between the adjective "realist" as pertaining to whoever or whatever is "addicted to realism" in the historical sense and "realistic" as something that is systematically "Characterized by artistic or literary realism; representing things as they really are."

This shift from a noun referring to an art concept apt to characterize an epoch, to an adjective designating the features typical of a style addresses a terminological conundrum that can be encountered in a variety of fields in the humanities but which is particularly virulent with regard to the term in question in the sense that, in the course of time, the adjective seems to develop generalizing repercussions on the noun, turning what originally pertains to an epoch into an overall stylistic feature of representation. It may precisely be due to this confusion or, as has been formulated in more polite terms, to its "exceptional elasticity" that the term "realism" today looks back on an impressive, albeit somewhat doubtful, success story.[20] Historically rooted, as we have seen, above all in the 1850s in France, it has rather unhistorically deployed its impact forward and backward in the sense that, prospectively, it even today still looks as if it were addressing an important—if not *the* important—aspect or feature of what is widely, and almost always epigonally, identified with, or commonly taken for, "literature," while at the same time, it is also used retrospectively to— anachronistically but, perhaps, to some extent also appropriately—describe, for example, eighteenth-century or even seventeenth-century prose or is taken as an epithet referring to the "novel" in general, going back to works like Cervantes's *Don Quixote* or even Homer's *Odyssey*.[21]

Considering this, one can say that the term today seems to have split into basically two complementary, if not contradictory, uses: (1) "realism" as a historical term referring to the literature of a certain distinct period, that is to say, (roughly) to the genre of the novel in the second half of the nineteenth century, and (2) "realism" as a typological (or systematic) term referring to a certain mode of re/presenting a text's contents in a way so as to make the process of transmission as self-denying or unobtrusive or direct or objective or transparent or consumable as possible.[22] In the first case, "realism" is used as a term referring to a specific period in time comparable to other periods such as "classicism," "romanticism," "modernism," "postmodernism," etc.; in the second, it is used as a term identifying a specific style or mode, a way of expressing things, presupposing some existence of what is being expressed and, more often than not, appearing rather in the adjectival form "realistic" than in its nominal equivalent.

The term's immense spread nowadays looks as if it were mainly based on its second meaning. It shows, for example, in Wayne C. Booth's classical list of unquestioned assumptions about the "literary" in his to some degree still seminal book on the (novelistic) *Rhetoric of Fiction*, which programmatically begins with "General Rules I: 'True Novels Must Be Realistic'";[23] it shows negatively in Catherine Belsey's highly influential philippic against "expressive realism" as being the last stultifying bulwark of an ignorant bourgeois hegemony against a long-due emancipatory liberation of the "common reader";[24] in a German context, it also shows encyclopedically in somewhat breathtaking attempts to sum up the entire history of "realism" by starting with Plato and leading up to the present moment, as in Stephan Kohl's undoubtedly useful, but still sweepingly courageous book *Realismus: Theorie und Geschichte*.[25] This typological use of the term "realism" can be found in practically all entries on "realism" in the currently relevant dictionaries of critical terms or in the various introductions to "realism," above all in the ones in English where such a use seems to have spread most widely, but also not least in those in German (or, as for that, French).[26] The development thus shows a marked drift from the strictly historical use of the term to its widened typological use: from "realism" as an epoch to "realisms" as different varieties of one and the same style through history.

Uses: "Realistic" and "Non-Realistic" Realisms?

Coining terms, defining them, and surveying the stability of their denotational content constitutes one of the decisive tasks in literary scholarship. This need for a reliable terminology is all the more important, since literary terms are "notational" in the sense that they usually do not refer to facts but to notions and ideas that have to be defined in order to "exist." In other words, from the point of view of their coining and description, they are "standardized predicators" that precisely have to be "standardized" before they can be used.[27] This entails the necessity to (hopefully) ensure some kind of constant, and consistent, use; it implies the avoidance of an unwanted dispersion of meaning and above all the avoidance of the risk of incurring unwanted connotations or free-floating associations apt to misguide or, in the last event, even prevent any kind of "controlled" scholarly communication. Imprecisions in terms and blurrings of ideas may unleash highly controversial, and at times not altogether uninteresting, discussions but do not conduce to scholarly debates (ideally) bent on the rational exchange of mutually understood ideas.

Like few others, the term "realism" has come to be one of the most overused terms in literary discourse as well as in art criticism in general. This may be due to the fact that it seems to respond to the most obvious and "natural" expectation readers have when reading a piece of literature, an expectation based on the idea that texts invariably and "naturally" talk about the reader's world in a way that makes the textual world look as if it were (or at least could be) theirs. As such, "realism" has become one of the most widespread, though at the same time perhaps also one of the most trivial and uninspired value judgments imposed on works of art. This accounts for its inimitable elasticity; it also accounts, however, for its self-disqualifying paradoxicality. No term can be used both historically and systematically at the same time. If "realism" is a term referring to an epoch, it cannot simultaneously be used to refer to a style without risking to lose its historical value. On the other hand, if "realism" is used for a representational mode that is apt to take us from the fifth century BC up until today, its value looks hollowed out right from the start, since it to some degree is made to refer to almost everything that we have got as textuality, which would make its discriminatory power as a term practically worthless (and it would have to be continuously modified by additional supplementary adjectives doing the desired terminological job).

To some extent, the second thing is what happened in the course of the twentieth century. It has brought us the ideas of a "Psychological Realism," a "Surrealism," a "Socialist Realism," a "Marxist Realism," a "Grotesque Realism," a "Magic or Magical or Marvellous Realism," even a "Fantastic Realism."[28] Rather than elasticity, this looks like terminological sloppiness. Just like a narratology that insists on calling theatrical plays or poems "narratives" invariably ends up differentiating "non-narrative narratives" from "narrative narratives," or like intermediality studies that includes both multimedial and monomedial artifacts in its field of investigation inevitably has to come up with a distinction between a "non-intermedial intermediality" and a truly "intermedial intermediality," the study of "realism" thus seems to end in a split between "non-realistic realism" and "realistic realism." This not only looks like a contradiction in terms, it is one. One way out of the dilemma might be to forget about the term altogether, another would be to use it where it still is endowed with some value. This would mean, I would like to suggest, to restrict its use to the epoch only: to novels largely of the second half of the nineteenth century that were, historically speaking, written precisely under the label of belonging to a movement that referred to, and understood, itself as "realism." In this sense "realism," I suggest, is a historical term referring to the moment when the skill of mimesis perfected itself to the degree of creating an effect of utmost recognizable aesthetic illusion; accordingly, "realist" is what a work of realism inevitably is from a historical point of view, and "realistic" is what it may as well also be systematically in its narrative technique or style. But this is no necessity. "The first author to create realism," runs a famous dictum by Argentinian author Jorge Luis Borges, "was the first one to destroy it."[29] Gustave Flaubert's *Sentimental Education* (1869) may well be a serious portrayal of two mediocre and provincial characters who, in the middle of the nineteenth century, did not quite make it, but it doubtless also is an impressive monument of an exceptionally ingenious prose writer's imagination.[30]

Notes

1 I take the cue for this and the following from Stefan Hartung, *Parnasse und Moderne: Théodore de Banvilles Odes Funambulesques (1857). Parisdichtung als Ästhetik des Heterogenen* (Stuttgart: Steiner, 1997), 163–178.

2 For further detail with regard to the Courbet painting, see ibid., 163–166. For a concise reconstruction of the debate on "realism" in the 1850s, see Uwe Dethloff, *Französischer Realismus* (Stuttgart and Weimar: J.B. Metzler, 1997), 45–69; see also the New Critical Idiom volume by Pam Morris, *Realism* (London: Routledge, 2003).

3 Théodore de Banville, *Odes funambulesques, édition de 1857*, ed. Joseph-Marc Bailbé (Paris: Lettres Modernes, 1993), 45–46; I indicate the lines in deep-set ciphers after the quote.

4 See Klaus W. Hempfer, "*Transposition d'art* und die Problematisierung der Mimesis in der Parnasse-Lyrik," in *Frankreich an der Freien Universität Berlin: Geschichte und Aktualität*, ed. Winfried Engler (Stuttgart: Steiner, 1997), 177–196; as well as Klaus W. Hempfer, ed., *Jenseits der Mimesis: Parnassische Transposition d'art und der Paradigmenwandel in der Lyrik des 19. Jahrhunderts* (Stuttgart: Steiner, 2000). For a brief summary of the discussion, see Andreas Mahler, "Sprache—Mimesis—Diskurs: Die Vexiertexte des Parnasse als Paradigma anti-mimetischer Sprachrevolution," *Zeitschrift für Französische Sprache und Literatur* 116, no. 1 (2006): 34–47; for a systematic distinction between the mimetic as a way or representing ("imitating") what already seems to exist elsewhere and the performative as a way of presenting ("symbolizing") what is created through the act of presentation only, see Wolfgang Iser, *The Fictive and the Imaginary: Charting Literary Anthropology*, trans. David Henry Wilson (Baltimore, MD: The Johns Hopkins University Press, 1993), 247–303.

5 For an exposition of the communicative levels in poetry, see Andreas Mahler, "Towards a Pragmasemiotics of Poetry," *Poetica* 38, no. 3–4 (2006): 234–254.

6 Erich Auerbach, *Mimesis: The Representation of Reality in Western Literature*, trans. Willard R. Trask (Princeton, NJ: Princeton University Press, 2003), 491.

7 For the idea of "eclipsing" narration, see Andreas Mahler, "Joyce's Bovarysm: Paradigmatic Disenchantment into Syntagmatic Progression," *Comparatio* 5, no. 2 (2013), 276–291. For attempts at summarizing semiotic features of "realism" such as "referential illusion," "transparency," and "verisimilitude," see Rosmarie Zeller, "Realismusprobleme in semiotischer Sicht," *Jahrbuch für Internationale Germanistik* 12, no. 1 (1980): 84–101; as well as the synoptic list of "normalities" in Werner Wolf, "Radikalität und Mäßigung: Tendenzen experimentellen Erzählens," in *Radikalität und Mäßigung: Der Englische Roman seit 1960*, ed. Annegret Maack and Rüdiger Imhof (Darmstadt: Wissenschaftliche Buchgesellschaft, 1993), 35.

8 See E. H. Gombrich, *Art and Illusion: A Study in the Psychology of Pictorial Representation* (Oxford: Phaidon, 1988), 99–152.

9 Ibid., 121.

10 For the novel as a literary mirror relentlessly reflecting both the "beautiful" and the "ugly," with the reader-"monsieur" all too willingly chiding the novelist-messenger for the message, see Stendhal, *Le Rouge et le Noir: Chronique du XIXe siècle*, ed. Pierre-Georges Castex (Paris: Classiques Garnier, 1973), 342: "Eh, monsieur, un roman est un miroir qui se promène sur une grande route. Tantôt il reflète à vos yeux l'azur des cieux, tantôt la fange des bourbiers de la route. Et l'homme qui porte le miroir dans sa hotte sera par vous accusé d'être immoral! Son miroir montre la fange, et vous accusez le miroir! Accusez bien plutôt le grand chemin où est le bourbier, et plus encore l'inspecteur des routes qui laisse l'eau croupir et le bourbier se former." [Well, sir, a novel is a mirror that is walking along a main road. Sometimes, it reflects to your eyes the blue of the sky, sometimes the dirt and mud of the road. And you accuse of immorality the man who is only carrying the mirror in his pannier! His mirror is showing the mud, and you accuse the mirror! You should rather accuse the big road with its mud and, what is more, the road inspector who allows the water to become stagnant and the mud to form.]

11 For a summary of his understanding of the concept of "aesthetic illusion" see Werner Wolf, "Illusion (Aesthetic)," in *Handbook of Narratology*. ed. Peter Hühn et al. (Berlin and New York: De Gruyter, 2009), 144–159; for a constructivist view of seeing "realism" as "plausible not because it reflects the world, but because it is constructed out of what is (discursively) familiar," thus opposing not so much "fiction" and "fact" but a manifest construct (the fiction) and a latent one ("reality"), see Catherine Belsey, *Critical Practice* (London: Methuen, 1980), 47.

12 See Roland Barthes, *Camera Lucida: Reflections on Photography*, trans. Richard Howard (New York: Hill and Wang, 1982).

13 For the idea of "illusion" as being the entry into a textual game (in the sense of "*in-lusio*"), see Roger Caillois, *Man, Play and Games*, trans. Meyer Barash (Glencoe, IL: The Free Press, 1958), 14–23, esp. 19.

14 See Nancy Armstrong, *Fiction in the Age of Photography: The Legacy of British Realism* (Cambridge, MA: Harvard University Press, 1999); as well as Daniel A. Novak, *Realism, Photography, and Nineteenth-Century Fiction* (Cambridge: Cambridge University Press, 2008); for a recent summary of the debate see also Julia Straub, "Nineteenth-Century Literature and Photography," in *Handbook of Intermediality: Literature—Image—Sound—Music*, ed. Gabriele Rippl (Berlin and Boston: De Gruyter, 2015), 161–163.

15 For this idea of an "*effet de réel*," with reference to Flaubert's mentioning of a barometre in his *Un cœur simple*, see (famously) Roland Barthes, "L'effet de réel," *Communications* 11 (1968): 84–89.

16 See Gustave Flaubert, "A Louise Colet" (Dec. 9, 1852), in *Extraits de la correspondance ou Préface à la vie d'écrivain*, ed. Geneviève Bollème (Paris: Seuil, 1963), 95; and James Joyce, *A Portrait of the Artist as a Young Man*, ed. Hans Walter Gabler and Walter Hettche (New York: Vintage, 1993), 207 (5.1467–9); the Joyce quote is, of course, relativized by its dependence on

Stephen's perspective, who at that moment in his development seems to see in someone like Flaubert the highest artistic achievement to be followed.

17 For a very useful collection of original texts reconstructing the debate in France, see the volume *Texte zur französischen Romantheorie des 19. Jahrhunderts*, ed. Winfried Engler (Tübingen: Niemeyer, 1970), esp. 35, 42, 49, 52 and 57 (the Stendhal quote also 30).

18 A writer like Dickens, for example, would not have seen himself as a "realist"; for the debate in England, which is much more concerned with the concept of "truth" than with the notion of "realism," see *English Theories of the Novel. Volume III: Nineteenth Century*, ed. Elke Platz-Waury (Tübingen: Niemeyer, 1972).

19 Already the 1856 quote, however, from Ruskin, starts on a negative note by implying, just as much as Banville did for Courbet, that what all this kind of art is about is a sham way "To try, by startling realism, to enforce the monstrosity that has no terror in itself."

20 Cp. the (slightly ironic) beginning of the entry "realism" in J. A. Cuddon, *The Penguin Dictionary of Literary Terms and Literary Theory*, 3rd ed. (London: Penguin, 1991), 772: "An exceptionally elastic critical term, often ambivalent and equivocal, which has acquired far too many (but seldom clarifying) adjectives, and is a term which many now feel we could do without." The term's "unmanageable elasticity" had already been deplored in the (old) Critical Idiom volume by Damian Grant, *Realism* (London: Methuen, 1970), 1. For a discussion of the term's revival in contexts of debates of literary "relevance," see also the respective entry in Jeremy Hawthorn, *A Glossary of Contemporary Literary Theory* (London: Edward Arnold, 1992).

21 This backward projection would precisely be what is addressed in the well-nigh Auerbachian description of Defoe's *Robinson Crusoe* in Ian Watt, *The Rise of the Novel: Studies in Defoe, Richardson and Fielding* (Harmondsworth: Penguin, 1963), 76: "*Robinson Crusoe* is certainly the first novel in the sense that it is the first fictional narrative in which an ordinary person's daily activities are the centre of continuous literary attention"; for a (Marxist) attempt to trace this even further back to the sixteenth century, see the volume *Realismus in der Renaissance: Aneignung der Welt in der erzählenden Prosa*, ed. Robert Weimann (Berlin and Weimar: Aufbau, 1977), esp. Weimann's chapter on the specificities of a "Renaissance Realism," 47–110.

22 Accordingly, the *Reallexikon der deutschen Literaturwissenschaft*. 3 vols. vol. 3, ed. Jan-Dirk Müller et al. (Berlin and New York: de Gruyter, 2003) has split the entry into "Realismus$_1$" in the typological sense (treated by Monika Ritzer, 217–221) and "Realismus$_2$" in the historical one (summarized by Gerhard Plumpe, 221–224).

23 Wayne C. Booth, *The Rhetoric of Fiction* (Chicago: The University of Chicago Press, 1975), 23–64.

24 For the common sense attitude that "literature reflects the *reality* of experience as it is perceived by one (especially gifted) individual, who *expresses* it in a

discourse," which she discusses under the label of "expressive realism," see Belsey, *Critical Practice*, 7–14, the quote 7 (her italics).

25 See Stephan Kohl, *Realismus: Theorie und Geschichte* (Munich: W. Fink, 1977). Kohl's book reads like an attempt to "out-Auerbach Auerbach"; but where Auerbach seems to be particularly careful in avoiding the term "realism" in hiding the representational character of the endeavor behind the overall activity (or "skill") of "mimesis," Kohl foregrounds the notion of "realism" all over the place at the risk of voiding the term of any meaning altogether.

26 See Cuddon, *The Penguin Dictionary of Literary Terms and Literary Theory*; Hawthorn, *A Glossary of Contemporary Literary Theory*, Morris, *Realism*; see also the historical collection of essays on the debate in *Begriffsbestimmung des literarischen Realismus*, ed. Richard Brinkmann, 2nd ed. (Darmstadt: Wissenschaftliche Buchgesellschaft, 1987); the large entry by Wolfgang Klein, "Realismus/realistisch," in *Ästhetische Grundbegriffe*. 6 vols., ed. Karlheinz Barck et al. (Stuttgart and Weimar: J.B. Metzler, 2003), vol. 5, 149–197; and the more recent summarizing discussion of the German debate in *Realismus: Epochen—Autoren—Werke*, ed. Christian Begemann (Darmstadt: Wissenschaftliche Buchgesellschaft, 2007).

27 For the concept of "notational term," developed with regard to the notion of "style," see Nils Erik Enkvist, *Linguistic Stylistics* (The Hague and Paris: Mouton, 1973) 17; for terms as "standardized" or "normed predicators" ("normierte Prädikatoren"), see Klaus W. Hempfer, *Gattungstheorie: Information und Synthese* (Munich: W. Fink, 1973), 26.

28 See the various dictionary entries; for the idea of a "Grotesque Realism" as opposed to the "Socialist Realism" largely propagated under Stalin, see Mikhail Bakhtin, *Rabelais and His World*, trans. Hélène Iswolsky (Bloomington: Indiana University Press, 1984); for a very circumspect discussion of "realisms" addressing the fantastic see the New Critical Idiom volume by Maggie Ann Bowers, *Magic(al) Realism* (Abingdon: Routledge, 2004).

29 "El hombre que con *Madame Bovary* forjó la novela realista fue también el primero en romperla." Jorge Luis Borges, "Vindicación de *Bouvard et Pécuchet*" (1932), in *Prosa completa*. 3 vols, ed. Carlos V. Frías (Barcelona: Bruguera, 1980), vol. 1, 209.

30 For a programmatic focus on the imaginary side of realism, see the important work by Rainer Warning, *Die Phantasie der Realisten* (Munich: W. Fink, 1999).

2

George Eliot's Realisms

Nadine Böhm-Schnitker

Introduction

It has become customary to say that "realism" as such does not exist. "Realism" has been dissolved into plural realisms, and the question of what kind of a realism a text, in this case a novel, lives up to has become contentious. The Victorian age is a particularly interesting period in that context because, as an age in which the Gutenberg Galaxy comes to full fruition,[1] it provides not only the technical contexts for mass production of print material; it also spawns a plethora of writers who shape their readership in turn and who find an increasingly professionalized group of critics that begin to observe, classify, and, of course, criticize their work.[2] Authors are key players in this emerging critical discourse themselves since many of them also deliver their own literary theories[3] and prove highly self-reflexive with regard to their writing in the respective technological, social, cultural, and economic contexts. George Eliot is a case in point. Not only is she "credited with first using the term 'realism' in English,"[4] her theoretical chapter on realism in *Adam Bede* can also be understood as "a nineteenth-century British realist manifesto,"[5] while numerous of her critical essays on literature expand on the viewpoints articulated in this novel. Eliot's own literary career extends from the 1850s to the 1880s and has been subject to very different theoretical approaches. While her kind of realism was initially described as "moral realism,"[6] the term was soon to be amended to "sympathetic realism"[7] or "ethical realism."[8] Indeed, Eliot's novels strive less to prescribe moral norms than to reflect on norms in the sense of an ethics in and of literature. However, Eliot's oeuvre cannot be reduced to the ethical function of literature. Her novels extend to different other disciplines such as science, psychology, or sociology and can be further classified as "organic realism,"[9] a "realism of surprise,"[10] psychological realism,[11] sociological realism,[12] and many others.[13] Even though "many critics would broadly agree that realist writers rejected allegory and symbol, romantic and sensational plots, supernatural explanations and idealized characters, and opted instead for the literal, credible, observable world of lived experience,"[14] this consensus is soon revealed to be highly problematic since this pragmatic distinction of genres such as sensationalism, realism, Gothicism, romance, or melodrama does not generally hold for the novel.[15] I concur with Caroline Levine, who argues that "when we look for realism, in the end what we find is a complex syndrome of linked, overlapping, and contending aims and forms."[16] Nevertheless, Levine argues that "'realism,' in its earliest articulation, was a form of cultural critique,"[17] which leaves room for an analysis of the target of this critique in particular cases. Her summary of what realist writers tried to achieve also provides some helpful stepping stones for the analysis of narrative strategies:

> The realists worked, first, to gesture to the radical otherness of the world, and they did so by pointing to the failures of representation. But this effort to acknowledge alterity slowly yielded to a sense of the impossibility of getting at an otherness outside of the language of representation—and the realist experiment turned inward, to investigate its own rhetorical practices.[18]

For Eliot's ethical realism, this is a helpful guiding principle and it emphasizes realism's great awareness of mediality, the situatedness of point of view, and the probing of the possibility of a representation of otherness.

The nineteenth-century debate on realism, which gathered momentum around the 1850s[19] but continued throughout the century, is hardly homogeneous. "Given its accumulation of 'realistic' descriptions and detail, its capacity to name and map out time and space as if it mirrored reality, realist fiction emerged as part of a culture obsessed with the truths and realities of an increasingly scientific and secular world."[20] Even though "truth," "nature," and "sincerity" loom large in the discourse on realism, realism is, of course, far from a mimetic relationship to "reality" in any naïve sense of a direct representation. Many Victorian critics were widely aware of the fact that there is no direct mirroring relationship between "art" and "reality"; rather, they reflected on the relevance of mediality[21] and the fact that art can only ever provide an asymptotic approximation to "truth." In the example of Eliot's ethical realism, a "faithful" representation comes to stand as an act of moral obligation in the contract between author and reader and is prioritized over any guarantee of an ontological or epistemological correspondence between fact and fiction. Eliot focuses on "the devious ways of the mind, the natural and psychological and social impediments to knowing or speaking the truth."²² Epistemology and mediality are thus guiding aspects for Eliot's theory of realism.

In this contribution, I am going to analyze Eliot's *Adam Bede* (1859), *Middlemarch* (1871), and *Daniel Deronda* (1876) as well as her work as a literary critic in order to sketch the development of key aspects in her realism. *Adam Bede* lays down foundational assumptions of Eliot's realism, *Middlemarch* expands them, while *Daniel Deronda* arguably brings them to an end. *Middlemarch*'s realism interrelates "public and private, psychological depth and social expansiveness, perspective and immersion; it seals together the individual and the social and intertwines the vertical movement of the *Bildungsroman* with the horizontal inclusiveness of the social-realist novel."²³ *Daniel Deronda*, "deliberately reminiscent of *Middlemarch*,"²⁴ is the novel in which "Eliot was already pushing to its limits sympathy and its relation to realist form."²⁵ Hence, these three novels lend themselves well to illustrate the development of Eliot's realism together with the genre's ethical impetus.

Eliot's realism is decidedly aisth-ethic in that it reveals the individual sense-perceptions of both characters and readers to performatively establish the "worlds" they live in; it also reveals that both characters and readers are nevertheless agents in these constructed sensescapes, which implies their ethical responsibility for themselves and for others. I am going to probe if and, if yes, to what extent these inherent enmeshments—of characters and readers into sensescapes, lifeworlds, and networks of responsibilities—live up to what Karen Barad describes as entanglements of matter and meaning or as "agential realism,"²⁶ an approach that might serve as an apt determiner that allows to fruitfully integrate the different established designators of Eliot's realism under a pertinent and encompassing term. Stacy Alaimo, whose concept of "trans-corporeality" draws on Barad's approach, illustrates Barad's reliance on Niels Bohr and succinctly summarizes central aspects of agential realism:

> Barad's account of Bohr's "intra-activity," as opposed to interactivity, rejects an ontology whereby "things" precede their relations. Instead, "relata" (as opposed to discrete "things") "do not preexist relations; rather, relata-within-phenomena emerge through specific intra-actions" (2003, 815). Barad's agential realism, which rejects representationalism in favor of a material-discursive form of performativity, "circumvents the problem of different materialities." Thus, "there is no mystery about how the materiality of language could possibly affect (through whatever mechanism and to any degree whatsoever) the materiality of the body" (1998, 108).²⁷

Intra-activity ties in with an understanding of Eliot's realism as "organic" in the sense that it provides "an experiential truth found in the material world at the molecular level of the human body's nerve tissue."[28] Eliot's characters unfold in a relational sense as they are thrown into relief in the close interaction with one another and with their environments. Eliot's realism can thus be said to focus on *material* contexts and intra-actions that can be understood performatively, creating subject and object in mutual performative processes. This is crucial for the character development in Eliot's novels that only allows characters to reflect on what occurred to them in retrospect, while narrators provide some greater overview.[29] Even if I would not claim that Eliot subscribes to new materialism *avant-la-lettre*, this current theoretical approach seems apt to elucidate character development in an ethical realism that has one strong foundation in characters' embodied experiences.[30]

Perception, Sympathy, and the Construction of Ethical Realism in *Adam Bede*

Eliot's novels strive for "the extension of our sympathies."[31] Kyriaki Hadjiafxendi emphasizes that the concept's etymological root, combining the Greek prefix for "with" and *pathos* for "feeling," "means 'with emotion', rather than being 'in an emotional state,'" so that sympathy is best defined as "the imaginative ability to understand otherness in its difference."[32] Her definition captures the great hermeneutic importance of Eliot's notion of sympathy, which raises key hermeneutic questions such as how an understanding of otherness is possible without assimilating or appropriating it to one's own cognitive concepts and schemata; sympathy is thus intricately intertwined with the question of an ethics of understanding. Crucially, Hadjiafxendi's definition highlights the importance of the imagination, which is a central prerequisite for any capacity for sympathy in Eliot's aisth-ethics and proves conducive to establishing imagined communities "beyond the bounds of our personal lot" within the novel form.[33] "The benefit we owe to the novelist," as T. H. Irwin summarizes, "is extended cognitive and affective sympathy, not practical sympathy or moral sentiment."[34] This ties in with Eliot's ideal of teaching by way of aesthetics[35] and reveals that novels are not necessarily designed to change readers' actual behavior. Correspondingly, Irwin concludes "that the direct promptings of the sympathetic feelings may also obstruct true moral development if they are not guided by true moral principles."[36] Eliot's novels are thus less pragmatic in the sense that they make the reader *do* things in actuality; rather, they are aesth-ethical in the sense that they make readers *reflect on* social stratifications, their corresponding subject positions and the consequent ways of seeing or perceiving. These, in turn, are calibrated by personal psychological dispositions not only of the characters but also of wider cultural contexts such as historically specific value systems, forms of conduct, acceptable ranges of expressible emotions etc. The "extension of our sympathies" can therefore be understood only as "the *raw material* of moral sentiment,"[37] not as moral sentiment as such. In the context of Eliot's ethical realism, her notion of sympathy is one marker of her aisth-ethics, which constructs, by way of a perceptive affinity created in the imagination, an interconnection between characters as well as between characters and readers. At the same time, it encourages individual interiority and self-reflexivity by providing embodied points of view that foster an empathetic reading position—which, however, is also offered for critical, ethical evaluation by means of variable narratological perspectives, vacillating between immersive and reflexive positions.[38]

Adam Bede not only posits the diegetic world as a virtual sensorium and constructs idealized middle-class identities,[39] but closely associates literary criticism with these novelistic assets by including a self-reflexive chapter on the notion of realism that it presents. In this chapter, George Eliot makes her narrator (who metaleptically coincides with the implied author here) formulate a theory of realism that is highly sensitive to the problems of mediality and the issue of the "faithfulness" of realist representation. The novel's famous chapter 17, "In Which the Story Pauses a Little," is a paradigmatic example of novelistic literary theory. It starts with a reflection on the conditions of the possibility of "truthful," "immediate" representation in the novel. Within the structure of *Adam Bede*, chapter 17 serves to specify the rules by which the narrative has to abide, stipulating what is and is not to be included. Since the chapter combines ethics and aesthetics, it calibrates the perspective that readers are invited to take. As regards the novel's temporality, this chapter is, of course, also a "pause," in the sense that the plot is not moving forward. As Caroline Levine argues, "Eliot's prose essay enforces a delay, stopping both the reader and Arthur Donnithorne from rushing headlong into the future"; consequently, the novel "carefully refuses the pleasures of suspense in favor of suspensions—gaps and pauses that do not stimulate the forward-looking impulses of desire. These suspensions replace the enigmas of suspense to encourage a new readerly relationship to alterity."[40] While the use of such essayistic and theoretical chapters can be traced back to the eighteenth century, in *Adam Bede* the chapter provides a break in the plot to allow some training in aesth-ethical realism: "presumably by schooling her readers in acceptance through art, the novelist will also school them in empathy in life."[41] The pause also provides an opportunity for reflection, which is central to Eliot's choice of genre: "Realism, as Eliot envisions it, requires the pause."[42] The pause allows for turning around, looking again more closely, reconsidering the past and reflecting on its impact on a present situation.

Representing a programmatic exposition of the realist contract with the reader, the chapter introduces an—albeit mediated—authenticity as a substitute for any concept of "truth" that relies on an exact correspondence between reality and representation. In doing so, it reveals Eliot's acute awareness of mediality. The possible distortions of "truth" in the process of representation are counterbalanced by the narrator's obligation in a religious, ethical, and legal sense to convey experience as authentically as possible.[43] As in a witness box, the implied author strives to transcode experience as authentically and faithfully as possible into writing—or, more precisely, into narration. With this transcoding of *experience*, the implied author introduces categories pertaining to a phenomenology of narration. Eliot's version of realistic writing presents ways of harnessing the senses to ethical obligations, to a contract with the readership to render storytelling reliable. What becomes represented in writing is a derivation of perception: the reflection of perception in the author's mind transferred into writing. Readers are required to give the implied author credit for "his" faithfulness in reflecting perception and experience, as well as the quasi-legal obligation to veracity in relating these experiences:

> I aspire to give no more than a *faithful account* of men and things as they have mirrored themselves in my *mind*. The mirror is doubtless defective; the outlines will sometimes be disturbed; the reflection faint or confused; but I *feel as much bound to tell you*, as precisely as I can, what that reflection is, as if I were in the *witness-box* narrating my experience on oath.[44]

Reality is twice refracted, once in the narrator's mind—documenting Eliot's keen insight into "the necessary distortions that perception will introduce into representation"[45] and indicating the relevance of psychology in the context of realist representation—and once in the translation of such reflections into the medium of language, as John Hillis Miller has highlighted: "From things to mental images to verbal account."[46] The narrator's truthfulness must be trebly secured, by ethical, religious, and juridical discourses ("on oath"). "The obligation is economic, legal, and ethical, all at once,"[47] Miller argues,[48] illustrating the fact that truthful representation had already been placed in doubt by Victorian reflections on mediality and required strategies of plausibilization. The "truth" aspired to in Eliot's realism is authenticity:[49] an authentic representation of the narrator's/author's "experience." The relation between that which is told and the mind of the author/narrator relies rhetorically on religious discourses—specifically, St Paul's distinction between human perception in a state of history, and that in a redemptive state (see 1 Cor. 13: 12). The "account" must be "faithful" precisely because the perception of the unredeemed world is poor; consequently, storytelling becomes an ethical act, based on an obligation to aspire to "truth" as far as possible. The narrative must be *faithful* and, legally speaking, related as if "on oath," to testify to the correctness of the description provided. In place of direct representation, Eliot establishes a sort of contract, a plea for adherence to a convention that promises faithfulness on the part of the author and expects faith on the part of recipients. This contract reveals the ways in which realism calibrates perception as well as judgment;[50] it induces readers to respond to realist literary representations *as if* they were truthful, a responsive reaction, which lives up to an "ethics of reading," as Miller understands it.[51] The claim to truthfulness is performatively produced, defended, and secured in literary criticism.

In *Adam Bede*, literary representation in itself becomes an ethical obligation, as representation is considered instrumental in the establishment of ethical communities. Large groups can retain notions of social communality only as imagined communities. Literature is instrumental in this, because it provides the imaginary space in which people can relate to one another. In Eliot's novels, "it is necessary that [the neighbors] make a detour through the mirroring of art in order to become visible and hence lovable," Miller maintains, revealing the writer's "obligation" to return the "reflection with 'interest'. . . that is, in a represented form."[52] Quintessentially, this implies that *ethical* relationships become possible only through aesthetic and aisth-ethic mediation. The ethical end of novels can be achieved through strategies of presentification, inviting readers to participate in the diegetic world metaleptically, where they serve as quasi-deictic centers and embodied entities, and turning them into fellow beings who, ideally, develop fellow feeling. Eliot's realism is installed as a means of establishing social cohesion through aisth-ethics. In *Adam Bede*, despite *and* because of its self-reflexivity, this is achieved through metalepses. On the one hand, there is the conflation, as already mentioned, of narrator and implied author, who materializes on the diegetic level from his previously extra- and heterodiegetic position to converse with the diegetic character Adam. On the other hand, Levine's notion that realism's genre conventions are supposed to suggest the epistemological conflation of the verbal representation with "reality" amounts to a second metalepsis, which Eliot further justifies in her criticism. In her review "The Natural History of German Life," for example, she suggests that "art is the nearest thing to life,"[53] a proximity or metonymic contiguity that may culminate in a substitution, in turn producing a reality effect.

Correspondingly, *Adam Bede*'s opening chapter applies strategies to make the reader see, hear, feel, and smell what is described in the diegetic world, introducing them to the novel's setting and characters by aligning their perspective with the "elderly horseman"[54] who comes as a stranger to the vicinity and later turns out to be Colonel Townley, the magistrate at Stoniton where Hetty awaits her sentence.[55] The reader's perspective is thus initially aligned with a character who can adopt the position of a detached observer,[56] but who also takes a compassionate interest in the other characters' fates. Although such "interested detachment" is a paradoxical phrase and attitude, I contend that it is a crucial requirement of the novel's ethics.

The novel's first ethical task is hence the *representation* of characters to sympathize with, an ethical task that is closely intertwined with its aesthetic function. For Eliot, the novel "works morally only . . . if it is aesthetically effective."[57] "Eliot was using aesthetics and realism to redefine each other,"[58] extending the representational range of the novel[59] and conceiving of aesthetics as aisth-ethics. While the latter aspect comes to full fruition in *Middlemarch*, the former is scrupulously justified in chapter 17 of *Adam Bede*:

> In this world there are so many of these common, coarse people, who have no picturesque sentimental wretchedness! It is so needful we should remember their existence, else we may happen to leave them quite out of our religion and philosophy, and frame lofty theories which only fit a world of extremes. Therefore let Art always remind us of them; therefore let us always have men ready to give the loving pains of a life to the faithful representing of commonplace things—men who see beauty in these commonplace things, and delight in showing how kindly the light of heaven falls on them.[60]

This claim is, of course, intended to demarcate realism off from the *dramatis personae* of the romance. More crucially, it illustrates the need to remember "coarse people" (162), who, in an increasingly stratified society, have to be portrayed to other social strata, predominantly the middle classes, in order to provide the fellow feeling that is a condition of possibility of social cohesion. Eliot's notion of sympathy converts "lofty theories" (162)— abstractions and propositional knowledge about people—into emotional, embodied, experienceable stories; in other words, sympathy enables a mediated, emotionally sublimated relationship to "common people." The novel, in turn, makes feelings accessible via aisth-ethic forms of showing. The lasting effect of novel reading, however, is achieved by witnessing the emergence of relations between characters—conceiving characters not as entities to be represented, but as relata that emerge in the process of the novel craft and that become cathected correspondingly for ethical reflection.

Middlemarch: Mediating Realism by Symbolic Forms

Middlemarch takes further *Adam Bede*'s exploration of the condition of possibility of novelistic truth-telling and intensifies its reflection on calibrations of perception by providing a "life like gallery," as John Blackwood calls the novel,[61] or a "panorama" of different perspectives.[62] Love and desire, one's imaginary relationship to one's life course, history, economics, politics, art, and science calibrate perception in *Middlemarch* and reveal the "inextricable web of affinities" that defines the multiplot-novel's variety of realism.[63] All these different discourses serve as general framings and affect the characters' individual schemata, defining how they "see" the diegetic world. These general framings can be understood as symbolic forms in Ernst Cassirer's sense:[64] symbolic forms shape the "'pathways' from the senses to meaning"[65] and thus modulate the contexts in which each individual character is able to interpret their perception within the "interconnection and interdependence of all parts of the social web,"[66] and hence within a historically specific set of cultural contexts calibrating perception. Aisth-ethics in *Middlemarch* presents the translation of Eliot's insight into the sociohistorical shaping power of contextual factors, which imbue "life courses" with more or less meaning for individual characters, into a novelistic aisth-ethics. Her aisth-ethics of the novel reflects the limitations of perspectives due to their embodiment. Correspondingly, the panoramic view created by the narrative instance meets the narratological requirement to render the complex interdependencies of characters and contexts palpable at all.

In her review of Mackay's *The Progress of the Intellect*, Eliot formulates an approach akin to symbolic forms when in her introduction, pondering the relevance of the past to the present, she argues that "each age and each race has had a faith and a symbolism suited to its need and its stage of development."[67] While this claim is rooted in evolutionary theory, affirming the notion that human susceptibilities change depending on the stage of development, it also illustrates Eliot's conviction that such susceptibilities are intertwined with corresponding semiotic systems adapted to particular historical requirements—in short, of symbolic forms. These may refer to "particular occurrences of meaning, to pervasive kinds of symbolic relations, and to cultural forms or ways of having a 'world,'" and can be further understood as "specific cultural matrices."[68] It is such matrices that structure perception in Eliot's novel on a macro-level; in *Middlemarch*, such framings of meaning comprise language, art, science, myth, and religion. In Cassirer's phenomenological approach, all symbolic forms have their own internal logic and provide systems that organize the ways in which the phenomenal world is conceived of as meaningful. In Eliot's novel, perceptions and impressions are similarly transmogrified into individual sensescapes,[69] in the double sense of what characters perceive and how they make sense of it. All characters serve as perceptive "filters" and, by virtue of that function, turn what they *perceive as* reality into their individual reality, their individual outlook, to be reflected on by readers in the wider panorama of Middlemarch.[70]

The novel thus portrays the ways in which the interaction between contextual and individual factors shapes what is considered to be "reality" at a particular historical moment. Given the novel's setting shortly before the 1832 Reform Act and its wider thematic concern with several different reform processes,[71] reform also becomes a shorthand for changes in "ways of seeing": questions about the ways in which political participation can be conceived of or how human bodies can be understood to reverberate in individual lives and shape characters' outlooks. Such processes of change draw attention to the fact that contextual factors have a bearing on individual structures of feeling, which a concentration on symbolic forms can throw into relief.

One of *Middlemarch*'s most famous passages outlines that "pure," universal perception without any filtering or calibrating is impossible, particularly for psychological reasons: "If we had a keen vision and feeling of all ordinary human life, it would be like hearing the grass grow and the squirrel's heart beat, and we should die of that roar which lies on the other side of silence. As it is, the quickest of us walk about well wadded with stupidity."[72] "Ordinary human life"[73] would be too overwhelming and overpowering if one could get full perceptive access to all of its expressions. The plethora of potential impressions is cloaked by silence, in opposition to universal perception. *Middlemarch* reveals the interdependences between perception and anesthesia, between individual implicit and explicit silencing processes or forms of "insulation" and mediated ways of expression.[74]

The impact of calibrations of perception on hermeneutics is underpinned by the novel's use of scientific metaphors. Mrs. Cadwallader's schemes relating to Dorothea's marriage(s), for instance, must be evaluated differently depending on whether stronger and weaker lenses determine one's perspective:

> Was there any ingenious plot, any hide-and-seek course of action, which might be detected by *a careful telescopic watch*? Not at all: a telescope might have swept the parishes of Tipton and Freshitt, the whole area visited by Mrs Cadwallader in her phaeton, without witnessing any interview that could excite suspicion, or any scene from which she did not return with the same unperturbed keenness of eye and the same high natural colour. . . . *Even with a microscope directed on a water-drop* we find ourselves making interpretations which turn out to be rather coarse; for whereas under a weak lens you may seem to see a creature exhibiting an active voracity into which other smaller creatures actively play as if they were so many animated tax-pennies, a stronger lens reveals to you certain tiniest hairlets which make vortices for these victims while the swallower waits passively at his receipt of custom.[75]

While greater distance would provide a good overview of Mrs. Cadwallader's "territory," it would not allow any insight into her motivations or "plots." However, a microscopic view would not facilitate closer inspection of these per se, as motivations appear differently depending on the lens used.[76] The narrator thus avoids a clear judgment on Mrs. Cadwallader and instead provides a digression on the possible views one can take, which amounts to a suspension of hermeneutic judgment. The novel's reflection on perceptive limitations results in an ethical demand to abstain from epistemic violence. More generally, *Middlemarch* illustrates the calibration of perception by symbolic forms and the effects of such calibration on the "psyche" of individual characters. Consequently, the readers' task is to synthesize of multiple plot strands and multiple limited perspectives, and to reflect on the conditions that make possible a synthesis of differences, as a substitute for hermeneutic closure.

Difference, for Eliot, is ingrained in the very *form* of the novel. In "Notes on Form in Art," Eliot poses the rhetorical question, "what is form but the limit of that difference by which we discriminate one object from another?—a limit determined partly by the intrinsic relations or composition of the object, and partly by the extrinsic action of other bodies upon it?"[77] *Middlemarch* explores this interaction of extrinsic and intrinsic factors both with regard to character construction and more generally on the level of composition and what I would call the novel's epistemology, referring to the fact that it performs the insight by its very composition and structure. The novel reflects on ways of knowing, on epistemology, by modulating the internal and external effects shaping characters' thoughts and feelings—on the diegetic level, the extradiegetic level and the level of the implied reader. On the macro-level, *Middlemarch* mediates perception through symbolic forms, while on the extradiegetic level it modulates the perspective structure and generalizes particular points of view, as in *Adam Bede*. Finally, on the level of characterization, it reveals the individual patterning of perception. Concentrating on vision, J. Hillis Miller has shown that "seeing . . . is for Eliot not a neutral, objective, dispassionate, or passive act. It is the creative projection of light from an egoistic center motivated by desire and need. This projected radiance orders the field of vision according to the presuppositions of the seer."[78] In *Middlemarch*, it relates to the web-metaphor that is used for society,[79] and the correspondingly shifting viewpoints of characters, depending on which position in this network they occupy at a particular moment in time. More generally, the sensescapes of individual characters are presented as effects of particular calibrations of perception.

Eliot reflects on the role played by literary forms as mediators of sense, as well as thought, and the interdependence of form and content, each of which serves to constitute the other:

> Poetic form was not begotten by thinking it out or framing it as a shell which should hold emotional expression, any more than the shell of an animal arises before the living creature; but emotion, by its tendency to repetition, i.e. rhythmic persistence in proportion as diversifying thought is absent, creates a form by the recurrence of its elements in adjustment with certain given conditions of sound, language, action, or environment. Just as the beautiful expanding curves of a bivalve shell are not first made

for the reception of the unstable inhabitant, but grow & are limited by the simple rhythmic conditions of its growing life.[80]

This interdependence of emotion and form—or "life" and form—as well as the emphasis on selection, rhythm, and composition, foreground the importance of relationality and the fundamental interdependence of a subject and its environment.[81] *Middlemarch*'s realism reveals complex interdependencies between macrocosm and microcosm played out on the level of individual characters. In *Middlemarch*, realism has a decidedly aisth-ethic quality, in that its very narrative performs the successive development of several embodied perspectives that coalesce to form a panorama of a community situated in a specific historical setting. This panorama's intricate interdependencies are gradually disclosed to the reader, enabling a "slow, experiential, physical mode of learning."[82] As in *Adam Bede*, the novel's perspective structure oscillates between immersive and reflective passages conducive to aisth-ethics. I concur with Star J. Summer's assessment of *Middlemarch*'s realism:

> Eliot was using aesthetics and realism to redefine each other: to reposition the former in the sphere of everyday life, in the spontaneous and bodily perception of form in one's surroundings; and to ground our reality-perception in a fundamentally aesthetic mode of perception, one thus particularly amenable to literary representation.[83]

Consequently, *Middlemarch*'s aisth-ethics can be related not only to the calibrations of perception by framing strategies but to the relevance of the aisth-ethic in its characters' everyday lives and to its focus on their embodied experience.

Outlook and Conclusion: The Case of *Daniel Deronda*

The plethora of Eliot's realisms might be summarized as an agential realism in which it is the primacy of relations—be it by way of characters' interrelations or interrelations between characters and environments—that provide the material for narratological representation and reflection. Characters only emerge through "entanglements of matter and meaning,"[84] psychological as well as physiological interactions with their social and material environments. While omniscient narrators still serve to reflect on these processes, this kind of realist representation nevertheless underlines the fact that it is not directly observable, it can only be traced in the process of its emergence. While *Adam Bede* is fundamental for defining Eliot's early aisth-ethics in the form of an ethical realism that reflects on questions of novelistic mediation, hermeneutics, and epistemologies, *Middlemarch* renders the interaction between matter and meaning even clearer by representing the diegetic world through symbolic forms that shape characters' individual outlooks and determine the emergence of meaning and social interaction.

With *Daniel Deronda*, finally, Eliot pushes "sympathy and realism beyond their limits."[85] Her last novel is particularly "renowned both for its aggressive expansion of novelistic scope—most obviously in its insistence on a post-national supra-English perspective, its strategic introduction of 'foreign' and 'Jewish' identities into the English novel and its countervailing attention to unconscious and semi-conscious states (what Eliot calls 'the unmapped country within us' [235; ch. 24])—and for its omissions, lacunas, and generic instabilities."[86] The novel's double plot, connecting an allegedly English plot with a Deronda or Jewish plot,[87] illustrates the complex entanglements of characters and storytelling that are based on intra-active processes of "transmission, transmutation, and transmigration."[88] Despite such strategies of interconnection, the double plot has long been criticized as dividing the novel into two separate ones.[89] Eliot herself responded by saying, "I meant everything in the book to be related to everything else (Letters 6: 290)."[90] In the Jewish plot, this is illustrated in the way in which Daniel Deronda comes to realize and acknowledge his Jewish inheritance:

> It is through your inspiration that I have discerned what may be my life's task. It is you who have given shape to what, I believe, was an inherited yearning—the effect of brooding, passionate thoughts in many ancestors—thoughts that seem to have been intensely present in my grandfather. Suppose the stolen offspring of some mountain tribe brought up in a city of the plain, or one with an inherited genius for painting, and born blind—the ancestral life would lie within them as a dim longing for unknown objects and sensations, and the spell-bound habit of their inherited frames would be like a cunningly-wrought musical instrument, never played on, but quivering throughout in uneasy mysterious moanings of its intricate structure that, under the right touch, gives music. Something like that, I think, has been my experience.[91]

While this passage presents a somewhat problematic notion of inherited religion and, with its musical metaphor, reveals that characters are attuned to their tradition, it also shows how it was Daniel's interaction and intra-action with Mordecai and Mirah that enabled his development as a character: a character, that is, that results from the primacy of relata. Despite the fact that, "by the end of *Daniel Deronda*, sympathy in its recognisably Eliotian form cannot mend the nation,"[92] social cohesion in the novel can be secured by way of intra-actions that allow for the integration of differences, be they social, sexual, or religious. Eliot's (late) realism is agential realism.

Notes

1. See Marshall McLuhan, *The Gutenberg Galaxy: The Making of Typographic Man* (London: Routledge and Kegan Paul, 1962).
2. See T. W. Heyck, *The Transformation of Intellectual Life in Victorian England* (London and Canberra: Croom Helm, 1982), 200–221.
3. See Nicholas Dames, "Realism and Theories of the Novel," in *The Nineteenth-Century Novel, 1820–1880*, ed. John Kucich and Jenny Bourne Taylor (Oxford: Oxford University Press, 2012), 291.
4. Ute Berns, "George Eliot, *Middlemarch* (1871–1872; 1874)," in *Handbook of the English Novel, 1830–1900*, ed. Martin Middeke and Monika Pietrzak-Franger (Berlin and Boston: De Gruyter, 2020), 403.
5. Dames, "Realism and Theories of the Novel," 299.
6. See Saverio Tomaiuolo, "Genres and Poetology: The Novel and the Way Towards Aesthetic Self-Consciousness," in *Handbook of the English Novel, 1830–1900*, ed. Martin Middeke and Monika Pietrzak-Franger (Berlin and Boston: De Gruyter, 2020), 93.
7. Anna-Maria Jones, "The Art of Novel Writing: Victorian Theories," in *Handbook of the English Novel, 1830–1900*, ed. Martin Middeke and Monika Pietrzak-Franger (Berlin and Boston: De Gruyter, 2020), 115.
8. See Caroline Levine, *The Serious Pleasures of Suspense: Victorian Realism and Narrative Doubt* (Charlottesville: University of Virginia Press, 2003), 108.
9. Jean Arnold, "Organic Realism in *Middlemarch*," in *George Eliot: Interdisciplinary Essays. A Bicentennial Collection*, ed. Jean Arnold and Lila Marz Harper (Cham: Palgrave Macmillan, 2019).
10. Caroline Levine, "Surprising Realism," in *A Companion to George Eliot*, ed. Amanda Anderson and Harry E. Shaw (Malden, MA: Wiley-Blackwell, 2013), 63. Levine builds on her previous study on *The Serious Pleasures of Suspense*, where she made the broader statement that "suspense became the perfect vehicle for a new aesthetic that writers in the 1850s began to call 'realism.'" Levine, *Serious Pleasures of Suspense*, 3.
11. Wilbur Cross, *The Development of the English Novel* (New York: Macmillan, 1899), 237.
12. See Levine, "Surprising Realism," 62.
13. Avrom Fleishman notes that, apart from sociology, the discipline that most influenced the composition of *Middlemarch* was "esthetic theory, the record of which is 'Notes on Form in Art' (1868)." Avrom Fleishman, *George Eliot's Intellectual Life* (Cambridge: Cambridge University Press, 2010), 161.
14. Caroline Levine, "Victorian Realism," in *The Cambridge Companion to the Victorian Novel*, ed. Deidre David (Cambridge: Cambridge University Press, 2012), 84.
15. Royce Mahawatte provides a study on generic overlaps between George Eliot's novels and the Gothic, see Royce Mahawatte, *George Eliot and the*

Gothic Novel: Genres, Gender, Feeling (Cardiff: University of Wales Press, 2013). Generally, it is by now established that novels such as *Adam Bede* or *The Mill on the Floss* incorporate conventions generally associated with the sensational; see for example Nancy Armstrong, "The Sensation Novel," in *The Nineteenth-Century Novel 1820–1880*, ed. John Kucich and Jenny Bourne Taylor (Oxford: Oxford University Press, 2012), 137–153.

16 Levine, "Victorian Realism," 104.
17 Levine, *Serious Pleasures of Suspense*, 12.
18 Ibid., 17.
19 See Levine, "Victorian Realism," 89.
20 Sean Purchase, *Key Concepts in Victorian Literature* (Basingstoke: Palgrave Macmillan, 2006), 185.
21 See George Levine, "Introduction: George Eliot and the Art of Realism," in *The Cambridge Companion to George Eliot*, ed. George Levine (Cambridge: Cambridge University Press, 2001), 15.
22 Levine, "Introduction," 10.
23 Alex Woloch, "*Daniel Deronda*: Late Form, or After *Middlemarch*," in *A Companion to George Eliot*, ed. Amanda Anderson and Harry E. Shaw (Malden, MA: Wiley-Blackwell, 2013), 168.
24 Woloch, "*Daniel Deronda*," 167.
25 Carolyn Burdett, "Sympathy," in *The History of British Women's Writing*, ed. Lucy Hartley (London: Palgrave Macmillan, 2018), 321. For a comprehensive discussion of Eliot's notion of sympathy, see T.H. Irwin, "Sympathy and the Basis of Morality," in *A Companion to George Eliot*, ed. Amanda Anderson and Harry E. Shaw (Malden et al.: Wiley-Blackwell, 2013). The proposition is that "the artist can do something to change people who lack ready-made sympathy and active moral sentiment. By making us aware in imagination of what it is like to be one of these people, through a detailed description of their environment and their mental life, the artist 'surprises even the trivial and the selfish into that attention to what is apart from themselves, which may be called the raw material of moral sentiment'" (284). This is an early understanding of sympathy that is strongly influenced by Adam Smith and that changes throughout Eliot's career. See Burdett, "Sympathy," 322.
26 Karen Barad, *Meeting the Universe Half-Way: Quantum Physics and the Entanglement of Matter and Meaning* (Durham, NC and London: Duke University Press, 2007).
27 Stacy Alaimo, "Trans-Corporeal Feminisms and the Ethical Space of Nature," in *Material Feminisms*, ed. Stacy Alaimo and Susan Hekman (Bloomington: Indiana University Press, 2008), 248.
28 Arnold, "Organic Realism in *Middlemarch*," 122.
29 See Nicholas Dames, "1825–1880: The Network of the Nerves," in *The Emergence of Mind: Representations of Consciousness in Narrative Discourse*

in English, ed. David Herman (Lincoln: University of Nebraska Press, 2011), 227, 229.

30 Eliot indeed "sought to explore the embodiedness of mind and the mutual dependency of mind and brain." Jill Matus, "George Eliot," *The Cambridge Companion to English Novelists*, ed. Adrian Poole (Cambridge: Cambridge University Press, 2009), 232.

31 George Eliot, "The Natural History of German Life," *Westminster Review* (July 1856): 30.

32 Kyriaki Hadjiafxendi, "Negotiating Fame: Mid-Victorian Women Writers and the Romantic Myth of the Gentlemanly Reviewer," in *Crafting the Woman Professional in the Long Nineteenth Century: Artistry and Industry in Britain*, ed. Kyriaki Hadjiafxendi and Patricia Zakreski (Farnham and Burlington: Ashgate, 2013), 191.

33 Eliot, "Natural History of German Life," 30.

34 Irwin, "Sympathy and the Basis of Morality," 285.

35 See Gordon Sherman Haight, *The George Eliot Letters* (New Haven, CT: Yale University Press, 1954–1978), 1956 IV: 300.

36 Irwin, "Sympathy and the Basis of Morality," 290.

37 Eliot, "Natural History of German Life," 30.

38 See Pauline Nestor, *George Eliot* (Basingstoke: Palgrave, 2002), 51, for a discussion of the relevance of Spinoza's ethics to Eliot's concept of self-reflexivity.

39 See Margaret Homans, "Dinah's Blush and Maggie's Arm: Class, Gender, and Sexuality in George Eliot's Early Novels," *Victorian Studies* 36, no. 2 (1993): 156, 158.

40 Levine, *Serious Pleasures of Suspense*, 104. See also Deanna Kreisel on the relevance of pauses in *Adam Bede*: Deanna Kreisel, "Incognito, Intervention, and Dismemberment in *Adam Bede*," *ELH* 70, no. 2 (2003): 553.

41 Kreisel, "Incognito, Intervention, and Dismemberment in *Adam Bede*," 547.

42 Ibid., 556.

43 See Joseph Hillis Miller, *The Ethics of Reading: Kant, de Man, Eliot, Trollope, James, and Benjamin* (New York: Columbia University Press, 1987), 63.

44 George Eliot, *Adam Bede* (Oxford: Oxford University Press, 2008), 159; my emphases.

45 Elaine Freedgood, "Nineteenth-Century British Critics of Realism," in *The Cambridge History of Literary Criticism*, ed. M.A.R. Habib (Cambridge: Cambridge University Press, 2013), 326.

46 Miller, *Ethics of Reading*, 65.

47 With regard to Eliot's criticism and reflection on literary markets, one might add economic discourses to the equation. Her most important review, which is frequently cited to illustrate her realism, indicates that she is well aware of the "vicissitudes of the market." George Eliot, "The Natural History of German

Life," *Essays of George Eliot*, ed. Thomas Pinney (London: Routledge and Kegan Paul, 1963), 281.
48 Miller, *Ethics of Reading*, 63.
49 Levine, "Introduction," 7.
50 See Mark Warren McLaughlin, "*Adam Bede*: History, Narrative, Culture," *Victorians Institute Journal* 22 (1994): 64.
51 Miller, *Ethics of Reading*, 2–3.
52 Ibid., 63.
53 Eliot, "Natural History of German Life," 30.
54 Eliot, *Adam Bede*, 12.
55 Ibid., 399. See also Deanna Kreisel, "Incognito, Intervention, and Dismemberment in *Adam Bede*," 551–555 who analyzes the pause in the narrative achieved by the horseman's gaze, which is connected to class difference and the leisure to observe the scene with an aesthetic predilection for the pastoral, a genre of which Eliot, in the tradition of Ruskin, is critical.
56 See Hugh Witemeyer, *George Eliot and the Visual Arts* (New Haven, CT: Yale University Press, 1979), 130.
57 Levine, "Introduction," 8.
58 Summer J. Star, "Feeling Real in *Middlemarch*," *ELH* 80 (2013): 840.
59 See Rae Greiner, "*Adam Bede*: History's Maggots," in *A Companion to George Eliot*, ed. Amanda Anderson and Harry E. Shaw (Malden, MA: John Wiley & Sons, 2013), 106.
60 Eliot, *Adam Bede*, 162.
61 George Eliot, *Middlemarch: An Authoritative Text, Backgrounds, Criticism*, ed. Bert G. Hornback (London and New York: Norton, 2000), 533.
62 Henry James, "*Middlemarch*," *The Critical Muse*, ed. Roger Gard (London: Penguin, 1987), 75.
63 Charles Darwin, qtd. in Gillian Beer, *Darwin's Plots: Evolutionary Narrative in Darwin, George Eliot and Nineteenth-Century Fiction* (Cambridge: Cambridge University Press, 2000), 156.
64 My definition of symbolic forms is derived from Cassirer's *The Philosophy of Symbolic Forms. Volume 1*, trans. Ralph Manheim (New Haven, CT: Yale University Press, 1955).
65 Ina Habermann, *Myth, Memory and the Middlebrow: Priestley, du Maurier and the Symbolic Form of Englishness* (New York: Palgrave Macmillan, 2010), 17. Cassirer himself describes this in a similar fashion as "roads by which the spirit proceeds towards its objectivization, i.e., its self-revelation." Cassirer, *Philosophy of Symbolic Forms*, 78.
66 Jill Matus, "George Eliot and the Sciences of Mind: The Silence That Lies on the Other Side of Roar," *A Companion to George Eliot*, ed. Amanda Anderson and Harry E. Shaw (Chichester: Wiley Blackwell, 2013), 460.

67 George Eliot, "*The Progress of the Intellect, as Exemplified in the Religious Development of the Greeks and Hebrews*. By Robert William Mackay. London: John Chapman. 1850," *Westminster Review* (January 1851), 178.

68 John Michael Krois, *Cassirer: Symbolic Forms and History* (New Haven, CT and London: Yale University Press, 1987), 44; 51.

69 See also Marcus K. Jones, "Forming Reality through Perception and Imagination in *Middlemarch*," *The Victorian* 3, no. 1 (2015): 2.

70 See Gage McWeeny, "The Sociology of the Novel: George Eliot's Strangers," *NOVEL: A Forum on Fiction* 42, no. 3 (2009): 539; for a discussion of how *Middlemarch* diverges from a sociological perspective, despite its attempt to create a panorama of Middlemarch's social world.

71 See Brian Reed, "Envisioning the Metaphysical Middle: A New Way of Seeing Probes the Heart of *Middlemarch*," *Interactions* 14, no. 1 (2005): 213.

72 Eliot, *Middlemarch*, 124. George Levine argues that this passage, "though it echoes Huxley, is directly related to the question of the connection between imagination and morality." George Levine, "George Eliot's Hypothesis of Reality," *Nineteenth-Century Fiction* 35, no. 1 (1980): 15.

73 Eliot, *Middlemarch*, 124.

74 In her "Quarry for 'Middlemarch,'" Eliot includes the entry "Mikroscopische Untersuchungen. By Schwann, 1838–1839," see Eliot, *Middlemarch*, 543. Schwann did important research on nerve cells and related cells such as the Schwann cell; in addition, he explored myelination, that is, the process by which nerve cells are insulated. The metaphor of "insulation" is justified because it corresponds to a basic neurological insight of which Eliot was well aware: the fact that nerve fibers are themselves "well wadded" with myelin so that they can transmit impulses more easily. The fibers require insulation in order to function properly in the first place, so that an organism may perceive something *as something*, rather than being overwhelmed by a myriad of impressions. Literary representation depends on a similar selectivity; the perceptions of characters are thus shaped by their individual "insulations," even though they, in turn, may then be subject to criticism.

75 Eliot, *Middlemarch*, 38; my emphasis.

76 See also Charlotte Sleigh, "The Novel as Observation and Experiment," *The Routledge Research Companion to Nineteenth-Century British Literature and Science*, ed. John Holmes and Sharon Ruston (London and New York: Routledge, 2017), 78–79. Here she observes that the microscope "de-familiarizes human observation and makes it possible to get closer to the truth."

77 George Eliot, "Notes on Form in Art (1868)," *Essays of George Eliot*, ed. Thomas Pinney (London: Routledge and Kegan Paul, 1963), 434.

78 J. Hillis Miller, "Optic and Semiotic in *Middlemarch*," *The Worlds of Victorian Fiction*, ed. Jerome H. Buckley (Cambridge, MA and London: Harvard University Press, 1975), 138.

79 Eliot, *Middlemarch*, 131.
80 Eliot, "Notes on Form in Art," 435.
81 Peter Garratt, "Scientific Literary Criticism," *The Routledge Research Companion to Nineteenth-Century British Literature and Science*, ed. John Holmes and Sharon Ruston (London and New York: Routledge, 2017), 120.
82 Star, "Feeling Real in *Middlemarch*," 841.
83 Ibid., 840.
84 Barad, *Meeting the Universe Half-Way*.
85 Burdett, "Sympathy," 333.
86 Woloch, "*Daniel Deronda*," 168.
87 See Sarah Gates, "'A Difference of Native Language': Gender, Genre, and Realism in *Daniel Deronda*," *ELH* 68 (2001): 699.
88 Burdett, "Sympathy," 331.
89 Gates, "'A Difference of Native Language,'" 699.
90 Woloch, "*Daniel Deronda*," 169.
91 George Eliot, *Daniel Deronda*, ed. Graham Handley (Oxford: Oxford University Press, 2014), 631.
92 Burdett, "Sympathy," 333.

3

Medical Realisms and the Magic of Reality

Art and Insight in Thomas Hardy's *The Woodlanders* and Émile Zola's *Le docteur Pascal*

Maren Scheurer

Introduction

Realism is almost always understood as a project of maximizing the representative potential of art—depicting reality with as little distortion as possible.[1] However, as Roman Jakobson has pointed out, this project can be read in two different ways. It may be understood as the "*conservative tendency to remain within the limits of a given artistic tradition, conceived as faithful to reality,*" but it also encompasses the "*tendency to deform given artistic norms conceived as an approximation of reality.*"[2] Even today, a significant amount of our debates over the limitations and achievements of realism are still linked to this fundamental disagreement over the direction of realism: Does realist art confirm a culture's established knowledge of reality with as little distortion as possible, or does it distort conventional knowledge and conventional modes of representation to achieve a less distorted sense of reality—even at the risk of being labeled "anti-realist"?

In the appreciation of any realist endeavor, then, it is important to take into account what contemporaries held to be true and how they believed knowledge might best be attained. In the course of the nineteenth century, science became an increasingly important standard by which truths were measured and knowledge was gained, and so it is not surprising that many realists embraced scientific models and were judged accordingly. French realists like Stendhal and Balzac "espoused the new authority of science with its disciplined observation of empirical reality,"[3] and although the British realists were always a bit more critical of "rational scientific models of knowledge" and their identification with the scientist less complete,[4] they were nevertheless intrigued by the narrative potential of scientific matters and methods.

It appears, however, that Jakobson's dual perception of realism also applies to scientific innovation: what is truly "scientific," where "science" ends and speculation begins, and what may be held as a scientific truth has been subject to historical development and debate. Therefore, even when writers claim to adhere to scientific methodology in their own variant of realism, it was far from certain that their attempts would be acknowledged as "realism," in both senses of the term. Zola's "Naturalism," for example, was designed as a scientific, ultra-realist program, but it has often been noted that his novels veer toward the mythical or the allegorical. Many critics have therefore concluded that Zola has failed to live up to his own naturalist pretensions.[5] Thomas Hardy did not share Zola's specific aesthetic convictions, but his interest in science as a driving force for his fiction cannot be denied. Citing an entry in Hardy's *Early Life*, "A Physician cannot cure a disease, but he can change his mode of expression," Tony Fincham argues that Hardy probably saw "his role as a writer as analogous to that of a doctor," in experimenting with modes of expression and "altering man's understanding" of life.[6] Some of these experiments, however, have earned Hardy the title of an "anti-realist,"[7] which opens further problems in a neat alignment of science and realist fiction. I propose that we may come to a more nuanced understanding of the contradictions of literary realism by looking more closely at one of its central interdisciplinary sparring partners in science—medicine—and examine how medicine's realist potential is reflected in the work of Zola and Hardy.

Among the sciences, medicine takes up a particularly prominent role in realist discourse, offering a diagnostic gaze that promises critical insight into the connections between the biological and the social—a particular interest of nineteenth-century realism. Lilian Furst notes that the "realist's and the physician's 'common reliance on their powers of observation' . . . as their primary methodology leads to a marked affinity between realism and medicine."[8] At the high point of nineteenth-century realism, medical discourse becomes "saturated with a special kind of quasi-avant-garde cultural (and even political) authority,"[9] so we may assume that it proved particularly attractive to writers who sought to align themselves with its legitimized practice of knowledge production: "Clinical medicine ... offered Balzac, Flaubert, Eliot, and James an ideology of professional exactitude, an ideology that was extremely useful to novelists when new conditions of the marketplace enabled writers to picture themselves as self-sufficient professionals."[10] However, in the transitional period between realism and modernism, this medical paradigm was ultimately abandoned: "As clinical medicine comes under epistemic attack from other sciences, and as it becomes institutionalized, its attractiveness as a radical model fades."[11] As a result, Lawrence Rothfield argues, modernism would ultimately adopt models wholly antithetical to the medical paradigm, while Naturalism problematically aligned itself with experimental medicine, which abandons the sympathetic focus on the individual that was so important to realism.[12] Rothfield's history of medical realism suggests that the "failure" of realism is closely linked to a failure of the medical model and its claims to objectivity, truth, and authority.

This narrative, however, creates "a distorted trajectory of the rise and fall of the medical profession,"[13] as Janis Caldwell argues. Although underlying theoretical notions and practices changed, the medical profession suffered no overall decline—just a transformation. Moreover, writers like Zola and Hardy were not necessarily and not only interested in medicine for the idea of clinical observation and the epistemic authority it conveyed. Zola, for instance, does conceive his most important literary manifesto *Le roman expérimental* (*The Experimental Novel*, 1879/1880) on the basis of Claude Bernard's *Introduction à l'étude de la médicine expérimentale* (*Introduction to the Study of Experimental Medicine*, 1865), but he argues explicitly that medicine may serve as a model for literature because it has not yet resolved the tension between clinical practice and experimental science—or, in short, the tension between art and science.[14] For Zola, the attraction of the medical model is at least in part derived from its incompleteness—from medicine's imaginative components as much as from its clinical and experimental rigor. In this way, the authority of medical knowledge was always a matter of debate. Physicians may have sought to construct the objective, realist stance we often attribute to science, but they also questioned their access to the truth—and writers like Zola and Hardy were not only aware of but fascinated by these instabilities in medical discourse. And indeed, as can be seen in their writings, the practice of the medical doctor, even as it is assailed from many sides, remains a focal point of aesthetic self-fashioning.

The medical doctors that appear in Hardy's and Zola's novels show that the link between realism and medical science is by no means as unidirectional as Furst and Rothfield suggest. Dr. Edred Fitzpiers in *The Woodlanders* (1887) and Dr. Pascal Rougon in *Le docteur Pascal* (*Doctor Pascal*, 1893) are self-reflexive characters that are used not simply to emulate the "clinical gaze" but to investigate the epistemological implications of the realist worldview. Fitzpiers is not just a "realist" but an idealist who navigates the boundaries between science and the supernatural. Similarly, Pascal appears at times as a sorcerer or priest rather than a rational man of science. Both novels seem to be more fascinated with the *magic* of medicine and thus seem to fail in a "realistic" representation of science and its practitioners. However, I will argue that instead of reading these novels as failures, we might more suitably use them to destabilize our notions of what constitutes "successful" realism and its negotiation of the known and the speculative.

In what follows, I will first discuss the productive instability of medicine as a point of reference for realism through a reading of Bernard and the British psychiatrist Henry Maudsley, whose work was studied thoroughly by Hardy.[15] Thereafter, I will investigate how Hardy's *The Woodlanders* and Zola's *Le docteur Pascal* traverse the intricate relations between scientific inquiry and poetic conjecture. Along the lines of their characters' "medical realisms," Hardy and Zola interrogate their own realist poetics and investigate the powers and limitations of the realist endeavor more generally. They show us that realism is driven by a fascination for all aspects of experience, even those beyond the material and visible world, and that rather than establishing clear epistemological boundaries it is interested in questioning where these boundaries lie in the first place.

Medical Realisms

Furst has characterized the second half of the nineteenth century as "the time of the most fundamental changes through the transformation of medicine from a largely speculative endeavor into a discipline governed by scientific principles."[16] Whereas physicians previously had to rely on experience and guesswork, pronouncing diagnoses and applying remedies that had proved effective in the past, with the development of modern laboratory equipment, advanced chemistry, and radiography, a new evidence-based medicine was established in medical schools in France and later all across Europe. As patients could now be measured and observed in new ways, new frameworks were developed to explain what makes them sick, diseases were targeted through more advanced medical techniques, and hospitals evolved from welfare institutions for the poor and elderly to advanced care facilities.[17] Such developments began to change the relationship between doctor and patient: while earlier in the century physicians had limited resources but attended closely to patients and their family members, they would now be able to better help their patients, but their specialized knowledge and professionalized methods turned them into more distant figures and reduced the quality of the therapeutic relationship:

"The scientific focus on localized disease reduced the attention paid to the patient's social context and personality."[18] Despite many improvements, however, the doctor's actual options for treating diseases advanced at a much slower pace than medical understanding. Many of the diseases that could now be explained could not yet be treated: antibiotics such as Paul Ehrlich's arsphenamine and Alexander Fleming's penicillin were not introduced until 1910 and 1928, respectively. The end of the nineteenth century thus looks toward medical science as a highly ambivalent entity: rapidly growing medical insight is still paired with therapeutic impotence; although specialized knowledge has generally increased, it has become inaccessible to a public that still widely believes in folk remedies; and even many doctors were afraid that the "art" of treating the patient would be forgotten in the wake of new discoveries.

This difficult positioning between art and science has attracted literary realists to the field, and it is a tension that medicine still struggles with. Reacting to the developments that started in the nineteenth century, many physicians now emphasize their reliance on empathetic, narrative modes of understanding. In her seminal work *Narrative Medicine*, Rita Charon invites doctors to acknowledge how much their everyday practice deviates from orthodox notions of objective scientific practice. Charon argues that medicine as a whole "emerged as a response to the perilous unknown" but works best when it doesn't attempt to gloss over the puzzling multiplicity of narratives that arise in the clinical encounter.[19] Instead, she urges doctors to acknowledge that their work requires an ethical and "aesthetic appreciation" of what is going on in the therapeutic relationship.[20] Charon thus identifies a common concern in literature and medicine, which is not limited to an observational stance but cultivates a specific interpretive and ethical position, with which physicians negotiate their relationship toward others and toward reality.

Such an awareness of the aesthetic and ethical components and contradictions of medical practice and research is already apparent in the writings of nineteenth-century scientists. It may be more than an ironic footnote in literary history that Claude Bernard originally went to Paris to pursue a literary career but became a medical doctor instead.[21] When he describes medical practice as a fetid terrain palpitating with life or as a "salon" that can only be reached by walking through a long, horrendous kitchen,[22] we sense that Bernard's fascination with the "muck" of life may have attracted Zola, who was often accused of wading through the dirt of the French Second Empire in his novels. Moreover, Bernard emphasizes the importance of giving free rein to one's imagination,[23] thus aligning medicine with art even as he strengthens its experimental base. Bernard freely admits to stumbling in the dark,[24] and like other scientists at the time, he develops mythogenic or poetogenic structures to gain orientation in his unchartered field.

The imagination remains an important aspect of nineteenth-century scientific discourse. In *Natural Causes and Supernatural Seemings* (1886), Henry Maudsley calls the imagination a "great source of error" that "hastens to fill the voids of knowledge with fictions."[25] And yet, he also acknowledges that the imagination "has enticed and stirred men to enter upon the unknown, the vague, vast and mysterious."[26] The imagination Maudsley wants his readers to cultivate is restricted and sober, but such "truly informed imagination . . . , inspired by the deepest affinities of nature, organically unites the essential qualities of things, creating a product which is . . . more perfect than individual experience, and in harmony with all possible experience of its kind."[27] Science, as Maudsley understands it, is interested not just in what is obvious and visible but also in what is invisible and mysterious, and it is a scientifically shaped *imagination* that leads the way on such an endeavor.

As Maudsley's title suggests, he rejects superstition and the supernatural, and, like Bernard, emphasizes a scientific understanding of medicine. But Maudsley's main argument—that we only believe in the supernatural as long as we haven't explained "supernatural seemings" with "natural causes"— actually testifies to a larger confusion that occupied Victorian culture. While, on the one hand, many supernatural or inexplicable phenomena suddenly received a scientific explanation, science and technology produced new miracles: "Disembodied voices over the telephone, the superhuman speed of the railway, near-instantaneous communication through telegraph wires: the collapsing of time and distance achieved by modern technologies."[28] Bernard Shaw commented that only a "very small class . . . understands by science something more than conjuring with retorts and spirit lamps . . . and discovering magical cures for disease. To a sufficiently ignorant man . . . every locomotive engine [is] a miracle."[29] It is no wonder that, as Shaw and Maudsley both deplored, science, superstition, and religion often became conflated and the "commonly understood boundaries between science and pseudo-science, or the natural and the supernatural" were actually under much dispute.[30]

Maudsley's reasoning about medicine is also remarkable for its realization of the limitations of science: "The history of medicine is hardly less fruitful than the history of religion in example of fallacious observations and of superstitious theories; and for the same reason—namely, the extreme difficulties of observation and the strong propensity to supernatural beliefs where mystery and fear prevail."[31] Maudsley acknowledges that the "human organism" is "the most intricate and complex structure in the world,"[32] and the infinite internal and external influences that work on it make it nearly impossible to set down definite knowledge, let alone guarantee that such knowledge will not "fall into disrepute" as more advanced times hit upon new discoveries.[33] For Maudsley, "observation is a process of growth, not a process of mental photography, slow and tedious necessarily, and only to be perfected by degrees";[34] the impossibility of judging without ever being influenced by prejudice and emotion necessitates that a "pure lover of truth ... would be an abstraction ... just as truth itself is";[35] and finally, language stands in the way of attaining such truth, for although we may "believe that a word must mean an entity," it is really "the sign of an abstraction only," and "may have very different meanings in different mouths or in the same mouth on different occasions."[36] For all his concern with "natural causes," Maudsley's perspective is far from naïvely realist; it is keenly aware of the constructedness of truth and the instable relationship between signifier and signified, even as he imagines a slow process of approaching toward knowledge. It is this self-critical science that Zola and Hardy take as their inspiration, and what is often judged as a failure in or a rejection of "scientific" realism is actually well in line with the imaginative, tentative, and experimental realism many scientists cultivated in the nineteenth century.

Hardy's and Zola's novels feature medical doctors who, albeit in a highly dissimilar fashion, are used to explore the dimensions of the scientific imagination. Hardy demonstrates the fragility of the scientific model by pointing out how much science—and the popular "reception" of science—partakes of the mystical and magical. Zola's *Le docteur Pascal* shows that it is not science's claim to objectivity alone that fascinates the naturalist; instead, science's similarities with religion and art—its very fragility in the face of a complex and resistant reality—provide a model for a literature that is conscious of its powerlessness to represent the world in all accuracy but nevertheless does not renounce its claims on reality.

The Woodlanders

Hardy's attitude toward the involvement of science in fiction-making was ambivalent. In "The Science of Fiction" (1891), he argues that even the "most devoted apostle of realism, the sheerest naturalist, cannot escape ... the exercise of Art in his labor or pleasure of telling a tale. Not until he becomes an automatic reproducer of all impressions whatsoever can he be called purely scientific, or even a manufacturer on scientific principles."[37] In other words, if the writer were to become purely scientific, he ceases to produce art; if he continues to "select and omit" for the purposes of art, he ceases to be a scientist. As we have just seen, neither Bernard nor Maudsley understood themselves as "automatic reproducers," which calls Hardy's neat separation of art and science into question. But it seems that Hardy is not wholly rejecting science but sets up a rhetorical stance to clarify his own understanding of the "science of fiction" and expose the "poetic" work involved in producing impressions of reality. His novels are actually pervaded with references to contemporary science, based on his extensive reading in medicine, evolutionary theory, natural philosophy, and physics. Convinced that fiction can only ultimately be successful if it strives for a "comprehensive and accurate knowledge of realities,"[38] Hardy studies the advances in modern science, for as human knowledge progresses, the "old illusions" are no longer convincing and "a more natural magic has to be supplied."[39] The notion of "natural magic" is rich in meaning, aligning Hardy's theory of fiction with science as well as with fields of inquiry that are usually seen as science's opposites: magic, the supernatural, the imagination, and art. Angelique Richardson supports this alignment when she observes that in Hardy's work, "science and the aesthetic are closely bound" in his search for "a synthesis between science and imagination."[40] Fittingly, Hardy's views on medicine were determined by his promotion of a "deeply sympathetic holistic approach to human pathology" and a belief in the importance of psychological determinants of disease and medical treatment.[41] Hardy's work apparently seeks to integrate the material and immaterial experiences of life in a holistic approach to science and fiction.

In the depiction of the physician Dr. Edred Fitzpiers, *The Woodlanders* grapples with the problems that arise out of the synthesis of science and imagination. In many ways, Fitzpiers is the novel's antagonist: because Grace Melbury's father believes that the woodsman Giles Winterborne, to whom she has been promised since her youth, is not a good enough match for her, he promotes Grace's marriage to Fitzpiers, who turns out to be unsteady and unfaithful. The novel is primarily concerned with the dissatisfactions of the institution of marriage, but through the doctor, it also allows Hardy to probe the limitations of the medical profession.

Ironically enough, Fitzpiers is regarded with awe by his patients. The cottagers see him as a "somewhat rare kind of gentleman and doctor to have descended, as from the clouds, upon Little Hintock."[42] Grace perceives him as "a remorseless Jehovah of the sciences" (124), saving lives "as Elijah drew down fire from Heaven" (330). Several times, the doctor is thus stylized as a divine or prophetic figure. The population of Hintock has a syncretistic mindset, which intermingles heathen practices with Christian faith. Mr. South, for instance, believes that a tree can haunt him "like an evil spirit" (101), and the local girls attempt a traditional "enchantment" to get "a glimpse of their future partners for life" (145). Contemporary perspectives on science are equally affected by such syncretism, as Mr. Melbury demonstrates. He believes that Grace's phrenological "fortune has been told by men of science" (76) and reads ancient medical treatises like the Bible (162). In this climate of creative superstition, the doctor's medical work is yet another arcane practice and potential belief system, as impenetrable to the woodlanders as divine intervention.

Fitzpiers himself does not outwardly embrace this juxtaposition of religion, superstition, and science. For his marriage with Grace, he wishes a service at "a registry office" (165), which clearly indicates his secular worldview. Nevertheless, he is not portrayed as a rational man of science either but appears as "a parody of the bohemian intellectual" in the style of George Eliot's Lydgate.⁴³ Fitzpiers "seemed likely to err rather in the possession of too many ideas than too few; to be a dreamy 'ist of some sort" (101). Indeed, instead of physics, he mostly reads metaphysics and "rank literatures of emotion and passion" (124–25), "for the doctor was not a practical man, except by fits, and much preferred the ideal world to the real" (112). He is not actually engaged in a rational pursuit of truth but gets lost in the ideal worlds of bad philosophy and fiction. It is crucial that these literary interests are not actually presented as a superior mode of gaining access to the truth, as one might imagine; instead, Fitzpiers errs on both sides: the rational and the irrational.

However, while Fitzpiers is clearly the butt of Hardy's critique of volatile intellectuality, something about his vision fascinates the narrator. He admits, "a real inquirer he honestly was" (124), and he finds a "depth of vision" in Fitzpiers's eyes, a "light either of energy or of susceptivity," which, in the best sense, fails to adhere to scientific standards: "That quick, glittering, empirical eye, sharp for the surface of things if for nothing beneath, he had not" (100). This judgment resonates with Hardy's exploration of the "science of fiction." For Hardy, the art of observation is a complicated interplay of perceptions and inferences, and it must be substantiated by a sense for things beyond external inspection:

> A sight for the finer qualities of existence . . . [is] not to be acquired by the outer senses alone. . . . What cannot be discerned by eye and ear, what may be apprehended only by the mental tactility that comes from a sympathetic appreciativeness of life in all its manifestations, this is the gift which renders its possessor a more accurate delineator of human nature than many another with twice his powers and means of external observation, but without that sympathy.⁴⁴

Observation is essential to the method of true fiction, but it must be "informed by a living heart" and rests on intuition.⁴⁵ As Megan Ward argues, Hardy's approach does not sit well with conventional models of mid-nineteenth-century realism, which are supposed to derive their "reality effect" from "material details."⁴⁶ For Hardy, "realism . . . means gesturing toward both the material and the immaterial."⁴⁷

In the novel, such a vision beyond the surface, toward a deeper level of reality, is often seen as essential to perceiving what is "really" going on. In a scene in which Melbury expects Fitzpiers to ask for Grace's hand in marriage, the narrator notes, "Could the real have been beheld instead of the corporeal merely, the corner of the room in which he sat would have been filled with a form typical of anxious suspense, large-eyed, tight-lipped, awaiting the issue" (163). Grace also once claims, "Appearance is no matter, when the reality is right" (301). Ward observes that these passages are often taken as evidence of a "rejection of realism";⁴⁸ however, as Hardy's intense interest in a truth beyond surface materiality shows, he is not actually abandoning the pursuit of reality but "challenge[s]" it to go beyond popular scientific thinking[49] toward an integration of readable surfaces and the inscrutable complexities of life.

In a sense, Fitzpiers's attitude, "being ready and zealous to interrogate all physical manifestations" (134), as well as his intention to "carry on simultaneously the study of physiology and transcendental philosophy, the material world and the ideal, so as to discover if possible a point of contact between them" (133), would seem to reflect Hardy's poetics. Although the narrator withholds judgment at first on whether Fitzpiers's "apparent depth of vision were real" (100), at the end of the novel he emphasizes "his professional skill," "insight," and "freedom from conventional errors and crusted prejudices" (316). And as an observer, he is not so far from the ironic social perception of many realist narrators, when "abstractedly looking out at the different pedestrians," Fitzpiers "perceived that the character of each of these travelers exhibited itself in a somewhat amusing manner by his or her method of handling the gate" (111).

Nevertheless, if we are still not quite ready to take Fitzpiers's vision as a reflection of Hardy's vision, the crucial difference between their concerns can be found in the malfunction of his medical practice. In one of the few scenes in which we observe Fitzpiers at work, we learn that the doctor lacks empathetic compassion and a social conscience:

> Mr. Fitzpiers entered the sick chamber as a doctor is wont to do on such occasions, and pre-eminently when the room is that of the humble cottager; looking round towards the patient with that preoccupied gaze which so plainly reveals that he has well-nigh forgotten all about the case and the circumstances since he dismissed them from his mind at his last exit from the same apartment. (100)

In other words, Fitzpiers is not really interested in the human beings he deals with, and even less so because they are poor. With inquisitive enthusiasm, he covets the brains of Grammer Oliver and John South for his research, but, as Jenny Bourne Taylor notes, fails to understand their anxieties: "despite his interest in the interior of their skulls, Fitzpiers shows little understanding of his patients' inner mental lives."[50] Reflecting the radical changes in nineteenth-century medical practice, Fitzpiers's observational powers fail to engage with the individual preoccupations of his patients and thus to penetrate the surface—and this is the reason why, his passion for metaphysics notwithstanding, he never actually attains a contact between the real and the ideal. Despite sharing many of Hardy's own preoccupations, Fitzpiers is treated with "ironic detachment" because he fails to find a suitable form and context to deploy his ideas.[51]

A better model for Hardy's realism is not Fitzpiers's limited medical outlook, but Marty South's and Giles Winterborne's "intelligent intercourse with Nature":

> They had been possessed of its finer mysteries as of commonplace knowledge; had been able to read its hieroglyphs as ordinary writing; to them the sights and sounds of night, winter, wind, storm, amid those dense boughs, which had to Grace a touch of the uncanny, and even of the supernatural, were simple occurrences whose origin, continuance, and laws they foreknew.... Together they had ... mentally collected those remoter signs and symbols which seen in few were of runic obscurity, but all together made an alphabet. (330–31)

Marty's and Giles's reading of nature is an example of an ideal Hardyan reading that goes beyond the surface by connecting apparent material phenomena with each other and with the environment that produces them—and thus highlighting aesthetic and epistemological relations without which reading and insight are impossible. Crucially, Marty and Giles do not simply abandon the material world; this is not another example of metaphysics replacing physics. Instead, in these characters, an innate aesthetic gift for perception is rooted in close observation of the natural world, which makes it readable and capable of producing meaning. This knowledge is associated with the supernatural, but only by those who are not acquainted with natural laws and endowed with a sensitive mode of perception. A true "realist" reading neither relies on nor simply discards material surfaces but seeks to connect them in order to achieve a more comprehensive understanding of life and unearthing a new language for an interaction with reality.

Le docteur Pascal

For Zola's experimental novel, medicine is the central conceptual model. At the beginning of *Le roman expérimental*, he claims: "It will often be but necessary for me to replace the word 'doctor' by the word 'novelist,' to make my meaning clear and to give it the rigidity of a scientific truth."[52] Zola does indeed base the entire argument on Bernard's *Introduction*, quoting or adapting his thoughts about experimental medicine to develop a literary-scientific method of his own.[53] For Zola, the novelist is an "observer" and an "experimentalist," for whom writing a scientific novel means studying the mechanisms of nature within the parameters of their environment: "Finally, you possess knowledge of the man, scientific knowledge of him, in both his individual and social relations."[54] Observation paired with scientific knowledge and decisive experimenting—using that knowledge to set up fictional thought experiments—would lead to an expansion of realism in literature. Medicine is particularly interesting for Zola because it hovers between science and art and is still in the process of development. Literature can thus serve as an extension of its modes of inquiry, adding—and here Zola meets Hardy—psychological to physiological insight: "We are making use, in a certain way, of scientific psychology to complete scientific physiology; ... we should operate on the characters, the passions, on the human and social data, in the same way that the chemist and the physicist operate on inanimate beings, and as the physiologist operates on living beings."[55]

These ideas are most fully explored in the last novel of Zola's Rougon-Macquart cycle, *Le docteur Pascal*. Nevertheless, critics have often found the novel to be anti-realistic. Rita Schober would argue that Zola's attempt to create a final, quasi-religious embodiment of his theory destroyed realism.[56] Friedrich Wolfzettel has also claimed that the novel, with its "fairy tale motifs," is worthless for any kind of realist literary inquiry.[57] I argue, on the contrary, that this novel highlights some of the most important concerns of Zola's realism, precisely because it stretches its boundaries. It calls into question simplistic categorizations of science and realism as based on "hard facts" and religion and art as their opposite. *Le docteur Pascal* complicates this opposition by highlighting that the scientific endeavor is always, in part, an imaginative one, geared toward exploring the unknown rather than setting down what is already known.

Pascal is a sexagenarian medical researcher who lives on an estate near the small town Plassans. Having made a modest fortune as a country doctor, he now focuses on his studies in heredity, hoping to find a general cure to all human ailments.[58] This research forms the background to the main plot, which focuses on the relationship between Pascal and his niece and foster daughter Clotilde. At first, she opposes his studies but then falls in love with him as he convinces her of his own scientific persuasions. Their controversial love affair turns them into outcasts but leads to the birth of a child—a source of hope, even after Pascal's death and the destruction of his work by his fanatical mother.

Pascal is an almost "mythical" representation of nineteenth-century medicine with all its contradictions and potentials.[59] As usual, Zola invested plenty of research into the matter, read widely in the medical literature of his time, especially as it pertained to heredity. In studying Prosper Lucas, Darwin, Spencer, Galton, Haeckel, Virchow, and August Weismann, he was guided by informants such as the neurologists Maurice de Fleury and Jules Déjerine as well as the comparative anatomist Georges Pouchet.[60] To a certain extent, Pascal is a portrait of Claude Bernard,[61] but, more importantly, he is also a portrait of Zola himself. Displaying the same interests and beliefs Zola accumulated throughout his writing life as well as pursuing similar goals in researching and writing a family history,[62] Pascal is described by Zola as "the mouthpiece" for his own convictions: the novel represents a "scientific work" that was to be "the logical deduction and conclusion of all

[his] preceding novels."[63] Thus, Zola not only allows but almost forces us to read the scientist Pascal as a reflection on his own work as a writer.

Strikingly, however, Pascal is not portrayed as a straightforward scientist but is in conflict with and simultaneously aligned with religion and magic. While Pascal stands for the new practices of science, his mother, his niece, and his servant all oppose his work on religious grounds. Clotilde has begun to follow the teachings of a capuchin monk, who preaches against modern science, "denying the reality of the world" and opening up new perspectives on the mysteries of the unknown (82). In Clotilde, Zola represents an increasing trend in late-nineteenth-century France to dismiss the prevailing models of science and return to religion.[64] Zola is clearly critical of this development, but he does not simply dismiss religious belief systems. Instead, an association between religious motifs and science pervades *Le docteur Pascal*, not unlike *The Woodlanders*. The novel is suffused with religious images and rhythms: the doctor is a prophet and a sorcerer,[65] who speaks of the injections he has developed as his "sorcerer's *liqueur*" (42);[66] in the language of the Song of Songs, Pascal and Clotilde are associated with a number of biblical lovers, and their son is deemed to be the coming messiah.[67] This is fitting because science and Pascal's trust in the life force emerge as a new belief system in the novel. Clotilde describes his speeches about science as religious sermons: "it seemed to me that you were talking of God, so full you were of faith and hope" (89).[68] And asked to spell out his "*Credo*," Pascal tells her: "I believe that the pursuit of truth through science is the divine ideal which man should have in view" (45).[69] Paradoxically, as Schober notes, Pascal (and with him Zola) seek to replace religious belief with a belief in science.[70] However, Pascal becomes a "clairvoyant," as the French original has it (108), not because he idealistically believes in an improvement of humanity through science, but because "he was fully aware of . . . all the stains and blemishes disfiguring humanity; for during thirty years he had busied himself in bringing them to light, investigating and cataloguing them" (55).[71] He does not stop at believing but continues to acquire knowledge. In short, he is considered a prophet because he never abandons his realist pursuit for understanding.

Along those lines, the novel destabilizes the differences between scientific and religious belief systems to arrive at a determination of the medical realist's methodology. Religion and science are thus first strategically aligned in their passionate quest for the unknown, but, in a second step, science is revealed as a practice that is ultimately more affirming of life's myriad possibilities and their resistance against human knowledge. In his arguments with Clotilde, Pascal reveals that *both* disciplines are driven by a common desire for knowledge. Science seems at first to be at odds with Clotilde's desire for the mystery and the unknown: "an irresistible call to that which was inaccessible, that which could not be known" (84).[72] She explains that she has turned away from science out of disappointment; on top of having robbed the world of its magic, it has yet failed to explain its mysteries: "At all events . . . science has swept everything away, the earth is bare, the heavens are empty. . . . Since science is too slow, and does not yield the results we had hoped for, we prefer to turn back—yes, to plunge back into the beliefs of former times" (91).[73] Utterly disabused of science's explanatory power, she declares roundabout, "There is no reality" (85),[74] but Pascal is not willing to accept her skeptical position. He concedes that humans are fallible beings with a limited capacity for understanding, but that never quenches his thirst for comprehension:

> Our senses are liable to err; it is only through our senses that we know the world, hence it may be that the world does not exist. . . . Cannot you see, however, that if you suppress nature there will be no rule of life left, and that the only interest in living lies in believing in life, in loving it, and in striving with all the strength of one's intelligence to know it better? (85)[75]

Pascal ultimately rejects the all too easy shortcut from fallible human understanding to the conclusion that there is no world or that he cannot know *anything* about it. For him, humans are *in* the world, in nature, which gives them a framework with which they have to find their place in reality. Unknowability is not a hindrance to understanding but its driving force, for we are told that Pascal is interested in heredity precisely because "it remained so dim, so vast and fathomless, like all the sciences which are yet immature, lisping but their first words, and over which imagination still reigns supreme" (38).[76] Science—if practiced properly—is attracted to the mysterious, vast, and inscrutable nature of reality; approaching the unknown, grasping what is perhaps unknowable, is the motor of both Pascal's medical research and Clotilde's fascination with religion, but whereas in the first, they lead to an affirmation of reality, in the latter, they lead to its negation.

"There is no health, no beauty even, possible, if we live out of reality" (85),[77] Pascal continues his argument, thus radicalizing the realist aesthetic. This does not only suggest, as Thomas Klinkert has argued, that scientific matters may be considered as aesthetic objects[78] but also that beauty—and with it most art—is wholly impossible outside the dominion of science and reality. The realms of science and aesthetics are thus not just closely intertwined[79] but, following the novel's larger argument, to be firmly located within the material world. In *Le roman expérimental*, Zola had linked medicine and literature as two arts progressing toward science, associated by the fact that they are both concerned with the indeterminate ("indéterminé") and a complexity ("complexité") that forces them to base their work largely on conjectures.[80] Crucially, however, Pascal identifies the imagination—and thus a faculty that, in Hardyan fashion, goes beyond the material—as their interface:

> Ah! these infantile sciences, . . . they are assuredly the domain of poets quite as much as of *savants*. The poets go forward in the advance guard as pioneers, and often discover virgin lands, and point out the solutions which are near at hand. Between the acquired truths, those that are completely established, and the Unknown, whence the truth of to-morrow will be wrested, there is a space which fairly belongs to the poets. (113)[81]

Far from simply turning the writer into a scientist, the connections Zola identifies between them serve to affirm the poetic qualities of science.

Science, and especially medical science, as understood by Zola, is thus not a straightforward positivistic enterprise but a constant, albeit methodical, struggle with uncertainty and a wealth of possible meanings. In crucial distinction to the religious beliefs Clotilde professes in the first half of the novel, Pascal is aware of the limitations of science and stresses the falsifiability of his findings: "And thus the Doctor fully expected that his theory would some day become antiquated, and contented himself with it only as a transitional explanation, which sufficed for the present phase of that perpetual inquiry into Life" (37).[82] Knowledge is transitory and can always change as new knowledge is acquired, which, for Pascal, also calls into question the extent of man's interference in nature. In the face of nature's endless complexities, how can we hope to do good if we meddle with its laws? Such doubts, however, do not lead Pascal to anti-scientific resignation but to a heightened emphasis on the quest for knowledge: "despite everything it is still necessary that one should know. . . . Happiness in ignorance is no longer possible; certainty alone can bring tranquil life" (197).[83] Despite epistemological and ethical limitations, the *pursuit* of knowledge remains the prime objective of Zola's *docteur*—because it grounds him in the world and offers joy and peace.

Zola's scientific understanding is thus far less simplistic than has been assumed: when he argues that literature is to become scientific, he thinks of science as an incomplete and incompletable project of experimentation in which the thought experiments of literature may fulfill the important function of formulating hypotheses and bringing together various scientific and non-scientific modes of thinking and knowing.[84] Zola's position is not that science and literature are identical but that they can mutually inform each other; in this way, literature can be an important ally to science in supporting and promoting its findings as well as enhancing its imaginative capacity.[85] Based on scientific facts, the novelist may actually proceed toward speculation and contribute to science through fiction: "then before the unknown, but only then, exercising our intuition and suggesting the way to science, free to make mistakes, happy if we produce any data toward the solution of the problem."[86] Zola's ultimate naturalist novel thus ends in the realization that, confronted with the unknown, with a reality that remains resistant and in flux, poeto-scientific measures are more productive than purely scientific measures.

Instead of taking a defeatist position and abandoning oneself to the "chimeras" (86), Pascal recommends that one might instead turn toward reality and life in all their complexity as something to love and to study (85). Zola's project, as reflected in Pascal, is neither naïvely positivistic nor does it abandon the pursuit of reality in the face of its unattainability. Instead, it argues for an unending, imaginative, and loving quest for knowledge.[87] Love and care emerge as the ethical driving force of realism's pursuit of understanding, which makes it all the more imperative to turn to the physician as a model for the realist—not the absent and distant doctor driven by abstract questions, who is represented in Fitzpiers, but the involved physician who cares for his patients as he cares for the world beyond his surgery.

Conclusion

The implicit de- and reconstruction of medical realism in Hardy and Zola has far-reaching implications for the realist projects they pursue. Hardy, critical of strictly scientific approaches to literature from the start, employs the doctor, a character with a lost potential for deeper insight, as an ironic antithesis to the true reader of nature. A better vision of humanity and nature is to be had neither through the material surface nor through some immaterial realm, but only through an intuitive intercourse with both. Zola, in contrast, models literary Naturalism after experimental medicine, but in his manifesto and in the last novel of his naturalist cycle, he insists on the poetic qualities of Claude Bernard's scientific program. In both novels, the doctor is not only a poet but a prophet, a practitioner of the arcane arts, rejecting and simultaneously embracing the unknown *in* science. Casting Fitzpiers or Pascal as poised between physics and metaphysics, scientific and artistic insight, however, is not a failure in realism but a self-reflexive exploration of its potential. Meddling with the unknown and the unknowable, they seek a reality that is never quite accessible to them; but for observers who are even less acquainted with scientific procedures, the little knowledge that they do have appears to be almost supernatural. The novels thus sketch different levels of approaching the "magic" of reality, in which scientific method and poetic imagination are not separate but interrelated pathways to the truth. Hardy's and Zola's characters are driven by not only a hope in truth's ultimate attainability but also a suspicion that the scientist's, like the writer's, knowledge will remain limited. However, this does not lead them to give up on the project of realism. Instead, they infuse it with an ethical perspective that stresses our connectedness with the world we seek to understand.

Notes

1. Roman Jakobson, "On Realism in Art," in *Language in Literature*, ed. Krystyna Pomorska and Stephen Rudy (Cambridge: Belknap, 1987), 22.
2. Ibid.
3. Pam Morris, *Realism* (London: Routledge, 2003), 53.
4. Ibid., 80.
5. See, for instance, Barbara Ventarola, "Der Experimentalroman zwischen Wissenschaft und Romanexperiment: Überlegungen zu einer Neubewertung des Naturalismus Zolas," *Poetica* 42, no. 3–4 (2010): 279.
6. Tony Fincham, *Hardy the Physician: Medical Aspects of the Wessex Tradition* (Basingstoke: Palgrave Macmillan, 2008), 77.
7. Linda M. Shires, "The Radical Aesthetic of *Tess of the d'Urbervilles*," in *The Cambridge Companion to Thomas Hardy*, ed. Dale Kramer (Cambridge: Cambridge University Press, 1999), 148.
8. Lilian R. Furst, "Realism and Hypertrophy: A Study of Three Medico-Historical 'Cases,'" *Nineteenth-Century French Studies* 22, no. 1–2 (1993–1994): 30.
9. Lawrence Rothfield, *Vital Signs: Medical Realism in Nineteenth-Century Fiction* (Princeton, NJ: Princeton University Press, 1994), xii.
10. Ibid., xiv.
11. Ibid.
12. Ibid., xv.
13. Janis McLarren Caldwell, *Literature and Medicine in Nineteenth-Century Britain: From Mary Shelley to George Eliot* (Cambridge: Cambridge University Press, 2004), 6.
14. Émile Zola, "The Experimental Novel," in *The Experimental Novel and Other Essays* by Émile Zola, trans. Belle M. Sherman (New York: Cassell, 1893), 32. Original: Émile Zola, "Le roman expérimental," in *Oeuvres complètes: Tome 9*, ed. Henri Mitterand (Paris: Nouveau Monde, 2004), 337.
15. Angelique Richardson, "Hardy and Science: A Chapter of Accidents," in *Palgrave Advances in Thomas Hardy Studies*, ed. Phillip Mallett (Basingstoke: Palgrave Macmillan, 2004), 162.
16. Lilian R. Furst, *Medical Progress and Social Reality: A Reader in Nineteenth-Century Medicine and Literature* (Albany: State University of New York Press, 2000), xii.
17. Ibid., 17.
18. Ibid., 18.
19. Rita Charon, *Narrative Medicine: Honoring the Stories of Illness* (Oxford: Oxford University Press, 2006), 49.
20. Ibid., 113.

21 Fiorenzo Conti and Silvana Irrera Conti, "On Science and Literature: A Lesson from the Bernard-Zola Case," *BioScience* 53, no. 9 (2003): 865.
22 Claude Bernard, *Introduction à l'étude de la medicine expérimentale* (Paris: Delgrave, 1898), 27.
23 Ibid., 41.
24 Ibid., 35.
25 Henry Maudsley, *Natural Causes and Supernatural Seemings* (London: Kegan Paul, 1886), 116.
26 Ibid., 122–123.
27 Ibid., 137.
28 Nicola Bown, Carolyn Burdett, and Pamela Thurschwell, "Introduction," in *The Victorian Supernatural*, ed. Nicola Bown, Carolyn Burdett and Pamela Thurschwell (Cambridge: Cambridge University Press, 2005), 1.
29 Bernard Shaw, "Preface on Doctors," in *The Bodley Head Bernard Shaw Collected Plays with Their Prefaces: Vol. III* (London: Bodley Head, 1971), 247.
30 Bown et al., "Introduction," 13.
31 Ibid., 44.
32 Ibid.
33 Ibid., 51.
34 Ibid., 52.
35 Ibid., 75–76.
36 Ibid., 98.
37 Thomas Hardy, "The Science of Fiction," in *Thomas Hardy's Public Voice: The Essays, Speeches, and Miscellaneous Prose*, ed. Michael Millgate (Oxford: Clarendon, 2001), 107.
38 Ibid., 106.
39 Ibid., 108.
40 Richardson, "Hardy and Science," 169, 164.
41 Fincham, *Hardy the Physician*, 2.
42 Thomas Hardy, *The Woodlanders* (London: Penguin, 1998), 101. Subsequent references in parentheses.
43 George Levine, "*The Woodlanders* and the Darwinian Grotesque," in *Thomas Hardy Reappraised: Essays in Honor of Michael Millgate*, ed. Keith Wilson (Toronto, ON: University of Toronto Press, 2006), 188.
44 Hardy, "The Science of Fiction," 109–110.
45 Ibid., 110.
46 Megan Ward, "*The Woodlanders* and the Cultivation of Realism," *SEL Studies in English Literature 1500–1900* 51, no. 4 (2011): 867.
47 Ibid., 867–868.

48 Ibid., 876.
49 Ibid., 868.
50 Jenny Bourne Taylor, "Psychology," in *Thomas Hardy in Context*, ed. Phillip Mallett (Cambridge: Cambridge University Press, 2013), 339.
51 Levine, "*The Woodlanders* and the Darwinian Grotesque," 191.
52 Zola, "The Experimental Novel," 1–2. Original: "Le plus souvent, il me suffira de remplacer le mot 'médecin' par le mot 'romancier,' pour rendre ma pensée claire et lui apporter la rigueur d'une vérité scientifique." Zola, "Le roman expérimental," 324.
53 I don't want to get into the particulars of Zola's program or judge its workability; I am more interested in how medical practice serves as a source of inspiration and a figure of reflexion for realism. Zola has been accused of a naïve optimism toward the sciences and his experimental novel has been castigated as a pseudo-experiment. For an overview of and a response to such criticism, see Ventarola, "Der Experimentalroman zwischen Wissenschaft und Romanexperiment," 284.
54 Zola, "The Experimental Novel," 8–9. Original: "Au bout, il y a la connaissance de l'homme, la connaissance scientifique, dans son action individuelle et sociale." Zola, "Le roman expérimental," 327.
55 Zola, "The Experimental Novel," 17–18. Original: "Nous faisons en quelque sorte de la psychologie scientifique, pour compléter la physiologie scientifique. ... [N]ous devons opérer sur les caractères, sur les passions, sur les faits humains et sociaux, comme le chimiste et le physicien opèrent sur les corps bruts, comme le physiologiste opère sur les corps vivants." Zola, "Le roman expérimental," 331.
56 Rita Schober, "Doktor Pascal oder vom Sinn des Lebens," in *Doktor Pascal* by Émile Zola (Munich: Winkler, 1977), 535.
57 Friedrich Wolfzettel, "*Le Docteur Pascal* und seine Bedeutung für den Rougon-Macquart-Zyklus Zolas," *Die neueren Sprachen* 21 (1972): 159. My translation.
58 Émile Zola, *Doctor Pascal or Life and Heredity* (London: Chatto & Windus, 1894), 34, 37. Original: Émile Zola, *Le docteur Pascal* (Paris: Folio, 1993), 86, 91. Subsequent references in parentheses.
59 Henri Mitterand, "Préface," in *Le docteur Pascal* by Émile Zola (Paris: Gallimard, 1993), 39. My translation.
60 Frederick Brown, *Zola: A Life* (London: Papermac, 1997), 652–653.
61 Schober, "Doktor Pascal oder vom Sinn des Lebens," 518.
62 Mitterand, "Préface," 17, 45.
63 Zola qtd. in David L. Schalk, "Tying Up the Loose Ends of an Epoch: Zola's *Docteur Pascal*," *French Historical Studies* 16, no. 1 (1989): 207.
64 Schober, "Doktor Pascal oder vom Sinn des Lebens," 511–512.
65 Mitterand, "Préface," 41–42.

66 Original: "ma liqueur de sorcier" (94).
67 Schober, "Doktor Pascal oder vom Sinn des Lebens," 528.
68 Original: "il me semblait que tu parlais du bon Dieu, tellement tu brûlais d'espérance et de foi" (143).
69 Original: "Je crois que la poursuite de la vérité par la science est l'idéal divin que l'homme doit se proposer" (97).
70 Schober, "Doktor Pascal oder vom Sinn des Lebens," 517.
71 Original: "il voyait au contraire les maux et les tares, les étalait, les fouillait, les cataloguait depuis trente ans" (108).
72 Original: "un appel irrésistible vers l'inaccessible, l'inconnaisable" (137).
73 Original: "En tout cas . . . la science a fait table rase, la terre est nue, le ciel est vide. . . . Puisque la science, trop lente, fait faillite, nous préférons nous rejeter en arrière, oui ! dans les croyances d'autrefois" (144).
74 Original: "Il n'y a pas de réalité" (139).
75 Original: Nos sens sont faillibles, nous ne connaissons le monde que par nos sens, donc il se peut que le monde n'existe pas . . . [. . .] Mais ne vois-tu donc pas qu'il n'est plus de règle, si tu supprimes la nature, et que le seul intérêt à vivre est de croire à la vie, de l'aimer et de mettre toutes les forces de son intelligence à la mieux connaître (139).
76 Original: "elle restait obscure, vaste et insondable, comme toutes les sciences balbutiantes encore, où l'imagination est maîtresse" (91).
77 Original: "Il n'y a ni santé, ni même beauté possible, en dehors de la réalité" (139).
78 Thomas Klinkert, "Savoir de la Science et savoir de la littérature: À propos du 'Docteur Pascal' de Zola et de 'Giacinta' de Capuana," *Epistémocritique*, December 27, 2015.
79 Ibid.
80 Zola, "Le roman expérimental," 338.
81 Original: "Ah ! ces sciences commençantes, . . . elles sont le domaine des poètes autant que des savants ! Les poètes vont en pionniers, à l'avant-garde, et souvent ils découvrent les pays vierges, indiquent les solutions prochaines. Il y a là une marge qui leur appartient, entre la vérité conquise, définitive, et l'inconnu, d'où l'on arrachera la vérité de demain. . . . Quelle fresque immense à peindre, quelle comédie et quelle tragédie humaines colossales à écrire" (165–166).
82 Original: "Et il s'attendait bien à ce que sa théorie fût caduque un jour, il ne s'en contentait que comme d'une explication transitoire, satisfaisante pour l'état actuel de la question, dans cette perpétuelle enquête sur la vie" (89).
83 Original: "il faut savoir, savoir quand même. . . . Aucun bonheur n'est possible dans l'ignorance, la certitude seule fait la vie calme" (261).
84 Ventarola, "Der Experimentalroman zwischen Wissenschaft und Romanexperiment," 291, 298–299.

85 Klinkert, "Savoir de la science et savoir de la littérature."
86 Zola, "The Experimental Novel," 52. Original: "devant l'inconnu, exercer notre intuition et précéder la science." Zola, "Le roman expérimental," 347.
87 I am indebted to Pam Morris for suggesting I follow up on the meaning of the doctor's love and care for the project of realism more generally.

4

Conrad on Epidemics

From *The Shadow-Line* to Covid-19 (and Back)

Nidesh Lawtoo

For a long time in literary studies, mimesis has been restricted to the problematic of aesthetic representation central to realism. In the mid-twentieth century this line of inquiry culminated in Erich Auerbach's *Mimesis: The Representation of Reality in Western Literature*, which remains one of the most influential philological accounts of Western literary aesthetics.[1] At the same time, since the first decades of the twenty-first century there has been a growing awareness that *mimēsis* is a protean, plastic, and heterogeneous concept that includes realism but has never been limited to it. Since the dawn of aesthetic theory, in fact, Plato and Aristotle disagreed in their evaluations of aesthetic representations but they fundamentally agreed that humans are mimetic creatures—for both good and ill.[2] This less-emphasized, marginalized, yet fundamental philosophical realization traverses Western thought as well; it is constitutive of what Walter Benjamin called "the mimetic faculty,"[3] and accounts for a thoroughly imitative species I call, for lack of a more original term, *homo mimeticus*. From different disciplinary perspectives, there are indeed numerous indications that mimesis, in its protean manifestations, is back on the critical and theoretical scene, generating a "mimetic turn, or return"[4] of attention to an affective, embodied, and relational conception of imitation central to new modernist studies—with broader ramifications for literary theory, continental philosophy, political theory, film/media studies, and different strands of critical theory more generally.[5]

And yet, if the mimetic turn generates a paradigm shift from a dominant tradition focused on aesthetic realism to a minor tradition more attentive to embodied forms of imitation, this does not mean that these two perspectives on mimesis are antithetical or antagonistic. On the contrary, they can turn to face, mirror, and supplement each other to better reflect *on* the critical and theoretical potential of a new mimetic theory for the present and future. This chapter, then, takes the *re*-turn of attention to mimesis as an occasion to develop mirroring reflections that reach into the present from the perspective of a modernist author who played a key role in promoting the mimetic turn in the first place: Joseph Conrad.[6]

Within literary studies, Conrad occupies a privileged position in the mimetic turn, perhaps because his uneasy relation with techniques of representation characteristic of mimetic realism was doubled by a career-long fascination with the *homo duplex* constitutive of *homo mimeticus*. It is well known that Conrad, while indebted to realism, is not, strictly speaking, a realist writer. He anticipates modernist aesthetic principles that foreground opacity, impressionism, ironic distance, and different layers of narrative framing and mediation that problematize transparent reflections of reality. This does not mean, however, that Conrad's narratives are disconnected from lived, affective, and embodied experiences rooted in referential reality. On the contrary, Conrad's fictions are urging new generations of critics and theorists to reflect on all too real, dark, and catastrophic scenarios that cast a realistic shadow on the present and future. For instance, Conrad cautioned not only against the escalating violence of total wars in military tales like "The Duel" (1908) but also against the threat of perfect storms to generate "mountainous waves" in *Typhoon* (1902) and "The Secret Sharer" (1910) in ways that prefigure climate storms to come; he not only took seriously the threat of terroristic attacks to tear innocent bodies to pieces in *The Secret Agent* (1907) but also warned against the danger of leaders who are "hollow at the core" yet are endowed with a voice to "electrify large meetings" on "the popular front" in *Heart of Darkness* (1899) in ways that foreshadow the rise of (new) fascist leaders, among other contemporary threats.[7]

What I would like to add as we sail deeper in the age of the Anthropocene, is that Conrad's tales of the sea urge future-oriented readers to turn to yet another catastrophe that casts a shadow on the past, modern, as well as the contemporary imagination: the spread of epidemic contagion. From the fever recorded in "The Congo Diary" to the "little fever" that renders Marlow scientifically interesting in *Heart of Darkness* to the plague of tuberculosis that affects the crew in *The Nigger of the "Narcissus"* (1897), Conrad's fictions repeatedly invite a diagnostic of different types of infectious pathologies. But it is a novella titled *The Shadow-Line: A Confession* (1917)[8] that deserves renewed attention today. One of the best tales of his later period, it dramatizes an epidemic contagion of malaria on board ship so vividly that it led the present author in the mid-2010s to warn against "the shadow of epidemics loom[ing] large on the horizon"⁹—a shadow that materialized as the Covid-19 pandemic spread across the globe in 2020, 2021, and 2022. With the benefit of hindsight, I now return to Conrad's mimetic poetics that made such an anticipation possible in the first place.

Modernist Mimesis: The Moon and the Halo

Mimesis is not an obvious aesthetic principle to account for literary modernism in general and Conrad's poetics in particular. Yet, at a closer look, a minor conception of mimesis shines through Conrad's impressionistically opaque narratives, nonetheless. Repeatedly in his tales, Conrad alludes to mimetic principles that a dominant tradition in Western aesthetics from Plato to Auerbach consistently frames via the trope of the "mirror" and the luminous reflections of reality from the outside-in it entails. And yet, if he does so, it is to foreground what he calls "the mirror of the sea" to offer impressionistic, opaque, often fluttering and obscure, but also strangely illuminating mimetic principles that encourage readers to reflect *on* referential phenomena surrounding his tales from the inside-out.

What Conrad says of his most influential narrative voice, Charlie Marlow, equally applies to his poetics as a whole: Conrad's mimetic poetics was "not typical."¹⁰ As the frame narrator famously continues in the opening pages of *Heart of Darkness*:

> to him [Marlow and, at one remove, Conrad] the meaning of an episode was not inside like a kernel but outside, enveloping the tale which brought it out only as a glow brings out a haze, in the likeness of one of these misty halos that, sometimes, are made visible by the spectral illumination of moonshine.¹¹

This is arguably one of the most discussed passages in Conrad's corpus. And rightly so for it condenses impressionistic principles central to his poetics. As J. Hillis Miller has admirably shown, this modernist poetics deconstructs the complex relation between narrative and meaning.¹² At the same time, there is also a poetics of mimesis emerging from different degrees of narrative reflections that have not been fully sketched out as yet. If we situate the interplay of contrasting yet related images that in-*form* (give form to) this parable—light/darkness, sun/moon, direct/reflected light, origin/copy, tale/meaning, fiction/truth, etc.—within a longer genealogy of mimesis that goes from antiquity to modernity, Conrad's poetics begins to shine through in a different, original, yet still mimetic light.

Traditionally, at least since the dawn of Western aesthetics in Plato's *Republic*, the sun is metaphorical of a direct source of light that operates as the *locus classicus* of meaning. In Plato's metaphysics, in fact, the sun stands for a true, intelligible, and universal Form that reduces the world of sensible phenomena to the status of illusory shadows, and the artistic representations thereof. The latter are thus reframed as shadows of shadows far removed from the sun-like reality of ideal Forms, as Plato famously pictures it in the parable of the Cave in Book 7 of the *Republic*.[13] From the other end of the metaphysical spectrum, in a playful and creative rearticulation of the light/shadow, origin/copy, truth/fiction binaries, Conrad inverses the trope of art as an illusory representation, or dark shadow, via the image of a mirroring and luminous reflection, or "glow," of Marlow's tale that is double-faced with respect to the Platonic tradition it mirrors, reflects (on), and subverts. At the most general level, Conrad is still partially in line with a longstanding Platonic tradition in Western aesthetics in the sense that the light of the moon, which is at the "origin" of the tale's "meaning," is not "original" in the sense that is not the primary origin of light. The moonlight is already a reflection of the sunlight, situating the "halo" at three removes, so to speak, from the original source of light.

With Plato, then, Conrad's parable initially assumes the mimetic, mirroring, or doubling nature of art. Even the relation between the tale and its meaning, which, within the parable, mirrors the relation between the moon and the halo, is not arbitrary. Rather, it is based on what J. Hillis Miller calls, using a Platonic term, a "correspondence" (or *homoiosis*) that is double: "the glow brings out the haze, the story brings out its meaning."[14] At the same time, *contra* Plato and the critiques of mimetic art as a dangerous illusion or appearance, Conrad playfully alludes to this metaphysical tradition only to better inverse its most fundamental aesthetic and ontological presuppositions. In fact, for Conrad, the refracted light of the tale qua moon-glow does not generate shadows at "the third remove from truth," as Plato posited at the dawn of mimetic theory.[15] On the contrary, for Conrad, the aesthetic reflection brings out a "haze" that like a "halo" illuminates the darkness surrounding the moon via an impressionistic, opaque, and far-removed source of light. Importantly, this second-order reflection is generative of a "meaning" Conrad considers "true" and "essential" nonetheless. Thus, he writes in his famous "Preface": "The artist then, like the thinker or the scientist, seeks the truth and makes his appeal," to bring out a reality he considers "enduring and essential."[16] Conrad's mimetic poetics, then, suggests that the farther removed from the original source of light the aesthetic reflection is, the closer to an "essential" meaning we get, an "enduring" meaning that is not based on a direct mirroring reflection of a transcendental or consensual truth, yet as we begin to sense, is based on mimetic principles that cast light on immanent realities all around us, nonetheless.

Conrad inverses the Platonic evaluation of mimesis as a mirror and the idealist metaphysics it entails by setting up different layers of interconnected narrative mediation. If we transfer the layers of mediation internal to the framing parable to Conrad's tale "itself," they can be summarized as follows: first, within the tale, meaning is "originally" located in Marlow's atypical oral narrative (first origin); second, Marlow's oral narrative is already mediated by the framing narrator (second origin) addressing the listeners on the *Nellie* sitting in the dark; and, at three removes, Conrad's mimetic poetics (the "origin" which is not one) mediates this twice-refracted tale for us readers, generating an illuminating "glow" of what may have "happened" in the Congo. To this day this multi-layered tale continues to generate reflections around what Philippe Lacoue-Labarthe influentially called "the horror of the West."[17] We could say that Conrad's modernist poetics is on the side of the illuminating light, or "lamp," rather than the reflecting "mirror," to borrow from M. H. Abrams's famous categories articulated in *The Mirror and the Lamp*.[18]

And yet, as always, aesthetic oppositions can be shadier than they appear to be at first sight. As Abrams already recognized, the line dividing the romantic or expressive theory of art from the mimetic theory of art is not always clear cut. Thus, Abrams reminds us that the romantic writer and philosopher William Hazlitt had troubled the distinction between the mirror and the lamp via an image replete with genealogical reflections we can now fully see as he writes: "The light of poetry is not only a direct but also a reflected light, that while it shews us the object, throws a sparkling radiance around out."[19] Already for Hazlitt, then, a reflected (mimetic) light can be the source of a romantic (anti-mimetic) glow; mimetic reflections can be the source of original creations. We shall go further and suggest that an anti-mimetic aesthetic reflection emerging from the mirror of the sea can give form to reflections *on* the reality of pandemic contagion constitutive of *homo mimeticus*. This modernist mimetic aesthetics is important because it relies on immanent impressions to register non-anthropocentric (viral, environmental, material) forces that are often not directly perceptible through vision but can be communicated quite directly via affective contagion. In sum, what Conrad's much-discussed passage already suggests in the space between reflections and refractions is that the powers of mimesis continue to animate conflicting theories of art that go from the ancients to the moderns, the romantics to the realists to the modernists, stretching to in-*form* contemporary shadows as well—including real, all too real shadows like the shadow of epidemics.

To be sure, not unlike the twice-refracted light of the moon in *Heart of Darkness*, the "mirror of the sea" in *The Shadow-Line* does not reflect clear, transparent, and stable images. The sea is, after all, a moving rather than stabilizing source of reflection. And yet, the moving shadows it generates urge mimetic theorists to reflect *on* the shadow-line that divides not only youth from adulthood but also the living from the dead, the individual and the collective, sovereignty and community, human agency and viral agency, past generations and future generations, all of which are vital to cast light on the logical and pathological dynamic of that mimetic phenomenon par excellence which is an epidemic.

Modernist Mimetic Theory: The Reality of Epidemics

Epidemics often occur in Conrad's tales of the *homo duplex*, suggesting secret continuities between physical and psychic contagion in ways that reveal mimetic principles operating at both the level of meaning and formal mediation. At the level of meaning, Conrad would have agreed with René Girard's account of "the plague in literature" as a reflection on the affective dynamic of mimetic contagion central to "social phenomena."[20] And yet, if Girard is particularly attentive to the metaphorical implications of the plague, Conrad uses the "mirror of the sea" to reflect (on) the literal effects of epidemic diseases in immanent ways congruent with our modernist mimetic theory.[21] In fact, writing from the position of a still relatively immune nation-state, Girard, in the past, has tended to downplay the medical side of contagion, treating it as a "disguise" of a more profound, universal, and transhistorical mimetic truth: "the properly medical aspects of the plague never were essential; in themselves they always played a minor role, serving mostly as disguise for an even more terrible threat no science has ever been able to conquer [i.e., mimetic violence]."[22] Girard's mimetic theory of the plague in literature is historically determined and can be dated to the post–Second World War period, which shaped Girard's theoretical imagination. Equally dated is Girard's diagnostic that we now live in "a world less and less threatened by real bacterial epidemics."[23] From the plague of HIV that spread across the world in the 1980s and 1990s and continues to infect the "wretched of the earth" (Frantz Fanon's term), to the Covid-19 pandemic, which Conrad's work put us in a position to foresee, to the future pandemics that will continue to threaten an increasingly globalized, permeable, and precarious world, the shadow of epidemics will further threaten future generations as well. Girard recognized this shadow in his last book but did not fully develop a diagnostic of the immanent dynamic of contagion, leaving this work for future theorists of mimesis.[24] Hence the need to supplement Girard's hermeneutics in light of what epidemiologists, already in the 2010s, called the shadow of "the coming plague"[25]—a shadow that has since materialized in the 2020s and will continue to reappear in the future. Hence the urgency to turn back to a writer like Conrad, who, well before contemporary theorists, puts readers back in touch with the literal effects of pathological contagion, encouraging new generations of critics to treat epidemic infections *à la lettre*.

At the level of formal mediation, Conrad's modernist mimesis makes us see and feel imperceptible forces that are not reducible to the logic of visual representation but affect and infect bodies, nonetheless. In the process his poetics of catastrophe transgresses anthropocentric principles that posit humans in the foreground while endowing agentic powers to nonhuman forces in the background (wind, sea currents, typhoons, parasites). Critics are thus urged to consider the dynamic interplay between human and nonhuman entanglements that are currently returning to the foreground in different critical turns—from the affective turn to the environmental turn, the new materialist turn to the posthuman turn—all of which promote a *re*-turn of attention to the powers of mimesis constitutive of what I call, the mimetic turn. It is this spiraling interplay between human and nonhuman forces that in-*form The Shadow-Line* in particular and Conrad's diagnostic of the effects of epidemic on individual bodies and the body politic in general.

One of the best tales of his final period, *The Shadow-Line* is often read as a tale of individual maturation based on Conrad's experience of "first-command." This part of the story already received much attention in the twentieth century. What we must add is that it is also a tale of an epidemic of malaria in the background that is entangled with issues of human sovereignty, communal belonging, and collective survival that should be foregrounded in the twenty-first century. If we want to do critical and theoretical justice to what Conrad calls "a fairly complex piece of work" (5) and sound the depth of his ethical thought for contemporary times characterized by a shared vulnerability to pandemic infections, a change of perspective is thus urgently in order: the process of individual maturation in the foreground needs to be reframed against the collective shadow of epidemic contagion in the background Conrad takes the trouble to represent. Conrad's mimetic poetics mediates viral contagion for us to see and feel.

The Shadow-Line focuses on the threat of epidemic contagion in order to offer a diagnostic account of the shared vulnerability, collective responsibility, intergenerational relations, and ethical care that is not limited to sovereign individuals but stretches to include the latter's dependency on the community as a whole. Ian Watt influentially framed Conrad's narrative concerns with the dependence on others and the risk of alienation it entails with this concise formula: "Alienation, of course; but how do we get out of it?"[26] This dependency on others is accentuated as Conrad urges us to confront an even more contemporary and, perhaps, less anthropocentric question, which we could formulate as follows: "Catastrophe, of course; but how do we survive it?" I argue that *The Shadow-Line* calls for the coming of a type of mimetic solidarity that cuts across distinctions between self and others, high and low ranks, present and past generations, in order to establish an ethos based on shared, intergenerational, and communal cooperation to affirm survival not only for the self but for others as well, not only in the present but for generations to come. Ultimately my mimetic hypothesis is that Conrad's poetics sets up an opaque yet magnifying mirror to reflect *on* the possibility of collective survival in the age of the Anthropocene—out of catastrophic situations that are entangled in political contexts in need of reevaluation.

Political (Con)Texts: The *Grand Miroir* of *The Shadow-Line*

Both personal and collective reflections on epidemics internal to *The Shadow-Line* are already mirrored before the tale begins. Subtitled "A Confession," the novella opens with an epigraph by Charles Baudelaire, which reads: "*D'autres fois, calme plat, grand miroir / De mon désespoir*" (11; At other times, dead calm, great mirror / Of my despair). This mirror reflects an existential, romantic despair that casts a shadow on an individual ego, yet Conrad also sets up a larger mirror for more general ethico-political shadows cast on Europe more generally. Written in 1916, in the midst of the Great War, the novella opens with a deeply personal dedication that stretches to include an entire generation, thereby suggesting that personal and political despair, fictional bonds and real bonds, cannot easily be dissociated: "To Borys and all others who like himself have crossed in early youth the shadow-line of their generation, with love." Conrad's son returned from the front; most of his generation did not. They crossed the "shadow-line" that divides not only youth from maturity but also the living from the dead. Retrospectively, we can see that this is probably one of the most intimately personal and, in the same breath, widely collective dedications in modern literature—if not literature *tout court*. More than 16 million people perished in the Great War. And this tragic number was soon amplified by the 1918 Spanish Flu Pandemic, which, one year after the publication of *The Shadow-Line*, spread around the world, generating a heartrending estimate of 50 to 100 million additional victims.

Conrad was, of course, not in a position to foresee how far his dedication would stretch. Within the novella, the phrase "the shadow-line" is taken to delineate a boundary that divides two periods in the life of an immature individual. That is, a shady impressionistic line in-between the youth/adulthood binary the captain-narrator needs to cross for personal maturation and successful collective navigation to occur. Still, Conrad's sensitivity to what he calls in the "Author's Note," "the supreme trial of a whole generation" (6), testifies to his painful awareness that, during those dark years, a long shadow had been cast on the referential world. As Owen Knowles recognized, lending realistic weight to the tale, the dedication "actively invites the reader to attend to the story's wartime origins."[27] And as Martin Bock specifies, Conrad was personally concerned with the Spanish Flu pandemics and his fictions gain from considering "germ theory," and its concern with "contagion" that were emerging at the time.[28] Attention to realistic referents is indeed already part of the tale. In the process, *The Shadow-Line*'s mimetic poetics invites us to challenge a series of supplementary binaries such as self/others, living/dead, fiction/history, sick/healthy, ship/state, microcosm/macrocosm, one generation/the next generation. Thus reframed, what then does this *"grand miroir"* reflect?

In light of such referential historical horrors that press in from the outside, the political metaphors that inform the tale from the inside-out initially sound strikingly conservative. The newly appointed captain relies on monarchic images of authority that inform his vision of what command is or should be. As he unexpectedly lands his first command, he says: "In that community I stood, like a king in his country in a class all by myself. I mean a hereditary king, not a mere elected head of state" (54). This ship is thus not simply a ship; it is representative of a "state." The crew is not only a crew; it stands for a "community." The captain is not solely a captain; he is the embodiment of a "king"—a "hereditary" king whose power is guaranteed by his alignment with a dynastic, aristocratic tradition. The image of the king as head of the state, whose power is conveyed transcendentally by the "Grace of God" (54), alludes to the political *topos* of the two bodies of the king, one mortal the other divine, a distinction the captain-narrator convokes in order to draw a line that divides him not only hierarchically, but also affectively, from his subjects. Thus, he specifies: "My sensations could not be like those of any other man on board" (23–24). The captain might be in the same boat as the crew, yet his "sensations" should not be confused with communal sensations; the head is attached to the body but should not be confused with the body. Such autonomous conceptions of sovereign subjectivity are of romantic inspiration, rely on transcendental accounts of divine creation, and find a formal medium of expression in the use of an equally detached, omniscient, and third-person (diegetic) narrative perspective dominant in nineteenth-century realism. This, at least, is the initial theoretical premise.

And yet, in narrative practice, boundaries are shadier than they appear to be. The hierarchical line the human head sets up can easily be transgressed by nonhuman forces internal to Conrad's mimetic poetics in general and the captain-narrator's first-person (mimetic) perspective in particular. Already the organic analogy of the human body that mirrors the body politic cuts both ways and opens up the possibility of infectious continuities that cut across affective discontinuities. If the head/body dichotomy introduces a distance from communal "sensations," it also opens up channels for contagious infections that can potentially penetrate, contaminate, and, eventually, undermine the authoritarian power structure on which the body politic of the ship *qua* "state" rests. This, at least, is what the captain realizes as his "abstract idea" (38) of what command is begins to give way to the empirical "experience" (3) of what command leads one to become. This tension between abstract idea and lived experience is central to Conrad's mimetic poetics in general and in-*forms* his account of the pandemic shadow we are tracking. In the context of *The Shadow-Line* it generates a limit(ing) nautical experience that confronts the captain-narrator's naively anthropocentric idea of monarchic power with the immanent reality of nonhuman forces that constrain the ability of the head to direct the social body, generating both epidemic pathologies and patho-*logies*—that is, critical accounts (*logoi*) on contagious affects (*pathos*).

Epidemic Patho(-)logies

From the outset of his nautical journey the captain is quick to learn a lesson many politicians during the Covid-19 pandemic were slower to learn: namely, that the human head which controls the communal body is not only as vulnerable to viral contagion as the body, it is also radically dependent on nonhuman factors beyond the control of his command of the body politic.[29] Trapped in a becalmed ship in a river, the captain finds himself unable to "get her out to sea" (55). This is a repetition of nautical situations already haunting previous tales, like "The Secret Sharer,"[30] but Conrad never sails in the same river twice. His mimetic poetics is based on repetitions with a difference that supplement important diagnostic insights. *The Shadow-Line*, in fact, stresses that adverse meteorological conditions not only passively impede nautical action, they also actively generate new catastrophic possibilities. Thus, as a consequence of being stuck in what the captain-narrator calls a "pestilential river" (55) an epidemic of malaria breaks out on board ship. We are told that "The first member of the crew ... [was] taken ashore (with choleric symptoms) and died there at the end of a week" (57). This is one of the slowest possible starts in the history of narratives of the sea (six weeks are spent in that poisonous river). The slow *nautical* start is thus mirrored by a slow *narrative* start, for the reader to see and feel, at one further remove. As the ship eventually reaches the Gulf of Siam, the epidemic, far from being cured, continues to determine the entire trajectory of the journey, eventually forcing a return to Singapore. The captain-narrator retrospectively says: "the infection . . . clung to the ship. It obviously did cling to the ship. Two men. One burning, one shivering" (66).[31] Confronted with this epidemic infection, the captain's initial faith in his sovereign, monarchic power to be left unaffected begins to give way to a form of fatalistic, anxious, and desperate sensation, as he admits: "I felt a distinct reluctance to go and look at them. What was the good? Poison is poison. Tropical fever is tropical fever" (66). Poison is, indeed, poison. It affects the head as much as the body, rendering the head not only unable to direct the body, but also as vulnerable as all the other members of the body politic. There is a subtle diagnostic lesson in this fictional realization that applies to real epidemics as well. Indifferent to all-too-human hierarchical distinctions between (human and divine) bodies, the narrative alerts readers that epidemic pathologies are mimetic in the sense that they are contagious and introduce (horizontal) sameness where there once was (vertical) difference, (shared) infection where there once was (divided) affection.

This is, indeed, the state of "undifferentiation" that Girard would consider "metaphorical" of the mimetic crisis that is hidden behind the mask of real epidemics. But while the shadow of mimetic doubles haunts the tale, no violent crisis ensues. On the contrary, solidarity and sympathy follow. Moreover, Conrad's diagnostic of undifferentiation remains quite realistic and referential: it opens up a holistic, environmental, and non-anthropocentric perspective that is attentive to the complex ecological interplay between human and nonhuman contagion. As an ex-seaman, Conrad is, in fact, painfully aware that meteorological and epidemiological factors are intimately connected. And as a seaman turned writer his narrative dramatizes the contagious pathologies that infect the bodies and souls of the entire body politic.

What Conrad makes us see and feel is that this mimetic patho(-)logy (both sickness and diagnostic) does not operate according to a billiard-ball causal logic. Rather, it generates a systemic feedback loop of contagious circulation that—not unlike a haze in darkness—escapes visual representation. And yet, Conrad's mimetic poetics brings out its meaning via a narrative light that shines throught it and makes it visible. The captain-narrator retrospectively diagnoses the logic of this poisonous pathology with incisive patho-*logical* precision:

> The fact was that disease played with us capriciously very much as the winds did. It would go from one man to another with a lighter or heavier touch, which always left its mark behind, staggering some, knocking others over for a time, leaving this one, returning to another, so that all of them had now an invalidish aspect and a hunted, apprehensive look in their eyes.... It was a double fight. The adverse weather held us in front; and the disease pressed on our rear. (70)

As with winds and hazes, so with contagious diseases: both cannot be seen or easily represented, yet their effects around them are intimately and sometimes violently felt, leaving impressions Conrad's tale brings out via mimetic means. The formal strategies are different from the moon/halo allegory at the opening of *Heart of Darkness* for we do not have different layers of narrative mediation at play in *The Shadow-Line*. And yet, Conrad's ability to bring out, via a retrospective first-person narrative, invisible forces that rest on the deeply felt experience of viral contagion for the reader to see and, perhaps, partially feel as well, remains fundamentally mimetic in the double sense that the pandemic is both rooted in a referential reality and generative of viral/affective contagion. What emerges from this patho(-)logical picture of epidemic contagion is that this fight is at least double: It confronts both climatic and epidemic factors, which, in turn, retroact to affect and infect both the bodies and souls of the crew, generating a vortex of contagious actions and reactions. The mimetic ecology emerging from this widening spiral of climatic, epidemic, and anthropogenic forces generates what Gregory Bateson calls a "systemic pathology," making us realize, along with the captain, that "we are not by any means the captains of our soul."[32] It also opens up a diagnostic of the pathological effects of the material vibrations that, as Jane Bennett aptly recognized—from viruses to winds, currents to storms—are reframing human agency along lines that "are more emergent than efficient, more fractal than linear."[33] There is thus a hidden sense in which Conrad's mimetic poetics paves the way for non-anthropocentric accounts of mimetic influences in critical theory that will have to wait a century to materialize.

The imperceptible spiraling patho-*logic* of this vibrant mimetic pathology could be schematically diagnosed as follows. First, *climatic* factors deprive the captain (or head) of the power to effectively direct the ship (or body politic), leaving the entire crew (or community) exposed and vulnerable to additional threats that escape anthropogenic control. Second, viral, *epidemic* factors join hands with adverse weather conditions and cause a generalized *physical* pathology whereby one body infects another body, progressively knocking over subject after subject. And third, epidemic, environmental, and somatic factors, affect the *psyche* of "all" the members of the crew, generating a "haunting" apprehension which, in yet another feedback loop, renders the *bodies* even more vulnerable to the circulating return of other waves of infection. Once caught in such a pathological spiral of environmental, epidemic, and anthropogenic infections, linear logic breaks down preventing the possibility of effective antidotes to be applied.

There is, indeed, a monstrous shadow beyond human control haunting this tale, what the captain-narrator also calls "an invisible monster ambushed in the air, in the water, in the mud of the river-bank" (57). This monster may be invisible, but clearly has a referential reality. It is thus not surprising that the captain's mind is infected by poisonous images of catastrophe. Once out of the pestilential river, and still followed by the infection, he says: "The intense loneliness of the sea acted like a poison on my brain. When I turned my eyes to the ship, I had a morbid vision of her as a floating grave" (74). This poisonous infection is as somatic as it is psychic, as personal as it is collective. Importantly, Conrad does not limit such a vision to the microcosm of the ship and the community it sustains but, by metonymic association, extends the spiral of epidemic contagion to imaginatively infect what he calls, nothing less and nothing more than "a planet flying vertiginously on its appointed path in a space of infinite silence" (62). This planet is not a moon, illuminating the darkness all around it for humans to see at night. Rather, it is planet Earth vertiginously moving in a space of infinite darkness we cannot see during the day. If the former image guided modernist reflections on the autonomy of art in the past century, I suggest that it is the second image that should serve as a compass for contemporary reflections on the limits of human autonomy and the possibility for a new poetics of mimesis in the present century. As William E. Connolly also recognized, these mimetic reflections are vital for "facing the planetary" via an entangled and mimetic humanism that goes beyond anthropocentrism and is attentive to the fragility of life on Earth.[34]

Conrad's mimetic narrative posits a diagnostic, patho-*logical* problem to its captain: namely, how to find a remedy that would, if not magically cure, at least contain the contagious effects of epidemic infection. There is, of course, the episode of the missing quinine. Thrown overboard by the previous captain gone mad, this episode leaves the new captain without medical antidotes to counter the pathology on board. And as the phantom of the late captain continues to mysteriously haunt the ship, this episode opens up the tale to supernatural, magical, and anti-realistic interpretative possibilities that have stimulated the critical imagination.[35] Conrad, for one, did not seem particularly fond of this line of inquiry. Thus, he stressed in a realistic mood his "invincible conviction that whatever falls under the dominion of our senses must be in nature" (5). While a transcendent touch unquestionably informs the tale, my focus here is less on supernatural ghosts than on natural shadows, less on subjective impressions and more on referential reflections. There is, in fact, a referential environmental awareness internal to Conrad's mimetic poetics that still needs to be foregrounded in a period that is, once again, in the grip of monstrous and quite realistic epidemic dangers.

Caught in the windless waters of the poisonous river, this adventure has not taken us physically far. And yet, despite the paralysis generated by the becalmed ship, the epidemic infection, and the contagious demoralization that ensues, this experience of first command constitutes a decisive step ahead in the captain's psycho-ethical development. It leads to the realization that there is no second, divine body divided from the human body, no transcendental head of the state apart from the immanent body politic—if only because the head remains, for better and worse, attached to the body. Consequently, the captain experiences that the head is not only as vulnerable to the danger of infection as the body; it is also radically dependent on the social body for the survival of the "community" as a whole. Indeed, a radical reform of the captain's psychology, politics, and ethics is urgently in order if he wants to navigate out of these poisonous waters.

The first slow chapters of *The Shadow-Line* are often considered to be marginal at best and totally dispensable at worst, but on closer inspection they reveal the push-pull of mimetic and anti-mimetic undercurrents that give form to the tale, beginning, middle, and end. The beginning already makes clear that a mimetic anxiety casts a shadow on the captain-narrator's process of maturation. The novel starts with the narrator's complaint about the lack of originality provided on board his previous ship, where he served as first mate before giving up his berth. Invoking a romantic dissatisfaction characteristic of what he calls "the green sickness of late youth" (12), he says: "one expects an uncommon or personal sensation—a bit of one's own" (11). And later, he echoes: "There was nothing original, nothing new . . . no opportunities to find out something about oneself" (25). Originality (something "one's own"), not imitative behavior (something "shared"), is what this romantic soul in search of adventure seeks as the cure to his youthful, existential despair. Interestingly, such a solipsistic self-sufficiency and narcissistic self-concern renders the newly appointed captain indifferent to catastrophic scenarios: "People might have been falling dead around me, houses crumbling, guns firing, I wouldn't have known" (35). It is thus not surprising that his entire attitude at the Officer's Home in Singapore, as he is waiting, demoralized and anxiously insecure, for a ship to take him on a passage home, is characterized by a fierce anti-mimetic stance toward kindly disposed, paternal figures who actively serve as helpers in his journey of maturation. This romantic anxiety of influence concerning "whiskered" father figures is not unusual in Conrad's nautical fictions, and the type of psychic rivalry it generates has traditionally been read in familial, psychoanalytical terms. This rivalry, and the ambivalences it generates, however, is not so much revealing of the subject's Oedipal complex (Freud)—though an anxiety of influence is at play; nor can it be fully understood within the triangular dynamic of "mimetic desire" (Girard)—though mimetic shadows have certainly been cast on his ego. Rather, it sets in motion the mimetic "influences" (Conrad) grounded on a mimetic unconscious that generates affective communal pathologies as much as narrative patho-logies, that is narrative accounts (*logoi*) on mimetic affect (or *pathos*) vital to surviving epidemics.

Surviving Epidemics

The captain-narrator is fundamentally aware that the qualities of command based on a genealogy of the composite of the composite soul can only be tested on the basis of an individual, unique, and, in this sense, always new experience of navigation. If the "compass" reminded the captain-narrator of the importance of "vigilance," it is time for him to put his hands on the helm, which he takes as "a symbol of mankind's claim to the direction of its own fate" (63). And it is in the confrontation with a catastrophic situation that affects and infects the social structure of the ship, and the "planet" it symbolizes, that the captain's composite soul and the social structures that compose it, come together as a cooperative community in which head and body are joined to jointly steer—and affirm the possibility of survival.

The affect of command internal to *The Shadow-Line* should not be read in terms of a solipsistic process of psychic maturation confined to the inner space of the cabin. Rather, this inner experience gives birth to what Conrad calls "a sort of composite soul, the soul of command" (47), which opens up the sympathetic channels of the sovereign experience of "command" to the wider, collective, and exterior question of what Conrad also calls "community" (54). Critics have noticed this concern before,[36] but the theoretical implications of Conrad's emphasis on community to sail past catastrophic situations still need to be articulated. In this concluding section, as "the feverish, enfeebled crew, in an additional turn of the racking screw" (91) is forced to face a storm that overshadows the "last gleam of light in the universe" (92), Conrad's mimetic poetics outlines an ethos of community by rendering it operative on the basis of affective forms of cooperation. This also entails supplementing past monocephalic or acephalic accounts of community that first emerged in a period haunted by the specter of communism and the shadow of fascism (Georges Bataille) and were more recently reframed by continental philosophers who, on the shoulders of Bataille, rethought the question of the "in-common" on the basis of a relational ontology of the subject (Jean-Luc Nancy).[37] Building on this tradition, I propose some steps toward sovereign, yet non-totalitarian forms of command based on sympathetic cooperation between the head and the social body, the composite soul and its social structure we have been tracing so far. For Conrad, in fact, it is on an immanent, communal ground based on shared affective foundations that we can affirm the possibility of survival.

The slow beginning of the first part of the tale has the function of generating underlying currents that, in the second part, are instrumental to bringing the narrative to a speedy end. After spending seemingly useless, yet instructive time in the Officers Home in Singapore and enduring an epidemic contamination that infects nearly all members of the crew stuck in windless waters, the ship, as well as the narrative, begins to pick up speed. And in a final nautical turn that faces the shadow of catastrophe, Conrad anchors the captain's composite soul (or head) in the social structure of the ship (or body) in order to fight for the survival of community via an experience of sovereign communication that is as interior as it is exterior, as individual as it is collective. Following a type of "training become instinct" through the formative influences of exemplary figures, the captain knows, or better feels, that "[t]he difficulties, the dangers, the problems of a ship at sea must be met on deck" (73). That is, from a position in which the "composite soul" of command can both animate and be animated by communal social bodies, on a sympathetic, we-centric, and non-violent basis. And indeed, as the narrative unfolds, and the captain's mind is progressively haunted by "visions of a ship drifting in calms and swinging in light airs, with all her crew dying slowly about her decks" (82), he is led to abandon his solipsistic, aristocratic stance that initially characterized him, in order to invest his soul—and thus his body—in the social structure, or "nerves" of the ship, so as to innervate—and thus reanimate—a feverish and moribund social body on "the common ground" of the deck. A confrontation with a shared catastrophe leads the captain to open up the sympathetic channels that transect his already "composite soul." And on this affective basis, emerges an ethics of communal cooperation that eventually allows the planet of the ship to sail past the Scylla of totalitarian command and the Charybdis of refusal of command, so as to return to a harbor with a community of infected—yet still living subjects.

Plagued by a contagious "epidemic," afflicted by "windless" waters, driven by "mysterious currents" and, eventually, "beset by hurricanes," the narrative generates wave after wave of calamitous factors we should get ready for in the Anthropocene. These catastrophes require a type of strenuous, breathtaking, and continuous endurance to keep affirming the possibility of survival to the end. As Conrad made clear from the beginning, it is via the systemic interplay of human interactions between the captain and the crew, the head and the body, that this possibility of survival can ultimately be affirmed. In particular, the concluding part of the journey, which takes the ship from the Island of Koh-ring back to Singapore, suggests that the captain-narrator's ethico-political commitment to the body politic the ship represents stems from the juncture of two seemingly incompatible ethical traditions the narrative has been delineating all along. That is, a vertical, aristocratic tradition that inscribes the captain's soul in a "dynasty" (47) of commanders whose "influences" are constitutive of his "composite soul" on the one hand, and a horizontal, social experience of "sympathy" (47) that anchors this soul within a social "community" represented by the microcosm of the contaminated ship, on the other hand. I suggest that it is from this paradoxical conjunction of vertical, aristocratic bonds that tie the captain to an aristocratic past tradition, and of the horizontal, democratic bonds that tie him to the present social relations, that Conrad's communal ethics of survival emerges.

The bonds of shared solidarity that tie the captain to his fellow sailors are not opposed to the aristocratic soul of command but, rather, provide the living affects that transect the channels of what is already a composite soul. We could, in fact, say that "the composite soul of command" the captain inherits, in *theory*, from a past "dynastic" tradition of shared "influences," "training," and above all, "conception of duty" (47) is, in *praxis*, already connected to the horizontal bonds that tie this head, or if you prefer, this soul, to the social duties that structure the "fine nerves" (48) of the ship. For Conrad in fact, it is *because* the soul of command is already informed by what Nietzsche calls in *Beyond Good and Evil* the "social structure of the drives and emotions"[38] that the social duties that structure the ship can exercise such an absorbing affective "claim" on his composite soul, generating a bond so intense that he "could imagine no claim that would be stronger and more absorbing than the claim of that ship" (60). The strength of this claim, in other words, stems from the fact that it is not simply an external claim addressed to a singular head. Rather, it comes from the entire social body on board, a communal body that is—via the ramified "nerves" of the ship—already neurologically connected to the head, part of an inner experience of a soul that is not singular but composite instead. Alternatively, the lived experience of command opens those sympathetic channels that already innervate, but do not yet irrigate, the composite structure of the soul.

In his account of the soul as multiplicity, Nietzsche had already stressed that command is an affective affair as he writes: "will is not only a complex of feeling and thinking, but above all an *affect*: and in fact the affect of command."[39] Conrad furthers this affective view by putting the composite soul of command mimetically in touch with the nerves that tie the ship as social structure. That the head is back in touch with the social body is clear. With a retrospective narrative distance, the captain-narrator realizes the power of mimetic pathos. For instance, he notes that "an order has a steadying influence upon him who has to give it" (96). The mimetic concept of "influence" is thus used again to account for a process of nonverbal communication. Yet this time it does not designate a personal, psychological experience; nor does it have its origin in a totalitarian figure. Rather, it designates a collective, psychic-social, and referential dynamic whereby an order on the social body retroacts on the sovereign head, influencing him in return. This mimetic circulation of reciprocal influences harmonizes the interior structure of the soul of command and the community on deck in a way that balances the microcosm of the social structure of the ship. We are in fact given to think that without these living, experiential bonds that tie the head to the social body and are constitutive of what the narrator calls "the strong magic" (30) of command, the latter is bound to remain what the captain calls in an anti-Platonic mood, "an abstract idea" (38)—a dead concept deprived of the living affects that animate this magical experience. In short, for Conrad, the hypothesis of a composite (mimetic) soul innervated by shared (contagious) experience is necessary to bring a social body (community) into being.

The communal ethics that emerges from Conrad's reflections on epidemics mediated via his mimetic poetics is the following: in situations haunted by the real possibility of catastrophe the composition rather than dissolution of community should be at the center of literary and philosophical thought, a community which, with its social body innervated by the head (and vice versa). To be sure, models of social cohesion based on an organicist view of society in which the head governs, by "influence," the body politic have not been popular in the second half of the twentieth century, and rightly so given the poisonous effects of popular *Gemeinschaften* predicated on fascist forms of will to power. While the dangers of authoritarian will to power should always be kept in mind for political reasons, and self-contained notions of organic unity have become suspicious for aesthetic reasons, the ancient metaphor of the living yet precarious and embedded organism is currently regaining traction for ethical and ecological reasons, especially concerning contemporary preoccupations with epidemic infections and contagious pathologies. Conrad contributes to debates on community by adding a diagnostic that shows how a social organism is vulnerable to forms of infection that have the potential to affect equally—and in this sense "democratically"—the head and the body. He also dramatizes democratic solutions in which the head cooperates with the entire social organism in order to fight off pathologies and jointly affirm the possibility of collective survival.

There is, indeed, an immanent, life-affirming tendency at work in Conrad's communal ethos that cannot afford to think of sharing only as an individual exposure to death but uses the shadow of death to affirm communal life. This is, indeed, what happens in the end. The ship is hit by a storm, which is not terrific in itself yet, given the pathological state of the crew, has catastrophic implications. Enfeebled by the epidemic, the crew and captain have to join forces to hoist a sail to keep the ship floating. Here is how Conrad pictures the scene:

> The shadows swayed away from me without a word. Those men were the ghosts of themselves and their weight on a rope could be no more than the weight of a bunch of ghosts. Indeed, if ever a sail was hauled up by sheer spiritual strength it must have been that sail for, properly speaking, there was no muscle enough for the task in the whole ship, let alone the miserable lot of us on deck. (88)

These subjects are reduced to mere "shadows," or "ghosts;" yet these living ghosts shine through with a narrative mimetic light as they cooperate in order to affirm life. They are animated by a "spiritual strength" that is not singular (the head) nor plural (the body), but is generated by the communal work of a composite crew in which in which the head works in organic communion with the social body. In the process, Conrad makes us see that in a catastrophic scenario, work has the power to generate the flow of affect that keeps the infected organism together. For Conrad, in fact, this type of communal work cannot be reduced to a materialistic and servile conception of life, if only because the "strength" involved is not simply physical but "spiritual," an indication that the type of work that is required to affirm survival in a catastrophic scenario does not belong to the sphere of the profane but to the sacred instead, not to servile and life-negating, passions but to sovereign and life-affirmative experiences. In short, in a mirroring inversion of *Heart of Darkness*, where human catastrophes are triggered by "hollow" narcissistic leaders on the "popular front" generating a "horror" of (fascist) mimesis that reaches into the present, the mimetic poetics of *The Shadow-Line* reveals that nonhuman catastrophes can potentially generate sovereign, mimetic (communal) experiences that affirm collective survival for the future.

It is perhaps no accident that at the final turning point in the narrative, of all affects, Conrad privileges a social, contagious, and sovereign effusion such as "laughter" in order to strengthen the communal bonds of solidarity that invisibly ties self to others, while at the same time exorcizing supernatural fears. "Well, then—laugh! Laugh—I tell you" (95), shouts insanely and somewhat comically, Mr. Burns. And in an attempt to spread this laughter by mimetic contagion to the whole crew, he adds: "Now then—all together. One, two, three—laugh!" (95). This scene is only slightly comic and does not make the crew burst out in laughter, yet the narrative suggests that it is not deprived of mimetic efficacy. In fact, it marks the end of the storm and the crossing of a "barrier" the captain had been trying to cross all along, a shadow-line that could not be crossed individually but required a communal affective cooperation. We are thus given to think that laughter is not only cathartic, it also opens up those sympathetic channels that tie self to others via sacred forms of mimetic communication based on joyful, contagious effusions that generate what I have called elsewhere "the laughter of community" that sets the foundations for a modernist theory of mimesis.[40] The mimetic experience of sovereign communication gives birth to the communal desire of survival; and out of this desire the possibility of cooperative communities to come is at last affirmed. Thus, the captain-narrator makes clear to his crew that "the best chance for the ship and the men was in the efforts all of us, sick and well, must make to get her along out of this" (78). The shift from a diegetic perspective which speaks of "the men" from a temporal distance to an immanent, mimetic perspective which includes the pathos of the narrator ("all of us") is indicative of the affective investment, sharing and cooperation between the head and the social body necessary to overcome a catastrophic conclusion. Thus understood, the ship becomes "a symbol of mankind's claim to the direction of its own fate" (63). This, at least, is what emerges at the moments of maximum vulnerability in which precarious lives take hold of the realization that their soul is a composite soul, their destiny is a shared destiny, their community a shared planetary community.

As we are sailing our planet deeper into the age of the Anthropocene navigating a perilous pandemic against the even larger shadow of rapid climate change, the picture of the infected yet communal ship qua "planet" effectively reflects our exposure to the changes of climate, vulnerability to the turbulence of currents, openness to epidemic contagion and, more generally, the fragility of our all-too-human and nonhuman foundations. Meanwhile, Conrad already suggested that as we continue to navigate the rapid changes that are currently reorienting "a planet flying vertiginously on its appointed path in a space of infinite silence" (62), we should continue developing those shared bonds of "solidarity" vital to sailing through the turbulent waters which both sustain and threaten to dissolve the small planet we ultimately share.

The picture of catastrophe Conrad invites us to consider via mimetic means is thus realistic in the end. As the future of our children looks increasingly uncertain, turning back to Conrad's nautical experiences also reminds us that what is needed to affirm the survival of community is a type of "solidarity" which, as he so presciently put it, "binds men to each other, which binds together all humanity—the dead to the living," but above all—"the living to the unborn."[41]

Acknowledgment

This project has received funding from the European Research Council (ERC) under the European Union's Horizon 2020 research and innovation programme (grant agreement n°716181: *Homo Mimeticus*)

Notes

1. Erich Auerbach, *Mimesis: The Representation of Reality in Western Literature*, trans. Willard R. Trask (Princeton, NJ: Princeton University Press, 2003).
2. For an informed overview, see Gunter Gebauer and Christopher Wulf, *Mimesis: Culture-Art-Society*, trans. Don Reneau (Berkeley: University of California Press, 1995). See also the special issue, "The Mimetic Condition," *CounterText* (2022), forthcoming.
3. Walter Benjamin, "On the Mimetic Faculty," in *Reflections: Essays, Aphorisms, Autobiographical Writings*, trans. Edmund Jephcott (New York: Schocken Books, 1986), 331–336.
4. One of the first theoretical mentions of the "mimetic turn" can be found in Nidesh Lawtoo, "The Plasticity of Mimesis," *MLN* 132, no. 5 (2017): 1201–1224, 1222.
5. For the mimetic turn in new modernist studies, see Nidesh Lawtoo, *The Phantom of the Ego: Modernism and the Mimetic Unconscious* (East Lansing: Michigan State University Press, 2013); for a dialogue on the mimetic turn in literary theory see, "The Critic and the Mime: J. Hillis Miller and Nidesh Lawtoo in Conversation," *Minnesota Review* 95 (2020): 93–119. For more transdisciplinary outputs on the return of mimesis, see http://www.homomimeticus.eu/publications/
6. See the chapters in *Conrad's Heart of Darkness and Contemporary Thought: Revisiting the Horror with Lacoue-Labarthe*, ed. Nidesh Lawtoo (London: Bloomsbury, 2012); and Nidesh Lawtoo, "Conrad's Mimetic Turn," *Conradiana* 48, no. 2–3 (2016): 129–142.
7. I discuss in detail the centrality of catastrophe in relation to mimesis in Conrad's poetics in Nidesh Lawtoo, *Conrad's Shadow: Catastrophe, Mimesis, Theory* (East Lansing: Michigan State University Press, 2013).
8. Joseph Conrad, *The Shadow-Line: A Confession*, ed. J.H. Stape, Allan H. Simmons and Owen Knowels (Cambridge: Cambridge University Press, 2013). Hereafter *SL* and quoted in parentheses in the text.
9. What follows is a revised version of a chapter titled, "The Cooperative Community: Surviving Epidemics in *The Shadow-Line*," in *Conrad's Shadow*,

91–125. Written in 2014 and published in 2016, this chapter already warned against the "contemporary pandemics that, every year, threaten to contaminate an increasingly globalized, permeable and precarious world" (92).

10 Joseph Conrad, *Heart of Darkness. Youth, Heart of Darkness, The End of the Tether*, ed. Owen Knowles (Cambridge: Cambridge University Press, 2010), 45.

11 Ibid.

12 J. Hillis Miller, "*Heart of Darkness* Revisited," in *Conrad's* Heart of Darkness *and Contemporary Thought*, 39–54, 41–46, 43.

13 Plato, *Republic*, in *The Collected Dialogues of Plato*, trans. P. Shorey, ed. E. Hamilton and H. Cairns (Princeton, NJ: Princeton University Press, 1963), 747–751.

14 Miller, "*Heart of Darkness* Revisited," 42, 46.

15 Plato, *Republic*, 827, 602c; Auerbach, *Mimesis*, 554.

16 Joseph Conrad, "Preface," in *The Nigger of the "Narcissus,"* ed. Allan H. Simmons (Cambridge: Cambridge University Press, 2017), xi. On the mimetic principles internal to the "Preface," see also Lawtoo, *Conrad's Shadow*, xxxiv–xxx, 211–239.

17 Philippe Lacoue-Labarthe, "The Horror of the West," trans. Nidesh Lawtoo and Hannes Opelz, in *Conrad's* Heart of Darkness *and Contemporary Thought*, 111–122.

18 See M.H. Abrams, *The Mirror and the Lamp: Romantic Theory and the Critical Tradition* (Oxford: Oxford University Press, 1953).

19 Hazlitt qtd. in Ibid., 52.

20 For Girard "an analysis of significant texts . . . reveals definite analogies between the plague, or rather all great epidemics, and social phenomena." René Girard, "The Plague in Literature and Myth," in *To Double Business Bound* (Baltimore, MD: Johns Hopkins University Press, 1979), 138.

21 On the difference between Girard's mimetic theory and my modernist mimetic theory, see for instance Lawtoo, *The Phantom of the Ego*, 1–19, 281–305.

22 Girard, "The Plague in Literature and Myth," 139, 148.

23 Ibid., 148.

24 René Girard, *Battling to the End: Conversations with Benoît Chantre*, trans. Mary Baker (East Lansing: Michigan State University Press, 2010), 23. For a mimetic account of pandemic contagion beyond Girard, see Nidesh Lawtoo, "Viral Mimesis: The Patho(-)Logies of the Coronavirus," *Paragrana* 30, no. 2 (2021).

25 Laurie Garrett, *The Coming Plague: Newly Emerging Diseases in a World Out of Balance* (New York: Penguin, 1995): see also, *Contagion: Health, Fear, Sovereignty*, ed. Bruce Magnusson and Zahi Zalloua (Seattle: University of Washington Press, 2012).

26 Ian Watt, *Conrad in the Nineteenth Century* (London: Chatto, 1980), 33.

27 Owen Knowles, "Introduction," in *The Shadow-Line*, xxvi, xviii; see also xxvi–xxxv.

28 Martin Bock, "Joseph Conrad and Germ Theory: Why Captain Allistoun Smiles Thoughtfully," *The Conradian* 31, no. 2 (2006): 1–14.

29 Significantly the list of politicians who downplayed the coronavirus, got infected by it, and showed poor command of the pandemic infection, include the US president (Donald Trump) and Britain's prime minister (Boris Johnson). Leaders like Jair Bolsonaro in Brazil, Narendra Modi in India, among others would have benefited from the insights of *The Shadow-Line*.

30 See Lawtoo, *Conrad's Shadow*, 49–57.

31 Martin Bock reminds us that "malaria was thought at the time to inhere in the environment" (miasmic theory) and reads this passage in *The Shadow Line* as evidence of Conrad's "miasmic" (as opposed to the contagious) "view of the disease"; but later he also adds that Conrad "may have known" about "germ theory" and makes a strong case for Conrad's concern with the dynamic of contagion in *The Nigger of the "Narcissus."* Bock, "Joseph Conrad and Germ Theory," 4, 5, 6.

32 Bateson, *Steps to an Ecology of Mind: A Revolutionary Approach to Man's Understanding of Himself* (New York: Ballantine Books, 1972), 438; on systemic pathologies internal to an ecology of catastrophe, see also, Nidesh Lawtoo, "Conrad in the Anthropocene: Steps toward an Ecology of Catastrophe," in *Conrad and Nature: Essays,* ed. Lissa Schneider-Rebozo, Jeffrey Mathes McCarthy, and John G. Peters (London: Routledge, 2019), 43–67.

33 Jane Bennett, *Vibrant Matter: A Political Ecology of Things* (London: Duke University Press, 2010), 33. The influence between the mimetic turn and the new materialist turn is reciprocal as mimesis and materiality are genealogically entangled via "encounters" registered elsewhere. See for instance Jane Bennett, "Mimesis: Paradox or Encounter," *MLN* 132, no. 5 (2017): 1186–1200; and Nidesh Lawtoo, "Vibrant Mimesis," November 20, 2020, https://www.youtube.com/watch?v=xBhEnaGjvaU.

34 William E. Connolly, *Facing the Planetary: Entangled Humanism and the Politics of Swarming* (Durham, NC: Duke University Press, 2017). See also William E. Connolly and Nidesh Lawtoo, "Planetary Conrad: William Connolly and Nidesh Lawtoo in Dialgoue," *The Conradian* (2022), forthcoming.

35 See Ian Watt, *The Deceptive Text: An Introduction to Cover Plots* (Sussex: Harvester Press, 1984), 90–99.

36 See Watt, *Conrad in the Nineteenth Century*, 3–21; Mark A. Wollaeger, *Joseph Conrad and the Fictions of Skepticism* (Stanford, CA: Stanford University Press, 1990), 14–15.

37 I discuss Bataille, Nancy, and community, in Nidesh Lawtoo, *(New) Fascism: Contagion, Community, Myth* (East Lansing: Michigan State University Press, 2019), 53–128; on community and epidemics, see also Nidesh Lawtoo and Jean-Luc Nancy, "Mimesis: Concept Singulier-Pluriel, entretien avec Jean-Luc Nancy," *L'Esprit Créateur* 61, no. 2 (2021): 147–167.

38 Friedrich Nietzsche, *Beyond Good and Evil*, trans. R. J. Hollingdale (New York: Penguin, 2003), 48.
39 Ibid.
40 Lawtoo, *Phantom of the Ego*, 295–304.
41 Conrad, "Preface," xii.

PART II

Experiments

5

"Should I Call It Horror?"

Reflecting Realism by Exploring Contingency in Ror Wolf's Adventure Series *Pilzer und Pelzer*

Barbara Bausch

Adventure of Writing and Realistic Technique

I rarely saw Funguson at that time. But maybe it was Furguson whom I rarely saw at that time, Funguson or Furguson, one of the two, I think the bigger of the two, but which one was bigger? Perhaps the fatter of both, well, but which one was fatter? I didn't know, it had slipped my mind.... I was looking for clues, for external differences, for special features. Funguson, I heard, always appeared with a bald head, Furguson however with a thick, dark head of hair, but as it is, I heard, Furguson lost his hair in the course of time and now really looks like Funguson, Funguson, of course, had bought a wig just at that time, and everything is now as before, only everything is now the other way round, because what used to be true for Funguson is true today for Furguson.

But one day Furguson after all. How have you been, he asked me.... We had a conversation about the events of the whole day, during which I asked for Funguson. Funguson? said Furguson, he knew nothing about Funguson, he did not believe in the existence of Funguson, Funguson existed only in my head, in reality the one I thought was Funguson was not Funguson, but another, perhaps Fulguson. Funguson, no, he did not exist, he never existed, but he, Furguson, the determined opponent of Funguson, existed.[1]

With a constant emphasis on the contingency of what is told, Ror Wolf's highly self-reflexive prose engages the fundamental capacity of fictional literary texts to present the possible. The confusion about the protagonists Pilzer and Pelzer (in the following: Funguson and Furguson) reads like a semiologically informed comedy of mistaken identities. However, neither the most obvious resemblance of the protagonists in the text, their almost homonymous names, nor their clearest distinguishing feature, the one differing vowel (in the English translation a consonant), is commented upon.[2] The narrator's persistent but empty attempts to determine which character is which are abruptly ended by the statement: "But one day Furguson after all," a classification that is now apparently no longer problematic. The seemingly restored sense of security does not last long. The character of Furguson already questions the narrative agent by denouncing Funguson as a mere invention of the narrator and arguing that, "in reality," there is no such character—only thereby to emphasize the reality of his own existence and in the same breath to distinguish himself as "the determined opponent of Funguson." Furguson's offhand answer, that the narrator must be referring to "Fulguson" ("Polzer"), also results from a metaleptically founded change between the different levels of the text: While the narrator searches for the differentiability of the characters on the diegetic level, the character Furguson solves the problem with a play on words and jumps from the level of the signified to the level of the signifier, by changing a single character in the name. Object and symbolization, matter and sign break up in an irritating and at the same time comical way; reality can no longer be understood as a fixed order that the subject could recognize and reflect with language. The previous scene is a humorous implosion of the mimetic project: Language as an arbitrary and differential system of signs becomes the focus of attention.

The so-called Adventure Series *Pilzer und Pelzer*, first published in 1967, emerges from the background of the literary neo-avant-garde movement of the 1950s and 1960s with its search for possibilities of valid descriptions of world and perception, for example in the *nouveau roman*. The influence of Beckett's dissolution of consistent egos is as evident as the playful examination of the semiotic nature and the referential function of language. As a consequence of the salience of language game and self-referentiality, research on Ror Wolf's work tends to focus on the linguistic virtuosity of the prose and its metanarrative arrangement, claiming that the Adventure Series forms an "artistic revue program,"[3] in which language becomes the protagonist and single agent of the text. From this point of view, *Pilzer und Pelzer* demonstrates solely the potency of language operating according to its own laws and "rejects as inadmissible any reference to reality which might exist outside of language."[4] The play with language indeed assumes a central position in Wolf's prose, and one could argue—alluding to the memorable quote by Jean Ricardou—that the Adventure Series is less focused on the writing of adventure than on the adventure of writing.[5] However, by investigating what I will call the "mode of the maybe" of *Pilzer und Pelzer*, I argue that the common conclusion that no reference to reality at all exists in Wolf's text cannot be upheld.

If literary realism is understood not only as a term specifying a certain era, but also (in a structuralist tradition) as a way of writing that puts no obstacles in the way of understanding by hiding its own procedure,[6] the prose of Ror Wolf is most certainly not to be called realistic. Realistic literature, in this understanding, is operating in the scope of our cultural codes, thus creating a consistent and stable diegesis. It is emphasizing mimetic representation shaped by traditional structural narrative features like plausible characters, consistent motivation, comprehensible action contexts, causal logic and linear time.[7] Wolfs Prose, in comparison, undercuts realistic illusion evoked through such procedures by self-reflectively drawing attention to the process of writing. I will debate that in terms of its technique non-realistic prose, nevertheless, *exposes reality*. By taking into account the arbitrary structure of language as well as the contingent character of reality itself, Wolf dissipates and displays the realistic synthesis that professes to represent world while at the same time bringing contingencies, sometimes radical, to conventionalized forms, linear plots and meaningful coherence. In fierce opposition to realistically operating prose, what is told in Ror Wolf's *Pilzer und Pelzer* can be revised at any time, everything could always be different—a stable or coherent diegesis is, as we have already seen in the passage cited earlier, far out of reach. The Adventure Series, in other words, is characterized fundamentally by contingency, that "specific indeterminacy in which something is neither necessary nor impossible."[8] The contingent, argues Michael Makropoulos,

> is what could be other because it has no necessary ground of existence. This general definition already indicates that the contingent is something utterly ambivalent that can be realized in two modalities. The contingent belongs, on the one hand, to the realm of chance and the incalculable. The contingent, on the other hand, is everything that can be manipulated, that can be the object of arbitrary constructions, which likewise could be other.[9]

In Wolf's prose, this two-sidedness of the contingent in relation to the narrative dissolves any certainty about the diegesis. The prose gains an ample scope to recreate and expose the multiplicity of reality by orchestrating the text as a wide range of possibilities. The representational mode of the *as if* is substituted by a "mode of the *maybe*."

In the following analysis I will ask how this mode that tries to keep ever-present the differently possible is staged in the prose of Ror Wolf, and how it can be described as a specific access to reality. To answer the first question, I will examine the Adventure Series with the help of Bakhtin's category of the chronotope, the "intrinsic connectedness of temporal and spatial relationships that are artistically expressed in literature."[10] I will demonstrate that *Pilzer und Pelzer* can be read as a reflection on the temporality and spatiality of the literary adventure genre as well as of the narration of adventure through an avant-garde mode by pointing out its problematization of representation of world as such. After all, contingency plays a crucial role in adventure literature, which uses procedures of narrating to *overcome* these contingencies.[11] The used procedures are realistic techniques in the understanding introduced earlier: What is "realistic" about the adventure, is its techniques of emplotment and structuring the narrative (and narrative world)—techniques, that it lends to realism.[12] For *Pilzer und Pelzer* the adventure genre, especially in its modern popular forms, proves as a backdrop against which realistic patterns and conventions (like, for example, the always succeeding male hero) can be distinctly highlighted and reflected precisely because they are so familiar.[13] On the basis of my close readings, I will show how concepts of reality are negotiated not in spite of but through this non-realistic self-reflexive form in Wolf's meta-adventure that is constantly exposing its own devices. Drawing on Hans Blumenberg's approach in "The Concept of Reality and the Possibility of the Novel,"[14] I will argue that Wolf's prose reflects on reality on the basis of its special focus on potentiality: By stretching the literary adventure between the poles of the available and the unavailable, *Pilzer und Pelzer* not only reflects on realistic ways of representation but also highlights contingency as the subject's unstable and double-sided relationship to reality, showing itself as simultaneously manufactured and resistive. Instead of focusing on the depiction of a specific reality, the Adventure Series realizes what Blumenberg describes as worldliness, *Welthaftigkeit*, by reflecting the subject's relation to reality in the structure of the text.

Writing in the "Mode of the Maybe": Explorations of Contingency

As the subtitle "Adventure Series" already suggests, *Pilzer und Pelzer* is written in an episodic fashion and follows no linear plot. The setting is a huge house characterized by an upper-class atmosphere of the nineteenth century, which, however, becomes all the more obscure as the narrative progresses. The opening sentences already establish a highly self-reflexive narration, which is marked by fundamental uncertainty:

Good, so from the beginning, starting at the point where I had stopped, the sky, how was that, indeed, the sky very blue, on the horizon suddenly a man running quickly. A memory just swimming up, washed out, good, emerging at this moment from a certain distance, really quite simple, faintly black, indeed, everything is already starting now. Maybe today, or rather at the beginning of the nice time of year.[15]

Together with the narrative agent, the readers begin "now" and "from the beginning" although without knowing what precedes the supposed discontinuation. The narrative is motivated by a memory that emerges "faintly black," "from a certain distance," which in two respects points to the layout of the entire text: Memory is the motor of narration, but at the same time both memory and perception of the narrator prove to be highly precarious; "How the rest of the day passed, I forgot" ("Wie der Rest des Tages verging, habe ich vergessen," 9), he states for example, or "It may be that I am badly remembering everything" ("Es mag sein, daß ich mich auf alles schlecht besinne," 61). *Pilzer und Pelzer* begins with the explicit establishment of a narrative agent saying "I" and reporting in the present about a past that turns out to be his own:

Here I am, I shouted, and raised my hat. So I will spare myself the introduction and approach the matter immediately. I remember opening the door in the way I described, everything went really very fast, a crackling opening, it was nothing decisive, but now I saw Funguson, the first person to be mentioned, in a bent posture or action tampering with the widow's black hand.[16]

Metanarrative insertions interlock narration and diegesis; narrative process and spatial movement are closely intertwined. Approaching "the matter" without further exposition, the narrative begins with the arrival of the internally focalized figure of the narrator in the house and the opening of a door that allows the entrance into the narrative space, which is clearly marked as a *literary* space by its crackling sound—atypical of a door but all the more characteristic of paper. Already the first lines of the text give us a glimpse into its procedure, which insists on the fact that what we are dealing with here is literature and the reality of representation. Against this backdrop it is not too surprising that neither narrative agent nor focalizer is described in any greater detail but are presented as structural functions of narration. As an extradiegetic narrating subject and an intradiegetic figure and actor they remain indeterminate and are present in the text primarily through metafictional commentaries and as the center of uncertain perception and memory. No sort of consistent authority of awareness or narration takes form; instead, an only loosely synthesized ego becomes visible, one that speaks but has largely liquidated itself as an individual.[17] The other characters too remain without a clearly definable subjectivity or fixed outline: as their names already indicate, Wolf does not portray psychologically comprehensible individuals but rather types fixed by names.[18]

Subjunctive Time, Subjunctive Characters, Subjunctive Spaces

The story-time is determined only loosely at the beginning of the text and corrected immediately ("Maybe today, or rather at the beginning of the nice time of year"). The narrator tries to counteract this doubtfulness of what is narrated with verbal gestures of confirmation ("yes," "indeed," "really quite simple"), which certainly question the narrative through their accumulation just as much as they seek to secure its credibility. The narrator tries to give the impression of correct reporting by suggesting a linear temporal course of action as well as narrative fidelity. Chapter headings such as *1 Starting Arriving (1 Anfangen Ankommen)*, *2 Second Night, Third Night (2 Zweite Nacht, Dritte Nacht)* or *25 July August (25 Juli August)* assign the events to specific and consecutive points in time. Descriptions like "Nothing the next day. Also on Wednesday nothing, nothing on Thursday, nothing on Friday" ("Am nächsten Tag nichts. Auch am Mittwoch nichts, nichts am Donnerstag, nichts am Freitag," 10) offer seemingly precise information. However, since these statements are not clearly related to each other, they never manage to form a coherent, overarching whole. Time remains an indefinable quantity in the text, which features predominantly as a component of narration without creating structural comprehensibility or clarity within the diegesis:

> The next morning, the next noon, I make a rough estimate of that time.
>
> *33 Four days passed*
>
> So yet back in bed when I opened my eyes. I suddenly noticed that I had something in my mouth, probably a long, slumberous time lay behind me.[19]

Since it is no longer possible to establish unambiguous temporal succession in the alternation between rough temporal estimates, exact dates, and what is happening right now, the narrator and with him the characters find themselves in a kind of unspecified eternal present, a sort of immediacy, in which everything happens "suddenly" and stands under the sign of the possible. Its serial structure is composed of episodes which correspond to individual "adventures" and which—as neither impossible nor necessary elements of a reality—can potentially be endlessly strung together without being pulled into a teleological thread.[20] In these episodes, the narrator's descriptions of sensory perceptions are mixed with memories and ideas as well as an exorbitant amount of intertextual allusions to literature, advertising, and film, in particular to the repertoire of popular forms and genres such as travel novels and reports, adventure fiction, horror, and crime stories. The text becomes a stream of particles of reality, references, and phantasmagoria that bundle into individual scenes: more and more episodes of such "adventures" follow each other without forming a compelling order, be it physical, historical, or biographical. The time in *Pilzer und Pelzer* corresponds to the "adventure-time" common already in the ancient adventure novel described by Bakhtin, in which inherent laws lie beyond human criteria: "In this kind of time nothing changes: . . . This empty time leaves no traces anywhere, no indications of its passing."[21] This particularity is prominently staged in *Pilzer und Pelzer*. For example, during a walk through the basement of the house, which at the beginning of the description seems mainly to serve as a storage for preserving jars and wrinkled potatoes, the atmosphere suddenly changes drastically:

> In the cold stinging air of this cellar vault, with bloody marks on the floor, with a black sarcophagus in the middle, whose heavy lid slowly began to lift up, pressed up by hairy hands with bluish palms, a gnawed, split face, so Furguson's face, appeared with very pointed, bared teeth, the iron lattice opened whimpering, I rushed out, behind me it came growling and creaking with slapping feet, the widow screamed, I saw her how should I call it horror.[22]

Considering this narrative array of generic horror features, the widow, to the focalizer's amazement, does not flee, but instead calls after him, "where to then where to then?" ("wohin denn wohin denn?" 83). And indeed, the cinematic scene has already changed completely in the next sentence. The widow now sits contentedly on Furguson's shoulders, whereupon the horror scenario dissolves into laughter as quickly as it began and ends succinctly with the remark "so much for this matter" ("soweit diese Sache," 83). The narrator still finds the time to search for the right expression at the moment of the narration of terror ("I saw her how should I call it horror"), which—considering the distance and deceleration it creates in view of a scene allegedly designed to generate tension—has a strange and comic effect. Here, Wolf takes the inconsequentiality of the adventure-time to extremes: the characters seem to know that the "empty time" of adventure has no effect on them, that it will pass them by without a trace. The scenes of terror and adventure are only relevant in the moment of their description and do not entail any consequences within the diegetic world. No matter how dangerous the trials of the heroes are, everything, the readers know (and expect!), will be fine at the end—a structural feature of narratives that shapes the ancient and medieval as well as the modern adventure genres and suggests how the narrative pull strongly overdetermines the perils and intensities of experience.²³

Within individual scenes of the adventure-time, time is organized technically: "What is important is to be able to escape, to catch up, to outstrip, to be or not to be in a given place at a given moment."²⁴ While the Greek adventure novels Bakhtin examines have an overarching storyline following a predetermined scheme within which the loose sequence of adventures takes place and the constant coincidences are legitimized at least superficially in terms of logic of action, in *Pilzer und Pelzer*, conversely, the principle of coincidence as a necessity of the adventure genre prevails in pure form:

> But it didn't last long and already I was lying in a narrow cabinet and the ceiling was slowly descending, crunching heavily on me, and pressing me more and more to the floor, the air hissing out, it squeezed, it groaned, I reckoned with everything this time, but one couldn't touch me with that either, my fingers suddenly at the last moment touched a button, that was all right with me, something snapped open now, a small opening through which I crawled out.²⁵

Once again, the focalizer finds himself in an existential emergency: the readers have to assume his certain death. At the decisive moment, though, namely "at the last," his fingers happen to "suddenly" find the "button" that offers a way out of this hopeless situation. However, this by no means causes a euphoric reaction; the appearance of the button is commented on rather casually, as if the intradiegetic "I" had expected to be rescued at the last second. While in prose texts aiming at realistic representation the characters of a text know nothing about their character-like nature and their existence only in the narrative world, in *Pilzer und Pelzer* on the contrary, the figure of the narrator as well as the other characters seem confident of their genre: they must and they will experience further adventures, and always by favorable coincidence, some "small opening" will be found, which makes it possible to escape from even the most inescapable situation. This metaleptically founded certainty penetrates that what is narrated as well as the narration, which produces comic effects due to the explicitness in dealing with narrative premises of the genre—namely, that in the structure of popular adventure novels, narration can only produce situations of testing that *confirm* the disposition of characters or the established order of the narrated world.²⁶ Since the time of adventure, marked by pure chance, is fundamentally determined by the mode of "suddenly" and "at just that moment,"²⁷ the initiative does not come from the heroes who experience the adventures. The characters do not even act in the actual sense, but the adventures as well as their dissolution or overcoming happen to them: suddenly the monster is transformed back into the familiar Furguson, suddenly the saving button appears. Suddenness presents itself as a relationship in which there is no causality; chance as a concrete actualization of contingency directs the fate of the adventure-time, and the person moving in it is a "person of chance."[28] In *Pilzer und Pelzer*, the characters conform to this random logic and adapt to their circumstances: they are outwardly open, changeable, subjunctive characters.

In the traditional and popular adventure genre, the dangerous contingency that characterizes the adventures of the protagonists is ultimately eliminated by narration. By using adventures to test the heroes, not only in the ancient novel or the medieval *âventiure* but also in modern popular fiction, the narrative scheme provides strategies for overcoming contingency.[29] Wolf's Adventure Series brings into effect the "Hautgout" of adventure and popular literature,[30] by constantly evoking and hyperbolizing conventionalized topoi and genre rules as well as the expectations associated with them. This works especially well with the adventure, the crime, horror, or travel genres, because they are ubiquitous and thus familiar, and follow, as shown, easily recognizable narrative patterns. These patterns that become visible here are—understood as techniques—narrative procedures that also characterize realism: by establishing consistent and meaningful narrated worlds, in which comprehensible and even expected actions take place, popular genres such as the adventure novel conceal their own contingencies as well as their status as narrations by precisely those conventionalized forms to guarantee both easy understanding and realistic illusion of a meaningful reality.[31] Yes, also in Wolf's prose, the characters have to face seemingly insurmountable obstacles and terrible things—after all, they are characters of an Adventure Series and as such are utterly determined by the genre and its norms. However, due to the fact that in *Pilzer und Pelzer* the narrative agent always highlights that adventures are *told* and contingency is *contrived*, the mechanics of narration remain clearly recognizable at all times and both prevent the emergence of illusion as well as a mediated and mediating narrative coherence.[32] Thus, Wolf's prose takes up a position in sharp contrast to realistic poetics, which is typically emphasizing mimetic representation by trying to conceal the textual construction and conventional framings which suspend contingency through narrative order to create the effect of probability and suggest a strong relation to reality. Instead of containing the daunting and continuously surging contingency of the narrated world with narrative means, in the prose of Ror Wolf the conventions of the adventure genre are exposed and contingency is revealed to be the very constitutional condition of narration.

This applies not only to the characters and temporal structure of the text. Also space in the Adventure Series is characterized by contingency and potentiality, thus losing the supposed self-evidence it gains through realistic writing procedures treating it as a stable entity, a fixed set in which the action can enroll. The bourgeois tranquility in the house, which is invoked at the beginning, slowly changes over the course of the text. More and more animals populate the rooms, and the interior is continuously overgrown by plants. The characters begin exploring the house, and the further the description of the characters' journey progresses, the more the space described resembles an exterior space; references to interior attributes, such as "I saw the cupboard shine in the thicket" ("Ich sah den Geschirrschrank im Dickicht glänzen" 108), become rarer. An expedition into strange, dangerous regions unfolds under adaptation of language and action patterns of adventure novels and travel reports. The succession of different regions becomes quicker, climatic zones rapidly replace each other.

> Our footsteps sank deep into the powdery sand, peaked heat, said Furguson, we passed thorny, leafless undergrowth, peaked heat. My khaki shirt was baked on the open flesh chafed by the sand, stiff from the blood-water, and in the glowing air that boiled and bubbled on the horizon, we dragged ourselves along.... Gradually this landscape took on a quite different character.... I suddenly found myself walking along hard on the abyss, some boulders came loose and fell down clattering.³³

A few sentences later, it is icecold, and blood and sweat freeze on the body. Instead of tropical helmets, the travelers now need crampons ("Steigeisen," 133), and after the descent, they find themselves in a sea of ice. Here, the exhausted intradiegetic "I" finally remains alone, while the others move on. Drifting on a floe through the sea, the cold does not last long. Instead, "the heat grew. Underneath me it melted, it shrank, it cracked" ("die Hitze wuchs. Unter mir schmolz es, schrumpfte es, knackte es," 134). Here, the memory ends and only returns when the figure of the narrator is waking up "in a great vacuum of darkness" ("in einer großen luftleeren Finsternis," 135) and recognizes that he is inside the hull of a ship. After having worked its way through many crates full of different loads, he finally pushes his way through the ceiling—and finds himself in the salon of the house, where Furguson is playing on the piano "On the high sea or On heavy sea" ("Auf hoher See oder Auf schwerer See," 138). At every moment, some spatial boundary is crossed, the overcoming of great distances takes place at high speed. While the time of narration is reduced to a minimum, the narrated space expands into the immeasurable, for in adventure, from a narratological perspective, spatial transgression always takes precedence over logical temporal connection. Just as time in *Pilzer und Pelzer* cannot be a logically plausible and thus concrete time, this seemingly boundless space does not represent a concretely defined space, but rather a potentially infinite, polymorphic one. Although particular spaces within the text are described concretely and in detail, these individual descriptions are not connected to one another in any identifiable way and therefore do neither create "referential illusion" nor do they form an overarching, concrete whole.³⁴ According to Bakhtin, in order to allow for all possibilities of chance, the time of adventure in literary texts requires precisely this: "an *abstract* expanse of space."[35] To experience adventure, one needs extensive spaces that can be crossed and spatial obstacles that can be overcome. However, this space does not demand concretion. After all, it is not the sea in a geographical sense that is interesting for the narration of adventure, but the sea as an existential danger to the life of the characters or the sea as a condition of certain episodes, like a shipwreck. Instead of evoking a concrete spatial setting, Wolf plays with narrated space as *topos*, as space of meaning, memory, or consciousness without offering the option of reducing the text to one of these concepts; different variants of representation and conception of space are tested, whereby common forms of realistic structuring and demarcation aiming at a coherent and plausible order are dismantled through the explicit staging of radical contingency.

The diegesis of *Pilzer und Pelzer* confronts us with a fundamentally foreign and indefinite world with its own spacetime—one that is historically and geographically indeterminate and in which potentially exchangeable episodes are lined up in an overflowing, indeterminable, relational, and dynamic space of potentiality. To describe that space only *once* is therefore not enough; this potential space demands ever new descriptions as concrete realizations of the possibilities of narration. In other words, while realistic texts purport to show *the* world (as a specific, believable, logical world), what is depicted, or rather evoked, in *Pilzer und Pelzer*, is *a* world that is just one of many other possible, thinkable worlds.[36] In the Adventure Series, the manifold realizations of contingent spaces in the text are used to sound out the potential space of narration.

"Probably all Invention": (Im)Possibilities of Narration

In the opening scene of *Pilzer und Pelzer*, the narrative space with its specific spacetime opens, as described earlier, with the opening of the door of the house. The intradiegetic "I" arrives at the house, apparently to condole with the widow, for whom he brought a "Bonbonniere" (8), and then decides to stay: "I stayed in this house under a false name, I pretended to be a painter who wanted to paint the landscape and actually painted, even if only apparently, this landscape with its tremendously pointed mountains."[37] Not only does this self-disclosure obscure more than it reveals, it is also revised at a later point, where the arrival of the ego is narrated in another way:

> Here I am, I shouted and raised my hat. I was, I think, on the road as a salesman for orthopedic devices, I was not bad, I came around a lot and therefore one day through this door. I was judged immediately by

my outward appearances and I was taken for the doctor, who had been expected.[38]

Different variations of the narrative are presented without comment as equivalent possibilities, without it being possible to resolve which variant is the "right one." Within the serial structure of the Adventure Series, constantly new realizations of the possible take place. The narrative is staged as pure potentiality, as an accumulation of mutually exclusive, alternative possibilities which mark the experience of time and space as an experience of radical contingency. This experience of contingency, identified as the epitome of the experience of the world, can also be traced back to the predisposition of the narrative subject, which repeatedly emphasizes that it cannot remember. While the *ars memoriae* aims at the banishment of chance, the unsecured memory of the narrator in this text leads to a totalized contingency in experience and representation.[39] Neither memory nor the correct recording of seemingly trivial observations can be guaranteed: "The sea, *as far as the eye could see of course*, smooth, gentle, bluish, a shimmering surface, a cloudless sky, *this time I was not mistaken*."[40] The difficulties of capturing reality result in an attempt to present what is perceived in an overly thorough manner. However, the detailed description too is staged as a major hurdle: "I found no suitable words, as usual" ("Ich fand keine passenden Worte, wie üblich," 25). Corresponding to the claim Adorno articulated in 1954, that the certainty of the given is replaced in contemporary literature by the admission of one's own powerlessness considering the "superior strength of the world of things," the Adventure Series is indeed characterized by a "deteriorated associative language of things."[41] Adorno's demand to take a stand against the "lie of representation"[42] gets a humorous touch in *Pilzer und Pelzer*. In order to do justice to the sensual impressions, the "world of things" is described very precisely in a playful doggedness by offering entire catalogs of supposed synonyms or reformulations. However, instead of gaining conciseness, the things seen or experienced disintegrate into their details, since they are mostly presented without interpretation, described, but often not actually named:

> Now I did see something, something panting with a short blunt head, something lean thin slim bowed, and I have to admit that I . . . was staring down, following these slow, heavy forward movements at the end of the patio.[43]

The fixation on details that neglects the larger context creates vagueness rather than plasticity.[44] The (at least ostensibly) attempted increase in the accuracy of description results in a humorous demonstration of the impossibility of depiction itself, while the contingent multiplicity of the individual, which reveals neither coherence nor hierarchy, is exhibited.

Reality balks at its meaningful description and thus appears as an arranged resistance in the text.[45]

In the midst of this abundance of described impressions, the narrator as an indefinite, only loosely synthesized ego with an exceedingly casual relationship to time can be identified as the very vague subjectivity that extends from the traveling knight to the modern adventure novel.[46] That this narrative agent combines the staged impossibility of narration with a playful pleasure in narrating may be founded precisely in this genre. As Jacob Grimm notes, the Middle High German word *âventiure* has the double meaning of both an event and the report of the same.[47] In the dictionary the lemma registers as meanings not only "daring start with uncertain outcome," "coincidental esp. fortunate event," but also "a poem of it" as well as the personification of the report in a female character, namely *adventura*.[48] Etymologically, adventure has always been located equally in the sphere of lifeworld *and* literature, experience and narrative—as the intrusion of chance into life on the one hand, and as a narrative scheme on the other hand. If you set out on an adventure, you set out to experience something that is at least potentially *narratable*:[49] the self-reflexive component is already inherent in the term. Consequently, the oscillation of Ror Wolf's Adventure Series between adventure plot and playful focus on the narrative act can be read as another volte reflecting the genre.[50]

The representation of fictional reality as a reality that does not let itself be mastered narratively, as described earlier, is accompanied by a celebration of fictionality by the narrator. Through omnipresent metafictional commentary, the diegetic world is exhibited as something in the process of becoming, as the narrator's imaginary draft: "all delusion probably all invention" ("alles Einbildung wahrscheinlich alles Erfindung," 56). By means of a snake winding its way through the thicket of the jungle, the narrative agent presents itself as the supremely reigning subject of the narrated world. There slides

> a very long, spotted, extraordinarily agile-looking or as it seemed or as it actually was initially the first part of the first piece of this body down . . . , and this head now pulled its very long and not so thick but obviously still much longer than expected body out of this mop of the tree and behind it and took no end at all . . . , because the tail still lay far in the distance, . . . but I say tail now, because the tail will never appear here in any other way, so the tail slid down smoothly from the branches, and Funguson shouted under this snake embrace.[51]

What is told and when it is told remains at the discretion of the narrative authority. It determines whether something looks, seems, or is: every process in the text, every topic, every matter finds its way in and out of the text only and precisely at the time it is initiated or ended by the narrator. He has his characters firmly under control, they scream (dutifully) under his "snake embrace," for which the readers are prepared with phonetic gimmicks ("slid ... smoothly"—"glitt glatt"). From the lush thicket of the possible, from which many snakes could still wind their way out, the narrator only has to choose and constellate the selection he has made. He does not attempt to conceal the great pretension of narrating. It is therefore not the thematic coherence of the narrative but rather the contingency of narrating itself that becomes the focus of attention. *Pilzer und Pelzer* showcases both the impossibility of narrating a reality obstructing its description and the ability of prose to invent and test possibilities on the threshold of reality on the basis of productive imagination.

In the end, this adventure arrives back where it began. In the final chapter, we find ourselves again in the tranquil atmosphere of the upper-class interior. The protagonists have gathered in the salon, where they are once more "introduced" to the readers, as if there had not occurred any horrors or catastrophes. Funguson, Furguson, the widow, and the narrator have made themselves comfortable in front of the television, because Furguson doesn't want to miss a "certain game."

> According to the pronunciation, it is Furguson who is saying something now. ... I don't know anything about him in particular. What I have to say about this cross, he asks me now. Nothing. No, I have nothing more to say. I'm completely calm. My only concern is that now, at the last moment, an unforeseen incident could still postpone the close of this matter, the end, until further notice.[52]

Just as the first sentence of the Adventure Series identifies the beginning as a continuation and thus problematizes it, these last sentences mark the ending of the text as a problem. Intradiegetic "I" and narrative agent merge at the end of the text. As a necessary positing of the writing subject the closure is supposedly threatened by "unforeseen" events outside the sphere of its influence that could disturb or delay it. The narrator, however, has already begun to withdraw from the diegesis and his role as reporter of events. The final chapter is titled *40 Already the Matter is Finished* (*40 Schon ist die Sache zuende*) and begins with the words "Yes, go on. We're coming to the end" ("Ja, wieder weiter. Wir kommen zum Schluss," 145). Therefore, it is not altogether surprising that now the narrator states, "No, I have nothing more to say," and starts to refuse to narrate. He no longer knows "anything in particular" about Furguson, and as a result, *Pilzer und Pelzer* actually draws to a close. However, in the German original the text concludes not only with an explicit reference to its own ending but also with the possibility of its continuation. It ends, more specifically, on a subjunctive phrase concluding with the modal verb "could"—thereby evoking further future eventualities.[53] And indeed, corresponding to the strictly speaking interminable internal structure of the episodic adventure genre, in 1978, an "extended edition" of *Pilzer und Pelzer*, which contains new chapters on the "return and final disappearance" of the main characters (*Rückkehr und endgültiges Verschwinden von Pilzer und Pelzer*), was published by Suhrkamp, followed by the "complete edition" published by Luchterhand in 1988, to which fourteen collages of Ror Wolf are attached. The option of further potentialities leaps to the extradiegetic level, to the form and materiality of the book.

What we observe in Wolf's prose is a critique of representation that could with Juliane Rebentisch be specified as a way of writing that "refers to the logic of representation in a negativist-ironic fashion."[54] By exposing the (semiotic, medial, material) reality of representation, as Rebentisch argues, "the form of depiction" assumes

> a potential independence from the depicted content, gaining a weight of its own and coming to the fore in its own material reality. This does not result in a formalism, however, but rather in a tension between the depiction and the depicted that disintegrates all evident meaning and calls the referential inference from the representation to the represented into question.[55]

The exhibition of conventions and common strategies of representing "reflectively blocks"[56] a reading that takes the depiction as a pure representation of something and subverts the idea of a natural relation of sign and matter. By this means, representation is not (as it is in realistically operating texts) disguised, but revealed and exposed in its rhetoricity. The text refers to reality on a superordinate level, by reflecting the paradigms of realistic writing techniques—for example by putting into the fore popular genre patterns as of adventure novels or horror stories—to point to the foregoing positings and images of world preceding representation, to display a world always already accessed through representation.[57] The reality to which the prose of Ror Wolf refers and to which it calls attention is always also the "reality of representation."[58] In this perspective, playful self-reflexiveness and reference to reality are not at all mutually exclusive. After modern writing techniques and the avant-gardes of the early twentieth century, reality in literature can only be thought as a "mediatized real," as a (exhibited) "reality effect of common procedures."[59] While realistic texts depend on being transparent, on disappearing as texts to show the depicted and in so doing establish and sustain the illusion of a representation of world, in *Pilzer und Pelzer* the fabrication of images of reality between the poles of determinant genre conventions and worldly contingency gains center stage. The realistic text conceals, partly by drawing on the narrative impulse of adventure, that it is emplotting radical contingencies with conventionalized forms—and this is exactly what Wolf's writing exposes. In this manner, as

I will debate in the following, the subject's understanding and concept of reality as such is taken into account.

"Potential Infinity": Reality as Possibility

Ror Wolf's prose is, as has become clear, entirely in the "mode of the maybe": every hint at causally structured spacetime, clearly comprehensible linear action, or consistent subjects dissolves in the face of other possibilities. By decomposing all classic structural features, the text focuses on potentiality and fundamental contingency of both, that which is narrated and the act of narrating itself. Manifest on the level of diegesis (in time and space as well as in the characters), on the level of narration (by displaying both the impossibility of narrating as well as the omnipotence of the narrator), and on the authorial level (by undermining the closure of the work), contingency becomes a principle constituting and generating text and evoked world.

As mentioned at the beginning, the contingent as something indeterminate, in which the ability to be different manifests itself as an actual alternative, combines two opposing options: After all, both the available and manipulable and the unavailable and accidental are "neither necessary nor impossible."[60] When it comes to asking about the text's relation toward reality, the contingency exposed in the narrative situation in particular is remarkable. On the one hand, the intradiegetic ego and the characters are exposed powerlessly to the conventions of the fictitious world with its spacetime of adventure: for the figures, the narrated reality lies beyond reach as the utterly unavailable. On the other hand, the prose text marks the narrated world as a construct and positing of a narrative agent, who commands it (acting by writing) from an external position, whereby this relationship too is staged as deeply precarious since it is constantly threatened by disturbances that cannot be influenced by the narrator. Through this exposed doublesidedness, the Adventure Series thematizes and reflects on the problem of contingency on a more general level as a relationship between possibility and reality.[61]

According to Hans Blumenberg's reflections on historically changing understandings of reality, modernity does not have a homogeneous concept of reality.[62] Instead, the consciousness of reality is a double one: reality in modernity is experienced both "as the result of an actualization,"[63] as manufactured reality, and *"that which cannot be mastered by the self,"* as an experience of resistance, as "that which is totally unavailable."[64] In other words, under the sign of worldly contingency, reality concretizes itself both in actions ascribable to certain actors and in groundless coincidences.[65] Wolf's prose reflects this ambivalent relationship between subject and world by evoking a starkly bottomless diegesis (subject to the dissolution of boundaries and constant change) that is represented as reluctant to its description, while at the same time exploring the possibilities and capabilities of fiction and narration. The Adventure Series, which not only unites many features that characterize the adventure chronotope but also explicitly thematizes them, is thus both a radicalization and a reflection of the adventure genre and the narrative patterns that it lends to realism. The literary adventure is negotiated in diegesis and narration and placed as an *event that can be narrated*[66] squarely between the poles of the available and the unavailable.

Modern literature, according to Blumenberg, confronts a concept of reality marked by contingency that takes into account that reality "can never be assured, is constantly in the process of being actualized."[67] Since in this understanding reality is always *one* among boundless other possible realities, the novel is geared to reference precisely the potentially infinite and inconclusive context of the real. Instead of mimetic imitation, its goal is to generate worldliness, *Welthaftigkeit*, by replicating the open-endedness of the experience of reality in the text by creating "*potential infinity*."[68] This is, I argue, at what Ror Wolf's Adventure Series aims. Realistic prose supposedly tells the truth by suggesting authenticity of a meaningful whole through creating narrative consistency and (teleological) coherence and through using language as an invisible window to look through at something "told." Wolf's prose instead models a problematic and precarious relation to reality, by generating "potential infinity" through a narrative process that constantly pushes forward and performatively presents an array of possibilities in unpredictable transformations. *Pilzer und Pelzer* explores the potential spaces of literature by presenting the prose text as a space of world-making, while at the same time referring to the unavailability of world through staging the impossibility of narration. The unsteady center on which the text orbits is the simultaneous existence of disjoint realities and the impossibility of dealing with reality by means of models of order and narrative codes.[69] What remains is the fictionally established abeyance of potentiality, a torn and impenetrable reality, in which the assumption of a fixed and logical structure of perception, events, or their mediation in narration is unmasked as a phantom. Within the framework of the reflexively mirrored adventure genre in *Pilzer und Pelzer* everything said can be revised at any time: what the text depicts always points to what it *could* but does not represent. Through alternatives offered in the text, any concrete actualization of something becomes one of potentially infinite possibilities: while each individual passage consists of a determinate representation, the text as a whole showcases potentiality and presents a constellation marked by radical contingency.[70] Representation in the text, therefore, serves only to a certain extent to represent something in particular; signification, though, takes place primarily at the level of form. What is represented, independent from a particular reality, becomes a model of the possible but uncertain emergence of reality through language.[71] By taking—with Blumenberg—its own possibilities and impossibilities as its subject, the Adventure Series itself becomes a "form of contingency,"[72] in this way recreating the simultaneity of heterogeneous worlds as an "aggregate of plural realities and temporary relations."[73]

The concept of reality reflected in *Pilzer und Pelzer* is that of an arbitrary and incoherent world and ultimately offers a representation of senselessness that cannot be glossed over. That the Adventure Series does not curb or mediate this impression with the conventionalized narrative contingency management strategies could be deeply harrowing, if the radical contingency as a vacancy of meaning was not at the same time embedded in a fundamentally humorous approach to what is narrated as well as the narrating act itself. According to Jean Paul, humor is to be understood as a consciously adopted *attitude*. As that kind of laughter "in which is still a pain and a greatness,"[74] it has its origin precisely in the precarious acceptance of the world's contingency opposed to unthinkable infinity. Given the nullity of reality, humor as an ability and attitude grants the license to ridicule the world.[75] Wolf's prose is clearly located in the area of the comic, but in the light of contingency voiding all meaning, the comic and the melancholic are closely intertwined. The sole possible mode beyond despair seems to be laughter as the attempt to fend off the daily horror, "billowing," as Wolf describes it, "from all cracks."[76] By humorous distance, *Pilzer und Pelzer* gives contingency as the upsetting "invasion of non-sense"[77] over to laughter.

Wolf's prose seeks to realize worldliness, *Welthaftigkeit*, as a "formal, overriding structure"[78] by reflecting the modern relation to reality marked by radical contingency in the literary mode. Becoming a form of contingency itself, it negotiates the possible, the potential, the contingent not only as generating principles of literary texts but also as basic principles shaping our experience of world. The comic play with potentialities performed in the text irritates and stirs up familiar orders and procedures of realistic representation and invites the readers to embark on the adventure of the abundance and multiplicity of reality.[79] With its "mode of the maybe" the Adventure Series shows that which allows realization in the first place, namely the "*reality of the possible.*"[80] It does so by establishing a literary form reflecting our precarious and contingent relationship to reality and still allowing us to laugh.

Notes

1 "Pilzer sah ich selten in dieser Zeit. Aber vielleicht war es Pelzer, den ich in dieser Zeit selten sah, Pilzer oder Pelzer, einer von beiden, ich glaube der größere von beiden, aber wer war der größere? Vielleicht der dickere von beiden, gut, aber wer war der dickere? Ich wußte es nicht, es war mir entfallen.... Ich suchte nach Anhaltspunkten, nach äußeren Unterschieden, besonderen Merkmalen. Pilzer, hörte ich, trete seit jeher mit einem Kahlkopf auf, Pelzer dagegen mit einem dunklen dicken Schopf, aber wie es so sei, hörte ich, habe Pelzer im Laufe der Zeit seine Haare verloren und sehe Pilzer nun tatsächlich ähnlich, Pilzer freilich habe

sich gerade zu dieser Zeit eine Perücke angeschafft, und alles sei nun wie vorher, nur alles jetzt umgekehrt, denn was früher für Pilzer galt, gelte heute für Pelzer/ Eines Tages aber doch Pelzer. Wie ist es Ihnen ergangen, fragte er mich. . . . Wir führten ein Gespräch über die Ereignisse dieses ganzen Tages, in dessen Verlauf ich nach Pilzer fragte. Pilzer? sagte Pelzer, er wisse nichts von Pilzer, er glaube nicht an die Existenz Pilzers, Pilzer existiere nur in meinem Kopf, in Wirklichkeit sei der, den ich für Pilzer hielt, nicht Pilzer, sondern ein anderer, vielleicht Polzer. Pilzer, nein, es gebe ihn nicht, es habe ihn nie gegeben, aber ihn, Pelzer, den entschiedenen Gegner Pilzers, gebe es . . . ." Ror Wolf, *Pilzer und Pelzer. Eine Abenteuerserie* (Frankfurt a. M.: Suhrkamp, 1967), 43–45; in the following quoted in the footnotes following the German original of the text.—*Pilzer und Pelzer* has not yet been translated to English. Unless otherwise indicated, all translations, including the secondary literature, are my own: They only aim to be working translations for the use in this chapter. The names Pilzer and Pelzer, translated as Funguson and Furguson, which are derived from the word stems "Pilz" (fungus) and "Pelz" (fur), are existing, but not common names. The name Polzer (Fulguson) has no semantic nucleus in German. I owe many thanks to Simon Friedland and Noah Zeldin for proofreading both the translations and the article.

2   The names clearly allude to the production of meaning by language organized through differentiality, while the signs themselves are arbitrary. See Ferdinand de Saussure, *Cours de linguistique Générale*, ed. Charles Bally and Albert Sechehaye (Paris: Payot, 1971), esp. 97–103.

3   Exemplary for this reading is Wolfgang Werth, "Vielleicht Polzer" [first published in *Der Monat*, April 1968], in *Über Ror Wolf*, ed. Lothar Baier (Frankfurt a. M.: Suhrkamp, 1972), 37. In opposition to such readings argues e.g. Michael Lentz, who regards Wolf as a "realistic artist". See Michael Lentz, "Das Imaginäre und das Konkrete. Ein 'Entzündungszustand,'" in *Neue Rundschau* 126, no. 1 (2015), 37-53. For analyses with a focus on *Pilzer und Pelzer* see Rolf Strube, "Eine Schule der Wahrnehmung" [first published in *Sprache im technischen Zeitalter* 76 (1980)], in *Anfang & vorläufiges Ende. 91 Ansichten über den Schriftsteller Ror Wolf* (Frankfurt a. M.: Frankfurter Verlagsanstalt, 1992) and Sabine Brocher, *Abenteuerliche Elemente im modernen Roman* (Munich and Vienna: Carl Hanser Verlag, 1981), 153–178.

4   Ibid.; see also 38.

5   "Ainsi un roman est-il pour nous moins *l'écriture d'une aventure que l'aventure d'une écriture*." Jean Ricardou, *Problèmes du Nouveau Roman* (Paris: Éditions du Seuil, 1967), 111.

6   See Moritz Baßler, *Deutsche Erzählprosa 1850–1950. Eine Geschichte literarischer Verfahren* (Berlin: Erich Schmidt, 2015), 11–30. The notion of "Verfahren" in Baßler's study stands in the tradition of Shklovsky's idea of "prijom" introduced in his seminal 1916 essay "Art as Technique" and is translated here as procedure or technique. For a short English résumé of Baßler's approach, see Moritz Baßler, "Realism(s) of the Avant-Garde: An Introduction," in *Realisms of the Avant-Garde*, ed. Moritz Baßler, Benedikt Hjartarson, Ursula Frohne, Sascha Bru and David Ayers (Berlin and Boston: De Gruyter, 2020), 3–10.

7   See Baßler, *Deutsche Erzählprosa 1850–1950*, 22.

8   Michael Makropoulos, "Kontingenz: Aspekte einer theoretischen Semantik der Moderne," *European Journal of Sociology* 45, no. 3 (2004): 371.

9   Michael Makropoulos, "Crisis and Contingency," *Thesis Eleven* 111, no. 1 (2012): 12.

10 Mikhail Bakhtin, "Forms of Time and of the Chronotope in the Novel," in *The Dialogic Imagination: Four Essays by M. M. Bakhtin*, ed. Michael Holquist, trans. Caryl Emerson and Michael Holquist (Austin: University of Texas Press, 1981), 84.

11 See for example Martin von Koppenfels et al., "Wissenschaftliches Programm der Forschungsgruppe," DFG-Forschungsgruppe *Philologie des Abenteuers* (FOR 2568), Ludwig-Maximilians-Universität München, 13-14, last accessed December 19, 2021, https://www.abenteuer.fak13.uni-muenchen.de/forschungsgruppe/wissenschaftliches-programm/wissenschaftliches-programm.pdf.

12 The focus of this analysis is, despite their many differences, on this fundamental common ground that adventure and realism share; on the narrative impulse, that realism draws of adventure. See also Jameson's reflections on the "narrative impulse" in *The Antinomies of Realism* (London: Verso, 2013), 15–26.

13 Not by chance did the Russian Formalists declare the adventure as a category of literaricity, as the adventure novel uncovers procedures due to its simple narrative structure: See Riccardo Nicolosi, "Der Abenteuerheld in der sowjetischen Literaturtheorie der 1920er Jahre (von Šklovskij bis Bachtin)," in *Abenteuer in der Moderne* (Philologie des Abenteuers, Bd. 2), ed. Oliver Grill and Brigitte Obermayr (Paderborn: Fink, 2020), 229–235. The "surprising historical durability" of the narrative scheme of adventure from antiquity to today state Martin von Koppenfels and Manuel Mühlbacher, "Einleitung," in *Abenteuer. Erzählmuster, Formprinzip, Genre* (Philologie des Abenteuers, Bd. 1), ed. Martin von Koppenfels and Manuel Mühlbacher (Paderborn: Fink, 2019), 1. For an outline of the changes of the (perception of) the genre through time and the connection of modern adventure to popular literature, see Oliver Grill and Brigitte Obermayr, "Einleitung," in *Abenteuer in der Moderne*, 1–14.

14 Hans Blumenberg, "The Concept of Reality and the Possibility of the Novel," in *New Perspectives in German Literary Criticism: A Collection of Essays*, ed. Richard E. Amacher and Victor Lange, trans. David Henry Wilson (Princeton, NJ: Princeton University Press, 2015), 29–48.

15 "Gut, also von vorn, an diesem Punkt einsetzen, wo ich abgebrochen habe, der Himmel, wie war das, jawohl, der Himmel sehr blau, am Horizont plötzlich ein rasch laufender Mann. Eine gerade heranschwimmende Erinnerung, herausgespült, gut, in diesem Moment auftauchend aus einer gewissen Entfernung, wirklich ganz einfach, schwach schwarz, jawohl, alles fängt jetzt schon an. Vielleicht heute, oder vielmehr zu Beginn der schönen Jahreszeit" (7).

16 "Hier bin ich, rief ich, und hob meinen Hut. Ich werde mir also die Einleitung sparen und sofort an die Sache herantreten. Ich erinnere mich, daß ich auf die beschriebene Weise die Tür öffnete, alles ging wirklich sehr schnell, ein

knisterndes Öffnen, es war nichts Entscheidendes, aber nun sah ich Pilzer, die erste Person, die genannt wird, in einer vorgebeugten Haltung oder Handlung sich an der schwarzen Hand der Witwe zu schaffen machen" (7).

17 See Theodor W. Adorno, "The Position of the Narrator in the Contemporary Novel," in *Notes to Literature: Volume One*, ed. Rolf Tiedemann, trans. Shierry Weber Nicholsen (New York: Columbia University Press, 1991), 35; and Devin Fore, *Realism after Modernism* (Cambridge, MA: MIT Press, 2012), who describes the continuous decomposition of sovereign narrative agencies and autonomous bourgeois subjects to decentered and de-individuated humans in the late nineteenth and early twentieth centuries.

18 For the analysis of the characters in Wolf's prose, see Marianne Kesting, "Das Wuchern der Wörter" [first published in *Die Zeit*, Oktober, 3, 1969], in *Über Ror Wolf*, 47–48; Helmut Heißenbüttel, "Bericht aus einer Traumlandschaft," in *Über Ror Wolf*, 20; Sabine Brocher, *Abenteuerliche Elemente im modernen Roman: Italo Calvino, Ernst Augustin, Luigi Malerba, Kurt Vonnegut und Ror Wolf* (Munich: Hanser, 1981), 158–161.

19 "Am nächsten Morgen, am nächsten Mittag, ich überschlage diese Zeit. / 33 Vier Tage vergangen / Also doch wieder im Bett, als ich die Augen aufschlug. Ich merkte plötzlich, dass ich etwas im Mund hatte, wahrscheinlich lag eine lange verschlafene Zeit hinter mir" (118).

20 A typical feature of the adventure genre in general. See Jutta Eming and Ralf Schlechtweg-Jahn, "Einleitung: Das Abenteuer als Narrativ," in *Aventiure und Eskapade. Narrative des Abenteuerlichen vom Mittelalter zur Moderne*, ed. Jutta Eming and Ralf Schlechtweg-Jahn (Göttingen: V & R unipress 2017), 25.

21 Bakhtin, "Forms of Time and of the Chronotope in the Novel," 91.

22 "In der kalt stechenden Luft dieses Kellergewölbes, mit blutigen Abdrücken auf dem Boden, mit einem schwarzen Sarkophag in der Mitte, dessen schwerer Deckel sich langsam zu heben begann, heraufgedrückt von haarigen Händen mit bläulichen Innenflächen, ein zerfressenes zerspaltenes Gesicht, also Pelzers Gesicht, erschien mit sehr spitzen gefletschten Zähnen, das Eisengitter öffnete sich wimmernd, ich stürzte hinaus, hinter mir kam es knurrend und knarrend heran mit klatschenden Füßen, die Witwe schrie, ich sah ihr wie soll ich es nennen Entsetzen" (82–83).

23 This can of course be observed not only in modern adventures (like, for example, the novels of Karl May), but also in other popular realistic genres as well. The genre rules guarantee a "pre-stabilized harmony of frames" ("prästabilisierte Frame-Harmonie"): The readers do not have to fear any surprises. Baßler, *Deutsche Erzählprosa 1850–1950*, 100–111.

24 Bakhtin, "Forms of Time and of the Chronotope in the Novel," 91.

25 "Es dauerte aber nicht lange und schon lag ich in einem schmalen Kabinett und die Decke senkte sich langsam knirschend schwer auf mich herab und drückte mich immer mehr an den Boden, die Luft fuhr fauchend heraus, es quetschte, es stöhnte, ich rechnete diesmal mit allem, doch auch damit konnte man mir nichts anhaben, meine Finger berührten plötzlich im letzten Moment einen Knopf, das war mir ganz recht, etwas schnappte jetzt auf, eine kleine Öffnung, durch die ich hinauskroch" (67).

26 See Baßler, *Deutsche Erzählprosa 1850–1950*, 107.
27 Bakhtin, "Forms of Time and of the Chronotope in the Novel," 92.
28 Ibid., 95.
29 See for example Eming and Schlechtweg-Jahn, "Einleitung," 9, 25–27.
30 Ror Wolf, "Meine Voraussetzungen," in *Über Ror Wolf*, 7–14, 12.
31 For a more general analysis of overcoming contingency by narration, see Rainer Warning, "Erzählen im Paradigma. Kontingenzbewältigung und Kontingenzexposition," *Romanistisches Jahrbuch* 52, no. 1 (2002): 176–209.
32 On exposed narration, see also Herbert Gamper, "Abenteuer der Sprache," in *Über Ror Wolf*, in *Über Ror Wolf*, 41–42.
33 "Unsere Schritte sanken tief in den pudrigen Sand, spitze Hitze, sagte Pelzer, wir kamen an dornigem blattlosem Gestrüpp vorbei, spitze Hitze. Mein Khakihemd war am offenen vom Sand aufgescheuerten Fleisch angebacken, vom Blutwasser steif, und in der glühenden Luft, die am Horizont kochte und brodelte, schleppten wir uns dahin.... Allmählich nahm diese Landschaft einen ganz anderen Charakter an.... Ich fand mich plötzlich hart am Abgrund dahingehend, etwas Geröll löste sich und fiel klappernd hinab" (131–132).
34 For Barthes, reality forms as a textual effect caused by descriptive details with no structural function punctuating the narrative flow: Roland Barthes, "The Reality Effect," in *French Literary Theory Today. A Reader*, ed. Tzvetan Todorov, trans. R. Carter (Cambridge: Cambridge University Press, 1982), 16. In *Pilzer und Pelzer*, however, a narrative that could be punctuated hardly forms at all, since the text mainly consists of "unnecessary" details. Wolf thus proceeds exactly opposite to techniques of narration described as realistic. To take another prominent example, Lukács claims for realistic literature to reflect "objective reality ... as it truly is" by showing its "essence," meaning its coherence and "totality" instead of the contingent abundance of surface appearances. Georg Lukács, "Realism in the Balance," in Theodor Adorno, Walter Benjamin, Ernst Bloch, Bertolt Brecht, and Georg Lukács, *Aesthetics and Politics*, afterword by Fredric Jameson, trans. and ed. Ronald Talyor (London: Verso, 2007), 33.
35 Bakhtin, "Forms of Time and of the Chronotope in the Novel," 99.
36 In his historical perspective, Jaques Rancière argues that such a way of writing is only possible in the era of the "aesthetic regime": a literary revolution, through which for the first time radical contingencies become narratable (*"grande parataxe"*), which was unthinkable in the antecedent so-called mimetic and representative regime. See Jaques Rancière, *Le partage du sensible, esthétique et politique* (Paris: La Fabrique, 2000), chap. 2 and 4; Jaques Rancière, *Le destin des images* (Paris: La Fabrique 2003), 55–64.
37 "Ich blieb in diesem Haus unter falschem Namen, ich gab mich als Maler aus, der hier die Landschaft malen wollte und malte tatsächlich, wenn auch nur dem Anschein nach, diese Landschaft mit ihren ungemein spitzen Bergen" (14).
38 "Hier bin ich, rief ich und hob meinen Hut. Ich war, glaube ich, als Vertreter für orthopädische Geräte unterwegs, es ging mir nicht schlecht, ich kam viel herum und eines Tages also zu dieser Tür herein. Man beurteilte

mich gleich nach Äußerlichkeiten und hielt mich für den Doktor, den man erwartet hatte" (98).

39 The *ars memoriae* is already laid out as a fortune banning coincidence in its founding legend. See Jürgen Trabant, "Memoria—fantasia—ingegno," in *Memoria—Vergessen und Erinnern* (Poetik und Hermeneutik XV), ed. Anselm Haverkamp and Renate Lachmann (Munich: Fink, 1993), 406–424; and Renate Lachmann, "Zum Zufall in der Literatur, insbesondere der Phantastischen," in *Kontingenz* (Poetik und Hermeneutik XVII), ed. Gerhart von Graevenitz and Odo Marquardt (Munich: Fink, 1998), 413–414.

40 "Das Meer, *soweit natürlich das Auge reichte*, glatt, sanft, bläulich, eine schimmernde Fläche, ein wolkenloser Himmel, *diesmal hatte ich mich nicht geirrt*" (100, emphasis added).

41 Adorno, "The Position of the Narrator in the Contemporary Novel," 35.

42 Ibid., 34.

43 "Nun sah ich doch etwas, etwas mit kurzem stumpfen Kopf schnaufend, etwas mager schmal dürr gebückt, und ich muß zugeben, daß ich . . . hinabstarrte, diesen langsamen schweren Vorwärtsbewegungen am Ende der Terrasse nach" (9).

44 On the analysis of variants of playing with language in the work of Wolf, see Werth, "Vielleicht Polzer," 39–40; Rolf Schütte, *Material, Konstruktion, Variabilität. Sprachbewegung im literarischen Werk von Ror Wolf* (Frankfurt: Peter Lang, 1987).

45 This of course is not a technique specific to Wolf but can also be observed, for example in the *nouveau roman* or, going further back, be compared to the procedure in Robert Musil's *Der Mann ohne Eigenschaften* as Blumenberg analyzes it. See Blumenberg, "The Concept of Reality and the Possibility of the Novel," 24.

46 On the narrating subject in the adventure genre, see Volker Klotz, *Abenteuer-Romane* (Munich: Hanser, 1979), 224.

47 See Jacob Grimm, *Frau Äventiure klopft an Beneckes Thür* (Berlin: Wilhelm Besser, 1842), 6.

48 Matthias Lexer, *Mittelhochdeutsches Taschenwörterbuch* (Stuttgart: S. Hirzel, 1961), 8.

49 See Mireille Schnyder, "Sieben Thesen zum Begriff der âventiure," in *Im Wortfeld des Textes: Worthistorische Beiträge zu den Bezeichnungen von Rede und Schrift im Mittelalter*, ed. Gerd Dicke, Manfred Eikelmann and Burkhard Hasebrink (Berlin and New York: De Gruyter, 2006), 369–370.

50 Already in Wolfram von Eschenbach's *Parzival* the adventure is staged as a self-reflexive procedure on the basis of the encounter with "frou Âventiure." A peak of literary adventure referring (parodically) to its own plot structures and narrative techniques can be found in the Russian avant-garde prose of the 1920s. See Aage A. Hansen-Löve, "'Wir sind zur einfachsten Kriminalhandlung unfähig . . .' Experimentelle Schundliteratur der russischen 20er Jahre," in *Abenteuer. Erzählmuster, Formprinzip, Genre*, 237–261; and Brigitte Obermayr, "Metaabenteuer. Vsevolod Ivanovs und Viktor Šklovskijs Roman *Iprit* im Kontext der frühsowjetischen Abenteuer-Konjunktur," in *Abenteuer in der Moderne*, 251–272.

51 "ein sehr langer gefleckter außerordentlich beweglich wirkender oder wie es schien oder wie es auch tatsächlich war zunächst der erste Teil das erste Stück dieses Körpers herab . . . , und dieser Kopf zog nun seinen sehr langen und gar nicht so dicken aber offenbar noch viel länger als erwarteten Körper aus diesem Baumschopf heraus und hinter sich her und nahm gar kein Ende . . . , denn der Schwanz lag noch in weiter Ferne, . . . doch ich sage jetzt Schwanz, weil der Schwanz auf andere Art hier nie erscheinen wird, also der Schwanz glitt glatt von den Ästen herab, und Pilzer schrie unter dieser Schlangenumarmung" (118–119).

52 "Der Aussprache nach ist es Pelzer, der nun etwas sagt . . . . Ich weiß nichts Bestimmtes von ihm. Was ich zu dieser Flanke zu sagen hätte, fragt er mich jetzt. Nichts. Nein, ich habe nichts mehr zu sagen. Ich bin vollkommen ruhig. Meine einzige Sorge besteht darin, daß jetzt, im letzten Moment, noch ein unvorhergesehener Zwischenfall den Schluß dieser Angelegenheit, das Ende, auf weitere Zeit hinausschieben könnte" (146).

53 For an analysis of this ending, see also Jörg Albrecht, *Abbrüche. Performanz und Poetik in Prosa und Hörspiel 1965–2002* (Göttingen: Wallstein, 2014), 240, who calls it an "ending without closure" ("Ende ohne Abschluß").

54 Juliane Rebentisch, "Realism Today. Art, Politics, and the Critique of Representation," in *Thinking-Resisting-Reading the Political*, ed. Anneka Esch-van Kan, Stephan Packard and Philipp Schulte (Berlin: diaphanes, 2013), 260.

55 Ibid., 259.

56 Ibid., 260.

57 Ibid., 256–261.

58 See ibid. 256.

59 Baßler, *Deutsche Erzählprosa 1850–1950*, 287. In this respect, although of course building on traditions of avant-garde writing, Wolf's prose differs fundamentally from the poetics of the historical avant-gardes, that conversely tried to break through to a primary reality with or in the text. See Baßler's chapter on modernist writing 1910–1925, esp. 213–216. For a reflection on a possible typology of relations between literary techniques and concepts of reality, see also Susanne Knaller, "Realitätskonzepte in der Moderne. Ein programmatischer Entwurf," in *Realitätskonzepte in der Moderne. Beiträge zu Literatur, Kunst, Philosophie und Wissenschaft*, ed. Susanne Knaller and Harro Müller (Munich: Fink, 2011), 11–23.

60 Makropoulos, "Crisis and Contingency," 12.

61 See Makropoulos, "Kontingenz," 370 and Michael Makropoulos, "Kontingenz und Handlungsraum," in *Kontingenz*, 23.

62 See Blumenberg, "The Concept of Reality and the Possibility of the Novel," 34. For Blumenberg's concept of modernity as a culture of contingency, see also Hans Blumenberg, *Säkularisierung und Selbstbehauptung* (Frankfurt a. M.: Suhrkamp 1974).

63 Ibid., 33.

64 Ibid., 34.

65 See Makropoulos, "Kontingenz," 376 and Makropoulos, "Kontingenz und Handlungsraum," 23–24.
66 See Schnyder, "Sieben Thesen zum Begriff der âventiure," 369–370.
67 Blumenberg, "The Concept of Reality and the Possibility of the Novel," 47.
68 Ibid., 42. Blumenberg's expression "Welthaftigkeit" is translated in the American edition as "fixing (or causing) a world," while in the given context I prefer to use the term *worldliness*.
69 This is not only true for *Pilzer und Pelzer*: Ina Appel reads Wolf's stories in *Nachrichten aus der bewohnten Welt* with Deleuze as a game of infinite folding. See Ina Appel, *Von Lust und Schrecken im Spiel ästhetischer Subjektivität. Über den Zusammenhang von Subjekt, Sprache und Existenz in Prosa von Brigitte Kronauer und Ror Wolf* (Würzburg: Königshausen & Neumann, 2000), esp. 125–126.
70 For an investigation on contingency as a formal principle of literary texts, see Philipp Erchinger, *Kontingenzformen. Realisierungsweisen des fiktionalen Erzählens bei Nashe, Sterne und Byron* (Würzburg: Königshausen & Neumann, 2009).
71 See Gamper, "Abenteuer der Sprache," 41, 43.
72 Erchinger, *Kontingenzformen*, 7.
73 Makropoulos, "Crisis and Contingency," 11.
74 Jean Paul, *Vorschule der Ästhetik* (Sämtliche Werke Abteilung I, 5), ed. Norbert Miller (Munich: Carl Hanser Verlag, 1963), 129.
75 See Jean Paul, *Vorschule der Ästhetik*, 125. See also Max Kommerell, *Jean Paul* (Frankfurt a. M.: Vittorio Klostermann, 1977), 318; for a specific focus on Paul's determination of humor in relation to contingency, Wolfgang Preisendanz, "Komik als Komplement der Erfassung von Kontingenzen," in *Kontingenz*, 388.
76 "[D]as Lachen [ist] auch der Versuch . . . , das alltägliche Grauen abzuwehren, das aus sämtlichen Ritzen quillt." Ror Wolf, "Spaß und Entsetzen," in *Der Bremer Literaturpreis 1954–1998. Reden der Preisträger und andere Texte*, ed. Wolfgang Emmerich (Bremerhaven: Wirtschafsverlag NW, 1999), 423.
77 David E. Wellbery, "Zur literaturwissenschaftlichen Relevanz des Kontingenzbegriffs. Eine Glosse zur Diskussion um den Poststrukturalismus," in *Poststrukturalismus—Dekonstruktion—Postmoderne*, ed. Klaus W. Hempfer (Stuttgart: Steiner, 1992), 167.
78 Blumenberg, "The Concept of Reality and the Possibility of the Novel," 48.
79 See also Erich Auerbach, who proposes that it is exactly the "fruitful irony" of Rabelais, "which, through the play of possibilities, casts a dawning light on the possibility of freedom" (281) and invites the readers to "deal directly with the world and its wealth of phenomena" (276). Erich Auerbach, *Mimesis. The Representation of Reality in Western Literature*, trans. Willard R. Trask (Princeton, NJ: Princeton University Press 2003).
80 Blumenberg, "The Concept of Reality and the Possibility of the Novel," 40.

6

Trawling Truth

B. S. Johnson's Evacuation of Realist Epistemology

André Otto

Representing Context

Bryan Stanley Johnson is a curious case. And probably a rather surprising inclusion in a discussion of realism. Forming the center of an informal group of writers in and around London in the 1960s and early 1970s, Johnson was, and saw himself, as the most prominent figure of a literary avant-garde. Reacting against what he perceived to be a resurgence of Victorian realism in post–Second World War Britain,[1] he energetically proposed a new aesthetics of the novel. In opposition to such economically and medially successful literary phenomena as the Angry Young Men and the Movement with their foregrounding of represented reality and story, Johnson developed a textuality that did not allow for a forgetting of the discursive dimension of the text nor of its materiality. His novels are highly self-reflexive and full of metafictional commentaries that disrupt the mimetic illusion and remind the readers of the fact that they are reading a text.

But what might sound like a postmodern aesthetics is in stark conflict with Johnson's claims for the epistemology of his texts. With their intended effects and their gathering of circumstantial detail, these claims point toward a realist heritage while manifesting a highly ambivalent and ambiguous stance toward realism. The epistemological framing clashes with an insistent experimentation with the novelistic form that Johnson sees at the service of a search for truth. This internal conflict places Johnson in a relation with realism that is full of unresolvable tensions—and indicates an epistemological environment in which the very notions of reality and representation produce a complex array of shifting parameters. The peculiarity of his aesthetic project therefore prompts us to interrogate what counts as realism in a particular historical moment, and what we do by discussing certain texts in the light of their relationship to realism.

Johnson's questioning of the form of the novel departs from the idea that the novel as genre and as form has to be in correspondence with contemporary concepts of reality. It has to find formal expressions for a sense of life's complexities, and it has to be geared toward what seems to be a very emphatic notion of truth. For Johnson, the literary text represents a crucial medium of knowledge, which primarily relies on an investigation of the self, a *recherche* of the lost self, as it were. Despite all the metafictional disruptions, his texts, therefore, perform a programmatic blurring of the boundaries between fiction, autofiction, and Johnson's own life. They strongly operate with, and are based on, his personal experiences, and test the fringes of the autobiographical. Foregrounding a mutually constitutive relationship between writing and memory, they not only question how literary texts deal with the writing of memory but also focus on the function the writing of memory has in literary texts. This both poses the fundamental problem of literary reference and investigates the role the relation to one's own experiences has *in* and *through* the novel.

As I will argue, the two central aspects of Johnson's renewal of the form of the novel create a fundamental tension with versions of realism. They imply a highly polemical mobilization of realism within Johnson's project, while relating to a tension that is at the heart of whatever one might consider as literary realism. The first aspect concerns the notion of representation against which Johnson measures his formal innovation. The second, his concept of truth in its relation to his concept of reality. Both aspects are crucial to any discussion of realism. Particularly, the defining term of reality, hovering uneasily between effective cause and reference of representation and representational effect, is a highly contentious one.

In 1981, Marshall Brown argued that realism, rather than presupposing a consistent notion of reality, in fact comes into its own in an epistemological situation of the nineteenth century when conflicting notions of reality cannot be reconciled anymore: "The age of realism is thus not the period when reality became the literary norm. On the contrary, realism developed into a central issue in mid-century precisely because the conception of reality had become increasingly problematic."[2] Accordingly, for Brown, "the realistic novel can be considered an exploratory investigation into the nature of reality."³ With regard to the function of representation, Brian McHale took up Roman Jakobson's notion of a progressive realism. This type of realism that "might better be called 'deviant realism,' or realism of estrangement,"⁴ highlights the conventions of representation within realism. It "is achieved precisely by violating the norms of received realism. The implicit argument of norm-violating realism is that received realism is faithful only to convention, that it nowhere breaks out of the closed circle of solidarity to touch 'reality.'"⁵

Systematically, the two aspects of the notion of reality and the traditions of representation seem to be generally conflated in literary realism. However, they concern different spheres and a discussion of realism would have to look at how they are being related. Neither aspect on its own is sufficient for a definition of realism or for a description of a particular historical text as realist. While realism associates a certain notion of reality with a certain conception of mimetic representation, the one does not necessarily follow from the other. Symptomatically, Pam Morris's two basic definitions of realism given at two different occasions tacitly refer to these different aspects separately. In *Realism* the stress on communicability foregrounds the possibility of a transparent representation: "As a starting point I shall define literary realism as any writing that is based upon an implicit or explicit assumption that it is possible to communicate about a reality beyond the writing."⁶ In a later definition, however, she focuses on knowability and connects it to communicability only in a second step: "The basic defining condition of any realist discourse, whether philosophic, scientific, or literary, is the implicit assumption that knowledge about the socio-physical world is possible and sharable."⁷ It is precisely this combination of knowability and communicability that at once blurs the linkage between reality and representation and reinforces a constitutive separation that disguises the intervention of the semiotic system by which one communicates.⁸

Communicability within fictional discourse relies on what Nelson summarizes as the main techniques for reinforcing mimetic illusion.

> The main techniques that reinforce the mimetic illusion are: a linear, chronological narrative based on causality; the use of coherent and "typical" characters; detailed notation of the physical world; a clearly evoked social and historical setting; and reference to an extratextual world shared by author and reader.⁹

These representational techniques, however, already entail a particular formulation of mimetic illusion. As Morris has pointed out, their particular understanding of plot development, temporality, and character and their historically specific concept of reality depend upon interrelated notions of truth and verisimilitude.

Realist plots and characters are constructed in accordance with secular empirical rules. Events and people in the story are explicable in terms of natural causation without resort to the supernatural or divine intervention. Whereas idealism is grounded upon a view of Truth as universal and timeless, empiricism finds its truths in the particular and specific.[10]

Realist truth is thus associated with a modern concept of reality that Hans Blumenberg has characterized as the result of an actualization within a context that is always open to the future and has to be established via the creation of consistency.[11] This truth, then, is not about the particular and specific in their own right; they have to be integrated into a consistent context that is neither preexisting nor transcendentally guaranteed. A realist world might seem chaotic at first glance—but is revealed to be determined by various causalities that, in the end, form the impression of a unified, consistent whole.[12] As Morris has argued, this way

> plot structure, in conjunction with narrative technique, also functions as a model of universal knowledge in which mastery of particularity is brought intellectually into a unified systematised whole. Readers are interpellated into this fictitious position of panoptic omniscience and rewarded by the plenitude of certainty, justice and transcendence at the conclusion of even the most harrowing of stories.[13]

Realizing consistency, these texts shape the "notation of the physical world" and the "social and historical setting"[14] into a unifying form. As George Levine has argued, this kind of consistent forming "plagued realism from the start" because of "the incompatibility of tight form with plausibility."[15] Tight forming collides not only with the sense of a more or less disordered reality of particulars but with the realist "attempt to use language to get beyond language, to discover some nonverbal truth out there."[16] For getting beyond language involves a high degree of linguistic consciousness and experimentation. In Levine's view, realist fiction is characterized by the struggle to achieve a linguistic form of representation that makes one forget the process of representation—and this requires ever new representational techniques. It is

> the struggle inherent in any "realist" effort—the struggle to avoid the inevitable conventionality of language in pursuit of the unmediated reality. Realism, as a literary method, can in these terms be defined as a self-conscious effort, usually in the name of some moral enterprise of truth telling and extending the limits of human sympathy, to make literature appear to be describing directly not some other language but

reality itself (whatever that may be taken to be); in this effort, the writer must self-contradictorily dismiss previous conventions of representation while, in effect, establishing new ones.[17]

This sounds surprisingly similar to what Johnson proposes for the renewal of the novel. The differences, however, are crucial. They relate to the notions of subjectivity, the function of truth and both the degree of the foregrounding of the medium of representation and the function this disruptive foregrounding has regarding the status of the novel as formative of subjectivity and truth.

Novel, Not Story

In the introduction to *Aren't You Rather Young to Be Writing Your Memoirs?* from 1973, Johnson retrospectively outlines the rationale for his approach to the novel. At the center of this belated manifesto lies Johnson's provocative contention that telling stories is telling lies, which was first put forward by the narrator of Johnson's second novel, *Albert Angelo* (1964).[18] It forms the cornerstone for a poetics of the novel that radically historicizes the genre by basing its legitimacy and specificity on its epistemological (and didactic[19]) function within society. In contrast to the "stultifyingly philistine" situation of "the general book culture" in post-war England that is dominated by "writers of romances, thrillers, and the bent but so-called straight novel," Johnson wants the novelists to be "writing as though it mattered, as though they meant it, as though they meant it to matter."[20] Writing that matters, however, requires more than a didactic aim or a social consciousness. It first and foremost necessitates a consciousness of writing itself and its formal and formative properties and effects. For Johnson, this is exactly what has been missing in an England that, after the war, has seen a suppression of the legacies of modernism and a return to realism. The problem with this predominant mode of writing shows itself most detrimentally in the novel: it forgets its own historical situatedness and its relation to the evolution of literary forms. What is more, it neglects, or irresponsibly veils, the fundamental distinction in Johnson's theory by equating novel with story. Whereas telling stories amounts to telling lies, the novel, for Johnson, should aspire to truth and be a medium for truth. In order to achieve this, it has to be conscious of the possibilities of the genre and enlist the entire media-technological apparatus at its disposal, "the precise use of language, exploitation of the technological fact of the book, the explication of thought."[21]

Behind this distinction lies a notion of representation as a conscious act that has to be made conscious. As in Levine, this hinges on the notion of form. In the process of forming, mere matter is transformed into a matter that matters because it carries an epistemological intention and an individuating function within the parameters of the social. Every story entails a process of "strict, close selection," by which the writer extracts something from life. These matters are then combined through different forms of overdetermination. For Johnson, this amounts to a falsification because it does not accord with the contemporary notion of reality. Life just does not work in neat segments, it "does not tell stories. Life is chaotic, fluid, random; it leaves myriads of ends untied, untidily. Writers can extract a story from life only by strict, close selection, and this must mean falsification."[22]

This falsification is then further exacerbated because telling stories hides its constitutive processes by disregarding the medium of representation itself. This marks the difference to the novel for Johnson. The novel is a historically particular way of giving form and it has to be conscious of this, since it is the attention to form that enables the novel to be a medium of truth: "The novel is a form in the same sense that the sonnet is a form; within that form, one may write truth or fiction. I choose to write truth in the form of a novel."[23] In order to not just write fiction, the writer needs an understanding of reality that is aware of its historicity, and a consciousness of the evolution of the form in which he or she is writing. This conceptualization of the historicity of the form of the novel and of its epistemological function marks a stark contrast to a realist truth claim since the novel's epistemological value rests on its constitutive mediality. Truth is achieved only within medial strategies of representation.

For Johnson's own historical position, the epistemological differentiation between novel and story has two major implications. First, his concept of reality is defined by chaotic contingency. This contingency is all the more pronounced as reality is accessible only through radically relative individual perception.[24] It is therefore no coincidence that he is referring to life rather than to reality in the passage quoted earlier,[25] since this distinction is at the heart of Woolf's rejection of Edwardian realism in her own programmatic statement about the modern novel.[26] The more decisive point of reference, however, is Joyce. Not only is it impossible for Johnson "to write as though the revolution that was *Ulysses* had never happened," and to "still rely on the crutch of storytelling,"[27] but form has to follow function. This does not imply, though, that Johnson argues for a new kind of formalism; he is looking for adequate forms for manifesting present-day reality. Everything else would amount to escapism:

> The novelist cannot legitimately or successfully embody present-day reality in exhausted forms. If he is serious, he will be making a statement which attempts to change society towards a condition he conceives to be better, and he will be making at least implicitly a statement of faith in the evolution of the form in which he is working. Both these aspects of making are radical; this is inescapable unless he chooses escapism.[28]

This historicizing functional argument is similar to the one with which Johnson starts his manifesto. Citing the anecdote that Joyce opened the first cinema in Dublin in 1909, he develops a media-historical approach to the necessity of the evolution of the novel. According to Johnson's reading of the anecdote, the changing media landscape, in conjunction with changing notions of reality, sets the conditions for a different function of the novel. As cinema and television are much better suited to serve realist purposes of representation, not for the first time in its history, storytelling has "passed from one medium to another."[29] This change in medial dominance requires a new legitimation of the novel, while liberating it from the subservience to story. It facilitates an engagement with the novel's medial and generic capacities, so that "the novel may not only survive but evolve to greater achievements by concentrating on those things it can still do best: the precise use of language, exploitation of the technological fact of the book, the explication of thought."[30]

Textual Trawling

Johnson draws important narratological consequences from this triple functional definition of the contemporary novel. Since the rise of other media "has seen large areas of the old territory of the novelist increasingly taken over," the territory proper to the novelist is not the representation of an external reality anymore. Instead, "the only thing the novelist can with any certainty call exclusively his own is the inside of his own skull." *Trawl* is the Johnsonian novel that most comprehensively puts his conclusion that "this is what the novelist should explore"[31] into practice. Through the way it relates its different medial, textual, and narratological dimensions to each other, it unfolds a pervasive meta-reflection on the implications of its fictional and linguistic parameters. Focusing, in its representation of life, with utmost intensity on the possibility of a truth that might lie outside of its representation, it at the same time bases this epistemological process on writing and the fiction of writing. This contradiction is already compounded in a title that both refers to the (fictive) occasional frame and constitutes the central epistemological as well as metafictional metaphor for what the novel is doing. It is this convergence that gives expression to the enfolding of a realist epistemology within an aesthetics that relies on the very opaqueness of its mediality and genre. On the one hand, the text insists on the possibility of truth, its knowability, and communicability by way of the novel. Through its radical partialization, its stress on individuality to the degree of solipsism and especially the deconstruction of the function of truth at the end, the novel, on the other hand and under the guise of an epistemological analysis, embodies the non-analytical effects of its rhetoricity and mediality.

In order to find a form for the novel not as fiction but as truth, *Trawl* combines its search for novelistic truthfulness with a highly metarepresentational set-up. It creates a fictional situation that makes the exclusive focus on the processes inside of a narrator's skull both plausible *and* available for metafictional questioning. This situation is very simple and yet immensely charged with allegorical cultural references and metafictional self-references. The unnamed narrator undertakes a voyage on a trawler to Norway and the Barents Sea as a supernumerary passenger. The trip is scheduled to last three weeks, in which the narrator proposes to confront his past. More specifically, he wants "to trace the causes of my isolation"[32] and possibly overcome his feeling of lack and social failure. As the reader becomes aware in the final pages of the novel, this need for a confrontation with the past arises out of an impending decisive moment in the narrator's life: after a number of disappointing relationships, the self-absorbed narrator has finally mustered the courage to propose to his girlfriend Ginnie and is about to marry her. At the end of the novel, the narrator apparently succeeds in letting go of his past and seems to be able to commit to a future with his fiancée.[33]

This relatively banal and almost melodramatic plot, however, serves as a vehicle for a sustained testing of the form of the novel and its parameters of representation that blurs the borders between the novel, the diary, and autobiography. This starts with the problem of autobiographical reference. The text quite openly mirrors a three-week journey Johnson undertook "from 14 October 1963 on the trawler Northern Jewel to the Barents Sea"[34] immediately after his proposal of marriage to Virginia Kimpton, whose name is clearly echoed in the narrator's name for his fiancée. As Andrew Hassam contends, *Trawl* therefore "cannot be read with ease either as fiction or autobiography: it is an indeterminate case and as such it explores the very basis of the fictive journal form, the embedding of a nonfiction form in a fictional frame."[35] But this generic obscurity is only the first of a variety of ways that point to the text's problematic framing and to the novel *as* problematic framing.

The next level is the typographic shape of the text. The book presents a tightly set body of text that looks like a continuous monolithic column[36] and is only interrupted occasionally by two different kinds of typographical spacing devices. The first kind are blank spaces that correspond to the space of two or three blank lines and divide the text into blocks of irregular length. Even more conspicuous, however, are the spatial interruptions within the lines that are marked by varying amounts of dots. These range from two to eleven dots at a time. The reader is confronted with both forms of typographical arrangement immediately when entering the text (Figure 6.1).

This beginning not only emphatically introduces the theme of isolation and personal introspection with a variation on "I," "one," "alone," and "sole" but the general "one" gives way to a first-person narrator that presents his stream

```
        I  · ·  always with I  · ·  one starts from  · ·
   one and I share the same character   · ·  are one  ·
   ·  ·  ·  ·   one always starts with I  · ·  one  · ·
   ·  ·  ·   alone  ·  ·  ·  ·  ·  ·  ·   sole  ·  ·  ·  ·
   ·  ·  ·  ·  ·  ·  ·   single  ·  ·  ·  ·  ·  ·  ·  ·
   ·  ·  I
```

I have no means of telling, here, down here, when

FIGURE 6.1 *Typeset as it appears on the opening page of* Trawl *(7).*

of consciousness. We are in the skull of the narrator, following the process of his thinking. Within this narratological framework, the typography fulfills a marked iconic function since Johnson uses the spacing to represent different kinds of interruptions of the thinking process that vary between pauses or vacillations and the suspension of the thinking process due to sleep. Both the literal and the figurative dimensions of the process of trawling thus blend with the representational techniques of the textual surface.

> *Trawl* is both figurative and literal: an account of his life and his experiences writing it while on a deep sea trawler, it includes elliptical breaks to represent the mind working when the voice does not speak, invokes rhythm to emulate the sea's swells, and shortened line length to accommodate the lack of paragraph breaks in order to write "a representation of the inside of my mind but at one stage removed; the closest one can come in writing."[37]

The complexity of the text derives from the narratological, metafictional, and epistemological implications of this basic constellation: in order to confront his sense of isolation, the narrator seeks the utter isolation on board a ship. The allegorical reverberations of the ship voyage are of course overwhelming, and I will return to them with regard to the cathartic conception of truth in the text. For the evolution of the narrative, however, it is important that the ship represents one of the most emblematic heterotopic spaces[38] and that Johnson uses the implications of the heterotopy by associating it with a sense of utter estrangement:

> why I was going to sea: . . . I could not just say, I want to give substantial yet symbolic form to an isolation I have felt most of my life by isolating myself in fact, by enacting the isolation in an extreme form, by cutting myself off as far as possible from everything I have ever known before. (105)

The narrator cuts himself off completely from his known environment and enters a radically restricted and absolutely placeless space while introducing himself into a homosocial environment that has its particular rules and rituals as well as a very specific language. The ever-increasing presence of a vocabulary associated with the ship and with fishing is part of a textual progression that is based on accumulation and enumeration—and, with every accumulation of particularity comes the problem of ordering and giving shape to the material.

Apart from its authenticating reality effect, the nautical vocabulary foregrounds the status of the world on the ship as a world apart. This has immediate meta-representational implications as the text combines the narratological restriction to the narrator's stream of consciousness with an utter limitation of the exterior world. There is hardly any perceptual stimulation from a world that is reduced to the goings on onboard. Since the ship is a trawler working on the open sea, there is no touristic aspect to this journey at all and the visuality characteristic of mimetic forms of the novel is reduced to a minimum. As if to stress this further, large portions of the journey are suffered by the narrator in the seclusion below deck due to recurrent bouts of seasickness. There, perceptions are predominantly of an acoustic nature and range from the sounds and noises of the ship itself to the teasing of the narrator by the crew. Thus, the narrator sets out on a decidedly "symbolic" journey that leads more into his inner world than into a world of seafaring adventure and worldly discovery. The linguistic accumulation of nautical terminology is an expressive correlate to this reduction of the present world of the narrator to the world on the ship. More importantly, however, the text, too, leaves the known world behind by deliberately leaving off representing an exterior world. The thematic and narratological isolation leads to an excessive focus on the solipsist subject and unfolds a highly ambiguous process of textual evacuation. In its course, evacuation and abjection will turn out to constitute the narrator's complex relationship to the details of reality. And they will also be the form the text's performative representation of truth takes.

Evacuations

In isolation and confronting the sources of his isolation, the narrator starts a process of memorial trawling that circles around the problem of evacuation. In addition to the thematic dimension, however, evacuation becomes a textual principle that presents a major challenge of the novel. It complicates both the narrator's relationship to his past and the textual representation of the performative recollection. By associating it with a process of abjection,[39] it not only leads to a questioning of subjectivity by establishing an ambivalent relationship to the self and its past, but the resulting estrangement also affects the purported epistemological value of the text and its concept of truth.

As a central theme of the text, evacuation relates the narrator's isolation to the historical effects of the Second World War. But just as isolation is both the problem and the means of an envisioned solution, evacuation traverses a variety of textual dimensions and acquires different meanings. While the experience of the wartime evacuation as a young boy and the enforced separation from his mother during the German air raids presents one of the reasons for the narrator's failing relationships and his sexual trawling,[40] evacuation also becomes a principle of the textual memorial poetics that oscillates between a rescuing recovery and a literal emptying out. In this ambiguity it manifests a process of abjection that characterizes the narrator's recovery of personal memories, which is simultaneously aimed at an identification with and an overcoming of the past self. It signifies both a recognition and a rejection of the self and thus gives expression to the strange subject formation through the paradoxical inclusion of that which is rejected that Kristeva describes as the foundational moment of subjectivity.[41] This has decisive effects on the major epistemological challenge of the text since it ironically turns the epistemological quest from an excavation that pretends to dig ever deeper into the personal past and to discover the originary causes of the narrator's isolation into a paradoxical progression of abject accumulation that defies any particular sense of order. Abject accumulation is thus both the way through which the narrator pretends to recover (a sense of) reality and the recognition of an estrangement that precludes an integration into a coherent contextual unity. Instead, the memorial fragments of reality can eventually only signify a truth through the acceptance of an abjection that establishes a metonymic relationship it at the same time rejects to integrate. This is the novel's way to treat (its) matter so that it matters.

The abjective evacuation not only comes about because of the deliberate isolation but also leads to an even stronger and enforced sense of isolation. As if the strangeness of the ship's environment and its placelessness were not enough, the narrator, upon entering the ship, almost immediately becomes seasick. On the level of narration, the rhythm of the seasickness structures the narrative flow of the text by connecting it to the hauling of the trawl. The noise of the counterweight announcing the trawl and beating virtually against the place where the narrator's head rests punctuates the narrator's ruminations as well as the textual surface through the typographic interruption of the onomatopoeia "*CRAANGK!*." Thus, the craangk reminds not only the narrator of his situation within the fictional world but also the readers of the fact that they are reading a text: "*CRAANGK!* · · Ah, they haul again, recall me again to this narrow bunk, the ventilation orifice which plays fresh air on my face" (59). What is more, the craangking represents a major point of intersection of the various textual temporalities. While anchoring the chronology of the present-tense narration that is constantly under threat by the effects of the seasickness, by the flow of the ruminations as well as by the smooth time-space of the sea voyage, its striations[42] crucially spark recollections of episodes in the past that are, for the most part, presented in a chronological order but with decisive gaps and a lack of coherence. The craangking, therefore, organizes the text's progressive accumulation of disjointed matter.

But the seasickness acquires further epistemological and metafictional importance. Being dysfunctional in various psychological, physiological, and social senses,[43] the narrator is restricted to his own bunk in the lower regions of the trawler for large stretches of the first two-thirds of the text. While this actually helps his original purpose as there is no distraction from his confrontation with the past—and thus almost no representation of external reality apart from the odd noise, visit, or reference to time— the effects of the seasickness constantly interrupt the thinking process by recalling the narrator to the embodiedness of experience, most insistently through the literal evacuation of the body by vomiting. In a marked parallel to what the trawling of memory brings up, this evacuation only feeds on the narrator's own body, since he is initially unable to eat or to keep down anything he has eaten. The body evacuates itself down to what the text uses as a central metaphor for the problems to be dealt with: the green bile.[44]

In the set-up of the text, then, isolation confronts isolation, evacuation counters evacuation. They form the empty center around which the process of "trawl[ing] the delicate mesh of my mind over the snagged and broken floor of my past" (21) revolves. The narrator starts from the thesis that his sense of isolation is due to the experiences during the evacuations of the Second World War. The traumatic separation from his mother is then repeated in the constant fear, and experience, of betrayal by a whole range of girls in a variety of sexual encounters that constitute the other major topic of the narrator's memories. Psychologically, the question would be whether the narrator manages to break through his fixation on his mother and his self-pity in order to become capable of recognizing his own responsibility for the repeated failures of engaging with the world and the women he selfishly used and emotionally abused.

Metafictionally, this narrative situation constitutes an intensification of Ian Watt's subject-philosophical precondition of the realist novel[45] almost to the extent of parody. Johnson presents an individual that is not autonomous but isolated and self-conscious to the degree of an anxious lack of control. Autonomy becomes isolation, self-consciousness obsessive self-interrogation. If this already subverts one crucial parameter of realism, the way the text progresses adds to this deconstruction. This involves three different aspects. First, the situation of remembering and the situations remembered constantly interact with, or interrupt, each other, making the memories dependent on the embodied process of remembering. This, secondly, results in a nonlinear textuality, which is most apparent in terms of the temporal structure. Even though the narrator variously exhorts himself to follow the chronology of past events, this chronology is constantly disrupted by the events on the ship or the metareflections on the thinking process, preventing any sense of temporal continuity and stressing instead the breakdown of mental activity, the gaps in memory and the jumps between episodes.

This problem of textual order, which is mirrored in a broken syntax, typographical interruptions and the blank spaces between the blocks of narrative, points, thirdly, to Johnson's fundamental critique of stories as lies. For the non-linearity relates to what Brown designates as the basic feature of realism: the silhouetting apparent in the overcoding integration of prominent detail.[46] Instead of furthering the illusion of integrative and consistent reality, Johnson ironically counters the "mimetic urge" of an "accurate representation of reality"[47] by a poetics of accumulating matter whose representational truth value will have to emerge out of the performance of accumulation. This means that there is no pre-existent unifying form that is applied to the matter, the accumulation rather confronts narrator and reader with the parameters of the formative ordering process.

The trawling catches a multiplicity of worldly details that conform to some of the most naturalist expectations in terms of their sordidness and the bleakness of social milieus. The very first episode is a paradigmatic case in point. It recalls in all graphic detail the problems of sexual and emotional intercourse with a married mother. These range from the logistic challenges in a shared bed-sit, to the physical challenge of sexual satisfaction in a vagina widened by having given birth to three children, to the economic and emotional challenge of not being able to provide the stability the woman might be looking for. There are a number of problems here that are exemplary not only for the way the narrator treats his materials but also for how readers might react to them. For how does one deal with an egotistical male's view of his past in which lachrymose self-pity alternates with genuine bafflement and short moments of analytical recognition of guilt and responsibility: "I begin to suspect I shall wish I had never started on this examination: I keep surprising myself with my own nastiness, with my own limitations. ·· But on" (82–83). This strange mixture not only manifests the narrator's abjective relation to an estranged and estranging self but extends abjection to the readers in their relationship with what they are reading.

As Kristeva argues, abjection confronts us with the constitutive moment of establishing a boundary (for the self, its interiority and what is to belong to it) in which, because of the violence of the reaction, the parameters of our ways of ordering become affectively apparent. In Johnson's trawling, this applies both to the wealth of circumstantial detail and to the kind of moral and ethical assimilation narrator and reader face. Neither are the events and episodes clearly delimited in themselves, nor are the relationships between them in any way obvious, nor can one be sure what the narrator's stance toward them is. Instead, the text creates lists of memorial findings, of the trawler's catches, and of nautical and fishing terms. Its mode is fundamentally paratactical. Its central gesture is the recurring question "what else?" (67) that expresses the crucial epistemological challenge of this text's confrontation with life and its novelistic forming. For the epistemological and psychological value of the cumulative effort is all but self-evident, as the narrator recognizes time and again in a concession the reader might at times feel more than justified: "This is tedious, has no relevance." (80) While the narrator's aim is to discover all the material that might explain his isolation, it is precisely the "all" that is the problem. Lacking parameters for the selection and integration, the gesture to include all effectively produces isolation and the compulsive need to go on: "All, all? ·· All? No, but go on now to Scale Lane, enough of the earlier past, this works in chronological order as far as it can, if it works" (82–83). The "all" does *not* result in a sense of wholeness, there is *no* transcendent leap that evidences a presumed order, and the cumulative method does *not* produce consistency in terms of a realist notion of cause and effect: "What use are analyses, reasons, causes? All I am left with are just things, happenings: things as they are, happenings as they have happened and go on happening through the unreliable filter of my memory. But try. What else is there to do?" (93–94). In the face of the overwhelming challenge of "things as they are" and their apparent resistance to signification, the text proceeds by evacuative exhaustion[48] and foregrounds a different kind of textual overdetermination. Both are crucial for the text's epistemology and for Johnson's concept of novelistic truth.

Cathartic Truth

What is obvious from the beginning is that coherence is provided by the interiority of the I. The non-linearity, the gaps, the jumps are all motivated by the thinking process and the strictly linear representation of the subject's consciousness. As symbolized by the enclosure on a trawler in a temporally and spatially delimited situation of heterotopic exception, the novel's representation is not directed outward, but at an interior reality. It departs from the notion that all sense of reality is not only mediated through individual experience and memories but solipsistic—there will always be distortions and fragmentations. This has important consequences for the epistemological process. Even though the narrator proposes an analytical approach to his past, this does not lead to an increasing self-awareness. The entire process is deceptive, not least because it resembles a psychotherapeutical approach. Through the accumulation of detail, the text lays bare what is consciously remembered, but also gradually reveals what the narrator seems to want to repress. It thus gives the teleological impression of a gaining of consciousness.

The central metaphor for this process, however, refers to the notion of evacuation and entails a non-rational mode that complicates the novel's epistemology. It is the green bile that is introduced roughly in the middle of the text, when the narrator remembers boarding the ship and being forewarned that he will be sick: "You'll be sick until you bring up your green bile, you've got to bring up the green bile that's been there maybe since you were a child. And once that green bile's gone, you'll be alright, he said, and his mate too said, You'll be sick, but you'll fooking eat afterward!" (105). The green bile constitutes the metaphor for the pivot of a cathartic process that confronts the concrete with the symbolic, the literal with the non-literal.

At the same time, it shows how the linguistic markers of repression work in the text as foreshadowings. For the green bile points to the most threatening and humiliating experience of the narrator: the encounter with a prostitute he remembers as the green pro. This encounter, which condenses all his failures of emotional interaction with women, announces itself through veiled references to the green pro throughout the text and through the recurrence of the word "green" in incomplete phrases. This metonymic as well as metaphoric dissemination superimposes the green bile not only with the green pro but also with the color of the sea. And it is ultimately this association with the color of the sea that makes the narrator confront this painfully embarrassing memory. For as the seasickness makes insistently clear, there is no shirking the pressure of the green sea.

A similar symptomatic dissemination occurs with references to the narrator's fiancée. The revelation that there is a fiancée at all comes very late in the text as quite a surprise. The narrator's name for his fiancée, Ginnie, however, is also prefigured in various instances through a number of references to small skates that the fishermen call "ginnies": "Ah! A ginnie, I must take special care of the ginnies, for her sake, for that is my name for her, I can't call you that, I said, when I first met her, I'll call you Ginnie" (150).

These two examples have to suffice in order to indicate how the epistemological process differs from a progression to a center and an origin. In fact, there is no final resolution as to the reasons for the narrator's sense of isolation. Rather he concedes, "I still do not know exactly why I felt isolated, how it had come about that I was isolated" (179), and poses the rhetorical question that effectively puts the epistemological project under erasure: "What use is knowing a reason?" (180). Nevertheless, the ruminations perform a healing process that does not follow the logic of cause and effect. The accumulation culminates in a sudden turning point that denies direct causality, just as the text denies any single principle that might organize its material and give it determinate shape: "I wake of a sudden, clear, my purpose in coming achieved. I do not know why. What did I consider last night?" (166). The accumulation does not coalesce into a truth of contextual coherence, but produces an emergence based on the constellation of all the threads and details, an embodiment of multiple possible relations: "Nothing there to precipitate it. ·· But everything, building up on this voyage, all the thinking, collectively, accumulatively, must have led to this sudden freedom I feel now, relievedly, relieved of all thinking" (166).

The effect of the solution remains one of speculative supposition: it must have led to this. Rather than a reconstruction of reasons and causalities, it is the possibilities arising from the accumulation that end the isolation and make the projection of a future and a commitment possible. They also enable something that sounds like the very subversion of Johnson's novelistic premise, since they relieve the narrator of a thinking process in favor of embracing embodied experience. However, this does not indicate a sublation into the fullness of truth. The epistemological process does not only remain radically partial and dependent on the faulty cognition of the solipsistic subject: "everything is relevant only to me, relative only to me, to be seen only from my eyes, solipsism is the only truth: can be the only truth: a thing is so only because I think it to be so: if I do not think it to be so, then it is not so: this must be the only truth: belief does not arise" (172). What is more, the epistemological goal of truth paradoxically rests on its abandonment in the encounter with the green bile. Truth becomes an effect not of heightened consciousness in a Blumenbergian subjective realization of a consistent context, but of a medial process of abjective evacuation.

> No, I need no more of these flashbacks, these autopsies performed on the past, I have all that, no, not all, only a part, there is so much, but what I wanted has been achieved, I have been purged of my past, of those things which have hurt me, or enough of them, to make me feel it has worked, this coming to sea, that I have no need now to shoot again, I am going home now. (174)

Ultimately, the confrontation with the accumulation of memories gives way to a letting go. The trawling, thus, evacuates isolation in a double sense. It rescues memories, but in order to get them out of the system, to vomit them into exteriority and empty them of their threat: "so the benefit must have come from the rehearsal of the experiences themselves, like writing an experience down, it fixes it, takes the hurt out of it: one remembers then that one has hurt, but not the hurt itself" (180).

The novel's truth is not a truth that can be found in exterior reality, neither is it a truth that can be represented. It emerges in an evacuation that establishes a relationship of abjection to the traces of the real in all the plenitude of detail. It gathers them in a way that deconstructs realist parameters of coherence in order to make the truth of their experiential matter emerge from the performative (textual) gathering. Thereby, the ambiguity of the evacuation extends to a possible realist project. In abjecting it, Johnson both tries to get rid of it *and* acknowledges the belief in a knowable truth of reality at its very core. But Johnson's novelistic truth is a truth of representation understood as a formative textual process. It works via the overdetermining organization of its materials and textual levels. In *Trawl*, this is paradigmatically enacted and exposed through the re-entry of the central allegories that relate the fictional setting to the narrative process and the linguistic material. The text's numerous traditional *topoi*, such as the trawling of memory, the voyage on the ship, the re-birth from the womb of the ship,[49] create a unifying structure for the text's deconstruction of mimetic order. That these allegories are rather obvious is the whole point, though. They are not only openly treated as a kind of cultural and generic baggage by the narrator but also abjected when the text at its very end turns against the same totalizing tropes that provided the motivation for its accumulation of detail.

The paradoxicality of this evacuation is summed up precisely at the cathartic moment of the text. In the triumphant moment when the narrator, having become the catch of his own trawling, hauls himself out of the womb of the ship into a therapeutic re-birth, all the major allegories are superimposed: "I climb through, up the companionway, strongly hauling myself by the arms, feeling the strength of my release in the power of my arms, for some reason, the decisiveness, the resolution, to haul myself through this hatch . . . into the air" (166–167). The appropriate counter-statement to the pathos of this teleological allegorical closure that proclaims what Blumenberg calls an "in sich einstimmigen Kontex[t]" (a univocal context)[50] comes three pages from the end by way of bathos: "what use is it pointing to this ship as a womb, for instance, as a symbol . . . and all that balls. What use would it be?" (180).

The irony between these two positions resonates right through the entire text up to its very end. Here it is not only a question of the truth of the narrator's catharsis. Whether or not he will overcome his auto-fixation and be able to take responsibility in the encounter with the other, remains crucially outside of the scope of the text. The end, though, is at least suspicious. Its circling back to the text's beginning could either indicate the progressive contrast in personality between the two framing moments of the text. Or it could indicate another turn of the screw, the same old enclosure of the I within itself. Is the narrator opening himself up to the position of the other, or is he again blaming her and shirking responsibility?

> If she had tried hard enough, of her own accord she might have tried to break my isolation in the only way it could be broken. Ginnie! But is it she? . . . It must be of her own accord, to contain, to accept the knowledge, the certainty. . . . . . I, always with I · · · · · one always starts with I · · · · · · · · And ends with I. (183)

With this fundamental irony, the text poses the alarmingly disruptive question over and over again as to how we can make sense of its accumulation of matter. If there are only conventional devices such as the allegories sanctioned by tradition that can provide the framing for an overdetermination, then how does this not lead into the mere accumulation of details that remain meaningless because there are no validated parameters for their sensible integration? If the end has not given an explicit answer to the initial question of the reasons for the feeling of isolation, then "what am I doing" (117) is more than a rhetorical question. It is the fundamental generic question of the novel's rhetoricity in relation to concepts of reality and realism, a problem that hovers between lying and estranging storytelling on the one hand and the utter estrangement of "just things, happenings: things as they are, happenings as they have happened and go on happening through the unreliable filter of my memory" (94) on the other hand, an estrangement that keeps raising the question: "But of what importance is it? Ah . . ." (88).

Through its aesthetics of evacuating abjection *Trawl* performs the openness of this question instead of providing the closure of a lying story. The abjection insists on the importance of worldly experience, with which the novel's end supplements the lack of solution: "the benefit must have come from the rehearsal of the experiences themselves, like writing an experience down, it fixes it, takes the hurt out of it: one remembers then that one has hurt, but not the hurt itself" (180). But instead of fixing it and taking the hurt out of it, abjection in the experience of a novel that is more than just a writing down, more than a fixing re-presentation of something remembered, confronts us with the way that we shape this novel's evacuations into a more or less meaningful form and position us toward it. The truth of Johnson's novel would then be this abject interrogation of the function of the novel's form.

Notes

1. See also Tracy Hargreaves, "'. . . to find a form that accommodates the mess': Truth Telling from Doris Lessing to B. S. Johnson," *Yearbook of English Studies* 42 (2012): 205, who states that post-war English writing "came to be viewed, as Nick Bentley summarizes, as 'antimodernist, anti-experimental and representing a return to traditional or conventional realist forms.' A 'crisis of writing' within a broader set of cultural crises is a not uncommon observation made about postwar literature."

2. Marshall Brown, "The Logic of Realism: A Hegelian Approach," *PMLA* 96, no. 2 (1981): 227.

3. Ibid., 228.

4. McHale, "Revisiting Realisms; Or, WWJD (What Would Jakobson Do?)," *The Journal of the Midwest Modern Language Association* 41, no. 2 (2008): 7.

5. Ibid., 7.

6. Pam Morris, *Realism*. The New Critical Idiom (London and New York: Routledge, 2003), 6.

7. Pam Morris, "Making the Case for Metonymic Realism," in *Realisms in Contemporary Culture: Theories, Politics, and Medial Configurations*, ed. Peter Auer et al. (Berlin and New York: De Gruyter, 2013), 16.

8 See also Brian Nelson, "Realism: Model or Mirage?," *Romance Studies* 1, no. 1 (1982), repr. *Romance Studies* 30, no. 3–4 (2012): 155; "The implication of these techniques is that mimetic narrative attempts to reduce, so to speak, its fictive status, to disguise its reality as a semiotic system, to close the gap between language and reality, and to suggest that form and content are easily separable one from the other."

9 Ibid.

10 Morris, *Realism*, 3.

11 Hans Blumenberg, "Wirklichkeitsbegriff und Möglichkeit des Romans," in *Nachahmung und Illusion*, ed. Hans Robert Jauß (Munich: Fink, 1964), in particular 12–13. An English translation of this text appeared as "The Concept of Reality and the Possibility of the Novel," in *New Perspectives in German Literary Criticism*, ed. Richard E. Amacher (Princeton, NJ: Princeton University Press, 1979), 29–48.

12 As with the always open context, this whole, though, can never reach a "total, final consistency" (Ibid., 33).

13 See Pam Morris, *Jane Austen, Virginia Woolf and Worldly Realism* (Edinburgh: Edinburgh University Press, 2017), 10. This promise, however, differs fundamentally from the transcendent notion of truth in Morris's earlier quote.

14 Nelson, "Realism," 155.

15 George Levine, *The Realistic Imagination. English Fiction from* Frankenstein *to* Lady Chatterley (Chicago and London: University of Chicago Press, 1981), 11.

16 Ibid., 6.

17 Ibid., 8.

18 B. S. Johnson, *Albert Angelo* (London: Picador, 2014), 170: "Faced with the enormous detail, vitality, size, of the complexity, of life, there is a great temptation for a writer to impose his own pattern which must falsify, cannot do anything other than falsify; or he invents, which is pure lying. Looking back and imposing a pattern to come to terms with the past must be avoided. Lies, lies, lies."

19 See Ibid., 175: "And another of my aims is didactic: The novel must be a vehicle for conceiving truth." It is, however, problematic to take any of these utterances as authoritative in a text that constantly contradicts, erases, and rewrites itself by assuming different positions and making this metafictionally explicit.

20 B. S. Johnson, "Introduction to *Aren't You Rather Young to Be Writing Your Memoirs?*," *Review of Contemporary Fiction* 5, no. 2 (1985): 13.

21 Ibid., 4.

22 Ibid., 5.

23 Ibid.

24 In this respect, Johnson's approach exemplifies Walter Benjamin's analysis of the novel as a symptom of modernity's epistemological fragmentation into the

"Ratlosigkeit" (perplexity, p. 442) of the isolated subject in contradistinction to the holistic and participatory experience of storytelling. See "Der Erzähler. Betrachtungen zum Werk Nicolai Lesskows," in *Gesammelte Schriften*, Vol. II, ed. Rolf Tiedemann and Hermann Schweppenhäuser (Frankfurt am Main: Suhrkamp, 1991), 438–465.

25 Johnson, "Introduction to *Aren't You Rather Young to Be Writing Your Memoirs?*," 5.

26 See Virginia Woolf, "Modern Fiction," in *The Essays of Virginia Woolf. Volume 4: 1925 to 1928*, ed. Andrew McNeille (London: The Hogarth Press, 1984), 157–164.

27 Johnson, "Introduction to *Aren't You Rather Young to Be Writing Your Memoirs?*," 6.

28 Ibid.

29 Ibid., 4.

30 Ibid.

31 Ibid.

32 B. S. Johnson, *Trawl* London: Picador, 2013), 53. All further references to this text will be made in brackets directly after the quoted passages.

33 For reasons I will specify later, I am cautious as to the narrator's self-presentation at the end of the book.

34 Philip Tew, "Early Influences and Aesthetic Emergence: *Travelling People* (1961), *Albert Angelo* (1964), *Trawl* (1966) and *The Unfortunates* (1969)," in *B. S. Johnson and Post-War Literature. Possibilities of the Avant Garde*, ed. Julia Jordan and Martin Ryle (Basingstoke: Palgrave Macmillan 2014), 25.

35 Andrew Hassam, "Literary Exploration: The Fictive Sea Journals of William Golding, Robert Nye, B. S. Johnson, and Malcolm Lowry," *Ariel* 19, no. 3 (1988): 40.

36 For the lack of chapter divisions and the typographic scansion of the text, see also Melanie Jane Seddon, "'Giving Feeling Form': B. S. Johnson's Literary Project" (PhD diss., University of Portsmouth, Portsmouth, 2016), 125.

37 Hargreaves, "Truth Telling," 217.

38 See Michel Foucault, "Of Other Spaces," trans. Jay Miskowiec, *diacritics* 16, no. 1 (1986): 27, who ends his delineation of what constitutes heterotopias precisely with the reference to ships as the paradigmatic heterotopic space: "The ship is the heterotopia par excellence. In civilizations without boats, dreams dry up, espionage takes the place of adventure, and the police take the place of pirates." For a reading of *Trawl* as a narration based on and in the heterotopic space of the ship and in the form of a ship log that fulfils the function of a heterotopia of crisis, see Seddon, "Giving Feeling Form," 123: "Through the 'different' space of the trawler ship Johnson seizes the possibility of investigating the relationships and connections of his life outside of the constraints of chronological narrative convention; time becomes warped. Such a process, like the voyage, is to be endured and is necessarily fraught with

abjection; it is a creative rite of passage aligned with Foucault's heterotopia of *crisis*, transformative but primitive."

39 For a reading of Johnson's novel based on Julia Kristeva's notion of abjection, see Seddon, "Giving Feeling Form," 131–135.

40 I am indebted to Pam Morris for pointing this colloquial meaning of trawling out to me.

41 See Julia Kristeva, *The Powers of Horror. An Essay on Abjection*, trans. Leon S. Roudiez (New York: Columbia University Press, 1982), particularly 1–13.

42 For the conceptual pairing of smooth and striated space, see Gilles Deleuze and Félix Guattari, *Thousand Plateaus. Capitalism and Schizophrenia II*, trans. Brian Massumi (Minneapolis and London: University of Minnesota Press, 1987), 361ff.

43 His status as the only dysfunctional "supernumerary passenger" marks a repetition of the narrator's failure of social integration: "I failed as a member of that group as I have failed as a member of all groups I ever joined . . . As here, too, it is repeated: For I am on this trawler, on the crew list a supernumerary, even, but not of the ship" (90–91).

44 I will discuss this central metaphor in the last section.

45 See Ian Watt, *The Rise of the Novel* (London: Chatto & Windus, 1957), 12–22.

46 See Brown, "The Logic of Realism," 231–233.

47 Nelson, "Realism," 154.

48 In the sense delineated by Gilles Deleuze's reading of Beckett in "The Exhausted," trans. Anthony Uhlmann, *SubStance* 78 (1995): 3–28.

49 For the equation of the consistently feminized ship with the mother's womb and the voyage as a rebirth that counteracts the early childhood abandonment, see Tew, "Early Influences and Aesthetic Emergence," 27. For a reading of the voyage as a *rite de passage* through a liminal phase, see Seddon, "Giving Feeling Form," 128 and 129: "*Trawl*'s imagery fixates it firmly in the liminal phase where, removed from society, original identity is discarded and a new means of defining the self must be found."

50 Blumenberg, "Wirklichkeitsbegriff und Möglichkeit des Romans," 5. This is the aim of the actualization in the third concept of reality that corresponds to the novel in Blumenberg. Instead of the important notion of the univocity of context, the English translation unfortunately only puts "*a context in itself*" (32).

7

Cultural Realism

Reconsidering Magical Realism in Louise Erdrich's *Love Medicine*

Nasrin Babakhani

> *Where there is a woman there is magic. If there is a moon falling from her mouth, she is a woman who knows her magic, who can share or not share her powers.*[1]

Realism, Magical Realism, Cultural Realism

The last three decades have seen an increased interest in magical realism as a narrative form often related to issues of cross-culturalism, postmodernism, and postcolonialism. While more than half a century has passed since the first appearance of the term "magical realism" in English, there is still no general consensus about its significance or even definition. Some critics see magical realism as a problematic trend that is either "an effect of and a vehicle for globalization"[2] or the "commercial imposition" of a cosmopolitan style "on a new generation of authors."[3] Others praise it as a way of inserting forgotten voices into realist conventions that otherwise exclude them. It is often described as a narrative strategy that subverts the line between realism and the fantastic so that supernatural events seem natural and congruent with everyday life. Yet, this definition seems to be incomplete when the literature of marginalized writers is taken into consideration, because it assumes a fundamental distinction between reality and magic, and between realism and fantasy that I want to problematize in this chapter by introducing the concept of "cultural realism."

Many "magical realist" authors, including Jack Hodgins, Gabriel Garcia Marquez, Ben Okri, Susan Power, Louise Erdrich, and Toni Morrison, have rejected the label of "magical realism" because they want to distance themselves from the often exoticized notion of magic and the fantastical approach to reality that it implies. Their arguments against magical realism raise some thought-provoking questions: What is realism? What is magical? And even more important to my discussion, who decides what is magic, what is real? The concepts of both realism and magic have changed over time and throughout different geographical places. This is the reason, I believe, that there is no agreed-upon definition of magical realism. In the following, I will look in more detail at various concepts of realism and magic to work out what I mean by "cultural realism."

According to *A Dictionary of Literary Terms and Literary Theory*, "realism is a copy of nature and reveals to us the literature of truth . . . it is clear that, according to the realist, an artist should concern himself with here and now, with everyday events, with his own environment."[4] Also, in *A Glossary of Literary Terms*, M. H. Abrams provides the following definition of realism: "representing human life and experience in literature . . . realism is said to represent life as it really is."[5] Definitions in literary dictionaries and encyclopedia tend to attribute a correlative set of qualities to realist novels: besides reflecting knowledge based on individual experience, realist novels are often marked by rational inquiry, plausible cause-and-effect-based plot structures, and well-defined, lifelike characters who usually face everyday problems in recognizable settings.

Realism is often historically dated back to the mid-nineteenth century, but it also can be traced to Aristotle's concept of "mimesis" and a more general ambition of art to perfect the imitation of nature. Nineteenth-century realism, in fact, draws attention to the connection between the concept of mimesis as a reflection of the exterior world and the projection of this coherent and detailed world in literary works. Basing his definition on Descartes' dualism and Locke's empricism, Ian Watt in *The Rise of the Novel* states that modern realism "begins from the position that truth can be discovered by the individual through the senses."[6] By this definition, the realist novel is supposed to evolve from the experiences of an individual who has liberated himself or herself—at least to a degree—from the transcendental constraints of religion, the past, and of tradition, and the representational conceptions of nature that they offered.

However, Marxist critics of realism such as Georg Lukács suggest that the concepts of experience and everydayness embedded in such definitions are products of a particular point of view or ideological orientation. For him, realism is neither the scientific objective form of "mirroring" reality, nor "empty artifices of formal experimentation."[7] Thus, unlike the nineteenth-century "emptiness of modern individualism,"[8] and unlike Ian Watt's emphasis on individual experience to understand reality, for Lukács realism portrays individuals and society as a totality. Rather than showing photographic and mechanical reality, he notes "the great realists always regard society from the viewpoint of a living and moving centre and this centre is present, visibly or invisibly, in every phenomenon."[9]

Lukács offers an important corrective to Watt, but neither social realists nor the nineteenth-century account of realism has examined the term through the lenses of colonized, marginalized people. With the publication of Roland Barthes's *S/Z*, realism was examined through a new perspective. For Barthes, realism is a system of codes that seem to signify reality only because it is so familiar and conventional. In his book, he argues that

> realism . . . consists not in copying the real but in copying a (depicted) copy of the real: this famous *reality*, as though suffering from a fearfulness which keeps it from being touched directly, is *set farther away*, postponed, or at least captured through the pictorial matrix in which it has been steeped before being put into words: code upon code, known as realism.[10]

Like Plato who sees the painter/creator at two removes from the truth of the idea, Barthes places realism as a replica of the original truth. Unlike Plato, the original form is not situated in the realms of ideas or even of nature but rather is a social phenomenon or social production that makes the texts meaningful to members of a specific society who are familiar with that signifying system. Therefore, a reader brings to the text a predetermined system of codes through which he/she can determine its meaning.

Postcolonial critics, in contrast, are concerned about the way knowledge about the Third World, the colonized subjects, is produced. For many of them the concept "real" or "reality" is problematic in a postcolonial context because it depends on the "pact between writer and readers," to borrow from Durix.[11] Therefore, what appears magical—or unrealistic—to the colonizers might seem quotidian or part of everyday life to the colonized/oppressed. With this in mind, Catherine Belsey describes twentieth-century realism in these terms: "realism is plausible not because it reflects the world, but because it is constructed out of what is familiar."[12] Finally, as Allison Lee notes, "realism has little to do with reality. It is, rather, a critical construct which developed in a particular social and ideological context."[13]

The ideological perspectives embedded in the concept of realism become even more evident when comparing realism to magic. To some critics, "magic" means escapism, a refutation of the real. For Patricia Hart, for instance, the magic within "magical realism" is best defined as "any phenomenon in the narrative that goes beyond what we understand as natural law."[14] It is not clear who "we" refers to in this account, whether only white men or women in the United States? Scholars such as Caroline Rody have argued: "fictional magic is not simply an efflorescence of the anti-rational elements of an indigenous culture or region; neither does a narrative mix of magic and realism merely imitate a strange cultural encounter."[15] For her, magic expresses a postcolonial attitude toward colonialism: "Magic works to figure the shaping persistence of colonial history in the postcolonial present ... [it] breaks down the realist barriers that would keep such potent history at a distance."[16] Exposing a reductive Western understanding of magic as anti-rational, Matthew Potolsky reminds us that "recent anthropologists have suggested that the entire category of magic is an artefact of European ethnocentrism, for which any unfamiliar forms of thought are defective or primitive rather than simply different."[17] These arguments reveal the fact that the concepts of realism and magic have changed throughout history and carry different meanings depending on the context in which they are mobilized. Unsurprisingly perhaps, there is no general agreement on their definition and signification.

A typology developed by William Spindler in 1996 recognizes three different kinds of magical realism. The first is "metaphysical magic realism" in which "a familiar scene is described as if it were something new and unknown."[18] This mode helps us see the metaphysics of the ordinary, which is to say the number of unnoticed assumptions that always go into our construction of reality, by provoking a sense of unreality in the readers or viewers. Examples of this kind include Franz Kafka's *Das Schloß* (1926), Joseph Conrad's *Heart of Darkness* (1899), and Patrick Süskind's *Das Parfüm* (1985). Next in Spindler's typology comes "anthropological magic realism ... which describes texts where two contrasting views of the world (one 'rational' and one 'magical') are presented as if they were not contradictory, by resorting to the myths and beliefs of ethnocultural groups for whom this contradiction does not arise."[19] Spindler argues that this form of magical realism corresponds to Latin American literature and is synonymous with Alejo Carpentier's notions of *lo real maravilloso*, the "marvellous real" of Latin American landscapes and cultural syncretism; however, Spindler believes that anthropological magical realism is a better description of this type. This is exemplified in the works of Jorge Luis Borges, Alejo Carpentier, Carlos Fuentes, Gabriel García Márquez, and Isabel Allende, to name a few. Lastly, Spindler introduces a third type of magical realism, which he describes as "ontological," which is defined by being "without recourse to any particular cultural perspective."[20] This type of magical realism blurs the line between reality, magic, and the supernatural so that no convincing explanation is given for supernatural events. The fantastic, in this mode, becomes indistinguishable from ordinary and everyday life. Kafka's *Die Verwandlung* (1916) is an example of this type.

In the terms proposed by Spindler's typology, my study focuses on anthropological magical realism. However, I will substitute the term "cultural realism" for "anthropological" magical realism because I find Spindler's terminology, and the assumptions behind it, problematic. Spindler claims that anthropological magical realism represents two different world views, one "rational" and one "magical." In the same way, Amaryll Beatrice Chanady's frequently cited book *Magical Realism and the Fantastic*, repeatedly claims that magical realism shows two opposing perspectives which are rational and irrational, natural and supernatural, "primitive" and "enlightened."[21] I would like to argue that the denomination "magical" realism, rather than providing a fusion, maintains a binary opposition between magic and realism, which—perhaps inadvertently—reproduces the valorization of Western science and Cartesian subjectivity over other forms of knowledge and identity. Likewise, many literary scholars and critics, consciously or not, label the cultural traditions of ethnic groups—Latin American, Native American, and African American—as irrational, supernatural, superstitious, primitive, and unreal. They, therefore, put the ethnic groups' cultural traditions on the inferior side of the rationality/irrationality binary to justify a hegemonic mode of reading and writing the world. Such labels impose a colonial set of distinctions on the literature of colonized people. In this, I position my argument with Alejo Carpentier's concept of *lo real maravilloso*, which insists that a "marvellous reality" was a fundamental feature of Latin America and "essentially" present there. He believes that magical realism was rooted in Latin American nature and culture, connected to the tangible reality of their lives. In his definition of *lo real maravilloso*, there is no binary opposition between rationality/irrationality, natural/supernatural, enlightened/primitive. For him, in Latin America "the strange is commonplace, and always was commonplace."[22] I would like to suggest that Carpentier sees magic in Latin America as an aspect of realism because magic—the "marvellous"—is part of everyday experience. Scholars who do not share the indigenous perspective tend to demystify the magic or reduce it to the status of an anthropological code. I am employing Carpentier's idea about *lo real maravilloso* to develop my own notion of cultural realism in different cultural contexts. Thus, I think what has been called magical can be interpreted as a strategic turn to magic in the service of an alternative cultural tradition. In this usage, cultural realism, to which I will return later, is a means of voicing cultural difference rather than simply a recent installment of a familiar cultural code.

While traditional realism may well thematize idiosyncrasies, irrationalities, and absurdities (most notably in Dickens) in modern European culture, it typically encodes reality with a dualist worldview that is rationalistic, scientific, and empirical. In that respect, historically, realism was related to imperial form[23] and its binaries of self and other, male and female, rationality and superstition. Cultural realism draws heavily on aspects of the marginalized culture such as folklore, myth, ritual, legend, oral tradition, and so on, as a means of resisting cultural oppression. These marginalized elements of culture are labeled "magical" by the dominant worldview. However, I believe that when magic is matched with myths and folklores of ethnic groups, the aim is neither to create a supernatural or magical effect nor is it simply escapism. Rather, the "magical" element in magical realism represents another layer of reality which points to the relevance of group experience, collective memory, and traditions, against the empiricism of individual perception. I would like to insist on the reality of cultural traditions, which, like many aspects of culture, do not have to be scientifically "true" in order to be "real." Many people who live on the "wrong" side of the political, gender, race, or class lines, such as Latin Americans, African Americans, or Native Americans, turn to this narrative mode as a strategy to express cultural traditions that have been deemed irrelevant or "unreal" by those defining what matters.

Drawing on a shared tradition cannot mean that Native American cultures are primitive and dedicated to otherworldly magic as opposed to reality. To prevent such hierarchies and binaries, which are central to definitions of magical realism and realism, I favor the term "cultural realism." I also reject the idea that the primary purpose of retelling cultural tradition stories is to return to the "native" culture or preserve it. In other words, writing from her ethnocultural background or calling her writing style "cultural realism" does not mean that a writer like Louise Erdrich is a regionalist or nativist. On the contrary, she reinvents old traditions to present narratives that are counter-historical, decolonial, anti-racist, and anti-patriarchal. Thus, cultural realism is neither an argument about cultural determinism or relativism. It is an argument about how culture helps transform what is real by reinventing traditions and inviting people from all sorts of different backgrounds to regard the world in new, potentially non-antagonistic ways.

I will illustrate the workings of cultural realism with a reading of Louise Erdrich's first critically acclaimed novel *Love Medicine*, published in 1984. Erdrich, like many other "magical" realists, expresses her dissatisfaction at being labeled magical realist when she says: "The thing is, the events people pick out as magical don't seem unreal to me. Unusual, yes, but I was raised believing in miracles and hearing of true events that may seem unbelievable."[24] If we would like to adopt a term that acknowledges both the cultural and the literary specificity of this type of realism in her writing, I suggest that we adopt cultural realism, as Erdrich evokes and elaborates some key aspects of Native American culture such as storytelling, the oral tradition, specific rituals, including love medicine, and the trickster narrative when she describes what does not seem unreal to her. However, she reworks these traditions to uproot the fundamental issues which still impede contemporary Native Americans. In my conception, cultural realism goes beyond affirming its cultural relevance; it also articulates an alternative representation of history and becomes a highly political literary device. If the reality is magical in this novel, it is not because it is about necromancy, spell, or the supernatural; it is because it points to the feminist and cultural realities that seem magical from a literary tradition that privileges patriarchy, individualism, and rationalism. Thus, I will point to the ways in which reality becomes magical from a decolonial perspective of cultural realism.

Cultural realism is political because it is collective, and the collective, I would like to argue, always seems magical to an individualist. Erdrich deliberately taps into a non-individualistic perspective, and thus an alternative form of realism, to write about Native Americans whose stories are "unrepresented or misrepresented in traditional historical narratives."[25] While Faris claims that "history is the weight that tethers the balloon of magic,"[26] I think the history of colonization inflates the balloon of magic. In other words, magic helps Erdrich portray the real and collective experiences of contemporary Native American survivors. In *Love Medicine*, the magic articulates collective memories, shared past and present experiences, and a cultural sense of community. In what follows, I would like to examine how magic manifests itself in the forms of memory and solidarity in *Love Medicine*.

Love Medicine as Cultural Realism

Love Medicine, as its title indicates, is based on a Native American love ritual and focuses on the relationships between couples, families, and the community. It presents the peripheral lives of several Native American families, the Kashpaws, Morrisseys, Lazarres, and the Nanapushes, whose members have interconnected relationships. With multiple narrators and nonlinear plots, *Love Medicine* narrates the process of healing through so-called magical elements. The first episode of *Love Medicine* begins with the description of a Chippewa woman, June Kashpaw, "walking down the clogged main street of oil boomtown Williston, North Dakota, killing time before the noon bus arrived that would take her home."[27] While killing time, she meets a man who "looked familiar like a lot of people looked familiar to her. *She had seen so many come and go*" (1, emphasis added). She spends time at a bar with the man, a mud engineer, named Andy. After meeting him at the bar, she thinks, "he could be different" (3). While she hesitates as to whether she wants to have sex with him or not, in her loneliness, she feels her "pure naked body," she, then, decides to be with him "even if he was no different" (4). Finally, "far out of town on a county road" (4), she let him have sex with her. When he fell asleep on top of her, June felt that "she would crack wide open not in one place but in many pieces . . . she thought to pull herself back together" (6). Instead of returning to the city and taking the bus, she decides to walk home through the watery road. Despite the freezing weather, even after her heart stopped and her skin became cold, "the pure and naked part of her went on" (7). The first chapter is closed with June's voluntary walk toward death: "The snow fell deeper that Easter than it had in forty years, but June walked over it like water and came home" (7). To be precise, June's deliberate choice to walk into stormy weather to return home is an act of committing suicide, but she may also find her action as a possible solution "to pull herself back together" (7). Although she is dead, the pure and naked part of her continued the road like water and came home. Allison E. Brown reads her journey as not only "spiritual and traditional" but also "supernatural, ghostly, and mythic."[28] However, from a cultural realist perspective, her journey is neither magical nor impossible. If we agree with Allison E. Brown that June's journey after her death is part of traditional Chippewa worldviews[29] and interpret her homecoming as a part of Chippewa cultural reality, it is also magical and collective, for her death and her memory become a metaphor for the whole community to reconstruct their lives. Her spirit and memory haunt the characters because what happens to her affects the whole community. Paula Gunn Allen argues that "the roots of oppression are to be found in the loss of tradition and memory."[30] bell hooks has made the same point when she writes: "Memory sustains a spirit of resistance."[31] As both Allen and hooks declare outright, memory is a strategy of resistance. In *Love Medicine*, magic often emphasizes the necessity of sustaining memory whether of a woman, June, who does not die but goes home, or of a collective Native American community who has the shared experience of perpetual colonization. Indeed, the memory of June and the mourning for her death and, later in the novel, for Nector's death become the most important magical part of the novel.

June's memory magically haunts not only Albertine, her niece, but also the rest of the community. The novel uses magical remembrance to address the complex landscape of trauma and memory. Jan Assmann argues that "memory is the faculty that enables us to form an awareness of selfhood (identity), both on the personal and on the collective level."[32] Assmann examines memory at two different levels: on the "inner level" and the "social level." He believes that Sigmund Freud's and Carl Gustav Jung's concept of collective memory still remains at the inner or personal level, as it digs into the unconscious of the human psyche. On the "inner level," June's memory is with Albertine before she finalizes her decision to return to the reservation after two months. While she is driving to the reservation, the sight of the lands reveals another side of her memory, which is collective. She thinks: "The policy of allotment was a joke ... I saw as usual how much of the reservation was sold to whites and lost forever!" (12). Although she feels at home in the reservation with her family, she is also conscious of its marginalized position politically, socially, and economically. She is aware of the exploitation and oppression of the tribes by whites and its impact on the collective memory of Native Americans. What the imperialist has done throughout history is to repress Native Americans' version of history and memory as grounded in their language, culture, and landscape. Albertina's first-person women-centered narration, however, taps into the collective memory of Native Americans who carry the burden of traumatic colonial practices.

On the social level, Albertine's memory needs social interactions and communications with other people on the reservation. Through these interactions, she notices her grandfather, Nector, who graduated from a white boarding school, loses his memory in his old age. His brother Eli, who lived in the woods and has no educational background, is still sharp. Albertine concludes his grandfather's loss of memory "was a protection from past, absolving him from whatever had happened"(19–20). She, then, explains, "His great-grand son King Junior, was happy because he hadn't yet acquired a memory while perhaps Grandpa's happiness was in losing his" (20). Loss of memory, therefore, becomes a source of joy.

Albertine emphasizes the power of the past and memory through stories not only on the inner level but also on social and collective. When she says of June: "She told me things you'd only tell another woman, full grown, and I had adored her wildly for . . . telling me everything she needed to tell, and it was true, I hadn't understood the words at the time. But she hadn't counted on my memory. Those words stayed with me" (17). As I have already mentioned, according to Allen, loss of memory and one's own past equates to a loss of self. Put differently, knowing about the past is the key to understanding oneself, the present, and even the future. Thus, the narrative device of cultural realism allows Erdrich to reveal other layers of representation of history and memory, which is not "merely" magical but also highly political.

The practices of remembrance for Marie Kashpaw have also worked at both the levels of the personal and the social. She remembers the time when she becomes the protégé of Sister Leopolda, a nun in the convent located outside of the reservation. Marie envisions a day when she will become a saint, and everybody kneels before her. After torturing by Leopolda who tries to exorcize the demon or the "Dark One" out of her, she falls unconscious. It was when Marie's memory stops responding: "I began to forget it; I couldn't hold on. I begin to wonder if she'd really scalded me with the kettle. I could not remember. To remember this seemed the most important thing in the world" (55). After Marie falls unconscious, Leopolda stabs her. To conceal the attack, she tells the other nuns that Marie has had a vision and ascribes the scars to miraculous stigmata. Thus, when Marie regains consciousness, Leopolda and other sisters kneel beside her. After repeated violence, Marie ends up fleeing from the convent. On her way back to the reservation, she encounters Nector Kashpaw, the tribe's chairman. Although Nector was in love with Lulu, he cannot resist Marie's enchantment and power. Marie then loses her virginity to Nector. This is how Nector takes her wounded hand in his and marries her. Marie's memories question the idea of Christian saintliness and magic learned in the convent. Instead, she becomes an Indian "saint" by doing some normal down-to-earth actions such as adopting other people's children or helping her husband to stabilize his authority as the chairman of the Chippewa Tribe.

In her old age, Marie's perceptions are tuned higher than what is fathomable, astonishing her grandson Lipsha with her powerful memory and impossible knowledge (240). Lipsha—June and Gerry Nanapush's son—believes that Marie's Chippewa blood gives her this magical power. Lipsha thinks if he asks her how she knows the things people do not, "she'll say she just had a feeling or ache in the scar of her hand or a creak in her shoulder. She is constantly being told things by little aggravations in her joints or by her household appliances" (240). Indeed, her magical vision overcomes saintliness. She gains a sense of herself as a person separate from her adolescent vision of saint but unites with her community and Chippewa culture.

Another aspect of Native American culture that Erdrich adopts in *Love Medicine* is the trickster. Critics seem to agree that some characters in the novel share the features of tricksters. Julie Barak proposes that "Nanapush, is one of the linguistic variants of the name of the Chippewa trickster. This name is shared by two other characters in the text: Lulu Nanapush, and her son Gerry Nanapush."[33] Before proceeding to examine Lulu and Gerry as trickster figures, I shall propose a working definition of the trickster. Paul Radin views the trickster as "the oldest of all figures in American Indian mythology, probably in all mythologies."[34] He goes on to explain some characteristics of tricksters in Indian American tribes. He believes that a trickster is always wandering, always hungry, has no normal conceptions of good or evil, is highly sexed, and has some divine traits.[35] For Jeanne Rosie Smith trickster is "a symbol of cultural survival,"[36] and according to her "tricksters are uninhibited by social constraints, free to dissolve boundaries and break taboos."[37] Victor Turner believes the trickster is "betwixt and between," in a "liminal" position that accommodates his/her ability to transgress boundaries.[38] Manzanas, Sanchéz, and Semal make a similar argument, calling tricksters "double-sided characters [who] act as mediators between this world and the other, between men and gods, and between the rational and the intuitive."[39] As border-crossing figures, tricksters disrupt the binary models of cultures often deployed in realist aesthetics. In other words, through a trickster aesthetic, a broader cultural aspect of reality is engendered.

Lulu is admittedly a trickster who uses sex to outwit the conditions and limits imposed on Native culture. Apparently, Lulu is known for her seduction of most of the town's men and for having sex with whomever she wants (see 231). She feels a superhuman love in her heart, which gives her strength and magical power. Her ability to "love the whole world" introduces her as a trickster figure. Like a conjurer, she is presented as both a human being and a goddess. Her "betwixt and between" position allows her to be a matriarch with an autonomous life; in other words, she is politically empowered. As a young woman, she goes off to the island where she can meet Moses Pillager, who is described as a "ghost" or an invisible person: "Nobody saw him" (75). The closest character to the Native American tribal culture, Moses is a trickster figure who is identified as "Old Man Pillager" (123). She chooses "Old Man Pillager" as her first lover, a perfect embodiment of Native American tribal culture. When Lulu meets him for the first time, she describes him as follows: "He was surprising, so beautiful to look at that I couldn't tell his age.... My mother's face was like that—too handsome to be real, constructed by Manitous" (77). Lulu's union with Moses both spiritually and sexually gives birth to the legendary Chippewa trickster, Gerry Nanapush.

Nanapush heritage has been passed on to Gerry Nanapush by Lulu and Moses. Whenever Gerry is captured by the police, he escapes, as if by magic, through the holes or windows. Quite literally, no jail can hold him. As I have mentioned earlier, critics largely seem to agree that Gerry Nanapush is a trickster figure. Alan Velie notes, "Gerry Nanapush is clearly a modern avatar of the trickster. Not only is he the consummate player of tricks (his miraculous escapes, for instance), but Nanapush is the name of the Chippewa Trickster Hare."[40] Because of his repeated escapes not only from prison but also from the confinement of dominant white American culture, Lydia A. Schultz calls him a "folk hero to the Native American community."[41] She continues to argue that Gerry "openly accepts his role as folk hero and trickster by becoming active in the leadership of AIM (American Indian Movement), challenging his people to seek a clear cultural identity."[42] By becoming active in the leadership of the AIM, he is chased and captured by the police, but each time he escapes "magically" through holes or windows— no jail can hold him. His son, Lipsha, describes him as a man "who could fly. He could strip and flee and change into shapes of swift release. Owls and bees, two-toned Ramblers, buzzards, cottontails, and motes of dust. These forms were interchangeable with his" (361). In the trickster figure, political resilience/resistance and magical powers become indistinguishable in a cultural realism that may be liminal to the ontologies of realism, but by no means simply antithetical to it. The trickster figures change the concept of reality by crossing back and forth between cultures, times, and spaces. The fluidity of the trickster, in other words, signifies the uncertainty and inconsistency of postcolonial American reality. The modern avatars of tricksters, Lulu and Gerry, transfer and transform Native American myth, tradition, and memory into postcolonial modernity. They, thereby, have a leading role to play in the multivocal, decentralizing aspects of the novel.

Nanapush heritage has also been passed on to Lipsha—Gerry and June's son and Lulu's grandson—who has the power of "touch" or healing. He describes his power as follows: "I am sometimes blessed with the talent to touch the sick and heal their individual problems without ever knowing what they are. I have some powers which, now that I think of it, was likely come down from Old Man Pillager" (341). However, he loses and regains the touch power repeatedly in the novel. His magical ability becomes weak or useless when his connection with the past, family, and community is broken. Yet, he is a healer when he maintains such a connection. An example of this is seen in an episode when Marie asks Lipsha's love medicine to win Nector's heart. Lipsha knows that "love medicine is something of an old Chippewa specialty" (241) and he must ask "Old Lady Pillager" (250) for advice. Since he is afraid of her, "like everybody else," he thinks to perform the ritual by himself. Unable to hunt the wild geese necessary for the ritual, Lipsha replaces frozen turkey's heart from the supermarket to do the ritual. When Marie and Lipsha ask Nector to eat the turkey heart, he chokes on it and dies. Lipsha seems impotent in the face of such a disaster, he thinks: "My touch had gone worthless" (250). Lipsha is convinced that the fake frozen turkey, which corrupts the Chippewa medicine, is responsible.

After Nector's funeral, his ghost appears first to Marie, then to Lipsha, and Lulu. For Marie, the reason why Nector's ghost returns is obvious. Marie credits love medicine as an effective remedy: "It [love medicine] was stronger than we thought. He came back even after death to claim me to his side" (255). When the ghost appears to Lipsha, he tries to persuade him to return where he belongs and wonders why the ghost comes back. He observes that it is not his medicine that brings him back, rather Nector's true love for Marie makes him return to the living world. Lipsha says: "Love medicine ain't what brings him back to you, Grandma. . . . It's true feeling, not no magic. No supermarket heart could have brought him back" (214). Thus, for Lipsha neither the reality of the existence of the ghost nor the reality of his touch is an issue. He reassures Marie that love has a power that does not have to be real to be true, even if it goes beyond the rational-scientific perspective. The magic, here called into question as such by its very practitioner, expresses a sense of bonding that is essential to this community and central to any realist projection of its practices. The attempt at magic succeeds despite its apparent failure: Nector's death allows the rivalry between the women, Marie and Lulu, to resolve into harmony, allowing each woman to fulfill her potential as a strong matriarch. It seems to me that Erdrich deliberately sacrifices a male character, Nector, whose memory is lost, to give women more power. Thus, the magic resurfaces in the shape of women's solidarity.

In that sense, the real magical ritual in *Love Medicine* seems to be sacrificing Nector, because it serves these women as a remedy to their pains. Mourning the man they both love helps build a closer relationship between the two women. It was after Nector's death that Marie volunteers to put eye drops into Lulu's eye. When Marie visits Lulu, she says: "Somebody had to put the tears into your eyes" (297). Lulu reports their visit as follows: "We mourned [Nector] the same way together. . . . For the first time I saw exactly how another woman felt, and it gave me deep comfort, surprising. It gave me the knowledge that whatever had happened . . . in the past, would finally be over once the bandages came off" (297). When Marie puts the eye drops, Lulu describes her "like a dim mountain, huge and blurred, the way a mother must look to her just-born child" (297). It is here that the novel's title gives one of its indications: Lulu did not weep throughout her life despite all the tragedies; she regains the ability to weep through Marie's love who cares for her like a mother for a child. Only when Lulu feels another woman's feelings, does she heal. Put differently, their solidarity is a magical achievement generated by love medicine.

The magic in Erdrich's *Love Medicine* appears and disappears several times, like Lipsha's touch power. Lipsha's practice of magic has to fail in order to empower the women—Lulu and Marie—who led the tribe after Nector's death. Even though Lipsha has magical abilities, which he frequently loses, he admits that his power comes from the connection he has with the other women: "I have some powers which, now that I think of it, was likely come down from Old Man Pillager. And then there is the newfound fact of insight inherited from Lulu, as well as the familiar teachings of Grandma Kashpaw on visioning what comes to pass within a lump of tinfoil" (341). According to what he says, his magical ability, then, comes from his relationship with both his ancestors, Old Man Pillager, and his grandmothers, Lulu and Marie, and hence they become the real source of his power. They not only have the ability of magical vision but also have social and political influence on the reservation. It is after Nector's death that Marie and Lulu become active in politics on behalf of Indian Affairs and manage to advise Lyman, Lulu's son, on his enterprise to set into motion a tribal souvenir factory.

Conclusion

In *Love Medicine*, Erdrich decolonizes the realist modes of storytelling by deconstructing the world of magic and reality. Magic conveys neither supernatural effect nor escapism but transmutes into women's memory, solidarity, and collectivity. Thus, instead of reinforcing the colonial either/or dichotomies and binary oppositions, Erdrich modifies the older Native American rituals like love medicine and trickster narrative to empower women and to achieve her political, feminist, and social concerns. In this sense, decolonization does not involve a return to Native American culture but rather it provides women with the chance to dismiss racial stereotypes and gain power.

In an interview conducted by Chavkin, Erdrich says, "I am on the edge, have always been on the edge, flourish on the edge, and I don't think I belong anywhere else."[43] Erdrich's representation of the "edge" is not a passive attitude, but rather resists colonial domination and cultural loss. It is from this site that she explores Native Americans' personal and national history as colonized people. The women in the novel are from the margin, yet they are not passive, powerless victims. By emphasizing the magic of memory and collectivity at both personal and social levels, Erdrich tells "the stories of contemporary Native American survivors"[44] whose histories are lost, and memories are denied or repressed. Erdrich deploys what I call cultural realism as a literary mode by drawing on stories from Native American cultural traditions such as the presence of the trickster figures, touch and vision power, or powerful matriarchs. However, Erdrich's narrative presents no fantastic or supernatural outcome, but the reality of complex cultural formations through the reality of love medicine. Without conveying any superior/inferior binaries, cultural realism is a highly political narrative mode as it explores the individual and collective memory of Native Americans. Thus, in this cultural realist narrative, magic often emphasizes memory and mourning in order to deepen and strengthen the bonds between individuals and the community.

In the final episode of the novel, Lipsha helps his father, Gerry Nanapush, escape to Canada. When the police fail to recapture and return him to prison, Lipsha comments: "I knew my dad would get away. He could fly" (361). Lipsha drives him to Canada, where he can join his wife and his child. While he drives June's car, he stops the car in the middle of the bridge to remember the traditional Native American ritual of "how the old ones used to offer tobacco to the water" (361). The thought of ritual evokes the strong memories of June and he resolves that "there was nothing to do but cross the water, and bring her home" (361). Erdrich closes the novel as she opens it with the magical image of June's homecoming. Her homecoming acts like a love medicine that helps her to heal even after her death. Perhaps she can find it in the reservation where people can offer the community. These real powers of community figures as magical, but only because they cannot otherwise be comprehended through a Eurocentric prism that identifies realism with an ethical and aesthetic emphasis on individual perspective. Against this limited conception of realism, cultural realism offers the power of collectivity, collaboration, and resistance. Only to a perspective trained in individualism does this really seem magical.

Notes

1. Ntozake Shange, *Sassafrass, Cypress & Indigo* (New York: St. Martin's Press, 1982), 3.
2. Michael Valdez Moses, "Magical Realism at World's End," *Literary Imagination* 3, no. 1 (2001): 105–133.
3. Wendy B. Faris, *Ordinary Enchantments: Magical Realism and the Remystification of Narrative* (Nashville, TN: Vanderbilt University Press, 2004), 62.

4 John Anthony Cuddon, *A Dictionary of Literary Terms and Literary Theory* (Malden, MA: John Wiley & Sons, 2012), 591.
5 Meyer Howard Abrams and Geoffrey Harpham, *A Glossary of Literary Terms* (Stamford, CT: Cengage Learning, 2014), 303.
6 Ian Watt, *The Rise of the Novel: Studies in Defoe, Richardson and Fielding* (Berkeley: University of California Press, 1962), 88–90.
7 Georg Lukács, "Narrate or Describe?" in *Writer and Critic and Other Essays*, trans. and ed. Artur Kahn (London: Merlin Press, 1971): 133.
8 Georg Lukács, *Studies in European Realism* (New York: Grosset & Dunlap, 1974), 240.
9 Lukács, "Narrate or Describe?" 145.
10 Roland Barthes, *S/Z*, trans. R. Miller (New York: Farrar Straus and Giroux, 1974), 55.
11 Jean-Pierre Durix, *Mimesis, Genres and Postcolonial Discourse: Deconstructing Magic Realism* (New York: Palgrave Macmillan, 1998), 73.
12 Catherine Belsey, *Critical Practice* (London and New York: Methuen, 1998), 40.
13 Alison Lee, *Realism and Power: Postmodern British Fiction* (London: Routledge, 1990), 30.
14 Patricia Hart, "Narrative Magic in the Fiction of Isabel Allende," PhD diss. (The University of North Carolina at Chapel Hill, 1987), 19.
15 Caroline Rody, *The Daughter's Return: African-American and Caribbean Women's Fictions of History* (New York: Oxford University Press, 2001), 64.
16 Ibid., 65.
17 Matthew Potolsky, *Mimesis* (London: Routledge, 2006), 139.
18 William Spindler, "Magic Realism: A Typology," *Forum for Modern Language Studies* 29, no. 1 (1993): 79.
19 Ibid., 78.
20 Ibid., 82.
21 Amaryll Beatrice Chanady, *Magical Realism and the Fantastic: Resolved versus Unresolved Antinomies* (New York: Garland Press, 1985), 21–22.
22 Alejo Carpentier, "On the Marvelous Real in America: Magic Realism," in *Magical Realism: Theory, History, Community*, ed. Lois Parkinson Zamora and Wendy B. Faris (Durham, NC: Duke University Press, 1995), 104.
23 Nicolas Guilhot, "Imperial Realism: Post-War IR Theory and Decolonisation," *The International History Review* 36, no. 4 (2014): 698–720.
24 Nancy Feyl Chavkin and Allan Chavkin, "An Interview with Louise Erdrich (1993)," in *Conversations with Louise Erdrich and Michael Dorris*, ed. Allan Chavkin and Nancy Feyl Chavkin (Jackson: University of Mississippi Press, 1994), 221.
25 Nancy J. Peterson, "History, Postmodernism, and Louise Erdrich's *Tracks*," *PMLA* 109, no. 5 (1994): 984.

26 Wendy B. Faris, "Scheherazade's Children: Magical Realism and Postmodern Fiction," in *Magical Realism: Theory, History, Community*, ed. Lois Parkinson Zamora and Wendy B. Faris (Durham, NC: Duke University Press, 1995), 169–170.
27 Louise Erdrich, *Love Medicine*. Expanded (New York: Henry Holt and Company, 1993), 1. Subsequent references in parantheses.
28 Allison E. Brown, "Blood Re(a)d: Native American Literature and the Emergence of the Mythic Real," in *Moments of Magical Realism in US Ethnic Literatures*, ed. Lyn Di Iorio Sandín and Richard Perez (Basingstoke: Palgrave Macmillan, 2012), 201.
29 Ibid., 201–203.
30 Paula Gunn Allen, *The Sacred Hoop: Recovering the Feminine in American Indian Traditions* (Boston: Beacon Press, 1992), 280.
31 bell hooks, *Black Looks, Race, and Representation* (Boston: South End Press, 1992), 191.
32 Jan Assmann, "Communicative and Cultural Memory," in *Cultural Memory Studies. An International and Interdisciplinary Handbook*, ed. Astrid Erll and Ansgar Nünning (Berlin and New York: De Gruyter, 2008), 109.
33 Julie Barak, "Blurs, Blends, Berdaches: Gender Mixing in the Novels of Louise Erdrich," *Studies in American Indian Literatures* 8, no. 3 (1996): 57.
34 Paul Radin, *The Trickster: A Study in American Indian Mythology* (New York: Philosophical Library, Inc., 1956), 164.
35 Ibid., 155.
36 Jeanne Rosier Smith, *Writing Tricksters: Mythic Gambols in American Ethnic Fiction* (Berkeley: University of California Press, 1997), 23.
37 Ibid., 7.
38 Victor W. Turner, "Betwixt and Between: The Liminal Period in Rites de Passage," in *The Forest of Symbols: Aspects of Ndembu Ritual*, ed. Victor W. Turner (Ithaca, NY: Cornell University Press, 1967), 576.
39 Jesús Benito Sánchez, Ana María Manzanas, and Begoña Simal, *Uncertain Mirrors: Magical Realisms in US Ethnic Literatures* (Amsterdam: Rodopi, 2009), 143.
40 Alan Velie, "The Trickster Novel," in *Narrative Chance: Postmodern Discourse on Native American Indian Literatures*, ed. Gerald Vizenor (Albuquerque: University of New Mexico Press, 1989), 122.
41 Lydia A Schultz, "Fragments and Ojibwe Stories: Narrative Strategies in Louise Erdrich's *Love Medicine*," *College Literature* 18, no. 3 (1991): 89.
42 Ibid.
43 Chavkin and Chavkin, "An Interview with Louise Erdrich," 111.
44 Ibid.

8

Narrative as Realistic Thinking

Kai Wiegandt

What is the benefit of embedding ideas in narratives? This chapter proposes that a specific answer to this question—because it allows the reader to think them realistically—can be found in contemporary literature. To present ideas realistically, contemporary works suggest, means presenting them in the conditions which allow them to exist in the first place: embodied by someone and embedded in history and culture. The chapter consists of two parts. In the first part, I outline the realism proposed in J. M. Coetzee's *Elizabeth Costello* (2003).[1] "Realism" does not refer here to a period in literary history nor to a mode of narrative that attempts to stay close to the facts of a historical time and place. Realism is Coetzee's term for an attitude toward ontology and epistemology that considers ideas inseparable from the things or people that embody them and from the situations in which these things or people are embedded. Realism is characteristic of narrative, but not of philosophical or scientific discourse, insofar as only narrative, by conveying the qualia of experience, allows the reader to think ideas in these conditions. In the second part, I read Rachel Cusk's *Outline* trilogy (2014–18) as an engagement with this notion of narrative realism. Like *Elizabeth Costello*, the trilogy sometimes breaks with realism as a conventional mode of evoking reality, but at the same time affirms realism as the ability of narrative to present ideas realistically. In contrast to *Elizabeth Costello*, however, Cusk's trilogy suggests that our ideas (including our idea of self) are culturally shared rather than unique to each of us because our thinking is inflected by similar historical-cultural coordinates.

Elizabeth Costello

J. M. Coetzee's book *Elizabeth Costello* consists of eight so-called lessons and a postscript. The lessons feature lectures on a range of topics from "Realism" (the first lesson) to "The Novel in Africa," "The Problem of Evil," and "Eros." At the book's center are two lessons called "The Philosophers and the Animals" and "The Poets and the Animals," which together are called "The Lives of Animals." All lectures are given by a character called Elizabeth Costello, an elderly and highly regarded Australian novelist best known for her novel *The House on Eccles Street*. Costello's lectures are embedded in narratives about her. In the case of "The Lives of Animals," for example, Costello is welcomed by her son John, who is the focalizer of the narrative and who happens to teach at a US college that will honor Costello at an award ceremony. Costello has a meal with John's wife Norma and the couple's children, during which her ostentatious vegetarianism is a thorn in Norma's side. John notices how much his mother has aged during the last two years; he escorts her from one event to the next, including the lecture, a dinner with members of the faculty, and a workshop with faculty and students the next day. This frame narrative inflects the reader's interpretation of Costello's lecture, and implicitly raises the question of whether we can understand Costello's ideas if we understand them without reference to her person.

At the most fundamental level, Costello's lecture on "The Philosophers and the Animals" aims at devaluing reason as a criterion of comparison between humans and animals. It instead aims to draw attention to the shared embodiedness of animals and humans. Both exist not only *in* a body but *as* that body. If humans did not shy away from what they share with animals, Costello suggests, this would elicit an attitude toward animals that would not allow for meat factories. She argues that philosophers have not *wanted* to acknowledge what humans and animals have in common. Augustine, for example, defines God as reason, and since humans are created in the image of God, they too are endowed with reason, whereas animals are not. Costello rejects the centrality of reason advanced by Augustine's argument and cites the example of the Indian intuitive mathematician Srinivasa Ramanujan, a self-taught man who presented ground-breaking mathematical results with no notion of mathematical proof or demonstration. It took professional mathematicians years of intellectual labor to prove the validity of his results. The lesson of Costello's anecdote is this: although Ramanujan's mind seems to be more closely affiliated with reason than the minds of most humans, we do not think of Ramanujan as closer to God and certainly not as more human than others—despite the fact that we tend to fetishize reason as human essence. If reason and humanity should not be seen in too close a conjunction, the reader is prompted to ask: Why should the gulf between humans and animals be insurmountable?[2]

For Costello, the example of the psychologist Wolfgang Köhler illuminates with particular clarity how an experimental focus on reason misjudges creatures under observation. Between 1908 and 1920, Köhler conducted experiments on the mental capabilities of primates for the Prussian Academy of Sciences, testing chimpanzees' ability to pile crates on top of one another. The primates had to reach bananas dangling from the cage ceiling or use a stick in order to fetch bananas lying outside the cage. With each of these experiments Köhler's primates were forced to think of themselves exclusively as organisms in need of feeding themselves. First they were trained to sacrifice all forms of thought for instrumental reason—the form of thought that Köhler essentialized as "thought"— then the primates' reasoning was compared with that of humans, and found lacking (see 71–4).

As Costello desires to make this point without relying on reason, she attempts to perform it. Costello sets herself up as the embodiment of Franz Kafka's ape, Red Peter, from the story "Report to an Academy." In Costello's view, Kafka modeled Red Peter on Köhler's most capable pupil, a chimpanzee called Sultan.[3] Kafka's Red Peter is captured in his native environment in order to stock the German Hagenbeck company's zoo and finds that he can escape confinement only by becoming human. Step by step, he learns the civil gestures and habits humans take as signs of humanity— shaking hands, drinking schnapps from a bottle, and so on—until he is able to address the learned society of the academy, making use of *logos*, the fetishized quintessence of "humanity." Like Costello, Red Peter does not deliver a lecture the academy expects, as he does not give account of his previous life as an ape.[4] Red Peter explains eloquently how he became human, and at the same time, his tale demonstrates how little he benefits from rationality. Making use of reason allows Red Peter only to perform on variety stages.[5] Kafka's story leaves no doubt that giving a report to an academy is performing on just such a stage, and Elizabeth Costello underlines the point when, from behind the lectern, she compares herself to Red Peter:

> The comparison I have just drawn between myself and Kafka's ape might be taken as . . . a light-hearted remark . . . . I want to say at the outset that that was not how my remark—the remark that I feel like Red Peter—was intended. I did not intend it ironically. It means what it says. I say what I mean. I am an old woman. I do not have the time any longer to say things I do not mean. (62)

The link between Costello's being both "an old woman" and Red Peter is addressed when she calls Red Peter's wound her own:

> Red Peter was not an investigator of primate behaviour but a branded, marked, wounded animal presenting himself as speaking testimony to

> a gathering of scholars. I am not a philosopher of mind but an animal exhibiting, yet not exhibiting, to a gathering of scholars, a wound, which I cover up under my clothes but touch on in every word I speak. (70–1)

Costello's implication that her advanced age links her to Red Peter, as well as her comment that she covers up a wound under her clothes, suggests that she shares with the animal a body that is vulnerable to wounding and to death. What she consistently covers up but touches on in every word she speaks is the wound of mortality. The members of the academy she addresses, like those addressed by Red Peter, have bodies, and even *are* such bodies, but the civil manners of humanity call for clothes deflecting from the condition of mortality not only to hide this condition but also to hide the animality of the human body.

In return for his "prodigious overdevelopment of the intellect" (75) and for his command "of lecture-hall etiquette and academic rhetoric," Red Peter had to give up more than exhibiting his animal body. He had to realize that he could not with a clear conscience make use of one of the vital functions of the body, the function of reproduction, for his hybrid nature would only father monsters. The point of Kafka's story, according to Costello, is that Red Peter stands for *human* nature as defined by the philosophers. He is literally an animal that has evolved into a human animal, and Kafka draws attention to a rift within human nature as defined by philosophy rendering humans, in the words of Costello, "monstrous thinking devices mounted inexplicably on suffering animal bodies" (75). In fact, the idea of the hybridity of the human goes back as far as Aristotle. When Aristotle faces the problem that he cannot define life, he chooses, in *De Anima*, to divide and categorize it by analyzing how and in which contexts the term is used. Animal or nutritive life and higher forms of life (which are supposed to make us human) conjoin in the human, but in practical terms they are always separated from each other.[6] The human has since been the site and the result of continuous separations and divisions.

Costello's performing Red Peter demonstrates not only the hybridity of the "human" but also that the "animal" part of the human has not been given its due weight. Costello contrasts Descartes's influential emphasis on reason in his view of the human with

> embodiedness, the sensation of being—not a consciousness of yourself as a kind of ghostly reasoning machine thinking thoughts, but on the contrary the sensation—the heavily affective sensation—of being a body with limbs that have extension in space, of being alive to the world. (78)

The issue, for Costello, is not that we must rationally understand that we inhabit a mortal body like other animals. Red Peter is not making the point of animal rights activists who argue that some animals should get rights similar to human rights because these animals share certain properties with humans, such as rationality, self-consciousness, or language. Red Peter does not want to be regarded as a mentally defective simpleton. In Costello's reading, "Report to an Academy" invites us to experience (not understand) our shared embodiedness with animals, and that is why her reading of Kafka is, in fact, a performance of Red Peter.

Costello's claims have been read as a call for a changed attitude toward animals, and Costello has been taken as a mouthpiece for Coetzee's vegan convictions. Yet a critical focus on the mere propositional content of the lessons misses the point. The philosopher Cora Diamond has argued that the moral virtue of *Elizabeth Costello*'s lessons does not lie in the propositional content but in performing Costello's own embodiedness. However, the virtue of performance is not only of a moral nature. Only the lessons' performative quality puts the propositional content in a perspective that allows the reader to see that a redefinition of the human is at stake. As Elizabeth Costello does not "ironically" but literally stand in for Red Peter, Red Peter literally stands in for the human as a hybrid creature. She thus challenges ideas of the human as a disengaged thinker contemplating the world in favor of an idea of the human always already engaged in the world through embodiedness and through embeddedness in practices. With Charles Taylor, we could say that embodiedness and embeddedness in practice are "that of which I am not simply unaware . . . because it makes intelligible what I am uncontestably aware of; but at the same time I cannot be said to be explicitly or focally aware of it, because that status is already occupied by what it is making intelligible."[7]

Only with this modified idea of the human does an ethics as charted by Diamond emerge. If a reader of "The Lives of Animals" focuses only on the moral problems inherent in the way we treat animals, he or she sees his or her own body merely as a fact that may or may not play a role in a moral argument;[8] whereas the difficulty of reality due to our being embodied creatures, if striking us directly, in the words of Diamond, "shoulders us from a familiar sense of moral life, from a sense of being able to take in and think a moral world."[9] According to Diamond, this difficulty is exhibited by Costello when she is faced with animal corpses in abattoirs, an experience that prompts her to say she knows what it feels like to be a corpse.[10] In other words, awareness that we share vulnerability to death with animals is wounding. It is a difficulty of reality from which humans escape into moral discussion, that is, a mere difficulty of philosophy obscuring the fact that our very ideas are embodied. The story in which Costello's lecture is embedded also shows that her moral views cannot be completely separated from her family relations, the competition between philosophy and literature in the university context, and other factors.[11] Coetzee's descriptions of Costello's physical frailty stress the fact that our arguments, views, and beliefs are influenced by the desires, instincts, rhythms, and aging of our bodies. Costello is aware of this. She is a skeptic because she is open to the difficulty of reality and to being confounded by accepting the impossible disentanglement of thought and physicality. The coming apart of thought and reality in skepticism belongs to our daily experience.[12] Costello's skeptical stance concerning her ideas and beliefs leads her to take only the fact of being a body for certain. Belief in the body is the rock upon which she builds her anthropology and her ethics: a *habeo corpus, ergo sum*, to use a phrase by Jean Améry[13] whose conviction also flows from a keen awareness of mortality, an alertness that arrests the ritualized motions of everyday life. Blinding ourselves to mortality might make life bearable; yet for Costello belief in the perishable body rests more securely in reality than does Descartes's belief in reason, and this is enough for her to cling to what she calls realism.

While "The Lives of Animals" stresses the perspective that individuals who embody ideas are in turn rooted in the body with its needs and instincts,[14] *Elizabeth Costello*'s other six lessons broaden that perspective. They show the complexity of the relations in which the ideas expressed in Costello's lectures are embedded, and the complexity of overlapping cultural expectations, social pressures, and personal interests that all have a bearing on these ideas. Embeddedness comprises all social and historical ways in which human thought is inflected. The beliefs Costello holds and the ideas she entertains are embedded in particular situations in the sense that she would possibly not hold or entertain them in other situations. There are hints that she would not entertain her ideas about the body if her own body did not show signs of decay and mortality. As she herself depends on her body, so do her beliefs and ideas because they do not exist as disembodied currency of reason. The novel's first lesson, "Realism," accordingly defines realism as being true to the embodiedness of ideas and to their embeddedness in social contexts:

> Realism is premised on the idea that ideas have no autonomous existence, can exist only in things. So when it needs to debate ideas, as here, realism is driven to invent situations—walks in the countryside, conversations—in which characters give voice to contending ideas and thereby in a certain sense embody them. The notion of *embodying* turns out to be pivotal. In such debates ideas do not and indeed cannot float free: they are tied to the speakers by whom they are enounced, and generated from the matrix of individual interests out of which their speakers act in the world—for instance, the son's concern that his mother not be treated as a Mickey Mouse post-colonial writer. (9)

To fully understand this statement, one must consider that the lesson "On Realism," in which it is embedded, undermines literary realism, or realism as a particular mode of writing, by showing up the arbitrary conventions on which it rests. For example, the lesson emphasizes that literary realism (as well as other modes of writing) offers a selective view of the reality it purports to present, because realist texts are full of gaps in which time passes:

between paragraphs, even phrases. Here the gaps are made explicit: "There is a scene in the restaurant, mainly dialogue, which we will skip" (7). The realism proposed in the long quote is of a different kind. Instead of a literary convention, realism here is an epistemological virtue if we acknowledge the embodiedness and embeddedness of ideas in "the matrix of individual interests out of which their speakers act in the world." The salient point, however, is that while literary realism is a period in literary history or a literary program, narrative turns out to be a privileged epistemological mode, because it accommodates—within the bounds of its historically contingent conventions—embodiedness and embeddedness that are the roots of what Diamond calls the difficulty of reality. Philosophy, as it has been practiced, does not; and the sciences, including the social sciences and psychology, are themselves only partial, as they focus on the psychological, the social, or the body in isolation and cannot offer integrated representations, and even less the experiential dimension of reality.

The magnitude of these claims is considerable. Kant's *Critique of Pure Reason* attempts to provide a solid foundation for epistemology by limiting its claims: our perception of the world is inflected by time and space, both of which are categories of our minds rather than of reality; we therefore do not see the world as it is, but within the aforementioned limitations we see it realistically, that is, reliably as the same. While Kant argues that time and space condition the possibility of thought, *Elizabeth Costello* suggests that it is conditioned by the body and social factors. We must take these factors into account if we want to approximate—even if we cannot reach—a realistic image of reality, and we can only do so through narrative. One can conceive of this redefinition as a narrative turn in which narrative—in all its generic forms—inherits the epistemological position claimed by Kantian philosophy, and in which the embodied mind inherits the position held by reason. Narratives are more convincing than philosophical arguments because they let the reader experience the difficulty of reality rather than attempting to solve it. The generalizations of reason do not hold according to the novel because embeddedness and embodiedness mean that no *particular* instance of reality is experienced like another.[15]

The idea of literature as a mode of thinking realistically is not as new as it may seem. Coetzee draws heavily on Mikhail Bakhtin's ideas from *Problems of Dostoevsky's Poetics*. "In Dostoevsky," Bakhtin writes, "two thoughts are already two people, for there are no thoughts belonging to no one and every thought represents an entire person."[16] *Elizabeth Costello* turns this poetological characterization of Dostoevsky into an ontological claim about ideas: there cannot be any thought at all if not an embodied and socially embedded thought. There are no thoughts, there is only thinking. Bakhtin only makes claims about Dostoevsky's creative method when he claims that the author "thought not in thoughts but in points of view, consciousnesses, voices," that he "tried to perceive and formulate each thought in such a way that a whole person was expressed and began to sound in it"; and that "this, in condensed form, is his entire worldview, from alpha to omega."[17] Coetzee radicalizes these thoughts by negating the existence of disembodied ideas and by consequently embodying them in speakers. This radicalization suggests that Dostoevsky invented the "realism" discussed in *Elizabeth Costello* and thus refined the novel into a privileged means of addressing, playing with and testing ideas. Earlier literary-philosophical genres attempted what, in this view, only Dostoevsky fully achieved. The Socratic/Platonic dialog influenced Dostoevsky's poetics and is premised on a belief in "the dialogic nature of truth" and its embodying of ideas in "ideologists."[18]

If realistic narrative (in Coetzee's sense) lets the reader experience the difficulty of reality, then the reader experiences "the human" neither as an abstract idea, nor only as an idea inflected and "made difficult" by reality but also as the very bedrock of reality: the specific forms of embeddedness and embodiedness which are the sources of reality's difficulty are properties of the human itself. They determine human experientiality; hence to show "what it is like" to be human, narrative must realistically convey this experientiality if it wants to go beyond philosophy's and science's abstract "ideas" of the human.

In the last two decades, narratology has come to define experientiality as narrative's core function: "the quasi-mimetic evocation of 'real-life experience.'"[19] Any attempt to make sense of narrative must proceed from the recognition of cognitive emotional states as the basic events of a narrative; it is not the plot that is the essence of narrative, but a theory of mind.[20] David Herman has ventured as far as arguing that "we cannot even have a notion of the felt quality of experience without narrative."[21] These claims echo *Elizabeth Costello*'s suggestion that the experientiality of embedded and embodied consciousness is not only the *sine qua non* of any narrative that can claim to give a truthful account of what it is like to be human, but that narrative is the form of language that can give such an account.

Philosophers have argued since the mid-twentieth century that conscious experience involves non-physical properties, which means that someone who has complete physical knowledge about another conscious being might still lack knowledge about how it feels to have the experiences of that being.[22] Narratological conceptualizations of experientiality have been particularly influenced by Thomas Nagel's concept of "qualia." These are the qualitative, experiential, or felt properties of mental states, which Nagel characterizes as the sense or feeling of what it is like for someone or something to undergo certain conscious experiences.[23] Drawing on both Nagel's and John Searle's work, Herman has argued that narrative is a mode of representation tailor-made for gauging qualia. Not only are qualia irreducibly subjective and thus unavailable for inspection in the way we can inspect objects in the world,[24] they also pose a problem for representation, because there is no way to step outside consciousness and observe it as it really is, since consciousness simply *is* the (act or process of) observing, i.e., the qualia associated with observing or experiencing the world from a particular, irreducibly subjective or first-person vantage-point.[25]

It follows that the qualia bound up with the content of my consciousness cannot be represented but only experienced. Herman argues that narrative enables us to experience other minds by emulating the what-it's-like dimension of conscious awareness, since it is isomorphic to qualias' elements of structure.[26] Herman acknowledges the explanatory gap here: cognitive science still has to explain what this isomorphism consists of. What is certain is that experientiality involves being a body. Narratology offers some conceptualizations of embodiedness that are helpful for reading *Elizabeth Costello*. Monika Fludernik has argued that embodiedness is the core of experientiality:

> The feature that is . . . most basic to experientiality is *embodiment* rather than specificity or individuality because these can in fact be subsumed under it. Embodiedness evokes all the parameters of a real-life schema of existence which always has to be situated in a specific time and space frame, and the motivational and experiential aspects of human actionality likewise relate to the knowledge about one's physical presence in the world. Embodiment and existence in human terms are indeed the same thing.[27]

Marco Caracciolo has recently refined Fludernik's approach, bringing narratology yet closer to *Elizabeth Costello*'s points about embodiedness and embeddedness. Building on Fludernik's insight that embodiment anchors narrative in experience, Caracciolo takes issue with her claim that narrative with realist intentions is a "mimetic *representation* of individual experience that cognitively and epistemically relies on real-world knowledge."[28] A narrator's and characters' historically situated bodies are not principally cognitive representations in the reader's mind but are pre-rationally inhabited by the reader: this pre-rational element of enactment is key to the relation between Costello's arguments and *Elizabeth Costello*'s literary performances (and performative contradictions) of these arguments. After all, it is the very point of Coetzee's book that the embedded and embodied nature of ideas is an experiential quality that cannot fully be grasped by Costello's or the reader's reasoning. Embodiedness and embeddedness cannot without loss be translated into propositional terms but can only be experienced. This is the reason why one must speak of "performances" enacted by narratives: allowing readers to inhabit and enact historically embedded fictional bodies, narrative performs what cannot be told in propositional terms because ideas gain their content only against the background of embodiedness and embeddedness.

Outline, Transit, and *Kudos*

I now turn to how Rachel Cusk's trilogy *Outline* (2014), *Transit* (2017), and *Kudos* (2018) engages with the realism proposed and performed in *Elizabeth Costello*. Like *Elizabeth Costello*, the Trilogy (as I will henceforth call it) features characters that often discuss philosophical questions in their speeches. Martin Puchner has aptly called Coetzee's novels "novels of thinking" rather than "novels of ideas" because they are premised on the belief that ideas only exist in characters engaged with each other and the world.[29] As Puchner observes, Coetzee's novels share this premise with Platonic dialog, a literary genre designed to explore the embodied nature of thinking, arguing, and debating.[30] Much the same can be said of the Trilogy which consists almost entirely of conversations. I will show that like *Elizabeth Costello*, the Trilogy emphasizes the embodiedness of ideas and their embeddedness in history and culture. Like that novel, the Trilogy suggests the idea of narrative as a realistic way of thinking. Unlike *Elizabeth Costello*, however, the Trilogy suggests that ideas, including ideas of self and of identity, are always *shared by and common to members of a particular culture*. According to the Trilogy, narrative can truthfully convey these common ideas but does not allow to think uniquely inflected ideas of single individuals because ideas themselves are common rather than singular.

The Trilogy's first-person narrator is named Faye. She is a writer in her fifties, mother of two sons, recently divorced at the beginning of *Outline* and remarried later. Faye travels frequently, attends literary festivals, and teaches writing classes. She buys and renovates a home in London, dealing simultaneously with a helpful contractor and the resentful neighbors downstairs. She debates the merits of coloring her hair with her hairdresser, goes on a date, and runs into her onetime lover in the street. Yet the Trilogy is a record not so much of Faye's thoughts and actions but of those described to her by the people she encounters. Without much prompting, these people speak in long, arcing monologues that swoop from banal personal experiences to philosophical claims and back again. They tell Faye about lost love, secrets, failures, and wounding and shameful experiences. Faye listens to each of them in turn, sometimes passing judgment, more often remaining silent. It is as if she has renounced all personal agency and narrative authority.[31] Faye's name appears only once and late in each book, always in one of the rare instances when we read the direct speech of a character.

The *New Yorker*, the *London Review of Books*, and other publications in rare unanimity credited Cusk with accomplishing nothing less than a "reinvention of the [novel] form," as reviewer Monica Ali put it in the *New York Times*.[32] A review in the *New Yorker* argued that the books merge fiction with oral history,[33] while others noted that the books convey the oral speech of characters in purposefully artificial ways.[34] Almost all reviewers mentioned the near-impersonality and near-invisibility of the first-person narrator.[35] Some focused on the Trilogy's affinity with autobiography and compared Cusk's books to Karl Ove Knausgård's *My Struggle* series.[36] The reviewer for the *Washington Post* argued that in *Kudos* Cusk's characters are also symbols and philosophical propositions, and that the dialog resembles Socratic questioning.[37]

I argue that these features are connected to one another. The Trilogy highlights that it presents ideas in embodied form not only insofar as all characters "have" and "propose" at length striking ideas, but also insofar as evoking *oral* forms of storytelling in Cusk's writing gives these ideas body. Like *Elizabeth Costello*, the Trilogy shows that realism as a literary mode is a mere convention, but that a realistic approach to ideas requires narrative as embodiment and embedding of ideas. Cusk breaks with realism as a conventional mode of evoking reality by simultaneously suggesting several irreconcilable forms of oral storytelling as frames of interpretation for the stories told to Faye. This method draws attention to the fact that a realistic rendering of ideas does not depend on any particular mode of storytelling but that it concerns storytelling as such.

The different forms of oral storytelling suggested by Cusk are

1) spontaneous conversational storytelling,
2) institutionalized oral storytelling specific to contexts such as psychotherapy or the interview, and
3) literary genres simulating oral storytelling such as the chorus speech in Greek tragedy, the Socratic dialog and the confession.

Simultaneously suggesting these forms of orality, the Trilogy plays off against each other two functions that written evocations of orality have had in literary history. On the one hand, the function of creating reality effects: contemporary readers are used to read it as a marker of unique speech and character, which are in turn read as signatures of the real.[38] On the other hand, the function of creating commonality effects: the sense that what is spoken aloud belongs to everyone, that it shares what is common and is no less real for it.[39] The Trilogy's mapping "oral" genres predating modernity onto conversational storytelling challenges the modern habit of reading written simulations of orality as signals of unique speech and character that supposedly realistically embody ideas. It shows that whether we consider such oral narrative as lifelike and as bringing a character to life depends on whether we read it dialogically in Bakhtin's sense as conversational narrative, or as part of an interview, or as the communal speech of a chorus. Our understanding of the ideas voiced (embodied) depends, in other words, on what we as readers take to be the specific context (embeddedness) of the speech: conversation, interview, chorus speech, and so on. None of these forms is "the" realistic one. The stories that people—mostly men—tell Faye about themselves show their unique characters. But the reader also learns to read them differently, because Faye, like a midwife, helps them deliver their stories only to reveal the similarities between them. These similarities suggest that the thoughts of which the stories tell, however idiosyncratic they may seem, are remarkably like those of other people; that thoughts are common social forms as much as individual expression; and that character may be a mask hiding a self that, in fact, is like other selves.

Outline, the first book of the Trilogy, starts with Faye on a plane to Athens where she will teach writing at a summer school.[40] Her neighbor, a short, old Greek man, starts a conversation with her. After some small talk he tells Faye about his previous marriages. During the following days, he will take her on two boat trips to islands near Athens (chapters 4 and 7). Each time they meet, the man corrects his previous stories and fills in the picture of these marriages. Most of the speech is reported by Faye, as she does throughout the Trilogy, including his signals that he is interested in Faye. Although we learn that Faye finds the man physically repulsive, she keeps accepting his invitations. She does not say why. On their second trip her neighbor—she always calls him that, her neighbor—awkwardly bends toward her face and kisses her. She withdraws.

The episodes of the Trilogy are unconnected to each other in terms of plot. In *Outline*, for example, Faye meets Ryan, a fellow writer and teacher at the summer school, who tells her how he balances work and his life with wife and children and about the differences to his previous marriage. Similar themes crop up in an episode in which Faye meets her friend Paniotis, who discusses the question of how meaningful talking about one's "character" is in marriage, where partners cannot define themselves without reference to what the other has made them. Another episode reports long speeches by Elena, an editor at a publishing house, and Melete, a lesbian poet. The episode moves from highly personal childhood experiences to a disagreement on the role that honesty should play in relationships. In each of these conversations, a level of abstract arguments is reached, on which the ideas gain their content if understood against the background of the embodied speaking self and of the situation that embeds the speech. Here are two examples from Faye's conversation with Paniotis. At one point, Paniotis notes:

> The human capacity for self-delusion is apparently infinite—and if that is the case, how are we ever meant to know, except by existing in a state of absolute pessimism, that once again we are fooling ourselves? I [Paniotis] had thought there was nothing, having lived my whole life in this tragic country, about which I could any longer deceive myself, but as you have so unhappily pointed out, it is the very thing you don't see, the thing you

take for granted, that deceives you. And how can you even know you have taken something for granted until it is no longer there? (95)

Ten pages later, Faye says:

I replied that I wasn't sure it was possible, in marriage, to know what you actually were, or indeed to separate what you were from what you had become through the other person. I thought the whole idea of a "real" self might be illusory: you might feel, in other words, as though you were some separate, autonomous self within you, but perhaps that self didn't actually exist. (105)

Narratives of personal experience lead up to such general ideas and follow after them; and it is only in the light of those experiences told, and of everything we know about the speakers' intentions and interests, that the general ideas gain their meaning. As Faye's neighbor on the plane, Ryan, Paniotis, Elena, and Melete talk about their romantic and domestic situations, echoes and symmetries emerge. The episodes make visible behind the details of these stories the outline of a common experience of partnership and family in a society and its particular domestic arrangements.[41] In other words, the sameness, or at least similarity, of the culture(s) in which these characters are embedded seems to result in a similarity of ideas, regardless of how specifically inflected these ideas are.

The conversation with the Greek on the plane is a good example of how storytelling *in* the episodes simultaneously suggests several kinds of oral storytelling as frames of interpretation for the experiences, ideas, and characters at hand, and thus breaks with a convention of realism attuned to evoking individual characters and their ideas. The conversation starts with a mixture of reported and direct speech:

The man to my right turned and asked me the reason for my visit in Athens. I said I was going there for work. "I hope you are staying there near water," he said. "Athens will be very hot." (6)

The dialogic nature of the speech is clearly visible even in the reported parts until the neighbor launches into the story of his life: he used to have a flat in London, his wealthy parents had at one point relocated the whole household to London, and so on. The turn-taking fades out. Faye no longer interrupts the Greek while the inquit-formulas "he said" or "he continued" signal Faye's presence: "But like all wealthy people, *he continued*, his parents had long outgrown their origins and moved in a borderless sphere among other people of wealth and importance" (8; my emphasis). Then the inquit-formula is dropped. Reported speech turns into free indirect discourse as we simply read: "Theirs had been the pre-eminent family of the island: two strands of the local aristocracy had been united by the parental marriage, and what's more, the shipping fortunes consolidated" (8). Faye, whose name points to the realm of fairies and to the unreal, gradually becomes invisible in the movement from direct speech to free indirect discourse and impersonality—techniques notably still associated with Flaubert who first methodically used them to heighten the realism of his prose and profoundly influenced the history of the "realist novel." Occasionally, an inquit-formula reminds us that she is still there. Only when the Greek has finished his tale, however, does she fully emerge again:

> I was dissatisfied by the story of his second marriage. It had lacked objectivity; it relied too heavily on extremes, and the moral properties it ascribed to those extremes were often incorrect. . . . I found I did not believe certain key facts, for instance that his wife had locked his son in the cellar . . . . [T]his was a story in which I sensed the truth was being sacrificed to the narrator's desire to win.
> My neighbour laughed, and said that I was probably right. (29–30)

Faye makes a claim about the man's narrative as such: a claim that, although not universal, moves to a meta-level about storytelling rather than responding to single claims made by the Greek. Her judgment is startling because she had dropped out of sight—and because it is only through the neighbor's laughter that we understand that her judgment is not her silent opinion but was spoken aloud.

The movement toward impersonality up to Faye's judgment is accompanied by invocations of different forms of oral narrative. The starting point is what narratologists call experiential conversational narrative, in which one person tells another an experience and comments on how the experience felt. This form of oral narrative is typically repetitive and marked by turn-taking, as listeners frequently interrupt; or at least this is what present-day, Western readers expect conversational narrative to be like.[42]

When written narrative tries to evoke conversational narrative, it typically does *not* transcribe conversational narrative. It stresses stereotypical features such as avoidance of literate vocabulary, dialect, repetitiveness, and contradictions.[43] Narratologists argue that such "pseudo-orality" can make a character come alive on the page. The beginning of the episode on the plane invites the reader to read the Greek as such a character.

Yet from the beginning there are also features untypical of real-life conversation. In novels, we can often sense individual speech characteristics even through reported speech. Not so in the Trilogy. There is a clarity to the diction that is not usually found in conversation.[44] Faye's neighbor never repeats himself, and Faye's dropping out of view undermines our sense that we are reading *conversational* narrative. The reader might explain this by attributing a special talent for storytelling to the Greek. Yet in the second, the third, and the fourth episodes of *Outline*, conversation likewise develops into unbroken storytelling.

In each case the social context seems to change from a casual conversation to a more formal, *institutionalized* situation in which one person is *expected* to tell a listener his or her story, for example in psychotherapy, in an interview, or in a situation in which a witness speaks to an oral historian. Such situations form the background of what narratology calls "institutionalized oral narrative," which can be longer and more complex than conversational narratives. In *Outline*'s three episodes with the Greek, the prominence of suffering, of guilt, and the confession of shameful experiences suggests that Faye acts as a kind of psychotherapist for her interlocutor: only occasionally asking questions and triggering further revelations, she helps him talk about experiences that in other situations resist verbalization. In other episodes, people talk as if they are interviewed by Faye. In *Kudos*, Faye herself is to be interviewed, but the literary journalist ends up telling *his* story to her until time is up. Faye's acting as a recorder of long narratives concerned with similar topics also evokes the methods of oral history. The Trilogy's episodic structure can be read as a record of voices testifying to a collective memory of loss and separation characteristic of a particular society at a particular time.

Helping her interlocutors deliver their stories, Faye performs the function of midwife. Her own frame narrative increases rather than diminishes her impersonality. We expect her narrative to be inflected by her subjective point of view, as narrative voice and focalization coincide in first-person narrative. Yet Faye's narrative does not describe what it is like for her to experience the events she talks about. She is a first-person narrator who much of the time performs the role of an impersonal, covert third-person narrator. It is the jarring between both points of view that impersonalizes Faye: if Cusk had chosen a covert third-person narrator, there would have been no one to impersonalize in the first place. The effect is disturbing because the communication of what an experience feels like is a central, some narratologists even claim *the* central, function of narrative: "the quasi-mimetic evocation of 'real-life experience,'" as Monika Fludernik puts it (see above). *Conversational* narrative has been described by these narratologists as the most common, even "natural" type of narrative. The Trilogy constantly invokes it, but denies access to how Faye experiences the events of her narrative.

In contrast to Faye, her mostly male interlocutors are vocal about their reactions to what happened to them. They comment on their stories and actively create their characters as they talk. Their talking seems excessive, their characters plausible only if we map onto the conversations the situations of psychotherapy, the interview, or oral history. Yet as we read on in *Outline* and continue with *Transit* and *Kudos*, the interpretive frame of institutionalized oral narrative holds no more plausibility than that of conversational narrative. The reported conversations attain a level of complexity, coherence, and abstraction that would not occur even in institutionalized oral narrative. The people conversing with Faye increasingly become indistinguishable. In *Transit*, a hairdresser is extremely eloquent and intelligent, but his language and phrasing do not tower over his job. In *Kudos*, everyone—a youthful city guide, a ski instructor, even Faye's son—speaks in hypotactic, measured, literary sentences, regardless of whether they are native English speakers or not.[45] It is as if the characters were writing in inverted commas.[46] This would seem a fault on Cusk's part if the Trilogy's critique of the idea of character were not so persistent, and if the spectacle of ideas overriding the characters who speak them was not so consistently performed. We might conclude that Faye is, in fact, not reporting stories but making them up.[47] The point, however, is that what we consider a realistic story depends itself on which social practice (conversation, interview, dramatic chorus, etc.) we take to embed the speeches of the characters. What sounds unnatural when read as conversational narrative may seem a perfectly realistic oral speech when read as literary genre. The creation of realistic speech and characters whose ideas are inflected in certain ways is not a function inherent to orality in writing, but rests on knowledge of practices common in a culture, and on the application of that knowledge for understanding speech.

When Cusk has characters speak as if they were writing, she adds a third form of orality to conversational and institutionalized oral narrative in writing: literary genres that invoke orality through their form rather than through pseudo-orality. In these genres, writing is not a secondary representation of primary orality but its own, still-born form of orality; an orality that suggests commonality rather than uniqueness as the signature of the real.

To begin with, the Trilogy's forming a collective voice out of collected voices all telling of and commenting on tragic loss invokes the chorus of Greek tragedy. The chorus returns to the audience the tragic character's fate *shown* onstage as story *told*. Partly set in Athens and frequently referring to Greek tragedy and mythology, the Trilogy's idea of character as mask rather than unique personality echoes the meaning of the Latin word "*persona*," derived from the ancient Greek, meaning "mask," particularly the mask worn in ancient dramatic performances. The blueprint of the Socratic dialog in Plato is also recognizable in Faye's wide-ranging conversations. Socrates says of himself he acts as midwife to truth. His *interlocutors* have to give birth to it, and *they* talk most of the time. Their words reveal common misconceptions rather than individual character. Plato's interest in the arguments and ideas at issue in the dialogs frequently overrides his concern for the speech habits of the characters who hold these ideas (see *Outline* 95), as do the conversations especially in *Kudos*. Just as visible is the Trilogy's affinity with the literary genre of confession, derived from Catholic confessional practice and intimately linked with autobiography since St. Augustine's *Confessiones*. The Greek neighbor's telling of his failed marriages, including his wavering between self-serving half-truths and the will to tell all, is a vivid example. Even the genre of the storytelling contest can be glimpsed. In Geoffrey Chaucer's *Canterbury Tales*, a frame narrative tells of a contest of storytellers. The tales (named "The Wife of Bath's Tale," "The Pardoner's Tale," etc.) are derived from story materials commonly known in Chaucer's day; like the Trilogy's episodes, they comment on each other and form symmetries. Margaret Atwood's novel *The Handmaid's Tale* (1985) is modeled in structure and title on Chaucer's tales. The first-person narrator Offred speaks her tale on tape. Her narrative alternates between short parts featuring her memories and parts telling the possible lives of the other women. The Trilogy shares Atwood's concern with the subjugation of women's voices in patriarchal societies. Faye's invisibility behind the stories told by men speaks to the male habit of overbearingly explaining things to women, or "mansplaining," as Rebecca Solnit has named the phenomenon.[48] More generally, it speaks to the fact that Western culture's valuing speech over writing and valuing men over women are interdependent biases, as Jacques Derrida's hybrid term "phallogocentrism" illustrates.

The wealth of genres invoked amidst conversational and institutionalized forms of oral narrative, and the evident overlaps between some of these forms, do not call upon the reader to find *the* realistic form. There is no single realistic one, the Trilogy suggests. The creation of supposedly unique speech and character has been only one of orality's conventional functions in written narrative. The innovative feature of Cusk's trilogy, then, is its enabling modern readers to rediscover orality as a sign of that which is common and belongs to everyone even though men claim a monopoly on it, and to understand themselves as social animals exchanging—or mimicking—ideas common to a culture rather than as singular individuals. Meanwhile, the Trilogy's embedding ideas and arguments in speech and simultaneously reflecting on their status in the narrative—its realism of giving substance to its propositions by performing them—is a feature that links *Outline*, *Transit*, and *Kudos* to Coetzee's *Elizabeth Costello*. The idea of the novel of thinking is itself a shared one.

Notes

1 For this part, I draw on my book *J. M. Coetzee's Revisions of the Human: Posthumanism and Narrative Form* (Basingstoke: Palgrave Macmillan, 2019), 18–35, 142–176.

2 See J. M. Coetzee, *Elizabeth Costello* (London: Vintage, 2003), 67, 69. Subsequent references in parentheses.

3 Köhler published the results of his experiments in 1917; Kafka's story was published in November of that year.

4 See Peter-André Alt, *Franz Kafka: Der ewige Sohn. Eine Biographie* (Munich: Beck, 2005), 522.
5 See Franz Kafka, *The Complete Stories*, trans. Willa and Edwin Muir (New York: Schocken, 1995), 281–291.
6 See Giorgio Agamben, *The Open: Man and Animal*, trans. Kevin Attell (Stanford, CA: Stanford University Press, 2004), 13–16.
7 Charles Taylor, "Engaged Agency and Background in Heidegger," in *The Cambridge Companion to Heidegger*, ed. Charles B. Guignon (Cambridge: Cambridge University Press, 1993), 325.
8 See Cora Diamond, "The Difficulty of Reality and the Difficulty of Philosophy," in *Philosophy and Animal Life*, ed. Stanley Cavell et al. (New York: Columbia University Press, 2008), 59.
9 Ibid., 64.
10 Ibid., 74.
11 Ibid., 55–56.
12 Ibid., 55–67.
13 Jean Amery, *Unmeisterliche Wanderjahre: Aufsätze* (Stuttgart: Klett-Cotta, 1971), 146.
14 See Stephen Mulhall, *The Wounded Animal: J.M. Coetzee and the Difficulty of Reality in Literature and Philosophy* (Princeton, NJ: Princeton University Press, 2009), 182.
15 See Ibid., 183.
16 Mikhail Bakhtin, *Problems of Dostoevsky's Poetics*, trans. Caryl Emerson (Minneapolis, MN: Minnesota University Press, 1984), 93.
17 Ibid., 93.
18 Ibid., 110, 111.
19 Monika Fludernik, *Towards a "Natural" Narratology* (London: Routledge, 1996), 12.
20 See Ibid., 12; see David Herman, *Story Logic: Problems and Possibilities of Narrative* (Lincoln: University of Nebraska Press, 2002), 115–169; David Herman, "Cognition, Emotion, and Consciousness," in *The Cambridge Companion to Narrative*, ed. David Herman (Cambridge: Cambridge University Press, 2007), 247; Alan Palmer, *Fictional Minds* (Lincoln: University of Nebraska Press, 2004), 170–239.
21 Herman, "Cognition, Emotion, and Consciousness," 257.
22 See Martine Nida-Rümelin, "Qualia: The Knowledge Argument," in *The Stanford Encyclopedia of Philosophy*, ed. Edward N. Zalta, https://plato.stanford.edu/archives/sum2015/entries/qualia-knowledge/.
23 See Thomas Nagel, "What Is it Like to Be a Bat?" *Philosophical Review* 83, no. 4 (1974): 435–450; Janet Levin, "Qualia," in *The MIT Encyclopedia of the Cognitive Sciences*, ed. Robert A. Wilson and Frank C. Keil (Cambridge, MA: MIT Press, 1999), 693.

24 See David Herman, *Basic Elements of Narrative* (West Sussex: Wiley Blackwell, 2004), 137–154.
25 Ibid., 155.
26 Ibid., 157.
27 Fludernik, *"Natural" Narratology*, 29–30.
28 Ibid., 28.
29 See Martin Puchner, "J.M. Coetzee's Novels of Thinking," *Raritan Review* 30, no. 4 (2011): 5–6, 11–12.
30 See Martin Puchner, *The Drama of Ideas: Platonic Provocations in Theatre and Philosophy* (Oxford: Oxford University Press, 2010), 3–35; Puchner, "Coetzee's Novels of Thinking," 7–12. For Bakhtin on the Platonic dialogue as a forerunner of the dialogic novel, see *Problems of Dostoevsky's Poetics*, 110–111.
31 See Francine Prose, "Real Talk: Rachel Cusk's *Kudos*," *Sewanee Review* 126, no. 3 (2018): 520–521; Alexandra Schwartz, "I Don't Think Character Exists Anymore": A Conversation with Rachel Cusk," *New Yorker*, November 18, 2018, https://www.newyorker.com/culture/the-new-yorker-interview/i-dont-think-character-exists-anymore-a-conversation-with-rachel-cusk.
32 See Monica Ali, "Monica Ali on Rachel Cusk's Risky, Revolutionary Novel," *The New York Times*, January 23, 2017, https://www.nytimes.com/2017/01/23/books/review/rachel-cusk-transit.html.
33 See Judith Thurman, "World of Interiors," *The New Yorker*, August 7, 2017, 48, *Academic OneFile*.
34 See Prose, "Real Talk"; Schwartz, "I Don't Think Character Exists Anymore"; Andrew Anthony, "*Kudos* by Rachel Cusk Review—Exquisite Control," *The Guardian*, April 30, 2018, https://www.theguardian.com/books/2018/apr/30/kudos-rachel-cusk-review-final-part-trilogy.
35 See Ali, "Monica Ali on Rachel Cusk's Risky, Revolutionary Novel"; Prose, "Real Talk"; Thurman, "World of Interiors"; Patricia Lockwood, "Why Do I Have to Know What McDonald's Is?" *London Review of Books*, May 10, 2018, https://www.lrb.co.uk/v40/n09/patricia-lockwood/why-do-i-have-to-know-what-mcdonalds-is.
36 See Elaine Blair, "All Told," *The New Yorker*, January 5, 2015, 70. *Academic OneFile*.
37 See Jamie Fisher, "Rachel Cusk Is Returning Fiction to Its Roots in Storytelling," *Washington Post*, January 13, 2017. *General OneFile*.
38 See Roland Barthes, "The Reality Effect," in *The Rustle of Language*, trans. Richard Howard (Los Angeles: University of California Press, 1989), 141–148. Barthes seminal essay names redundancy and superfluousness, so characteristic of the repetitive structures of oral speech, as mechanism for the production of what he calls reality effects. Importantly, Barthes associates such production of reality effects with "modern" literature; his examples are especially from Flaubert.

39 As will become clear, "commonality" in the sense I use it goes beyond the fact that oral speech always requires the minimal presence two persons: a speaker and a listener. For an argument along these lines that oral speech forms community, see Walter J. Ong, *Orality and Literacy* (London, New York: Routledge, 2002), 73: "Because in its physical constitution as sound, the spoken word proceeds from the human interior and manifests human beings to one another as conscious interiors, as persons, the spoken word forms human beings into close-knit groups. When a speaker is addressing an audience, the members of the audience normally become a unity, with themselves and with the speaker."

40 Rachel Cusk, *Outline* (London: Faber & Faber, 2014). Subsequent references in parantheses.

41 See Blair, "All Told."

42 See Fludernik, *"Natural" Narratology*, 42–47.

43 See Monika Fludernik, "Conversational Narration, Oral Narration," *the living handbbook of narratology*, ed. Peter Hühn et al., September 9, 2013, http://hup.sub.uni-hamburg.de/lhn/index.php?title=Conversational_Narration_-_Oral_Narration&oldid=2040.

44 See Schwartz, "I Don't Think Character Exists Anymore."

45 See Anthony, "*Kudos* by Rachel Cusk Review—Exquisite Control."

46 See Schwartz, "I Don't Think Character Exists Anymore."

47 See Prose, "Real Talk"; David Wagner, "Es zu erzählen: Rachel Cusks Lebensromane," *Merkur* 73 (2019): 62.

48 See Rebecca Solnit, *Men Explain Things to Me* (Chicago: Haymarket, 2014).

PART III

Politics

9

Realism for Sustainability

Caroline Levine

What does literary studies scholarship have to offer us in this moment of climate emergency? In recent years, literary critics have offered three main responses. The first concerns the imagination. Scholars have made the case that experimental and speculative art works jolt us out of entrenched habits of thought and feeling in order to allow us to imagine radically new futures for human and nonhuman lives. Lynn Keller, for example, argues for experimental poetry as a challenge to conventional thinking that can help us to engage in a "radical reconception" of our world.[1] Gerry Canavan makes a case for science fiction as "our culture's vast, shared, polyvocal archive of the possible" with two centuries of productive thinking about systemic planetary transformation.[2]

The second response is to understand the history of our current conditions. Literary scholars have tracked the cultural values and beliefs that have led us into our present climate catastrophe, from European imperialism to the US love affair with petroleum. Amitav Ghosh and Stephanie LeMenager are powerful examples of thinkers who have argued that we need to understand deep and longstanding traditions in order to disrupt them and usher in a new set of values.[3]

The third response is the work of political critique. Literary critics have argued that we are caught in the grips of ideologies that we must resolutely dismantle. These scholars warn us to be especially wary of projects associated with progressives, like "sustainability," which pretend to be steering us toward a more just and livable planet but in fact are just ways to entrench consumer capitalism, racial hierarchy, and fossil fuel extraction.[4]

What all of these approaches share is the insistence that we can and should resist the status quo. And that is hardly a surprise. For more than a century, literary studies has been focusing on the work of disrupting and dismantling. The field has valued the literary texts that are challenging and subversive. In the classroom, we often focus on the surprising moment in a text that surprises us or unsettles expectations. This version of art is powerful, in part, because it brings our politics and our aesthetics together into a neat revolutionary bundle. Because art resists convention and expectation, we say, it can also challenge oppressive structures, systems, and standards.[5]

In fact, there is no value more fundamental to literary studies than the capacity to break from the familiar. From Percy Shelley to Viktor Shklovsky, critics have argued that the very purpose of art is to interrupt entrenched habits of perception. And this version of the aesthetic as a disruptive force continues, alive and well, across almost every school of thought in the field today. Thinkers as different as Fred Moten and Tobin Siebers, Timothy Morton and Derek Attridge, Edouard Glissant and Jack Halberstam argue that the strange challenges of the aesthetic work against existing systems.[6]

So, why *not* rupture? Let me offer three reasons that emerge from our particular historical moment. The first and most important is that we are now living in an age of acute precarity. As neoliberal economics undoes hopes of secure work, and as fossil fuels radically disrupt longstanding ecosystems, we are faced not with oppressive stasis but with rapid and destructive change—the warming of the upper atmosphere, the eruption of fast-moving wildfires and the melting of ice caps, the destruction of ecosystems, desertification, the extinction of species, the growing mass of plastics in the ocean, storms, and droughts and floods both more frequent and more severe than ever before. As millions of people struggle against food insecurity and the loss of safe and stable shelter, the conditions artists and intellectuals have so long reviled—stability, security, and predictability—have become rare and precious. And our longstanding preference for unsettling and unmaking does not help us to figure out how to build stable and predictable conditions to sustain collective life over time.

The second reason is that disruption today does not always align with the radical left or even with progressives. Both right-wing leaders and massive global corporations, for example, have embraced the disruption of rules and the shattering of institutions in order to resist what they cast as the oppressions of the status quo. Authoritarian populists like Trump and Bolsonaro deliberately wreck norms and institutions in the interests—they say—of freeing ordinary people from entrenched norms, elite values, and state regulations. This is particularly troubling when it comes to climate justice. In the name of freedom, the Trump administration rolled back over ninety-five environmental regulations, including fracking on Native lands, drilling in wildlife preserves, and dumping toxins in waterways.[7] From this perspective, the drive to resist norms and institutions has hastened the worst effects of climate catastrophe. Technology companies, too, have vaunted innovation and disruption, claiming to free work from traditional office cubicles, regulations, bureaucracy, schedules, and hierarchies in favor of sharing, convenience, and "personal empowerment." This emancipation from traditional constraints has brought with it a terrible precarity for much of the labor force, as workers struggle to make ends meet by stringing together multiple unpredictable gigs.[8] The neoliberal right is as in love with rupture and unpredictability as any avant-garde artist. And so it becomes clear that the work of unsettling and resisting constraints is not the same as justice.

The third reason to turn away from rupture is that it is contributing to a paralyzing pessimism. Because it is slow and laborious to work against such massive global forces as capitalism and imperialism, literary scholars—and many others on the left—have been overwhelmingly gloomy about the prospects of reshaping global attitudes in time to forestall the most devastating effects of climate change. For this reason, many scholars today have turned their attention to *mourning*, casting their proper work as addressing the "traumatic knowledge that climate catastrophe is certain and unfathomable."[9] Since grief "does not offer any direct recourse for action or redemption," the best we can do is to "document . . . the tragic loss of all hope."[10]

In this chapter, I propose to reconsider our attachment to revolutionary rupture in favor of the project of maintaining life at a moment when most of the world's species are under existential threat. We may need to break with dominant systems in order to get to new political and economic conditions, but if stability is itself a desirable element of social justice, we must also think our way beyond ruptures, treating them not as goals in themselves, but as waystations on the route to another, more reliable, set of conditions. In our long love affair with rupture, we have lost sight of the hard, ongoing work of maintaining life.

Indeed, while radicals emphasize the shattering of the status quo, the actual labor of sustaining life has always hummed away in the background, even through revolutionary upheaval, most of it performed by women—care for the sick, the preparation of food, and the daily upkeep of environments. This kind of labor is not necessarily creative or radically emancipatory. It has to happen in many of the same ways every day. But no human sociality has ever taken shape without it. And right now, as the climate catastrophe worsens, the project of keeping life going cannot be taken for granted. To this end, I argue, we must revalue *maintenance*: the dull, literally conservative work of keeping ordinary life going.

A focus on maintenance presents an aesthetic challenge. The most basic goods, like the steady provision of food and water, clean air, and shelter, are by definition unexciting. They may even seem too obvious to name. After all, we do not argue about whether or not we all need to breathe air. But right now, as the most fundamental conditions of survival are unequally distributed and under ever-increasing threat, we cannot take these basic conditions for granted as the ordinary, dull backdrop to more exciting activity.

It is in this context that I want to turn away from the experimental poetry and speculative fiction beloved of ecocriticism and back toward realism, which is well known—and often reviled—for its focus on the mundane. Critics have long argued that realism is troubling politically because it naturalizes the ordinary life of a particular historical moment, seeking, as Franco Moretti writes, "to inscribe the present so deeply in the past that alternatives became simply unimaginable."[11] But this does not do realism justice. Realist fictions are often interested in focusing our attention precisely on the repetitive work of keeping life going, and far from taking this labor for granted, they work to slow down perception so that we do not rush past the everyday activity of maintenance to more exciting events and adventures. To this end, realist texts engage in a range of specific practices which I call here *realist defamiliarization*. These are strategies texts use to turn our attention from our usual interest in thrills and exceptions to the mundane forms necessary for maintaining ordinary life and carefully invite us to appreciate their importance. I want to suggest that these strategies are politically urgent in this moment of climate crisis, as the arduous, necessary, unglamorous work of sustaining life over time—securing basic food, water, and shelter—is under immediate threat.

I use the term "sustainability" here, although there have been lots of persuasive critiques of the term. What I want to suggest is that sustainability is in fact a kind of neutral term: it refers to the capacity to keep any state of affairs going over time. In this sense, sustainability can refer to just or unjust conditions, to environmental or social worlds. It is true that if we work to sustain current economic systems, we become complicit with the most rapacious forces on earth. The goal should not be to sustain neoliberalism or gas-guzzling lifestyles for the rich. But it is also clear that our dominant systems are in fact dramatically *un*sustainable: the pace of emissions is quickly making the planet uninhabitable for almost all living beings. And as precarity becomes an increasingly pervasive condition—both economically and environmentally catastrophic for most of the world—we are faced with a struggle to keep collective life going at all. Those already struggling hardest to sustain livelihoods and lifeworlds over time are the world's poorest and most vulnerable. It is in this context that the fight to preserve habitable conditions for human and nonhuman lives over the long term—stable planetary temperatures, arable land, clean air and water, and stable shelter—should, I believe, be our highest political priority.

Revaluing Routine

What would it mean, then, for literary studies to reclaim the project of a genuine sustainability—the ongoing work of maintaining life? I will argue here that we should begin by revaluing routine. Since the romantics, critics have defined art against routine, casting the shocks of a genuine art as the best or only ways to free ourselves from the numbing automatism of modern life. In Victor Shklovsky's famous line: "Habitualization devours works, clothes, furniture, one's wife, and the fear of war." For Shklovsky, art is defined by its capacity to counter the terrifying mindlessness of routine: "The purpose of art is to make objects 'unfamiliar.'"[12]

But what if routines are both necessary and desirable forms for sustainability? Routines and their close relations—habits—are ways of organizing experience. They are what I would call *forms*.[13] Specifically, they are arrangements of action into sequences so repetitive that they come to feel automatic and unthinking. Since they maintain everyday life, routines are conservative. They require little, if any, consciousness. They free us from decision-making. They are in this sense the opposite of thought, creativity, and critique. Modern thinkers have most often associated routines with industrial labor and the mechanization of experience. But human bodies have a periodic need for sleep, water, and food, which means that we return, day in and day out, to face the same necessities. In order to conserve health and well-being, humans have always needed—and probably will always need—ongoing, regular provisions of nourishment and rest, as well as the repetitive labor that makes those possible.

Of course, it is possible to survive with unpredictable food and radically disrupted sleep, and some people opt for that, but for most, the irregularity is painful, even catastrophic. US adults who do not have enough to eat report that they suffer not only from faintness, pain, and weakness but also from excruciating, ongoing anxiety about the uncertainty of their food supply: "I am worried. Worried each day where the next meal is going to come from"; "I am always thinking where to get the next meal"; "Always there a sense of anxiety I am feeling"; "I am worried sick. How am I going to feed the children?"[14]

It is worth noting, too, that routines are not only necessary but also can be pleasurable. One can be soothed by the ritual of morning coffee, for example, or refreshed by regular sleep. All cultures, too, are shaped by repetitive practices—from harvesting crops to religious observance to a weekly poker game—that keep social worlds going.

In short, routines are essential forms for sustaining collective life over time. And so, while it is urgent that we end current routines of fossil fuel extraction and wasteful consumption, the goal cannot be to do away with routines altogether. The challenge is to figure out how to replace unequal and destructive routines with those that can sustain both human and nonhuman species over time.

It is here that realism can help us. The critical tradition that shuns routine in favor of defamiliarizing shock tends to turn to avant-garde and modernist work for its exemplary aesthetics. As Rita Felski writes: "Modernism especially, with its roughened verbal textures and often startling juxtapositions, can inject a sense of strangeness and surprise into its portrayal of the most commonplace phenomena. It makes the familiar seem newly uncanny, jolting us out of atrophied perceptions and ready-to-hand formulae."[15] Realism, by contrast, is interested in prompting audiences to become alert to routines—and to recognize their immense importance. I will use Shklovsky against himself here to make the paradoxical case that we literary critics should pause to reconsider our automatic rejections of regularity and stability, our routine dismissals of routine. And I will make the case that many realist writers, both in the nineteenth century and in our own time, seek to defamiliarize routine itself, in part to help us to cultivate an appreciation for the necessary, unending work of sustaining ordinary life.

Nineteenth-century realism in particular is explicit about its goal of moving us away from a reflexive enthusiasm for *exceptions*—exciting events and extraordinary persons—in favor of recognizing that which is neither special nor astonishing. A wide range of realist writers seek to unsettle our habits of being drawn to special and remarkable people and events. Consider, for example, one of the most famous passages in *Middlemarch*, where we find Dorothea surprised to be sobbing on her honeymoon:

> Not that this inward amazement of Dorothea's was anything very exceptional: many souls in their young nudity are tumbled out among incongruities and left to "find their feet" among them, while their elders go about their business. Nor can I suppose that when Mrs. Casaubon is discovered in a fit of weeping six weeks after her wedding, the situation will be regarded as tragic. Some discouragement, some faintness of heart at the new real future which replaces the imaginary, is not unusual, and we do not expect people to be deeply moved by what is not unusual. That element of tragedy which lies in the very fact of frequency, has not yet wrought itself into the coarse emotion of mankind; and perhaps our frames could hardly bear much of it. If we had a keen vision and feeling of all ordinary human life, it would be like hearing the grass grow and the squirrel's heart beat, and we should die of that roar which lies on the other side of silence. As it is, the quickest of us walk about well wadded with stupidity.[16]

Dorothea is astonished to find herself miserable, but hers is actually a very routine kind of unhappiness, so frequent that elders ignore it, immersed in their own routines: they just "go about their business." Meanwhile, we readers too are stupefied by habit. "Well wadded with stupidity," our perceptions are dull; we are inattentive. Specifically, we cannot focus on ordinary unhappiness because it is just too common. Eventually, perhaps, we might develop new habits of perception, as the tragedy of ordinary suffering gets "wrought" into our emotions. In the meanwhile, however, the realist novelist has to develop aesthetic strategies that register the frequency of ordinary experience while also distancing us from it, making it feel less ordinary, so that we experience some shock of recognition.

A similar logic drives another famous realist passage. Here, Charles Dickens's *Bleak House* draws our attention to the fact that Jo the crossing-sweeper is dying from poverty and neglect:

> He is not one of Mrs. Pardiggle's Tockahoopo Indians; he is not one of Mrs. Jellyby's lambs, being wholly unconnected with Borrioboola-Gha; he is not softened by distance and unfamiliarity; he is not a genuine foreign-grown savage; he is the ordinary home-made article. Dirty, ugly, disagreeable to all the senses, in body a common creature of the common streets, only in soul a heathen. Homely filth begrimes him, homely parasites devour him, homely sores are in him, homely rags are on him: native ignorance, the growth of English soil and climate, sinks his immortal nature lower than the beasts that perish. Stand forth, Jo, in uncompromising colours! From the sole of thy foot to the crown of thy head, there is nothing interesting about thee.[17]

Distance and unfamiliarity, according to Dickens, "soften" our image of the remote heathen, making him seem appealing and interesting. By contrast, Jo's closeness and familiarity make him both repellent *and* uninteresting. There is a kind of circular logic at work here: first, we ignore the poor because they are all around us and so feel too familiar for us to take any interest; then we become so used to ignoring poverty that we fail to notice how shockingly everyday it is. Not only is one boy dead, but others are also "dying thus around us every day" (572). It is the common things we are inclined to ignore, but their commonness is, in fact, precisely what is shocking about them. What Dickens needs, then, is a representational strategy that will shock us into a recognition of the familiar—as both everyday *and* shocking. We ignore poor children like Jo because they are too familiar and ordinary for us to take any interest. But the commonness of Jo's fate is, in fact, *precisely* what should be most shocking to us. The really astonishing fact about Jo's death is how everyday it is.

Although Eliot and Dickens are otherwise vastly different, these passages suggest a shared concern, which is what I am calling realist defamiliarization. Neither text seeks to naturalize the commonplace; but nor do they struggle to reject the everyday in favor of radical newness and unfamiliarity. Rather, Eliot and Dickens alike seek to freshen perception of what is precisely not fresh—to jolt us into alertness to the "very fact of frequency," the "nothing interesting" that is human suffering. Since the ordinary is worse and more horrifying than the exceptional, the point is to shock us into recognizing its magnitude, the vast scale of its sheer unremarkableness. Shklovsky's concern is that we have dulled our perceptions in the face of an interesting world, while realist defamiliarization as I define it here struggles to generate an alert, attentive perception to the world's very dullness.

Defamiliarization for Sustainability

In some ways, the work Eliot and Dickens undertake to jolt us into a recognition of the suffering that is all around us is the opposite of revaluing routine. They are trying to reveal the horrors of the humdrum. But as these realist texts work to defamiliarize the ordinary, they hint at an unfamiliar critical practice that will serve the ends of sustainability well: the task of bringing routines from the background into the spotlight, paying a close attention to the work that they do. In this section of the chapter, I will point to four specific strategies of realist defamiliarization that prompt us not only to recognize the importance of routines but to appreciate their crucial value to the project of maintaining life.

Narrative Closure

The term "closure" suggests that narratives endings bring all action to a close. But that is not in fact quite accurate. Even classic happy endings tend to conclude with patterns of activity that extend predictably into the future. In Antony Trollope's *Barchester Towers* (1857), for example, the two male protagonists conclude the novel engaged in the steady performance of their obligations: Mr. Arabin "is a studious, thoughtful, hard-working man. He lives constantly at the deanery and preaches nearly every Sunday." Mr. Harding "does such duties as fall to his lot well and conscientiously."[18] Here, narrative closure does not entail the end of all action, but specifically the end of uncertain, sensational, *plotted* action, in favor of stable ongoing routines.

Of course, critics have often dismissed endings like these as consummately conservative, as shutting down revolutionary desires and falsely resolving social conflicts. Trollope's dutiful conclusion certainly seems exemplary of the least revolutionary impulses of the realist novel. But I want to suggest here that the routines that govern narrative endings can also point to a more promising politics of justice. Take, for example, George Moore's 1894 novel about an illiterate servant, *Esther Waters*. For most of the novel, we follow the character through crises and instabilities, including a pregnancy out of wedlock, unemployment, gambling wins and losses, near starvation, trouble with the police, and a long struggle to raise an illegitimate child. The novel ends, however, with Esther falling into a life of regularity with her employer. "In the evening they sat in the library sewing, or Mrs. Barfield read aloud, or they talked of their sons. On Sundays they had their meetings." In this smooth final stage of the novel, Esther's employer asks her if she would like to marry, and she responds: "Marry and begin life over again! All the worry and bother over again! Why should I marry?"[19] In place of the "worry and bother" of the marriage plot, the two women agree to "Work on, work on to the end," the exact duplication of the phrase conveying the sameness of the sequence to follow.[20] This is not the stuff of narratable adventure, but it is for Esther the first genuine prospect of a sustainable life—reliable food and the regular rituals of labor and religious observance. It is hard-won relief from the trials of poverty, the pleasurable prospect of predictable work rather than plotted worry.

If we read this ending as deliberately drawing our attention away from the conventional illusion of happiness in marriage and toward the actual material routines that sustain bodies and communities, we can see this as a kind of realist defamiliarization that is especially valuable in a moment of radical precarity. This is art that breaks us out of routinized perception—the assumption that marriage will always bring a woman's story to an end—precisely so that we will recognize and appreciate routine—the economic security that marriage supposedly promises but too often fails to deliver.

Even more subtly, this ending defamiliarizes the very idea of narrative closure itself. If we assume that closure brings action to an end, we see here something more precise: the end offers us a conclusion to the excitements of plotted action, but what it promises us is ongoing repetition, the prospect of stable routines like food, labor, and companionship stretching on into the future. Although critics have often read domestic endings in particular as nostalgic and ideologically oppressive, Susan Fraiman has recently made a case for the radical political potential of domesticity itself: "Desiring shelter is not necessarily conservative."[21] One of Fraiman's memorable examples is a passage near the end of *Stone Butch Blues* (1993), one of the first and most influential works of transgender literature. The main character Jess finally has a chance to create a home after a long period of homelessness, financial precarity, and violence. Jess paints, cleans, and buys linens and bath soaps at a department store, which is not weakly consumerist in this context, Fraiman argues, but rather "an audacious effort to produce a basic sense of physical and psychic security by someone who has been repeatedly violated."[22] This is an ending like Moore's, in other words, that is not so much offering a facile illusion of stability as it is slowly and lovingly lingering on the ordinary work of sustaining life over time in the wake of acute precarity and violence—defamiliarizing it in Shklovsky's sense.

The Perspective of the Outsider

The second strategy of realist defamiliarization I want to explore here is one of the most time honored: the perspective of the outsider. Although this literary technique in itself will not feel particularly new or surprising, I want to suggest here that it could be especially valuable for jolting wealthy and privileged readers into an appreciation for comforts that feel so ordinary that they cease to draw notice. Since the ordinary lives of the rich—including car and air travel, air conditioning, and meat consumption—are disproportionately responsible for the carbon emissions that are driving climate change, and since the uneven distribution of basic comforts is a major cause of injustice and suffering both now and to come, on political grounds the dramatic differences in what constitutes routine comforts for some and not for others should in fact be inviting our closest attention.

Chimamanda Ngozi Adichie's 2013 novel, *Americanah*, is my example here. The novel is interested in the ways that luxuries and conveniences become so routine that those who enjoy them quickly come to take them for granted. Early in the narrative, for example, Aunty Uju's life is transformed when she becomes the mistress of a powerful and wealthy general. "Do you know I've forgotten what it feels like to be in a bus?" she asks the main character, Ifemulu. "It's so easy to get used to all this."[23] Adichie, like Dickens and Eliot, works to shock readers into recognizing habituation as itself shocking.

In order to train us into a more alert attentiveness to the ordinary comforts wealth and privilege bring, Adichie gives us the changing perspectives of two migrant protagonists who move between countries and who rise and fall in personal wealth. As they move, these outsiders observe the changing routines of their social worlds, and this allows them to register the artifice, the sheer unnaturalness, of comforts and conveniences so familiar that those who benefit most simply take them for granted.

One example is the habituation of Americans to the steady provision of electricity. When Ifemulu's mother in Nigeria tells her that there's been no electric light for two weeks, home "seemed suddenly foreign to her" (196). Later, when Ifemulu comes back to Lagos, she is struck by "the loud, discordant drone of generators, too many generators" (478). In Lagos, electricity is impossible to ignore because its provision literally makes a lot of noise. When Ifemulu visits a wealthy home, her friend asks her if she had noticed its "completely noiseless" generator. The fact that she has not paid attention startles Ifemulu into the uncomfortable recognition that she has become too Americanized. She no longer notices what she is now in the habit of ignoring: "a true Lagosian," she says, would have noticed "the generator house, the generator size" (485). The protagonist's movement between the United States and Nigeria is what jolts her into a recognition of her own habituation.

The difference between electricity flow in the two nations—the United States and Nigeria—is not strictly a matter of wealth: rich Nigerians pay for their own steady provision of electricity. What the noisy generators defamiliarize is the absence of public investment in an electricity infrastructure. Or to put this another way, a smoothly working national electrical grid leads to a dangerous deadening of perception on the part of those who benefit from it. Habituated to the quiet flow of electricity, most Americans can afford to treat it as uninteresting. And so Adichie's turn to a plot organized around mobility across national borders might sharpen many US readers' attention to our own habits of taking the steady flow of electricity for granted, her plain description alerting us to a comfort which middle-class Americans habitually treat as too ordinary to draw our notice.

Convenience itself, the easy, steady provision of goods and services, is what blunts perception. Like her Aunty Uju, Ifemulu is temporarily seduced by the life offered to her by a wealthy boyfriend who brings her "the gift of contentment and ease." Unlike her aunt, however, she leaves this relationship because she is troubled by the narrowing and dulling of her own observations. "How quickly she had become used to their life" (246). As the character starts to write about race in the United States, she wants to see the world in a clear-eyed way that convenience always threatens to obscure. And so Adichie suggests that the realist project itself depends on a defamiliarization of ease and comfort.

Obinze, the novel's other protagonist, worries that his wealth is corrupting him and preventing him from seeing the world plainly. He decries garish colors and displays of wealth. And at one point he gets nostalgic for a past when he could not take the steady flow of electricity for granted: when the "neighbor downstairs used to shout, 'Praise the Lord!' whenever the light came back and how even for me there was something so beautiful about the light coming back, when it's out of your control because you don't have a generator" (533). This is beauty that comes not from splendor or subtlety but from the surprise of not being able to depend on the steady provision of electric light, which allows one literally to perceive the ordinariness of one's surroundings, and which, in becoming too routine, loses its capacity to move us.

Adichie's version of realist defamiliarization could be particularly valuable now. Given the deterioration of public infrastructures in wealthy countries and the opportunity to invest in new green infrastructures that could help us to sustain life over the long term—such as renewable power grids and zero-emissions public transportation systems—Adichie's strategies draw our attention to what too often seems like background noise for the rich and the comfortable, too uninteresting to invite our attention. Training ourselves not to take our comforts for granted is a crucial task in this moment of climate emergency, when we would do well to figure out what our infrastructures are costing, why they are crumbling, and what we can do to build sustainable systems for the long term.

Historical Defamiliarization

The third realist strategy I want to explore here is similar to the perspective of the outsider we have seen in Adichie, but this one revolves on temporal rather than spatial difference. I call it historical defamiliarization. My central example here is *Call the Midwife* (2012–), the BBC drama based on the memoir of a midwife working for the new National Health Service in London in the 1950s. *Call the Midwife* invites us to appreciate the National Health Service by repeatedly reminding us of life before the welfare state as well as its deterioration in our own time.

The series frequently looks backward to remind us of the Victorian workhouse system, acknowledging that the workhouse did provide basic food and shelter for the poorest British subjects. As one character in *Call the Midwife* says, "It was a roof over people's heads. They didn't starve." But this was a far cry from supporting their well-being. "I imagine none of you girls have ever been inside a workhouse," Sister Evangelina scolds the young nurses. "They were designed to break the spirit, worse than dying."[24] In one early episode, we hear the story of two orphans, Peg and Frank, who spend their lives trying to repair the damage done to them by the workhouse system. "It got a hold on you. Got inside your head," says Peg, who still finds herself muttering compulsive apologies to the workhouse administrators even decades after she has been free of them.

The most painful aspect of the organization of the workhouse for these two characters is that it deliberately separated family members. Divided from each other in childhood, Peg and her brother are so traumatized by their separation that they refuse to leave each other's sides even in death.[25] By contrast, the new public health infrastructure is organized around home visits, which bring the state to the family. The goal of the midwife in particular is to support the integrity and well-being of life within the home, as the laboring mothers give birth in their own beds, surrounded by friends and relatives, and encouraged to form loving bonds with their newborns.

The National Health Service could certainly be criticized for being much too focused on the traditional heterosexual family—with mostly married mothers laboring inside domestic walls. But I want to suggest that *Call the Midwife* deliberately offers a more inclusive politics than that. It shows us over and over that it is not only the conventional married couple who are entitled to connectedness. We are invited to feel sorrow for Mary, for example, a fifteen-year-old Irish sex worker who is thrown into unbearable misery by her enforced separation from her child. And even after we learn that Peg and Frank's relationship is incestuous, we are invited to understand it as a worthy form of love relation, better in many ways than a conventional marriage. In short, the crucial difference between the two state infrastructures ends up having everything to do with their capacity to sustain relationships: while the workhouse enforced separation, the welfare state works to support intimate connections.

Like Adichie, the BBC series invites us to appreciate public infrastructures by asking us to keep in mind what it is like not to have them, but unlike *Americanah*, it does not do so only to spark an alert awareness among the privileged to stop taking it all for granted—because it is already too late for that. In the midst of ongoing cuts to state programs, *Call the Midwife* invites a contrast not only to an earlier time but also to a later one, such as contemporary Britain, where home health visits, public housing, and full university tuition benefits have become a distant memory. It also invites an American audience to contrast the British welfare state of the 1950s to a contemporary United States, where no national health service ever took shape. Like Adichie, *Call the Midwife* teaches us to feel desire for the routines of a smoothly functioning public infrastructure. And the particular genius of this series is to invite us to recognize that the dreariest conduits of public works can carry not only bodies and basic services but also—a little shockingly—love.

The Narrative of the Struggling Team

While many literary critics have turned to science fiction to help us to imagine alternative futures in the Anthropocene, I am drawn to realism in part because I am especially concerned with the practical work that needs to be done urgently to slow the pace of global warming and to build routines of food and water security and green infrastructures for all. In place of mourning, I want to think the *how* of social change, and to put our minds to the movement from here to there as feasible—workable—including the nitty-gritty of organizing for economic and ecological sustainability. Literary scholars have not been disposed to use our work to draw conclusions about the practicalities of political organizing—and for a number of reasons: first, because institutions and norms have seemed repressive and instrumentalizing, the enemies of aesthetic autonomy, oppositionality, resistance, and emancipation; second, because we have understood our role as critical unpacking and unsettling rather than as planning or designing; and third, because the texts we study rarely invite an attention to the nuts and bolts of creating institutions, or setting down rules, or organizing movements.

And yet, while it is true that few canonical works of art and literature are explicitly about effective political organizing, several of the formal components of successful organizing for political action are in fact alive and well in cultural circulation around us, and in a surprising place—popular television and movies. My example of realist defamiliarization in this section is not a single text, but a popular plot that is by now so familiar that we are probably inclined to dismiss it as too clichéd for our attention. I call it "the narrative of the struggling team." This is a plot that often revolves around sports, but it can focus on music, dance, military, or academic teams: examples range from *The Sandlot* (1993) to *Friday Night Lights* (2006–11), from *Revenge of the Nerds* (1984) to *Overcomer* (2019), from *Fame* (1980) to *Glee* (2009–15), from *Stand and Deliver* (1988) to *The Great Debaters* (2007). While I myself know English-language examples best, this story also gives shape to popular films in China (*Shaolin Soccer*, 2001) and India (*Iqbal*, 2005; *Say Salaam India*, 2007; *Victory*, 2013), and to more than one Japanese manga and anime series (*Akakichi No Eleven*, 1970–1; *Eyeshield 21*, 2002–9).

You know the drill. The story starts off with a motley assemblage of underdogs, seemingly unable to meet the challenges of the sports season or the performance competition. The group then encounters a series of obstacles, from an undisciplined member of the team to trouble at home. But thanks to a charismatic coach or team leader, the team submits to rigorous training and careful practice. They pull together. Specifically, they subordinate individual desires to hours of free throw practice or the tight, unyielding choreography of the dance.

What is important here is that the narrative of the struggling team goes to some trouble to focus attention on the routines required for people to work in a coordinated fashion toward a shared goal. We might think of the classic montage sequence that shows the arduous routines involved in coordinating collective action behind the scenes: untold hours of free throw practice, running laps, pushup sequences, and dance rehearsal. *Remember the Titans* (2000), for instance, tells the story of a real Black coach, Herman Boone, who struggled to integrate a high school football team in Virginia in 1971. In the practice montage, we see teammates learning to move in perfectly coordinated formations. The soundtrack synchronizes musical rhythms with the bodily movements of the athletes as they train to hit, jump, do sit-ups, and roll together. We see Boone drag one straggler off the field and all of the coaches constantly correcting and penalizing. Becoming a unified team takes rigorous discipline, and the deliberate channeling of anger and aggression, the coach explains, into "perfect" coordination.

In a neoliberal cultural context whose preferred pleasures are individual choice and consumption, the montage sequence might come as a surprise, since it typically focuses us on the opposite—the arduous repetitiveness and sacrifice involved in drawing together as a team. It shows that success is not the result of raw talent but of long stretches of practice, the monotonous work of trying again and again to synchronize bodies into collective actions. To be sure, sometimes the montage sequence focuses on individual training, and in this sense reinforces the neoliberal value of the fit body as a personal achievement,[26] but the focus on teamwork in many popular stories carefully trains our attention on the subordination of individual preferences and desires to the demands of the collective.

And the endings to these plots do not simply soothe us into accepting the status quo but afford the realization of collective aspirations of all kinds. Sometimes the team loses the competition but has learned the joys of working together. The end of *Fame* is not a competition at all but a showcase of the students' skills: the orchestra, solo singers, a chorus, and ballet and modern dancers come together to perform a piece that moves across styles, including classical, rock, jazz, and a cappella, called, "I Sing the Body Electric." This line from Walt Whitman, self-styled poet of democracy, brings disparate characters and art forms together not into a sorting of winners and losers but into a coordinated, collective act of beauty. The camera shows us that the performance joins not only team members but also joyful audiences who leap from their seats to cheer the rousing performances that bring each story to a familiar end. To assume that all end-oriented narrative reinforces capitalism or sexism is to miss the fact that it can give shape to exquisitely shared pleasures, including democracy—and art itself. The final action is often gloriously aesthetic—the ball caught elegantly in the end zone, or the song performed in breathtaking harmony, with gestures and voices perfectly coordinated across bodies.

The narrative of the struggling team not only valorizes routine; it is itself highly repetitive and predictable. Since Adorno and Horkheimer condemned the culture industry, literary and cultural studies have often imagined the repetitiveness of mass culture as anesthetizing—the oppressive reinforcement of dominant ideologies.[27] But I have suggested that routines are also crucial to the projects of both social welfare—such as the ongoing, reliable provision of food, water, health care, and shelter—and environmental sustainability, the project of keeping the planet livable. And what if progressive and radical movements learned from the narrative of the struggling team to celebrate the joys of collective action also? That is, what if we grasped the work of coming together into coordinated groups both as a sacrifice, demanding the subordination of impulses to a larger end, and also as one of our most satisfying, exciting, and nourishing pleasures? The narrative of the struggling team points us to the potential for desiring the world otherwise and then figuring out how to make it so. This is not an argument for covering over the horrors of exploitation and violence, but a hypothesis and a gambit—that activism for environmental and economic justice has some heady and exciting pleasures to offer and that a successful movement for change might work best from the joined promise of disciplined sacrifice and collective joy.

All of these techniques of realist defamiliarization are valuable, then, in turning us from the excitements of rupture to the necessity and desirability of routine. Realist texts train our attention on the mundane work of sustaining life over time, and this means recognizing the ordinariness of suffering, appreciating regular provisions of adequate nutrition, clean air and water, and health care, becoming aware of the ways that our own comforts and conveniences are blunting our perceptions of labor and infrastructure, and figuring out how to work together, as a struggling team, to practice making the world more sustainable and more just.

Notes

1 Lynn Keller, *Recomposing Ecopoetics: North American Poetry of the Self-Conscious Anthropocene* (Charlottesville: University of Virginia Press, 2018).

2 "If This Goes On," in Gerry Canavan and Kim Stanley Robinson, *Green Planets: Ecology and Science Fiction* (Middletown, CT: Wesleyan University Press, 2014), 16.

3 Notable examples include Amitav Ghosh, *The Great Derangement: Climate Change and the Unthinkable* (Chicago and London: University of Chicago Press, 2016), 87–88; and Stephanie LeMenager, *Living Oil: Petroleum Culture in the American Century* (Oxford: Oxford University Press, 2014).

4 Leerom Medovoi, "Contribution to the Critique of Political Ecology: Sustainability as Disavowal," *New Formations* 69 (winter 2009): 129–143.

5 An elegant example of this argument around poetry and the environment is Joan Retallack's "What Is Experimental Poetry & Why Do We Need It?" *Jacket*, April 2007, http://jacketmagazine.com/32/p-retallack.shtml.

6 Fred Moten and Stefano Harney write of a Black aesthetics that is "(in) the invention of escape, stealing away in the confines, in the form, of a break." *The Undercommons: Fugitive Planning and Black Study* (Minor Compositions, 2013), 51; Tobin Siebers argues that the artistic display of disabled bodies and oozing bodily fluids challenges established standards of beauty and belonging in *Disability Aesthetics* (Ann Arbor: University of Michigan Press, 2010), 62; Edouard Glissant calls for "an aesthetics of disruption and intrusion" in response to a global culture shaped by capitalist consumption. *Poetics of Relation*, trans. Betsy Wing (Ann Arbor: The University of Michigan Press, 2010), 151; Timothy Morton writes "Poetry is astonishingly important ... because poetry tampers directly with causality." "An Object Oriented Defense of Poetry," *New Literary History* 43, no. 2 (spring 2012): 216; Derek Attridge argues that art is characterized by a certain "inventiveness and singularity" that "introduce into the culture the hitherto unthinkable." *The Singularity of Literature* (Abingdon: Routledge, 2004), 121; Jack Halberstam writes in *The Queer Art of Failure* of "a truly political negativity, one that promises, this time, to fail, to make a mess, to fuck shit up, to be loud, unruly, impolite, to

breed resentment, to bash back, to speak up and out, to disrupt, assassinate, shock, and annihilate" (Durham, NC: Duke University Press, 2011), 110.

7   Nadja Popovich Livia Albeck-Ripka, and Kendra Pierre-Louis, "95 Environmental Rules Being Rolled Back Under Trump," *New York Times*, December 21, 2019, https://www.nytimes.com/interactive/2019/climate/trump-environment-rollbacks.html.

8   Juliet Schor, William Attwood-Charles, and Mehmet Cansoy, *After the Gig: How the Sharing Economy Got Hijacked and How to Win It Back* (Berkeley and Los Angeles: University of California Press, 2020).

9   Anahid Nersessian, "Romantic Ecocriticism Lately," *Literature Compass* 15, no. 1 (January 2018): 1–15.

10 Cameron Clark, "Grief, Ecocritical Negativity, and the Queer Anti-Pastoral," *New Review of Film and Television Studies* 17, no. 2 (2019): 211–235.

11 Franco Moretti, *The Bourgeois: Between History and Literature* (London: Verso, 2013), 93.

12 Viktor Shklovsky, "Art as Technique," in *Russian Formalist Criticism: Four Essays*, trans. Lee T. Lemon and Marion J. Reis (Lincoln: University of Nebraska Press, 1965), 12.

13 See Caroline Levine, *Forms: Whole, Rhythm, Hierarchy, Network* (Princeton, NJ: Princeton University Press, 2015).

14 Mohan Jyoti Dutta, LaReina Hingson, Agaptus Anaele, Soumitro Sen, and Kyle Jones, "Narratives of Food Insecurity in Tippecanoe County, Indiana," *Health Communication* 31, no. 6 (2016): 647–658. See also Rebecca M. Aldrich and Virginia A. Dickie, "'It's hard to plan your day when you have no money': Discouraged Workers' Occupational Possibilities and the Need to Reconceptualize Routine," *Work* 45 (2013): 5–15.

15 Rita Felski, "Introduction. Everyday Life," *New Literary History* 33, no. 4 (2002): 608.

16 George Eliot, *Middlemarch* (Harmondsworth: Penguin, 1994), 194.

17 Charles Dickens, *Bleak House* (Oxford: World's Classics, 1996), 668. Subsequent references in parentheses.

18 Anthony Trollope, *Barchester Towers* (London: Dent, 1906), 462.

19 George Moore, *Esther Waters* (Oxford: Oxford World's Classics, 2012), 322, 324.

20 Ibid., 325.

21 Susan Fraiman, *Extreme Domesticity: A View from the Margins* (New York: Columbia University Press, 2017), 39.

22 Ibid., 41.

23 Chimamanda Ngozi Adichie, *Americanah* (New York: Anchor Books, 2014), 94. Subsequent references in parentheses.

24 *Call the Midwife*, dir. Jamie Payne. Season 1, episode 5 (October 28, 2012).

25 *Call the Midwife*, series 1, episode 5.

26 See Jürgen Martschukat, *The Age of Fitness: How the Body Came to Symbolize Success and Achievement*, trans. Alex Skinner (Cambridge and Medford, MA: Polity Press, 2021).

27 Max Horkheimer and Theodor W. Adorno, *The Dialectic of Enlightenment: Philosophical Fragments*, ed. Gunzelin Schmid Noerr, trans. Edmund Jephcott (Stanford, CA: Stanford University Press, 2002).

10

Network Realism/ Capitalist Realism

Dirk Wiemann

"All realism could, in some sense, be said to be capitalist realism,"[1] claims Leigh Claire La Berge in her reading of the fifth season of *The Wire*, one of the most frequently discussed specimen of that medial format that numerous cultural theorists have discovered as the twenty-first-century successor of the novel: the TV serial. In these speculations on the realism of *The Wire* or comparable programs, or the serial format as such, aspects of form and narrative structure are conspicuously central. More specifically, critics often put particular emphasis on two interrelated features, namely the gappy and episodic form ensuing from the strong chapterization (the division of the whole into consecutive "seasons"), and the interlacement of different plot strands into a more or less coherent ensemble.[2] In this vein, for example, John Kraniauskas describes *The Wire* as a text that

> signals, on the one hand, its own partiality and, on the other, its consequent status as a work of narrative totalization that is always already incomplete. In this sense, the program emerges not only from a realist desire to accumulate social content ... but also from a modernist acknowledgment of its own narrative limits (imposed by narrative form) and thus not so much as a representation as an invention.[3]

Kraniauskas's diction is copiously saturated with contrastive pairs, with at least four striking dichotomies squeezed into the space of the two concluding sentences of the cited passage: totalization—incompleteness; content—form; realist—modernist; representation—invention. These binaries are summoned up not in order to get triumphantly deconstructed but rather to enable the work of dialectics proper, where, for example, the form-content dichotomy gets sublated into the notion of form as sedimented content, or the opposition of totality and fragmentation into the concept of the networked world. What such analyses construe is a processing operation or "style" of mimetic representation (whether narrative, iconic or otherwise) that is itself dialectically articulated with the social universe it "registers" (not least by way of formal correlation or isomorphism) but also co-constitutes. As already indicated, two of the most pervasive topoi in these debates are the emphasis on incompleteness and on the more or less loose configuration of distinct but "somehow" entangled narrative strands—formal specifics that, as I will argue in the following pages, are not only characteristic of TV series like *The Wire* but which can safely be identified as hallmark features of a recent "realist turn" in literary production and reception as well. More specifically, I would like to pursue the question as to whether and in what ways these features may indeed be read as symptomatic of some textual engagement with, or at least "registering" of, a distinctly *capitalist* reality so that, as a consequence, some kind of "capitalist realism" would emerge. Such a horizon of expectation is of course strongly steeped in the venerable tradition of Marxist criticism with its penchant for the dialectics of form and content, from Lukács and Macherey via Jameson and Moretti to their current successors who address and/or confront "capitalist realism" across the entire spectrum of cultural production. Before turning, in the second section of this chapter, to literature proper by focusing on debates on the "global novel" today, I will first briefly and roughly delineate a couple of distinct yet interrelated strands of the current debate(s) on capitalist realism.

Mapping the Network of Capitalist Realism

Mark Fisher's influential manifesto, *Capitalist Realism: Is There No Alternative?* (2009), introduces itself as a merely slightly updated version of Fredric Jameson's magisterial work on postmodernism as "the cultural logic of late capitalism." And indeed, many an old acquaintance from the well-worn Jamesonian repertoire makes a cameo appearance in Fisher's narrative—from the waning of affect to the privileging of surface over depth, from the end, not of history but of historical consciousness to the idea of the postmodern as the complete obliteration of temporal heterogeneity. Fisher first takes the reader to the museum in order to familiarize her with his notion of capitalist realism as a kind of meta-realism whose power, at least in part, derives from its capacity to "subsume and consume all of previous history" by integrating it into its omnivorous system of equivalence:

Walk around the British Museum, where you see objects torn from their lifeworlds and assembled as if on the deck of some Predator spacecraft, and you have a powerful image of this process at work. In the conversion of practices and rituals into merely aesthetic objects, the beliefs of previous cultures are objectively ironized, transformed into *artifacts*. Capitalist realism is therefore not a particular type of realism; it is more like realism in itself.[4]

Disembedded and decontextualized ("torn form their lifeworlds"), objects are being transformed into exhibits and arbitrarily assembled and re-configured with other objects from widely discrepant origins and contexts. Where older museological hermeneutics put premium on the syntax of the exhibition at hand and attempted to identify its interpellative force by which the visitor got rendered into the virtual performer *and* reader of a "walking narrative" she herself enacted *and* construed,[5] Fisher's museum, very much in the footsteps of Jameson's diagnoses of the waning of the temporal, appears as an almost purely spatial assemblage, a constellation rather than a plot. Here, objects are juxtaposed and configured without necessarily encouraging (or enforcing) any one particular emplotment. The space of the museum, in the words of Susana Bautista and Anne Balsamo, becomes itself a network, as "dispersed, individualized, practised, and nonlinear as is the space of the digital age."[6] In this perspective, the museum as an institution has undergone a dramatic passage from a centralized authoritative centerpiece of the "exhibitionary complex"[7] to "one of the primary nodes" in the vast network of postmodern culture.[8] Some critics may embrace and endorse this development of the museum into a "distributed network" for its obvious de-hierarchizing impact; in such a reading

> truth, rather than being disseminated outwards from a center point, is discovered in its intersections and interstices, through the (sometimes surprising) juxtapositions that can happen when experiences are assembled collaboratively along the many-branched paths of a rhizome. In the museum as distributed network, content and experience creation resembles atoms coming together and reforming on new platforms to create new molecules, or "choose your own ending" adventure stories.[9]

Yet what appears as a spontaneous and *naturwüchsig* free play here ("atoms coming together to form new molecules") will from the perspective of capitalist realism turn out as an effect and function of precisely that radical de-ontologization and pervasive abstraction that the untrammeled triumph of the "system of equivalence" of postmodern capital entails, namely the instantiation of a decentered space in which everything can be assembled with everything else. As far as the museum is concerned, its revamping into a distributed network then turns out to be nothing more (and nothing less) than one among many instances of that much larger transition which is the passage from the society of discipline to the society of control; and, in terms of capitalist realism, to a fully globalized, transnational capitalism that creates "a networked world," where "the term 'network' is . . . the term most frequently used to connect up elements that are in fact highly disparate."[10] Whatever the ontological status of this "networked world," its defining paradigm is, as in Fisher's museum-as-network, the implementation of a pervasive interconnectivity of all the items that are included in it. This interconnectivity rests on the fundamental principle of commensurability thanks to the universal equivalent, which is, of course, money. Hence Fisher's reiteration of the well-worn lament of the waning of the object world in its transformation into a fundus of commodities: "one effect of its 'system of equivalence' which can assign all cultural objects, whether they are religious iconography, pornography, or *Das Kapital*, a monetary value."[11] And it is precisely by way of the relentless enactment, over and over again and with less and less exceptions, of this principle of equivalence that capitalism presents itself as more and more "natural" and self-evident. It materializes as reality by way of its performativity. "Capitalist realism" is therefore a name not only for a processing operation or "style" of mimetic representation (whether narrative, iconic, or otherwise) but just as much for the pervasive ideology, or structure of feeling, attendant on the social reality that postmodern capital constantly implements and simultaneously enacts *as given*. In Fisher's own formulation,

> capitalist realism . . . cannot be confined to art or to the quasi-propagandistic way in which advertising functions. It is more like a pervasive atmosphere, conditioning not only the production of culture but also the regulation of work and education, and acting as a kind of invisible barrier constraining thought and action.[12]

The reality to which capitalist realism refers, then, is first and foremost an ideological effect. In this vein, Boltanski and Chiapello reconstruct the "networked world," which they so elaborately describe as the result of essentially linguistic projections—more specifically, metaphoric operations—that are routinely rehearsed in the 1990s management literature they meticulously analyze. This, of course, does not mean that "the network" was not real; however, its status is not that of some inert given to whose non-negotiable existence one would have to acquiesce but rather that of a reality effect in the Barthesian sense; or it exists as a Latourian "factish," that is, as the outcome of a series of operations through which an object which can be traced back to a genealogy of construction (of "thing-making") yet achieves the solid and virtually natural facticity of an apparent given so that "construction and reality are synonyms."[13] Indeed, if

Latour proposes a realistic constructivism in order to outflank the ostensible dichotomy of realism and constructivism in the social sciences, then such a project is, perhaps to some extent surprisingly, germane to the analysis and critique of capitalist realism as well: not because Fisher, Boltanski, or even Hardt and Negri held any substantial affinities with actor-network theory (nor, vice versa, ANT with neo-Marxism) but because of the fact that Marxist theory itself has always seen it as instrumental to address the complex entanglements that pertain between actors and *Umwelt*. This, emphatically, includes the whole epistemological and aesthetic dimension of representation, thereby marking the Marxist tradition as particularly prone to engaging with the complexities of world-making. In fact, Fredric Jameson has long ago exemplarily formularized the dialectics that complicate the notion of capitalist realism with regards to the realist novel in the moment of its ascendancy, when it assumes

> the task of producing as though for the first time that very life world, that very "referent"—the newly quantifiable space of extension and market equivalence, the new rhythms of measurable time, the new secular and "disenchanted" object world of the commodity system, with its post-traditional daily life and its bewilderingly empirical, "meaningless," and contingent *Umwelt*—of which this new narrative discourse will then claim to be the "realistic" reflection.[14]

The reality effect is therefore always also an anteriority effect: that which is constructed by some operation is presented in the course of that same operation as always already there prior to any intervention. What assumes the guise of posterior "reflection" is, in other words, constitutively involved in the making of the very thing it purports to merely "represent." This suggestion, to be sure, is neither radically new nor restricted to Marxist theory. In fact, already Aristotle posits mimesis as an act not simply of copying but also of making—which leads Paul Ricoeur to glean from the *Poetics* an "almost exclusive interest in mimesis as inventive,"[15] and Rita Felski to assert that the world that mimesis allegedly merely reproduces is always already "*pre-figured*" in prior semiotic and narrative splinters that mimesis, then, re-assembles by skimming and recombining material "enmeshed within semiotic and social networks of meaning"[16]—perhaps as arbitrarily and randomly as the museum according to Fisher. To the extent that reality is not to be grasped in itself, but always only as that which is accessible by way of prior textualization; to the extent, then, that realism and constructivism (as we have seen) merge into some version of "realistic constructivism," mimesis too shades off into *poiesis*, representation into invention. And yet it would be not only counterintuitive but probably also counterproductive to fully discard the distinction between realist writing and its manifold "others" altogether, whether these others can be identified as "romantic," "modernist," "experimentalist," "escapist," "genre" fiction, or whatever. Instead of simply clinging to the assertion that "realism" does not have any stable and fixed reality to refer to in the first place and therewith triumphantly proclaiming that there is neither realism nor non-realism but simply "writing" as such,[17] it appears much more productive to attempt to distinguish between different praxes, perhaps in a loose reappropriation of Jakobson's notion of "the dominant."[18] This would enable the critic to hold apart, or locate on a heuristic spectrum, texts that foreground the constructedness of the factish and texts that highlight the factishness of the constructed. The "dominant" of the former would probably be the metatextual reflection of the very conditions of (im)possibility of signification and representation, while the latter texts' dominant would likely consist of various devices of creating *vraisemblance*: more simply put, where the former texts would signpost "invention" the latter ones would emphasize "representation."

Registration Forms

This last pair leads me back to Kraniauskas's reading of *The Wire*, and from there to a brief survey of current debates on realism, capitalist, or otherwise. As we have seen, the polarity of "representation" and "invention" is explicitly summoned up in Kraniauskas's text, where the former appears to emanate from "a realist desire to accumulate social content" and the latter to answer to the reflexive "modernist" (and by extension, for sure, also postmodernist) insight into some ineluctable limitation inherent to narrative, if not language as such. Of course, Kraniauskas is not explicitly asserting that realist representation were a mere passive reflection of some given pre-discursive reality. But by suggesting that realism is a quest for the accumulation of social content, and by contrasting "representation" and "invention," he implies that these are mutually exclusive operations. What the realist text does, then, is not to "invent" but to "represent," not to construct but to "register" social content. In this way, *The Wire* for Kraniauskas "register[s] an important, though banal, truth . . . : the excess of history."[19] To "register" implies, still for Kraniauskas, a marked proximity to classic paradigms of realist writing (reminiscent of Isherwood's "quite passive" camera with its open shutter) where "the novel, as a written form, acts as a recording machine, registering the co-existence of other semiotic systems,"[20] and where "to register" easily slides into that more drastic marker of some well-nigh naturalist realism, "to document," so that a film sequence may "register and document" at the same time.[21] To be sure, Kraniauskas's penchant for the verb "to register" is neither insignificant nor idiosyncratic; instead, it could be argued, the term has become a virtual buzzword, albeit an inconspicuous and hence often overlooked one, in current critical writing of what Jed Esty has called the "realist turn" (it being understood that the term does not denote some return to a realist mode of writing that had been allegedly abandoned in literary practice but a turning of the tides of critical appreciation). Esty reconstructs a Cold-War orthodoxy that put a premium on modernist or postmodernist experimentalism and reflexivity and hence favored texts that overtly and self-referentially "imagine" the world over realist texts that "merely registered, described, and chronicled" it.[22] Inasmuch as this Cold-War ideology privileged imagination over "mere registration," self-referential and metafictional experimentalism over clear-window style, it deeply entrenched a disfavoring of realism for most of the second half of the twentieth century.

By contrast, the current critical climate seems to have substantially changed in favor of realism, arguably in close affinity with literary production itself which, too, has rehabilitated realist writing styles. In light of the reflections in the previous paragraphs, it could be argued that this "turn" has something to do with the perception of a newly intensified exposure to a reality experienced as massively "out of joint": a new sensibility for all kinds of crisis that make pressingly urgent the need of what Donna Haraway has called "big-enough stories" to make sense of what appears utterly meaningless.[23] Of course it can be argued that such writing had never disappeared in the first place; but there is arguably a shift from the older postmodernist orthodoxy that stories have primarily to refer to themselves *as stories,* to the current preference for a mode of neo-realist writing that has its commitment to the extratextual world writ large on its sleeve, be this in terms of the ecology, the waning of democracy worldwide, or the excesses of global capitalism. What novels do today, it seems, is not so much to imagine but, precisely, to "register" these tendencies—an act of literature that should not be grasped simply as the "reflection" of a given reality but equally as the co-constitution of that which is registered. In this vein, Lauren Goodlad describes realist literature as both "*worlded* (in taking the material world for its premise) and *worlding* (in making new ways of seeing, knowing, thinking, and being palpable to those worlds)," and hastens to add that it is this doubleness that enables realist literature "to register the unregistered."[24] This is an almost verbatim rehearsal of Fredric Jameson's earlier distinction of realism's alleged task of "seeing things and finding out things that have not been registered before."[25] More systematically, the Warwick Research Collective around Neil Lazarus, Stephen Shapiro, Benita Parry, and Sharae Deckard define world literature as the realist "literary registration of the world system,"[26] elegantly bypassing the obvious circumstance that "the world-system" is of course not self-evidently given and very certainly does *not* have a concrete referent "out there." Rather it is a complex and contentious paradigm and not some non-negotiable fact readily available for "registration."

Narrating the Global

If the "literary registration of the world system" is one of the tenets of contemporary debates on realism; if, in other words, realism today is somehow perceived to be located within the horizon of the global rather than the local or even the national, then the appropriate setting for capitalist realism as a literary style would have to be that cherished object of contemporary literary criticism, namely world literature—a term which, in the Anglophone humanities, "gained momentum in the period when capital reassembled itself after the 2008 crisis."[27] Of course the world-literary turn in criticism and theory is a complex, internally contradictory, and ongoing process which so far has had numerous transformative effects (whether salutary or damaging), the discussion of which would clearly exceed the scope of this chapter. For the remaining considerations, however, I would wish to focus only on the somewhat disturbing circumstance that, whatever may have changed in Anglophone literary criticism under the auspices of world literature studies, at least one thing has remained stubbornly in place, namely that myopic bias that Clifford Siskin has long ago identified and decried as "novelism," that is, "the now habitual subordination of writing to the novel."[28] The extent to which literature tends to get identified with (and reduced to) novels alone is impressively indexed by the proliferation of qualifiers deemed to introduce appropriate compound terms for the "global novel" or "world novel" as a privileged object of literary studies today: terms that have been applied to those contemporary novels that center on aspects of globalization, the experience of transnationalism, planetarity, and the neoliberal world order. Critics have suggested a variety of qualifiers for these texts, including, among others, the "cosmopolitan,"[29] the "transnational,"[30] the "geopolitical,"[31] the "global,"[32] the "transcultural,"[33] the "planetary,"[34] the "maximalist,"[35] the "cosmodern,"[36] or the "neoliberal."[37] What emerges from contributions like these is the consensus that if not literature in general then at least the practices of the novel have entered into a decidedly postnational dynamics in which the "world novel"[38] serves as an experimental form whose function is "to offer a networked model of social and economic interaction, one in which globalization, for good and for ill, is no longer simply equivalent with Americanization (or even Westernization), in which the links between former peripheries are as significant, and potentially as disruptive, as more familiar patterns of North-South relations."[39]

The keyword here is "networked": a specific form of connectivity that appears to take center stage in the global imaginary of novelistic articulation, but which the "global novel" obviously holds in common with the vast corpus of management literature that, according to Boltanski and Chiapello, establishes the network as the central paradigm and concept metaphor of the neoliberal economy. Capitalist realism, then, will tend to "register" the networked architecture of the neoliberal regime in equally networked formal features. What ensues, then, is a literary form of expression, a new kind of realism that blogger James Bridle has dubbed "network realism." Bridle introduces this term in a discussion of the later works of William Gibson: a sort of fiction that he defines, in a rather vague and thin theorization, as "a mode of writing that is of and about the network."[40] According to Bridle, Gibson's novels fit the bill because they are set in the present or in the conceivable near future, media-saturated, and set in an environment marked by global or at least transnational interconnections. Of course, the "network" realism of the "world novel" participates in a much larger discursive ensemble that posits a networked world. Long before Boltanski and Chiapello, this imaginary has been influentially theorized in Manuel Castell's notion of a global network society powered by microelectronics-based information and communication technologies. Importantly, for Castells, the network society is not a homogeneous global village but rather a structure of combined and uneven development: it "diffuses selectively throughout the planet, working on the pre-existing sites, organizations, and institutions that still make up most of the material environment of people's lives"[41] but all the same increasingly arranges human relations of production and consumption, experience, and power in sets of interconnected nodes. Thus, while the network society is much more flexibly stratified than prior formations of the social, it does by no means create an even or level playing field; instead, hierarchies pertain between the various positions that the different nodes inhabit within the dynamic architecture of the web, whose logic is not only integrative and expansive but also exclusive and expulsive: "everything, and everyone, which does not have value, according to what is valued in the networks, or ceases to have value, is switched off the networks, and ultimately discarded."[42]

Similarly, in Caroline Levine's new formalist scenario, networks are introduced as forms "that link people and objects, including multinational trade, terrorism and transportation."[43] Inasmuch as "all networks afford connectivity; all create links between disconnected nodes,"[44] Levine's claim that forms live and flourish in all domains and dimensions of the social, from materialized institutions to literary patterns, is particularly persuasive in the context of a discussion of the world novel. Here, E. M. Forster's old imperative to network "Only connect!" spectacularly reappears in the form of the interlaced, multi-strand, often loosely, and episodically entangled "plot of globalization" that Alexander Beecroft identifies as a "device ... to project onto the level of form the paranoiac interconnectedness of life in a globalized era."[45] Beecroft is here clearly indebted to the diagnoses of postmodern claustrophobia so powerfully put forth by Fredric Jameson in his theses on conspiracy paranoia as a surrogate for an ever-receding grip on totality.[46] Therefore, his interlaced "plot of globalization" appears as a network that not simply connects but actually ensnares: a reiteration, then, of the "entrapment model"[47] that, whether in Althusserian Marxism, Adorno-style Frankfurt School thought, classic structuralism, or New Historicism, assumes that dissident (not to mention subversive) impulses along with agency as such will always remain contained within the insurmountable limits defined by discourse as a positive "*historical a priori*."[48] Where culture as a whole is conceived "as a mutually intelligible network of signs,"[49] the historically available code assumes the givenness and naturalness of a matrix and turns into "a context too rich and complex to be unmade."[50] This is, of course, only one part of the story. Even New Historicism allows for connective networks that are loosely knit instead of tight-meshed, and that may enable experiential and conceptual alternatives to the great postmodern dilemma of oscillating between the paranoid anxiety with overdetermination and the panic with entropy:

> If we reject both the totalizing of a universal mythology and the radical particularizing of relativism, what are we left with? We are left with networks of lived and narrated stories, practices, strategies, representations, fantasies, negotiations, and exchanges that . . . fashion our experience of the past, of others, and of ourselves.[51]

That networks, therefore, do not have to be construed and experienced as snares only does not mean that they are automatically enabling. More accurately, they "are neither consistently emancipatory—freeing us from a fixed or dominant order—nor always threatening,"[52] as they come in a multitude of patterns and densities, from the grid to the rhizome. Rigid or flexible, settled or precarious, they "can thus be nouns as well as verbs."[53] More than that, the figure of the network has a particular affinity to the notion of incompleteness, not only because networks tend to be open-ended and thus averse to closure and consummation but also because their nodes are primarily defined not by some singular set of essential properties but by the interrelations and interdependencies between them.

This aspect is especially crucial in two areas, namely in actor-network theories in the wake of Latour and his followers and in theorizations of current political practices of affiliation and assembly. The former have been highly influential in the emergence of neo-Spinozist new materialism with its tendency to horizontalize the relation between the human and the nonhuman, if not the animate and the inanimate. In this perspective, "humanity and nonhumanity have always performed an intricate dance with each other. There was never a time when human agency was anything other than an interfolding network of humanity and nonhumanity."[54] As I have argued elsewhere,[55] this "geoaffective" vitalist turn in the human sciences bears a strong formal affinity with current radically materialist reconceptualizations of literature that designate the latter with a vital force all its own—a force that is strictly grounded in the reassertion that literature "matters." For inasmuch as writing itself forms "the most concrete trace of the materiality of thought,"[56] literature cannot possibly be conceived as disembodied abstraction nor, however, as inert and ossified stuff. Instead, embedded as it is in an open network of animate materiality, literature becomes conceivable as the domain where materialized thought attains a vibrancy of its own: the "wordlife"[57] of literature as aesthetic event that pushes the reader "into a zone of indeterminacy where . . . thought bursts into atoms that are in unity with atoms of matter."[58] No "great divide," then, persists between the text and the world, the word and the flesh: The materiality of the text allows for its "unity" with other matter in analogy to the horizontal continuity between, say, the human and the nonhuman, the animate and the abiotic in those tentacular networks and interlacements that the world novel's "globalization plot" (re-)enacts. In this understanding, the network aesthetics of the "world novel" appears to project onto a global screen the "materialist, non-hierarchical and encompassing perception of existence" that, following Pam Morris, has defined earlier, more provincial variants of "worldly realism" ever since Jane Austen.[59]

The second area in which network thinking is specifically prominent at present is the theorization of contemporary political practices of forming alliances and affiliations. While these increasingly operate on the formal principle of the non-hierarchical, non-centered rhizomatic network instead of older structured models like the party, the union or the marching column, they share their network structure with the powers against which they constitute themselves: postmodern neoliberal sovereignty, or "network power," consolidates and reproduces itself through the interplay of "a whole series of powers that regulate themselves and arrange themselves in networks" of production, exploitation, expropriation, communication, and policing.[60] In polemic response to these acquisitive and restrictive networks but never outside their ambit, counter-power emerges in the form of networks, too: "It takes a network to fight a network."[61] In this vein, capital's contemporary creative antagonist, the multitude, forms itself as "an open and expansive network in which all differences can be expressed freely and equally, a network that provides the means of encounter so that we can live and work in common."[62] Inasmuch as the multitude articulates "its constituent capacity in networks . . . and in a process of dynamic and expansive self-regulation,"[63] it flourishes in continuous cooperative processes of sympoiesis and manifests its collective agency in forms of street politics and "network struggles" where "creativity, communication, and self-organized cooperation are primary values."[64] The visceral as the site and medium of affective affiliations and alliances is crucially important in these processes, giving rise to the assumption that "the body is bound up in a network of relations . . . , and that the body, despite its clear boundaries, or perhaps precisely by virtue of those clear boundaries, is defined by those relations that make its own life and action possible."[65] Therefore, in interconnectivity and assembly, the body acts as a node defined by its relations with others in sympoietic networks. As a consequence, "other lives, understood as part of life that exceeds me, are a condition of who I am. . . . To be alive is already to be connected . . . and no human and no self can live without this connection to a biological network of life":[66] incompleteness, in other words, is the indispensable precondition for being part of the network, which itself is constantly evolving and becoming in permanent incompleteness. This, then, would be a redefinition of agency beyond humanist speciocentrism, acknowledging the embeddedness of the human actor in what Jason Moore has called the "web of life," or the *oikos*.[67] If, as Rosi Braidotti posits, "for posthuman theory, the subject is a transversal entity, fully immersed in and immanent to a network of nonhuman (animal, vegetable, viral) relations," then it is precisely this immersion, this being interconnected to a variety of others, human and nonhuman, that opens up situational spaces of agency: "the power that each and every one of us exercises in the everyday network of social relations, at both the micro- and macropolitical levels."[68]

I would now like to come back to the "world novel" and its essentially *networked* structure—a structure that, I argue, is the prerequisite of its realism, more precisely, its *capitalist* realism. If the world system (or whichever term we prefer for the current capitalist global order) is as much structured as a network as the counter-forces that combat it, whether as organized terrorist networks or as loose affiliations and assemblies of the multitude; and if the world novel tends to register these networked structures in its own formal composition, then the isomorphic correlations between these various domains appear to either encourage a return to older formalist reflection theories (perhaps in the style of Alfred Sohn-Rethel's theses on Greek tragedy or Lucien Goldmann's reading of the bourgeois novel), or to invite to the far more preferable exploration of the world novel's *poein*,[69] that is, its capacity to co-construct the very reality it represents. In this perspective, capitalist/network realism emerges as a mode that reconciles the mimetic and the poietic.

As mentioned earlier, James Bridle introduced the term "network realism" with respect to William Gibson's later novels, especially *Zero History* (2010) and *Pattern Recognition* (2003). He focuses on the specific mediascapes of Gibson's chronotopes and discusses these texts as mimetic representations of the network society as theorized by Castells and others. However, he fails to mention that the networked structures of Gibson's fictional worlds are presented by the texts not simply as given social contents of the diegetic universe; rather these pervasive interconnections result from characters' and by extension also readers' apophenic activities. They are, in short, not merely mimetic but essentially poietic, that is the product of some imaginative agency that *does* the connecting. In psychological discourse the term "apophenia" describes the tendency of human perception to routinely search, and find or rather construct, patterns of meaning even within wholly contingent structures. Like the network according to Boltanski and Chiapello, then, apophenia "connects up elements that are in fact highly disparate."[70] As long as we conceive of apophenia as pathology, such a reading would immediately relegate us back to the paranoia of classic (post)modern critiques of overdetermination, fetishism, or mystification; however, the apophenia of Gibson's characters (and of the network-realist world novel in general) is *also* an active performance of meaning-making, akin to what Fredric Jameson has proposed as cognitive mapping: an epistemological and phenomenological procedure of self-identification in the post-subject environment of global capital. On the one hand, cognitive mapping has its share in the paranoia of the network-as-snare perception as it is itself concerned with the disorienting effects of networked capital and the concomitant "incapacity of our minds, at least at present, to map the greater global multinational and decentered communicational network in which we find ourselves caught as individual subjects";[71] on the other hand, however, cognitive mapping proceeds from the very premise that "the global totality which was to have been mapped" is and will remain essentially "unrepresentable, imaginary" so that the act of "mapping" (much like the dialectically entangled "tasks" of the early realist novel) involves the very *production* rather than the *reproduction* of the space to be charted cognitively. As I have observed elsewhere, the same holds true for the always already displaced and decentered subject that is supposed to perform the mapping in the first place.[72] Whether conceived as "totality" or "network" (or both), the global reality of capital is here both an absent cause whose representation remains impossible and the result of a figuration in structural terms, which is why, as Jameson tongue-in-cheek asserts, "achieved cognitive mapping will be a matter of form."[73]

Apophenia, pattern recognition, the construction of apparently willful connections: it is this duality of paranoia and *poiein* that characterizes network realism. In formal terms, this duality gains its perhaps most immediately tangible profile in the works of David Mitchell, to which Robert Selisker (fully independent of Bridle's blog) applied the very same term that Bridle had suggested for Gibson's later fiction: network realism. Apropos Mitchell's interlaced and multi-strand plot structures Selisker asserts that,

> while the content of these contemporary novels skews toward the realm of speculative fiction, their form might be best described as network realism. These novels make a project of describing complex worlds and their unfathomable contours while at the same time portraying characters who attempt to act within a world of which they have only partial knowledge. This emphasis on complexity ... is essentially antitotalitarian and antifundamentalist in its political orientation. It also brings to the fore the kinds of partial and networked agency that are difficult but necessary to describe.[74]

It is of course true that Mitchell foregrounds some form of networked agency in many of his texts, especially those of his novels that explore innovative, at times extravagant modes of figuring planetary interdependences and transsubjective porosities (a phenomenon of soul nomadism for which

Mitchell has coined the neologism of "psychosoterica"), as in his début *Ghostwritten* (1999), in *The Bone Clocks* (2014), and most elaborately in *Cloud Atlas* (2004)—a composite novel made up of six independent yet loosely interlinked narrative strands. Here, a cast of characters who inhabit widely discrepant times from the early nineteenth century to the far future (and who accordingly "never meet") are somehow connected by virtue of a comet-shaped birthmark: an instance of "psychosoterica" across the boundaries of time, space, and selves. Berthold Schoene suggests that Mitchell's device of the birthmark "has to be seen as a general rather than specific symbol of humanity's potential for communal affiliation" so that an "all-embracing cosmopolitan network"[75] of humanity becomes visible—network humanism rather than network realism, then. Yet as Jason Mezey observes apropos *Cloud Atlas*, it is precisely by virtue of its interlaced structure that the novel as a whole attains a realistic character. Its very form corresponds to the social world that this text configures not as a "totality" but as a network: "There is no totality of social structures in *Cloud Atlas*; . . . characters and readers are oriented not in relation to some vast social whole, but in relation to others—distinct points in a vast network of transhistorical and transglobal connections."[76]

As an open-ended, decentered structure, the network, like modernity itself, resists totalization. Its "adequate" realist formal representation would have to represent the network as a network by assuming a network structure for itself. What remains mostly thematic (as apophenia) in Gibson's novels but fully becomes a "matter of form" in Mitchell's texts is precisely that contingency containment that cognitive mapping is all about. The constellations and configurations that *Cloud Atlas* exemplarily presents leave the gaps between the nodes—the "distinct points in the vast network of transglobal connections"—decidedly undetermined so that a "gappy" realism ensues; one whose poietic force exhausts itself in the construction of an archipelagic and heterogeneous space, "a world made up of fragments of many worlds,"[77] that are yet held together by some nebulous instance like a birthmark, that on closer inspection turns out to be nothing but a textual device or, worse, a full-blown mystification of that *ens realissimum* that the scholastics (and after them Kant and Marx) posited as that which made the world cohere. It would be tempting and probably facile to point out that earlier programs of realist world figurations were more ambitious than the current network realism in identifying such leitmotifs that were deemed to permeate all society akin to the *ens realissimum*, that idea of a continuous ultimate reality like an ether that, as Adorno has it, "is anything but ethereal . . . . If it seems abstract, this is the fault not of fantastic, willful thinking, hostile to the facts, but of the objective abstraction to which the social process of life is subject—the exchange relation."[78]

However, it may be precisely due to this tendency toward ever more intensifying abstraction of social processes and relations that network realism with its gappy structures emerges as the one possible mode of practicing today something like an "epic 'realism' of capitalism [which] can only be a polemical demonstration of the ultimate impossibility of imaging those forms of abstraction"[79] that network capital imposes. In this perspective, the network-realist novel is nothing more (but also nothing less) than the current variant of what the novel, according to the young Georg Lukács, has always done: it "carr[ies] the fragmentary nature of the world's structure into the world of forms."[80]

Notes

1   Leigh Claire La Berge, "Capitalist Realism and Serial Form: The Fifth Season of *The Wire*," *Reading Capitalist Realism*, ed. Alison Shonkweiler and Leigh Claire La Berge (Iowa City: University of Iowa Press, 2014), 135.

2   See for example Ted Nannicelli, "It's All Connected: Televisual Narrative Complexity," *The Wire: Urban Decay and American Television* (London and New York: Continuum, 2009), 190–201; Fredric Jameson, "Realism and Utopia in *The Wire*," *Criticism* 52 (2010): 359–372; Caroline Levine, *Forms: Whole, Rhythm, Hierarchy, Network* (Princeton, NJ: Princeton University Press, 2015), 132–150.

3   John Kraniauskas, *Capitalism and its Discontents: Power and Accumulation in Latin American Culture* (Cardiff: University of Wales Press, 2017), 183.

4   Mark Fisher, *Capitalist Realism: Is There No Alternative?* (London: Zero Books, 2009), 4.

5   See Mieke Bal, "Telling, Showing, Showing Off," *Critical Inquiry* 18, no. 3 (1992): 566.

6   Anne Balsano and Susana Bautista, "Understanding the Distributed Museum: Mapping the Spaces of Museology in Contemporary Culture," *Museums and the Web* (2011), https://www.museumsandtheweb.com/mw2011/papers/understanding_the_distributed_museum_mapping_t.html (last retrieved September 15, 2019).

7   Tony Bennett, *The Birth of the Museum: History, Theory, Politics* (New York: Routledge, 1995).

8   See Balsamo and Bautista, "Understanding the Distributed Museum."

9   Nancy Proctor, "The Museum as Distributed Network: A 21st-Century Model," *MuseumID* 21 (2017), https://museum-id.com/museum-distributed-network-21st-century-model-nancy-proctor/ (last retrieved September 15, 2019).

10 Luc Boltanski and Ève Chiapello, *The New Spirit of Capitalism* (London: Verso, 2005), 24, 103.

11 Fisher, *Capitalist Realism*, 4.
12 Ibid., 16.
13 Bruno Latour, *On the Modern Cult of the Factish Gods* (Durham, NC and London: Duke University Press, 2010) 24.
14 Fredric Jameson, *The Political Unconscious: Narrative as a Socially Symbolic Act* (London: Methuen, 1981), 152.
15 Paul Ricoeur, *Time and Narrative. Vol. 1*, trans. Kathleen McLaughlin and David Pellauer (Chicago and London: University of Chicago Press, 1984), 51.
16 Rita Felski, *Uses of Literature* (Malden, MA: Blackwell, 2008), 85.
17 See Fredric Jameson, *The Antinomies of Realism* (London: Verso, 2013), 292–293.
18 Roman Jakobson, "The Dominant," in *Language in Literature*, ed. Krsytyna Pomorska and Stephen Rudy (Cambridge, MA: Harvard University Press, 1987), 41–46.
19 Kraniauskas, *Capitalism and Its Discontents*, 183.
20 Ibid., 31.
21 Ibid., 171.
22 Jed Esty, "Realism Wars," *NOVEL: A Forum on Fiction* 49, no. 2 (2016): 334.
23 Donna Haraway, *Staying With the Trouble: Making Kin in the Chthulucene* (Durham, NC: Duke University Press, 2016), 54.
24 Lauren M. E. Goodlad, "Introduction: Worlding Realisms Now," *Novel* 49, no. 2 (2016): 184.
25 Fredric Jameson, "Realism and Utopia in *The Wire*," *Criticism* 52 (2010): 362.
26 WReC Warwick Research Collective, *Combined and Uneven Development: Towards a New Theory of World-Literature* (Liverpool: Liverpool University Press, 2015), 15.
27 Sharare Deckard and Stephen Shapiro, "World-Culture and the Neoliberal World System: An Introduction," in *World Literature, Neoliberalism and the Culture of Discontent* (Basingstoke: Palgrave Macmillan, 2019), 21.
28 Cliffors Siskin, "Epilogue: The Rise of Novelism," *Cultural Institutions of the Novel*, ed. Deidre Lynch and William B. Warner (Durham, NC: Duke University Press, 1996), 423.
29 Berthold Schoene, *The Cosmopolitan Novel* (Edinburgh: Edinburgh University Press, 2009).
30 Paul Jay, *Global Matters: The Transnational Turn in Literary Studies* (Ithaca, NY: Cornell University Press, 2010).
31 Caren Irr, "Toward the World Novel: Genre Shifts in Twenty-First-Century Expatriate Fiction," *American Literary History* 23, no. 3 (2011): 660–679.
32 Alexander Beecroft, *An Ecology of World Literature: From Antiquity to the Present Day* (London: Verso, 2015).

33 Arianna Dagnino, "Transcultural Literature and Contemporary World Literature(s)," *CLCWeb: Comparative Literature and Culture* 15, no. 5 (2013): https://doi.org/10.7771/1481-4374.2339.

34 Min Hyuong Song, "Becoming Planetary," *American Literary History* 23, no. 3, (2011): 555–573.

35 Stefano Ercolino, *The Maximalist Novel: From Thomas Pynchon's* Gravity's Rainbow *to Roberto Bolaño's* 2666, trans. Albert Sbagria (London: Bloomsbury, 2014).

36 Theo D'Haen, "European Postmodernism: The Cosmodern Turn," *Narrative* 21, no. 3 (2013): 271–283.

37 Alissa G. Karl, "Things Break Apart: James Kelman, Ali Smith, and the Neoliberal Novel," in *Reading Capitalist Realism*, ed. Alison Shonkweiler and Leigh Claire La Berge (Iowa City: University of Iowa Press, 2014), 64–87.

38 Debjani Ganguly, *This Thing Called the World* (Durham, NC and London: Duke University Press, 2016), 2.

39 Beecroft, *An Ecology of World Literature*, 283–284.

40 James Bridle, "Network Realism: William Gibson and New Forms of Fiction," *booktwo.org*, October 25, 2010, http://booktwo.org/notebook/network-realism/.

41 Manuel Castells, *Communication Power* (Oxford: Oxford University Press, 2009), 25.

42 Manuel Castells, *The Rise of the Network Society* (Oxford: Blackwell, 1996), 134.

43 Levine, *Forms*, 21.

44 Ibid., 114.

45 Beecroft, *An Ecology of World Literature*, 283.

46 Fredric Jameson, "Cognitive Mapping," *Marxism and the Interpretation of Culture*, ed. Cary Nelson and Lawrence Grossberg (Basingstoke: Macmillan, 1988) 356; Fredric Jameson, *The Geopolitical Aesthetic: Cinema and Space in the World System* (London: BFI, 1995), 13.

47 Alan Sinfield, *Faultlines: Cultural Materialism and the Politics of Dissident Reading* (Berkeley: University of California Press 1992), 41.

48 Michel Foucault, *The Archaeology of Knowledge*, trans. A. M. Sheridan Smith (New York: Routledge, 2005), 143.

49 Catherine Gallagher and Stephen Greenblatt, "Introduction," in *Practicing New Historicism*, ed. Catherine Gallagher and Stephen Greenblatt (Chicago: University of Chicago Press, 2000), 7.

50 J. G. A. Pocock, *Politics, Language and Time: Essays on Politics and History* (Chicago: University of Chicago Press, 1989), xi.

51 Stephen Greenblatt, *Learning to Curse: Essays in Early Modern Culture* (London: Routledge, 1992), 138.

52 Levine, *Forms*, 145.

53 Sara Ahmed, *On Being Included: Racism and Diversity in Institutional Life* (Durham, NC: Duke University Press, 2012), 197.

54 Jane Bennett, *Vibrant Matter: A Political Ecology of Things* (Durham, NC and London: Duke University Press, 2010), 31.

55 Dirk Wiemann, "Passive Voice: Democratic Indifference and the Vibrant Matter of Literature," in *Theory Matters: The Place of Theory in Literary and Cultural Studies Today*, ed. Martin Middeke and Christoph Reinfandt (New York: Palgrave, 2016), 167–180.

56 Stathis Gourgouris, *Does Literature Think? Literature as Theory for an Antimythical Era* (Stanford, CA: Stanford University Press, 2003), xx.

57 Nicholas Royle, *Veering: A Theory of Literature* (Edinburgh: Edinburgh University Press, 2010), 162.

58 Jacques Rancière, *The Politics of Aesthetics: The Distribution of the Sensible*, trans. Gabriel Rockhill (London: Continuum, 2004), 149.

59 Pam Morris, *Jane Austen, Virginia Woolf and Worldly Realism* (Edinburgh: Edinburgh University Press, 2017), 5.

60 Michael Hardt and Antonio Negri, *Empire* (Cambridge, MA: Harvard University Press, 2001), 163.

61 Michael Hardt and Antonio Negri, *Multitude: War and Democracy in the Age of Empire* (London: Penguin, 2004), 58.

62 Ibid., viv.

63 Hardt and Negri, *Empire*, 163.

64 Hardt and Negri, *Multitude*, 83.

65 Judith Butler, *Notes Towards a Performative Theory of Assembly* (Cambridge, MA: Harvard University Press, 2013), 130.

66 Ibid., 43.

67 Jason Moore, *Capitalism and the Web of Life: Ecology and the Accumulation of Capital* (London: Verso, 2015).

68 Rosi Braidotti, *The Posthuman* (Cambridge: Polity, 2013), 193, 12.

69 Gourgouris, *Does Literature Think?* 54.

70 Boltanski and Chiapello, *New Spirit of Capitalism*, 103.

71 Jameson, "Cognitive Mapping," 254.

72 Dirk Wiemann, *Genres of Modernity: Contemporary Indian Novels in English* (Amsterdam: Brill, 2008), 170.

73 Jameson, "Cognitive Mapping," 356.

74 Scott Selisker, "The Cult and the World System," *NOVEL: A Forum on Fiction* 47, no. 3 (2014): 455–456.

75 Schoene, *Cosmopolitan Novel*, 116.

76 Jacob Howard Mezey, "'A Multitude of Drops': Recursion and Globalization in David Mitchell's *Cloud Atlas*," *MLS* 40, no. 2 (2011): 23.

77 Brian McHale, *The Obligation Towards the Difficult Whole: Postmodernist Long Poems* (Tuscaloosa: University of Alabama Press, 2004), 15–16.

78 Theodor W. Adorno, "Late Capitalism or Industrial Society? The Fundamental Question of the Present Structure of Society," in *Can One Live After Auschwitz? A Philosophical Reader*, trans. Rodney Livingstone (Stanford, CA: Stanford University Press, 2003), 121.

79 David Cunningham, "Capitalist Epics: Abstraction, Totality and the Theory of the Novel," *Radical Philosophy* 163 (2010): 19.

80 Georg Lukács, *The Theory of the Novel: A Historico-Philosophical Essay on the Forms of Great Epic Literature*, trans. Anna Bostock (London: Merlin Press, 1988), 39.

11

Postcolonial Realism and Rohinton Mistry's *Family Matters*

Eli Park Sorensen

Introduction

Within the field of postcolonial studies, scholars and critics have for a long time been reluctant to engage with literary realism. From the outset, the field embraced anti-realist literary styles as aesthetic vehicles of radical politics, emancipation, subversion, resistance, plurality, hybridity, pastiche, parody, catachresis, irony, and so on. Conversely, literary realism came to be associated with anachronism, naïve humanism, bad faith, ideology (capitalist/imperialist/racist etc.), commodified culture, false consciousness, totality and totalitarianism, illusion, delusion, essentialism, and spurious epistemology. Rarely was this juxtaposition questioned, quite the contrary; it guided a surprisingly large amount of postcolonial literary discussions in the 1980s, 1990s, and 2000s. In retrospect, it seems that the field's often caricatured, and surprisingly monolithic version of realism, more than actually referring to realism as such, essentially played the crucial role of postcolonial studies' *other*, against which it was easy to claim a position of political radicalism.[1]

Within the last decade or so, perhaps in conjunction with the general feeling of postcolonial studies' decline in popularity, the sense that the field has been surpassed by other adjacent fields,[2] or perhaps simply a renewed interest in notions of "the real" following "unreal" events like the 2008 financial crisis, Brexit, the Trump presidency, and most recently the pandemic—literary realism has made a sort of qualified comeback. Thus, *Journal of Narrative Theory* (2008), *Modern Language Quarterly* (2012), and *NOVEL: A Forum on Fiction* (2016) have all run special issues in which critics have approached literary realism within or in relation to postcolonial contexts, while others have approached realism in new and exciting ways such as realism and finance capitalism, realism and race, realism and slavery, telegraphic realism, urban realism, speculative realism, and other topics combined with a focus on realism. Furthermore, a number of books and scholarly articles have approached the specific issue of *postcolonial realism*, addressing both the paradox of the previous resistance to realism within a postcolonial perspective in spite of the fact that a large part of postcolonial literature could be categorized as realist, *and* offering sophisticated and more productive ways of understanding the potential of realism within a postcolonial context.[3] The recent interest in literary realism thus offers new ways of reconceptualizing this aesthetic mode within a postcolonial perspective, and the argument I want to develop here should be seen as an extension of this line of work.

One of the problems with realism in a postcolonial context, I believe, is that it has largely been approached as an *epistemological-mimetic-representational* problematic both by those who dismiss it and those who defend it. And since postcolonial studies as an academic field essentially situated its critical identity around a sophisticated (largely poststructuralist) critique of Western epistemological-representational models, a revaluation of literary realism defined primarily as an epistemological style would potentially run into many of the problems identified by the field. It is this notion of realism as an essentially epistemological-representational problematic that I would like to expand by reorienting the concept more in the direction of the *specifically political*. The political dimension of realism, I argue, has often been overlooked in the debates about realism's mimetic representation, where the main issue is to argue either for or against the effects of realism's epistemological dimension. By "political" in realist aesthetics, I am primarily referring to the notion of realism as a stylistic or aesthetic-formal articulation of the concept of reality understood or defined in terms of the premise of a collective unity—or more specifically the formation, production, protection, and normalization of an autonomous political community. J. P. Stern has described realism's implicit "premise of a single, undivided reality,"[4] while Ayelet Ben-Yishai defines realism as embodying a notion of "what is commonly accepted as real."[5] The notion of realism that I am interested in exploring here—using Rohinton Mistry's *Family Matters* as an "indirect" example—follows recent critical studies that seek to expand realism's potential, a potential that in addition to its epistemological value also contains important aesthetic work on dynamics related to consensus, commonality, common identity, collectivities, and communities—in short, the political.[6] It should be mentioned here that the kinds, variations, and degrees of realism and realist aesthetic aspects emerging within postcolonial contexts can by no means be reduced to a question solely about the specifically political, and I hope to make this point clearer in the following by looking at a text—*Family Matters*—which is particularly interesting in this context precisely because it *deviates* (without thereby necessarily becoming *less* realist), I argue, quite significantly from Mistry's previous novels and from more overtly politicized realist novels in general. Realism as a literary style comes in many different shapes and forms—and is used and engaged in many different contexts; the argument I present in this chapter relates to a narrow set of observations about the specifically political within Mistry's realist style, which may inductively point toward some broader tendencies within literary histories of postcolonial realism.

Another, related, issue that I hope to address in this chapter relates to what Chantal Mouffe, albeit in a different context, has described as the tendency to replace the political with the moral: "What is happening is that nowadays the political is played out in a *moralizing register* . . . in place of a struggle between 'right and left' we are faced with a struggle between 'right and wrong.'"[7] Much postcolonial scholarship, one could argue, has contributed to this moralization of the political. Meanwhile, Neil Lazarus laments that the field of postcolonial studies generally has failed to produce much writing about ongoing state violence:

> But the depiction of state violence has been central . . . to the literature that has emerged everywhere in the formerly colonial world since decolonization—hence the repeated representation of state-decreed "resettlement" schemes, land theft, slum clearances, forced sterilization campaigns, the crushing of opposition movements and parties, mass imprisonment, torture, political murder, and so on. This specifically *post*colonial depiction has received relatively little sustained attention from critics in postcolonial studies.[8]

The list of aspects Lazarus believes postcolonial critics have failed to address in a sustained way pertains directly to the effects of what I call the specifically political. Aside from the specificities and singularities of concrete, particular postcolonial situations, postcolonial intellectuals and writers at the most general level were faced with the realities of complicated power transitions, an unstable state, a divided community inhabiting a contested social space, and the challenges of constructing a notion of "the people," often out of myriad local communities brought together arbitrarily and violently through colonization. And it is because of these *specifically political challenges* that we see the emergence of a realist style that involves a distinct political significance. Conversely, it follows that once this focus changes—once there is an underlying stability securing the *reality* of a consensual-collective framework—the purposes, effects, and dynamics of postcolonial realism likewise develop according to a different set of coordinates; it is this development I hope to demonstrate in this chapter through a close reading of Mistry's *Family Matters*.

Rohinton Mistry's *Family Matters*

The notion of literary realism as an exploration of the political implications of collectivity vs. individualism is central to the works of the Canadian-Indian novelist Rohinton Mistry. Born in 1952, Mistry left India at the age of twenty-three and moved to Toronto, Canada, where he embarked on a successful career as a writer in the late 1980s. However, India figures centrally in all his works. His first novel *Such a Long Journey* (1991) tells the story of a bank clerk in Mumbai set during the Indo-Pakistani war in 1971. In the novel *Family Matters* (2002), we follow an old man with Parkinson's disease living in Mumbai during the 1990s, while the story in Mistry's perhaps most popular novel to date, *A Fine Balance* from 1995, takes place in Mumbai around the time of Indira Gandhi's state of emergency in 1975.

Mistry's three novels no doubt all belong to the realist genre, but *Family Matters* in many ways differs from the two previous texts, and this is an issue I want to explore further in this chapter. While the scholarship on Mistry has largely ignored the author's realist style (that is, as *realism*),[9] it has also (or perhaps because of that) largely overlooked the *internal* aesthetic-formal development of Mistry's novelistic oeuvre. Whereas the narrative trajectories of the first two novels take place during the turbulent 1970s, the third novel's plot is set in the 1990s. Furthermore, the solid, omniscient third-person perspective dominating both *Such a Long Journey* and *A Fine Balance* is gradually replaced by more intimate, focalized narratorial perspectives as well as an introverted first-person perspective in *Family Matters*. The themes in Mistry's third novel primarily pertain to private issues and concerns, rather than public-historical conflicts (e.g. the Indo-Pakistani war in *Such a Long Journey* or Indira Gandhi's state of emergency in *A Fine Balance*).[10] It does occasionally refer to public-historical events—for example, the massacre in the Babri mosque, Shiv Sena's political progress—but these seem pushed into the background, rather than constituting a force that actually has a determining impact on the development of the plot and the characters' lives.

What I am interested in here is how and why *Family Matters* at formal and thematic levels differs from his previous novels because I think these differences not only may tell us something important about the development of Mistry's realist style but perhaps provide a deeper understanding of the political implications of literary realism as such, its emergences and disappearances, intensities and apathies, as well as its ongoing relevance or irrelevance. Ultimately, I want to explore the argument that Mistry's realism is intimately connected to creating narrative trajectories and connectivities within situations entailing some form of political instability, when something collectively is at stake—and that the latter involves a crucial dimension of postcoloniality, what it means to be *situated* within postcolonial realities; once these realities cease to have a direct and determining impact, or once the focus changes from a dialectic between historical-collective forces and individual agency to endeavors mainly of a private nature, Mistry's realist style likewise demonstrates a noticeable change. Or, to put it differently; when Mistry's realism is no longer engaged in *creating* an overall, stabilizing framework of causal trajectories in an unstable world, a fractured reality—largely because the latter is no longer unstable or fractured in a *political* sense—its *realism* noticeably gives way to other aesthetic modalities better suited to capturing the fragmented, introspective, and private-intimate aspects of life. These "other aesthetic modalities"—for example, impressionism, psychological realism, allegory—may of course still overlap with or be labeled as realism, although it would be a realist style to a larger extent emphasizing the epistemological-mimetic-representational function and to a lesser extent the specifically political.

The Disintegration of Communal Identities

All of Mistry's novels employ complex, almost labyrinthine, plot structures in which the fate of the individual stands in a tense relationship to collective history. Like the first two novels, *Family Matters* explores the complicated relationship between the individual and the historical, albeit in a less direct way. Whereas Mistry described the fates of individuals during the 1971 Indo-Pakistani war in his first novel, and the violent events in the wake of the 1975 state of emergency in his second novel, the story in *Family Matters* takes place approximately twenty years later, during the 1990s, not in the shadow of some major historical event, but instead with an intense focus on the disintegration and disappearance of communal identities.

Family Matters tells the story of a generational conflict within a specific historical context: the dwindling Parsi community in India during the mid-1990s. The Indian Parsi community, whose members primarily belong to the middle class, finds itself at this point in a kind of existential crisis.[11] As it becomes clear during the novel, the present generation is on the brink of committing the same errors and mistakes as earlier generations.[12] The life of the novel's main character, Vakeel, in many ways reflects the conflicts and problems haunting the Parsi community during the post-independence epoch.[13] In Mistry's text, the Parsi community during the 1990s is a tormented people, externally as well as internally—the former, among other reasons, because of the increasingly popular nationalist Hindu Shiv Sena party, heavily criticized throughout the novel, and the latter because of a dwindling population due to low birthrates, Western influence, and secularization, as well as the possibility of collective extinction in the near future.[14]

The world that Mistry portrays in *Family Matters* is one that to some extent still lives in the aftermath of the political struggles fought out in the 1970s, the period in which Mistry's two first novels are set. It is a novel desperately in search of connectivity and causality in a world experienced as more bewildering and confusing to the individual than ever. What Mistry emphasizes in *Family Matters* is the *time after*, and the accumulated backlog erupting in the present. It is a present haunted by fragmentation, a time during which the sense of the historical seems lost in an ever-increasing chaos of smaller narratives, all of which indicate that the grand historical trajectory has come to an end. With *Family Matters*, Mistry reaches the present. After this point, there is in a sense only *more present*. The historical has here reached a kind of equilibrium, a time in which individuals are left undisturbed to attend to their small individual dramas and private concerns. What is missing here is precisely this dialectic between historical-collective forces and individual agency so characteristic in Mistry's previous novels—an absence, I argue, that has a profound impact on the way in which Mistry's realism is articulated.

The Private Sphere

As the title indicates, Mistry's third novel more than any of his previous ones revolves around the private-domestic sphere, the realm of the family. In *Family Matters*, the traditional notion of family is under pressure, and is perhaps on the verge of collapse. The novel portrays family life as rife with minor tensions and unresolved conflicts. Vakeel, the family patriarch, is in many ways the product of the collision between the traditional and the modern. His love for a Catholic woman creates problems for both families, and eventually he gives up his individual desire, succumbs to the will of his family, and marries a Parsi widow. There is a sense in which the novel suggests that Vakeel originally sowed the seeds of present family tensions with his unresolved individual desire early in his life; that is, when he insisted on marrying a woman from a Catholic family, but eventually gave in to the pressure from his family, and subsequently lived an unhappy life filled with regrets.[15]

The novel vaguely draws the contours of a causal chain of events, beginning generations ago with Vakeel's attempt to break away from family traditions. His guilt is passed on to his wife, as well as the woman he loved, and his children through a trajectory that becomes increasingly detached from its origins. To Coomy, Vakeel's wife's daughter from a previous marriage, her stepfather is the cause of all the family's misfortunes, and her passive-aggressive bitterness is reflected in most of her thoughts and actions until her death. Later, Roxana feels guilty over Coomy's death, while Yezad feels guilty over Mr. Kapur's death.[16] Guilt here signifies the individual's reaction to the unforeseen consequences of the past. The characters in *Family Matters* have mostly good or relatively harmless individual intentions that unexpectedly go in different directions, with unforeseen and often terrible consequences.

This discrepancy between individual intentions followed by unexpected and tragic consequences indicates a temporal framework that no longer operates in unison, but rather acts dissymmetrically through delays and postponements. Postponement here constitutes a dynamic that creates pockets of individual temporality outside collective, homogenous empty time. In Mistry's previous two novels, *Such a Long Journey* and *A Fine Balance*, we find a similar realist framework exploring the relationship between temporalities of the individual and the collective, albeit crucially framed within a larger historical discourse (the political crises of the 1970s) that ultimately reinscribes and to some extent redeems the fragmentary nature of individual experience. No such historical discourse frames the dissymmetrical delays and postponements in *Family Matters*. Coomy and Jal keep *postponing* their father's homecoming, while Yezad desperately *waits* for the matka number to be announced, although when it finally happens the police carry out a raid, which means that he loses all his money despite having picked the winning number. In these instances, the characters' attempts to *individualize* time are ambushed by randomness and external accidents, that is, instances of the dissymmetrical. Early in the novel, Yezad angrily prevents Murad from winding up an old clock, a fragile family heirloom (82). Later, Murad defiantly attempts to do it on his own, secretly, without his father's permission (198–200). Near the end of the novel, Murad receives a new clock as a birthday gift from Yezad. Moments later, Yezad casually asks him to wind up the old clock, thus indicating that Murad is now old enough to take responsibility, and perhaps in a wider sense that it is time for the family to move on.

More generally, the novel portrays individuals growing up or moving on from the sins of the past and the unintended consequences of their individual intentions, which they never quite manage to resolve or atone for properly. The figure of the "too late" is one that the characters individually can never entirely free themselves from, and which is never really redeemed at a collective level in *Family Matters*. At some point people simply die, move on, or grow up. There is, ultimately, very little resolved in the novel, at least in a collective sense. The private world portrayed in *Family Matters* is a disjointed world, temporally as well as spatially—a dissymmetrical world of many individual wills. And yet, at a collective level, the political reality of this world is solid, that is, the community is not threatened by anything external; the threat is entirely internal. The world may be falling apart for the individuals, but precisely because their problems primarily relate to the private individual, there is very little at stake politically. It is important to clarify here that while *Family Matters'* prose is no doubt still realism, it is a realist style that revolves around the instability of the idiosyncratically individualized life rather than the problem of collective reality.

Causes and Effects

Family Matters is a novel obsessed with family genealogies, which constitute the novel's perhaps most persistent forces of connectivity. However, *when* the concept of the family makes its entrance the first time in the novel, it is in the form of rupture; if the novel has a beginning, it is one that is haunted by fractures and the desire to break traditions—namely, Vakeel's unhappy love-relationship with the non-Parsi woman Lucy. When Lucy refuses to let Vakeel go, while Vakeel himself has difficulties cutting the ties, despite having followed tradition and married a Parsi woman, the course of events derails badly with both women ending up dead after a fatal fall from a rooftop. Since that time (thirty-six years) Coomy has been unable to forgive Vakeel, her stepfather, whom she still accuses of having caused her mother's death. Like circles in the water, the ruinous beginning produces effects all the way up to the novel's present time, when Coomy and Jal send the by-now-helpless Vakeel to Roxana's small apartment, apparently because of a ceiling in need of repair, but which they themselves in fact have smashed to prevent Vakeel from living there. Roxana persuades a local handyman—an unfortunate, clumsy fellow, happy to carry out all sorts of jobs but not very good at it—to fix the ceiling, and Coomy cunningly hopes that the man will only cause damage, so that even more time will pass before Vakeel may return to the apartment. However, not only does the handyman damage the ceiling; his work results in a catastrophic accident that causes his own and Coomy's death. Meanwhile, Roxana and Yezad suffer from a severely strained budget due to Vakeel's medicinal expenses. To solve their financial problems, Yezad plots a crooked plan that tragically backfires, leading to his boss Mr. Kapur's death. Thus, both Roxana and Yezad unwittingly and indirectly cause the death of others.

In this way, the novel creates (at times unlikely, perhaps even sensational) trajectories of causality encompassing different temporal epochs as well as different spatial levels—the highest levels as well as the most banal ones—although crucially without ever seriously undermining its realist diegetic framework. At one point in the novel, a teacher discovers that Jehangir, Yezad and Roxana's youngest son, has received bribe money from classmates while supervising their homework.[17] When Yezad learns about his son's dishonesty, he delivers a grandiose speech to Roxana: "There's only one way to explain it. The same corruption that pollutes the country is right here, in your own family. . . . Is it any wonder Jehangla took the bribe?" (283). Roxana retorts that Jehangir only took the money "to help his parents with food, and with Grandpa's medicines" (283).[18] Yezad, in return, understands this as an indirect accusation that he is unable to earn enough money for the family. A little later, Yezad becomes involved in the aforementioned shady piece of business, leading to his boss's death, in an attempt to get a pay rise so he can pay for the family's extra expenses. The strained family budget is of course related to Vakeel's health issues and general helplessness, a person who is possibly the cause of several people's tragic fates, including those of his wife, the woman he loved, and his stepdaughter, Coomy. The point here, again, is that it is not the external political-historical circumstances that drive the plot ahead, as in Mistry's previous two novels; what moves the plot forward are inner private conflicts.

Whereas *A Fine Balance* addresses the ruthlessness of global capitalism, and *Such a Long Journey* looks at governmental financial corruption, Mistry's third novel focuses closely on the individual middle-class economy, the cost of welfare, and the individual household budget.[19] Vakeel used his savings on the small flat for Roxana and Yezad.[20] The hospital bill eats away most of his remaining money (72), we are told early in the novel; this is why Coomy and Jal apparently cannot take care of their stepfather—but at the same time we are told that they spend a lot of money on toys and other unnecessary things. At one point, Yezad is so desperate for money that he makes a huge, ill-fated gamble on matka, losing a considerable sum. Jehangir and Murad discuss intensely how to raise money for the family, which only lands them in trouble. Meanwhile, we hear about Mr. Kapur's large suitcase full of money, which was supposed to have been spent on realizing his political vision, but which in the end leads to his violent death.

Money thus suggests something deeply problematic in the novel. The theme of money is of course central to many realist novels, although in *Family Matters* the futile individual pursuit of money seems at times to take over the narrative dynamic; almost everyone attempts to raise money, with little success and often catastrophic results. There is no real accumulation of money in this system. Nor will the novel allow any shortcuts; when people try to raise or save money through illicit or immoral means, punishment tends to follow promptly.[21] At the end of the novel, the family resolves the financial situation by selling Roxana's apartment, after which everyone moves back to the old apartment, whose size is appropriate now that Vakeel and Coomy are dead. The novel overall suggests that family values are the exact opposite to what money represents, and that the latter potentially ruins family values. But money is also what drives the characters, not for the sake of money itself, but rather the opposite—as a necessary means to keep the family together. The title *Family Matters* is thus ambiguous, since it refers both to the importance of the family—*that* family matters—but also matters concerning the material and the economic eventually leading to division and discord, that is, the dissolution of family.

Storytelling and Reality

The collision of grandiose rhetoric and the banalities of everyday life, or between collective visions and individual concerns, is one of the leading motifs in all of Mistry's novels. An example of this narrative dynamic in *Family Matters* is allegorically illustrated through the letters the bookstore owner Vilas Rane, one of Yezad's friends who works near the sports equipment store, composes for poor and illiterate people: "He was a writer of letters for those who couldn't, who poured out, into his willing ear, their thoughts, feelings, concerns, their very hearts, which he transformed into words upon paper at the nominal rate of three rupees per page" (139). Vilas Rane narrates stories about child births, money problems, diseases, weddings, family tragedies about young couples condemned to death because of religious issues, children being sold, and many other individual stories that taken together form a confusing jumble of intertwined human lives and destinies with no apparent connections. And yet, Vilas insists that the letters together constitute an overall pattern: "He felt that chance events, random cruelty, unexplainable kindness, meaningless disaster, unexpected generosity could, together, form a design that was otherwise invisible" (142). There is a sense in which Mistry, indirectly at least, inserts an allegorical or meta-reflective figure here, which in many ways resembles the very text in which it appears, as if to suggest that the novel as a whole is no more or no less than a series of letters that might seem disconnected, randomly put together, but which actually form a design of some kind.

However, the notion of a design amidst what seem like disconnected and randomly arranged components is considerably more pronounced in Mistry's previous novels, precisely because of their dominant historical frames. Thus, in *Such a Long Journey* there is a scene in which the dialog between the main character Gustad and a pavement artist almost turns into a metafictional reflection on the novel's compositional principles when the latter observes: "You see, I don't like to weaken anyone's faith. Miracle, magic, mechanical trick, coincidence—does it matter what it is, as long as it helps? Why analyse the strength of the imagination. . . . Looking too closely is destructive, makes everything disintegrate" (289). Gustad agrees with the pavement artist on this occasion, but one of the novel's great themes is ironically that Gustad in the end *does* look a little too closely at the illusion, the illusion of history, the nation, and the individual's relation to these. In *Family Matters*, the speculation on the overall pattern or design of Vilas Rane's many letters remains an isolated occasion, and plays no further role in the novel.

More generally, there is notable doubt about ideas of narrativity and forces of connections in *Family Matters*. Thus, on several occasions Yezad reflects on the strange appearance of coincidences, for example in connection with Villie Cardmaster's uncanny ability to predict winning numbers in the before-mentioned matka game. Much later in the novel, after the family has moved back to the old apartment, Chateau Felicity, Roxana is convinced that her father would have lived longer if they had looked after him instead of letting a caretaker look after him. "The proof is in the bedsores," says Roxana, "For almost a year I washed Papa and kept him clean and dry, and he was fine. Soon as the ayah and wardboy came, the bedsores appeared"—which Yezad rejects: "In bed for so long, he would have got sores no matter who was nursing him. Just coincidence." Roxana replies: "You say there is no such thing as coincidence. . . . You call it another word for the Hand of God" (495). As Roxana points out, Yezad seems to believe in destiny as well as coincidences whenever the situation suits him, in an entirely inconsistent and individualistic way.

After the wretched business in the sports equipment store during which Mr. Kapur dies, Yezad increasingly becomes religious. Much earlier in the novel, Yezad ridicules religious belief and believers.[22] But as he passes the fire-temple one day, by chance, he is suddenly overwhelmed with a sense of peace and tranquility. Going to fire-temple becomes a daily habit for him, a religious ritual that reconnects him to a lost communal identity in a world that—from the perspective of the individual—seems to be falling apart.[23] To Yezad, the only way to explain his conversion is, as he observes at one point, that "[w]e are not meant to understand everything. We just make ourselves miserable, trying to" (410). While the reader may assume that his sudden turn to religion would be related somehow to a sense of guilt for being implicated in his former employer's death, Yezad convinces himself, as well as Roxana, that "the entire chain of events, starting with Grandpa's accident and ending with Mr. Kapur's murder, was God's way of bringing him to prayer" (464).

However, while the novel overall shows a gently doubtful attitude toward the force of narrative connectivity in Vilas Rane's letters, as well as Villie Cardmaster's mystical abilities, it seems even more skeptical and ironic about Yezad's religious path. His rediscovered religiosity, which becomes more and more extreme, and which in the closing pages of the novel almost transforms him into a different person, threatens to undermine the newly established harmony in the family. Uncle Jal becomes more and more withdrawn, while Murad increasingly takes on a defiant attitude toward his father's insistence on Parsi traditions: "This is the twenty-first century . . . and you still believe such nonsense. It's sad" (463). When Murad wants to invite a non-Parsi girlfriend to his eighteenth birthday party, Yezad protests: "I'm warning you, in this there can be no compromise. The rules, the laws of our religion are absolute, this Maharashtrian cannot be your girlfriend" (482). The fact that Yezad in the end does agree to a compromise and lets Murad invite the girl home, thus seems to indicate that the present generation will not commit the same mistakes and errors as past generations, and perhaps that religion is not capable of guaranteeing meaning, continuity, or communal stability either.

Jehangir, the youngest member of the family, here represents at one and the same time a figure auguring reconciliation (between generations) but also fragmentation (of the Parsi tradition). At one point in the novel, he develops a close friendship with a girl called Farah Arjani, whose late great-grandfather once had a mean-spirited dispute with Vakeel Nariman regarding religious matters, which the latter won. However, Mr. Arjani subsequently hired Lucy, Nariman's first (and only) love, as a maid simply for the purpose of humiliating his neighbor. It is in this light of possible reconciliation among the younger generations, but also loss of loyalty toward Parsi traditions, that one should understand the plot's late turn to religion through the figure of Yezad, and the fear that his family's religious affiliations will decline and disappear. At the same time, ironically, it was religious fanaticism that almost destroyed the family in the first place.

As we have seen, *Family Matters*' realist style differs from Mistry's first two novels in several ways. The style is far more oriented toward the subjective-psychological, and thus more centered around the intense cultivation of the private-domestic—with the implication that the trajectories of the main characters are generally more complex and inscrutable than those in Mistry's two previous novels, but at the same time less significant in a political sense. In the novelistic world of *Family Matters*, individual economic concerns are more important than notions of the political. This is perhaps one of the reasons why the figure of Mr. Kapur, Yezad's boss in a small sports equipment store, an upper-middle-class Hindu who loves Mumbai, or Bombay, as he insists on calling the city, is ridiculed more than anyone else in the novel, and why his death is so meaningless. When Mr. Kapur decides to run for office, Yezad eagerly supports him, not because Yezad believes in his boss's political visions, but rather because it presents a chance to get promoted to manager and hence earn a higher salary, since Mr. Kapur will be busy running his election campaign. Yezad has no patience for Mr. Kapur's cosmopolitan vision of a better society where everyone lives in harmony with each other; in Yezad's view, Mr. Kapur is a man entirely detached from the realities of the city. Here we find another example of a collision between grandiose rhetoric and the banalities of everyday life. When Mr. Kapur compares Bombay to an aging woman, with "[a]ll her blemishes, her slums, her broken sewers, her corrupt and criminal politicians" (361), Yezad interrupts: "Hang on, Mr. Kapur. I don't think crime or corruption can be called a blemish. More a cancerous tumour. When a person has cancer in their body, they should bloody well fight it" (361).

The Reality of Words

In *Such a Long Journey* and *A Fine Balance*, we find countless of examples of words being taken out of their context, words becoming unreal, although crucially without the realist diegetic framework ever seriously being undermined. *Family Matters* likewise never really problematizes its own diegetic discourse to the extent that its realism is dissolved, even though one could argue that the novel's exploration of the rupture between things and their references has become intensified. It is an intensification that does *not*—unlike Mistry's two previous novels, which operate in a much more explicit sense with a dialectic between individual-private trajectories and notions of collectivity and historicity—*strengthen* the novel's realism, but on the contrary point toward its inherent instabilities and fragilities. In *Family Matters*, the overall realist framework thus at times disintegrates into irreconcilable and un-redeemable private-individual dramas. Through the focus on individualization, the novel continuously destabilizes words, names, buildings, relations, family, society, and history. Time and again, the same words come to signify different things to different people. Words and visions begin to refer to realities and memories that do not exist, or which orient themselves according to different coordinates—for example, Mr. Kapur's conviction that Parsi people are honest all the while Yezad, a Parsi, attempts to cheat him, or when Mr. Kapur comically misidentifies a scene at a busy train station as a manifestation of his vision of cosmopolitan collectivity. The novel contains several scenes in which characters ponder nostalgically on names, and what it means when the names of streets are changed.[24] Countless scenes involve misunderstandings, ironies (e.g. Mr. Kapur's death because of a verbal misunderstanding[25]), intentions misinterpreted because of words used wrongly or simply missing,[26] or the before-mentioned confrontations between grandiose rhetoric and practical everyday life.

Vakeel is a professor emeritus of English literature, fully aware of the power of words; and yet it is ironically uncontrollable words that come to play a fateful role in his life. In a sense, there are too many words in his life, and too little of an actually lived life. Vakeel ignored his own (and Lucy's) desires, and instead followed the words of his parents. He ends up having lived the wrong life, a character in the wrong story—a story written not by himself, but by family tradition. When Vakeel visits the local doctor, the latter wants a literary quote from the professor, but at this point he is tired of words; he simply wants to be cured.[27] Due to his Parkinson's disease, Vakeel becomes more feeble day by day; as his world shrinks, the only things left are, ironically, treacherous words and memories.

It is a word that lies behind one of the novel's great misunderstandings; what did Yasmin say when she fell to the ground from the rooftop after fighting with Lucy over Vakeel? Late in the novel, Jehangir meets Dr. Fitter.

This was the doctor who attended Yasmin and Lucy after their fatal fall. Dr. Fitter tells the young boy that at the time a lot of rumors circulated: "was it a double murder, was it double suicide, was it pure accident?" (489). But the old doctor explains that no one actually heard Yasmin's last word except him: "all the confusion was due to one word in her sentence: did she say 'he' or 'we'? . . . I know what she said. She said, 'What did we do!' But there were other people gathered around. Some of them heard, 'What did he do!' and they claimed it incriminated Nariman" (490). According to the doctor, Yasmin's last words were not an accusation against her husband, merely a lament of a kind: that they had all wasted their lives, making the wrong decisions based on misguided assumptions and flawed values. The novel's continued emphasis on the problematic of language—misunderstandings, ironies, and displacements—suggests an aesthetic style less occupied with the exploration of what J. P. Stern, as quoted earlier, describes as realism's "premise of a single, undivided reality,"[28] but rather the opposite; a fractured, fragmented world almost entirely centered around the private-individual sphere. It is a realist style that in this sense differs quite noticeably from Mistry's two previous novels.

Dr. Fitter's revelation ironically appears late in the text, after the novel throughout has insisted on the emptiness of the word compared to reality; for example, Mr. Kapur's rhetorical escapades, as well as Yezad's brutally rejected Canadian immigration visa application that contained quotes from both Churchill and Shakespeare. On this pivotal occasion, however, words *do* matter, albeit in an ironic sense. Only much later, that is, at a time when everything related to the story has become largely irrelevant (Coomy and Vakeel Nariman both being dead at this point), does the novel reveal the words to us, as if the text suggests that the power of words, their truth, can only emerge at the time of the "too late." The episode regarding Yasmin's last word, misunderstood by an entire generation, underlines the idea of fragmentation, dissolution, separation; but also, at the same time, the hope that words may yet again find their right form—that at some point, they will be reconnected to and understood in their right context, albeit belatedly.

The figure of lateness is one we find in all of Mistry's novels; in *Such a Long Journey*, Gustad only just meets Major Bilimoria one last time before he dies (and Dinshawji only just manages to withdraw all the mysterious government money from the secret bank account in time); in *A Fine Balance*, Maneck returns to India too late, discovering that everything he once cared deeply about has fallen apart during his absence. *A Fine Balance*'s epilogue, set eight years after the main events in the novel, reveals a tragic awareness of the problematic of late temporality, which eventually leads to Maneck's suicide. In contrast, *Family Matters* is a novel in which this temporal experience of lateness no longer plays a significant role. Words eventually find their meanings, albeit ironically at a time when the individuals to whom this meaning was significant are no longer there; that is to say, on a collective level, it is largely insignificant.

Set in the 1990s, *Family Matters* is a novel that is much less troubled by the collective historical trajectory than Mistry's previous novels, which also means that the relationship between individuals and the state is much less intense or relevant in the third novel. Occasionally, we hear about Shiv Sena's political initiatives, although the political generally plays an inconspicuous role. The point here is that whereas in the previous two novels, the external political-historical circumstances drive the plot ahead, often by way of disrupting the characters' lives, the individuals in *Family Matters*' plot are largely undisturbed by these circumstances. When the identity and structure of the state apparatus appears as undisputed fact, a self-evident, unquestioned reality—the more intense Mistry's realist style tends to focus on the private sphere. Stylistically, one could say that *Family Matters*' realism is less interested in exploring the dialectic between individual-private trajectories and notions of collectivity and historicity, and thus less interested in articulating a political subject-position, a collective-communal notion of a "we" emerging within a politically unstable and hence *historical* context. It is a novel, as I observed earlier, which in some sense situates itself in the aftermath of the postcolonial—a post-historical novel whose realism no longer orients itself toward the specifically political, but rather toward the private-intimate aspects of life.

Conclusion

Family Matters is essentially a novel about individuals whose individuality threatens traditional communal structures, family relations eroding and disintegrating—an aspect reflected in the novel's changing narrative perspectives; the novel begins with a third-person focalization mixed with Nariman Vakeel's meandering stream-of-consciousness memories (italicized in the text), which halfway through the novel shifts to Yezad's perspective. The novel ends with a first-person focalization of Jehangir in immediate present tense. These narratorial changes again underline the novel's exploration of individual realities, and to a lesser extent the pursuit after the political coordinates of a common level of reality.

Overall, *Family Matters* generates a vague or uncertain sense of causality and connectivity, albeit too weak to lead to specific conclusions. It would perhaps be possible to trace an overall causal trajectory underlying the majority of the novel's stories and anecdotes, but at the same time, as we have seen, the novel's realist style generally discourages such an interpretive endeavor. The novel's formal dynamic does not seek to consolidate a unified, causal trajectory, even if it vaguely indicates one, but instead offers a myriad of individual trajectories, tangentially and peripherally connected in what seems a kind of jigsaw puzzle, albeit one that remains unfinished, incomplete.

In the novel's epilogue, set five years after the main plot ends, the narratorial perspective as mentioned centers around Jehangir's first-person perspective. Jehangir studies an old jigsaw puzzle showing an image of Lake Como. The puzzle, he remembers, used to occupy him for hours; now, it only reminds him of his family's strangely entangled history:

> I go to my room and lie on the bed. I think of all the things I've heard, over the years, about Grandpa and Lucy and my grandmother. And the picture is still not complete. Like some strange jigsaw puzzle of indefinite size. Each time I think it's done, I find a few more pieces. And its form changes again, ever so slightly. My old jigsaws, including the beautiful Lake Como puzzle, are still on my shelf. . . . I wonder what it was about them that so fascinated me. They seem like a waste of time now. (491)

Like Yasmin, who expressed regret over time wasted in her last moment, and which subsequently was misheard and thus misunderstood with unfortunate consequences for the generations coming after—Jehangir seems to express a temporal awareness that transcends the longing for meaning, connectivity, and questions of guilt, although from an individual perspective. Time constitutes one of the most central narrative dimensions in *Family Matters*, albeit one that does not reconcile differences among the family members, but instead seems to exacerbate their distinct individualities.

Family Matters is a novel deeply concerned with themes such as individual aging, retrospection, and questions about guilt, forgiveness, and reconciliation. Vakeel remembers when as a young man he used to say to the older generation (which appears in the novel only as a collective voice): "*You've grown old without growing wise*" (17). Near the end of the novel, Yezad tells his own son: "Learn from this, Jehangoo. Listen to the advice of elders. When we grow up, we think we know everything. We assume old people are not right in their heads. Too much pride we acquire with our years. And then it brings us down" (494). However, when Vakeel is forced out of his own apartment by Coomy and Jal, he reflects: "To so many classes I taught *Lear*, learning nothing myself. What kind of teacher is that, as foolish at the end of his life as at the beginning?" (197)—as if the novel suggests that even old age does not bring desired wisdom to the individual. It is this discrepancy that the novel so persistently traces as it narrates the story of individual members of a family—and in a wider sense a people, a community, and a nation—moving from one generation to another, or from one epoch to another. During the last pages of the novel, Jehangir ponders: "I try to recall an earlier time, before Grandpa arrived, a time when the world was so safe and small and manageable. . . . I wonder what lies ahead for our family in this house, my grandfather's house, in this world that is more confusing than ever" (500). It is a world, one could add, which in many ways has moved on—a world no longer granting much space to traditional communities, and where these are increasingly being dissolved and eradicated not by history as such, but by fragmentation and the individualization of its members.

Read together, Mistry's three published novels illustrate an interesting formal development regarding the issue of literary realism. Mistry begins with a realist style still largely dependent on a historical discourse (*Such a Long Journey*), moves on to a more panoramic and expansive style (*A Fine Balance*), and finally ends with a style centered more narrowly on the private-domestic sphere (*Family Matters*). Although all three texts are clearly molded in the realist tradition, they each demonstrate important formal differences. While Mistry's first novel stylistically and thematically largely adheres to the norms of the Lukácsian historical novel,[29] his second (and, to some, the most classically *realist*) novel, *A Fine Balance*, is in many ways the text that comes closest to the nineteenth-century Balzacian novel. The historical background still plays a crucial role in *A Fine Balance*, although the novel places much stronger emphasis on the dynamics of interpersonal relations and stylistic heterogeneity, the interplay between collective forces and individual agency, as well as digressive, panoramic, and multiple plot developments. The story of *Family Matters* begins some twenty years after the timeframes of his first two novels (the 1970s), that is, the beginning of the 1990s. The novel occasionally alludes to history, although only in passing, and without it having any real consequences or impact in terms of the plot development. The realist style is not only more complex, detailed, inward-looking, introspect, reflective, and nuanced but also—and perhaps because of that—less energetic, dynamic, and ultimately less *political*. With *Family Matters*, we seem to arrive at a point where the urgency of the political questions of what constitutes a common reality has decreased. It is in many ways what one could call a post-historical novel, writing the *present*. The novel's world is thus one in which the realist style— or more concretely its specifically political dimension—ultimately seems less purposeful, perhaps because the memories of the national wars and crises of the 1960s and 1970s at this point are fading, even if the present (the 1990s) from an individual point of view seems even more disparate and heterogeneous.

The point here is that it is precisely *when* the outer frames of reality have been consolidated—to the extent that there are few significant political questions left to ask—that the stage is set for a private-individual realm to flourish, unhindered by fears of collective crisis, the existential threat of war. What I am addressing here is, I believe, a context intimately connected to postcolonial realities; that is, a cluster of themes revolving around questions about the collective "we," the body politic not as a self-evident fact but one in the process of becoming, that is, when the consensual-collective framework is no longer a natural given. The implication here is that once the political negotiation of what constitutes common reality is over, Mistry's realism and perhaps realism more generally *as an aesthetic form of political imagination* becomes less effective; at this point, aesthetic means and literary modalities more perceptive to the complexities and nuances of the private-individual realm (e.g. impressionism, psychological realism, quotidian realism, magical realism, symbolism, expressionism, surrealism, modernism, anti-realism) present themselves more readily and with greater relevance and force.

Notes

1. See Bruce Robbins, "Modernism and Literary Realism: Response," in *Realism and Representation: Essays on the Problem of Realism in Relation to Science, Literature and Culture*, ed. George Levine (Madison: Wisconsin University Press, 1993), 227.
2. For example, fields like globalization studies, critical race studies, world literature, and diaspora studies.
3. For example, see Ulka Anjaria, *Realism in the Twentieth-Century Indian Novel* (Cambridge: Cambridge University Press, 2012); Hamish Dalley, *The Postcolonial Historical Novel: Realism, Allegory, and the Representation of Contested Pasts* (Basingstoke: Palgrave Macmillan, 2014); and more recently Sourit Bhattacharya, *Postcolonial Modernity and the Indian Novel: On Catastrophic Realism* (Basingstoke: Palgrave Macmillan, 2020).
4. J. P. Stern, *On Realism* (London: Routledge, 1973), 63.
5. Ayelet Ben-Yishai, *Common Precedents: The Presentness of the Past in Victorian Law and Fiction* (Oxford: Oxford University Press, 2013), 15.
6. See in particular: Ibid; Ian Duncan, *Scott's Shadow: The Novel in Romantic Edinburgh* (Princeton, NJ: Princeton University Press, 2007); Elizabeth Deeds Ermarth, *Realism and Consensus in the English Novel* (Edinburgh: Edinburgh University Press, 1998); Catherine Gallagher, *Nobody's Story: The Vanishing Acts of Women Writers in the Marketplace 1670–1820* (Berkeley: University of California Press, 1994); Rae Greiner, *Sympathetic Realism in Nineteenth-Century British Fiction* (Baltimore, MD: The Johns Hopkins University Press, 2012); Sandy Petrey, *Realism and Revolution: Balzac, Stendhal, Zola, and the Performances of History* (Ithaca, NY: Cornell University Press, 1988); Harry E. Shaw, *Narrating Reality: Austen, Scott, Eliot* (Ithaca, NY: Cornell University Press, 1999).
7. Chantal Mouffe, *On the Political* (London: Routledge, 2005), 5.
8. Neil Lazarus, "The Politics of Postcolonial Modernism," *The European Legacy* 7, no. 6 (2002): 779.
9. See Laura Moss, "Can Rohinton Mistry's Realism Rescue the Novel?" in *Postcolonizing the Commonwealth: Studies in Literature and Culture*, ed. Rowland Smith (Waterloo, ON: Wilfrid Laurier University Press, 2000), 157–165 for one of the few exceptions to this tendency.

10 As McNamara observes, "whereas [Mistry's] previous novels were more directly engaged in the political issues of the day ... *Family Matters* is predominantly concerned with debates over religious identity within the Parsi community." Roger McNamara, "Developing 'A Fine Balance': Secularism, Religion, and Minority Politics in Rohinton Mistry's *Family Matters*," *South Asia: Journal of South Asian Studies* 40, no. 1 (2017): 56–57.

11 More generally, the novel presents a series of complex challenges facing traditional communities as such in an increasingly modern, individualistic, and fragmented world.

12 Thus, when Yezad's son decides to invite his non-Parsi girlfriend to his birthday party, Yezad protests by referring to Orthodox Parsi rules, a situation that echoes Vakeel's situation a generation earlier. See Mistry, *Family*, 481.

13 The Parsis played an important intermediary role during British colonial rule, but subsequently lost this position in the post-independent era; hence the nostalgic, anxious tone in the novel. For a discussion of this issue, see Tanya Luhrmann, *The Good Parsi: The Fate of a Colonial Elite in a Postcolonial Society* (Cambridge, MA: Harvard University Press, 1996), 59–60; and McNamara, "Developing," 54–70.

14 Mistry, *Family*, 411–417.

15 As McNamara, points out, the novel explores "how the desire for racial purity leads to suffering for the individual and the family." "Developing," 62.

16 Late in the novel, Roxana feels "terrible. At a time like this, suddenly the ceiling came into my mind" (401). It was Roxana who suggested that Coomy and Jal ask Edul Munshi to fix the ceiling (see 300).

17 Jehangir accepts a bribe from his wealthy classmate, allowing the latter to skip homework, and puts the extra money in the family's food money envelope (see 214–221).

18 Jehangir's act thus echoes Yezad's own, desperate attempt to raise money for the family.

19 There are three main narrative coordinates in the novel: money, religion, and family. Kapur, Vakeel's parents, along with Yezad traverse through the political-religious coordinate; Jal, Coomy, Jehangir and Murad, Roxana and Yezad are characters affiliated with money concerns; and the family coordinate relates to all the main characters in the novel.

20 See Mistry, *Family*, 88.

21 For example, Yezad's plan to deceive Mr. Kapur backfires; his hope to win money in the matka lottery is dashed; Jehangir's acceptance of bribery money is revealed; and Coomy and Jal's plan expel Vakeel from the apartment ends in tragedy.

22 See Mistry, *Family*, 24–25.

23 Jehangir at one point observes that the world seems to be "falling apart" (201).

24 For example, when Mr. Kapur shows a photo of the Marine Lines Station from the 1930s (see 53). Later, Mr. Kapur agrees to pay an enormous sum of money

to keep the old name of his sports equipment store (instead of changing it to "Mumbai Sporting Goods")—largely because of his nostalgia for the history of the name (see 325–329).

25 When Mr. Kapur refuses to change the shop's name to include "Mumbai" instead of "Bombay," he is attacked and killed by two Shiv Sena representatives.

26 Many of the characters in *Family Matters* are engaged in elaborate games of mindreading (characters speculating on what the other might be thinking, etc.), for example, in connection with Vakeel's eviction from his own apartment (see 192–193). This is one of the stylistic aspects that sets it apart from Mistry's two previous novels.

27 See Mistry, *Family*, 55.

28 Stern, *On Realism*, 63.

29 For a discussion of this issue, see Eli Park Sorensen, "Between the Private and the Public Spheres: The Politics of Realism in Rohinton Mistry's *Such a Long Journey*," *Studies in Canadian Literature/Études en littérature Canadienne* 45, no. 1 (2021): 182–203.

12

Settler-Colonial Realism

Naturalizing and Denaturalizing the Frontier

Hamish Dalley

It is now a critical commonplace that literary analysis should be grounded in contexts not limited to the boundaries of the nation-state. Under the banner of transnationalism, oceanic studies, globalization theory, or world literature (among others), contemporary criticism aims to diversify literary history and understand how literature develops through movement, translation, adaptation, hybridization, and re-contextualization.[1] In this chapter, I argue that the settler-colonial frontier is a zone shaped by economic, ideological, and cultural forces that are of profound significance for modern world literature, and that as such it represents an important global context for critics to consider. A comparative approach to the literatures of modern settler-colonial societies reveals narrative commonalities that attest to the entanglement of material forces and aesthetics. Settler-colonial literatures have unfortunately been treated as peripheral to metropolitan forms, with even cultural nationalists adopting a rhetoric of belatedness to position frontier texts behind the "advanced" zones of global modernity. Developments in the theoretical analysis of settler colonialism now create an opportunity to escape this trap. By recognizing that settler colonialism is a specific socio-cultural construct that is integral to global modernity, we can reframe otherwise perplexing aspects of settler literatures as aesthetic responses to their conditions of production. This approach especially allows us to shed new light on the aesthetic most strongly associated with settler-colonial novel writing: realism.

This chapter is divided into three sections. The first contextualizes the rhetoric of belatedness, found in both metropolitan literary theory and cultural nationalist discourse, which tends to peripheralize settler-colonial cultures. The second summarizes developments in settler-colonial theory that reframe peripheral belatedness as a structural effect of the frontier's material-ideological constructs. This perspective allows us to recognize settler literatures not as derivatives of metropolitan models, nor necessarily as postcolonial attempts at writing back, but as aesthetic responses to a contextually specific variant of global modernity. The third section sketches some shared features of settler-colonial realism, comparing examples of Anglophone writing from Africa and Australia. It identifies two tropes—"metamorphosis" and "revelation"—that recur in numerous instances of white writing. These tropes render legible some of the ideological paradoxes of settler colonialism, a project of "making known" a *new* place as one *already* understood. This contradiction is refracted aesthetically as a kind of ambivalent realism, fractured by an eternal frontier that is both reified and divided, naturalized and denaturalized, slipping in and out of narrative realization.

The Rhetoric of Belatedness on the Settler Frontier

The settler-colonial literatures of what historian James Belich has termed the "Anglo-world" have insistently been framed by a discourse of belatedness.[2] The ramshackle huts that marked the frontiers of European settlement in the eighteenth and nineteenth centuries were seldom inhabited by writers, and, even if they were, the cities mushrooming along the coasts of the new colonies usually lacked the economic infrastructure to support large-scale literary production. As Simon During notes, "the primary institutions of a literary culture were largely absent in the new territories" of the frontier, a lack not usually remedied until a generation or so after the settlement's foundation.[3] Modern settler colonies have therefore often been imagined, by their inhabitants no less than metropolitan taste-makers, as lands without high culture. In the nineteenth century, the word "colonialism," which referenced settler-colonial customs, "connoted that which was local, parochial, provincial, insular and hence narrow, restrictive, [and] inferior."[4]

Against this backdrop, the discourses of settler cultural nationalism that emerged across the Anglo-world in the late nineteenth and early twentieth centuries braided together the concepts of cultural belatedness and literary realism. The project to transcend the anachronistic traditions of frontier culture was understood as a quest for correspondence between aesthetics and the material realities of the new society. Cynthia Sugars writes of the attempt in nineteenth-century Canada "to assert and overcome cultural-historical belatedness through the invention and implantation of a resonant and rooted cultural tradition"—a project that entailed re-grounding historical fiction in a continent felt to be lacking a meaningful past.[5] Lawrence Jones observes that New Zealand's cultural nationalism of the 1930s posited a dialectic between its *realist* avant-gardism and the alleged "falsity, unreality, and sentimentality" of previous generations.[6] In 1952, novelist and essayist Bill Pearson diagnosed New Zealand's backwardness as a symptom of "unreality," a blindness to cultural specificity caused by the settlers' preference for British traditions: "The importation of our culture has always meant an accompanying unreality," he argued.[7] National maturity and cultural plenitude were thereby posited as future achievements in which representation and reality would finally align. As Allen Curnow expressed it in 1951, "We have allowed ourselves to feel protected always, hiding from actuality behind the maternal screen of England . . . We are stunted emotionally because we have not dealt direct with life, but through intermediaries."[8]

The irony of this discourse is that while the cultural nationalists were defining realism as the aesthetic signifier of having transcended colonial status, European and American critics were conceptualizing realism as a superseded form: the signifier of provincial anachronism par excellence. This framework still retains critical authority. Franco Moretti's *Modern Epic* (1996), for instance, presents experimental texts like *Ulysses* (1922) and *The Waste Land* (1922) as the formal analogs of the expanding world system, in contrast to which the novel is "not exactly a conservative, but certainly a *moderating* form: . . . a symbolic brake upon modernity."[9] Pascale Casanova's attempt at a universal theory of literature, *The World Republic of Letters* (1999; trans. 2004), outlines a similar trajectory in which parochial *national* authors, especially in former colonies, transcend their politically committed realism in the direction of aesthetic "autonomy" to acquire cultural capital and global credibility.[10] While it is true that the scholarly discourse on realism is vast and diverse, these examples indicate a structure of feeling that aligns realism with tradition, positioning authors who prefer realistic styles behind the times.[11]

Progressivist theories of realism reinforce an implicitly stadialist conception of cultural development that has been fundamental to how frontier societies have been imagined for at least 300 years. From the earliest attempts to theorize settler colonialism in the seventeenth century, the frontier has been understood as a museum where Europe's past is recapitulated: a view encapsulated by John Locke's 1689 declaration that "in the beginning all the world was America."[12] Stadialist discourse constructs metropolitan socioeconomic forms as normative, temporalizing the distance to the frontier as a measure of historical retardation. In the 1829 book that marked the consolidation of Anglophone "settlerism,"[13] Edward Gibbon Wakefield characterized the frontier as a site of civilizational regression, declaring that settler populations are unique in that, "though they continually increase in number, [they] make no progress in the art of living."[14] Stadialist discourse persisted throughout the nineteenth and twentieth centuries, appearing in popular anxieties about settler backwardness—the "cultural cringe" that nationalists tended to reinforce in their efforts to transcend—and, conversely, in expectations that settler societies would eventually surpass their metropolitan progenitors.[15] As late as 1964, the social scientist Louis Hartz was advancing a stadial model of settler societies, arguing that they could be understood as "fragments" chipped from the historical trajectory of their mother country, condemned to stasis by their isolation from the progressivist dialectic of Europe.[16]

Within this interpretive framework, the literatures of settler-colonial societies could be understood either as belated imitators of, or insurgents against, metropolitan norms. Cultural cringe or ressentiment—either way, the progressive engine-room of literary history is located in Europe. In Hartz's words, "when a part of a European nation is detached from the whole of it, and hurled outward onto new soil, it loses the stimulus toward change that the whole provides. It lapses into a kind of immobility."[17] This model explains Lukács's assumption that literary innovation was incommensurable with settler-colonial conditions.[18] It also structures Casanova's assertion that the pace of world-literary change is calibrated to the "Greenwich Mean Time" of Paris—with politically engaged realism relegated to the peripheries. If we are to escape this trap and integrate settler traditions into a non-teleological model of world literature, we must therefore disrupt the stadialist association of peripherality, derivativeness, and realism.

Settler-Colonial Studies: Theorizing Frontier Cultures

In the last twenty years, settler-colonial studies has emerged as a distinctive academic subfield. Building upon postcolonial theory and the work of indigenous scholars, it adopts a comparatist approach focused on structural continuities across a range of geographically and historically diverse examples. The field's central insight is that establishing a new society on appropriated territory has legal, economic, and cultural effects that persist over time, and which continue to organize social praxis even after the frontier has officially "closed." This chapter highlights three salient elements of settler-colonial society: the settler contract, the logic of elimination, and settler indigenization. These elements help explain why settler literature demands an understanding of realism beyond the stadialist model.

The material and legal specificities of the "settler contract" arise from the fact that settler colonialism—unlike imperialisms based on slavery or the economic exploitation of indigenous peoples—entails a primary, defining relationship between a *population* and a *territory*. In the Americas, Southern, Eastern and Northern Africa, and Australasia, Europeans established settlements with the primary intention of acquiring land. Appropriation could happen through treaty, purchase, conquest, or informal seizure (and how the conquest took place was of the utmost importance for indigenous survival), but the structural principle was the same: occupied territory was constructed as a "state of nature" superseded by the "civil society" founded by the settler population. Carol Pateman observes that

> a civil society created out of a state of nature has (is understood to have) its origin in an original contract. In a *terra nullius* the original contract takes the form of a *settler contract*. The settlers alone (can be said to) conclude the original pact. It is a racial as well as a social contract. The Native peoples are not part of the settler contract—but they are henceforth subject to it, and their lives, lands, and nations are reordered by it.[19]

This founding juridical act entails spatial and temporal paradoxes. Settler sovereignty is *mobile*, activated when settler citizens leave their heartland and travel to the extra-juridical spaces of the "new" world—territories defined as states of nature.[20] This process constructs a simultaneously *retroactive* and *proleptic* temporality: settler history begins with a political foundation that retroactively defines the indigenous society—regardless of whether or not native legal and cultural structures are acknowledged to have existed or to retain legal salience[21]—as belonging to the state of nature, and thus signifying the land's *prehistory*. The settler polity renders the indigenous population abject to civil society, yet simultaneously constructs indigeneity as *natural, autochthonous,* and *timeless*. Veracini calls this the "intractable historiographical paradox" of settler colonialism: the settler contract is premised on the necessary juridical primacy of the settler, *and at the same time*, it posits native belonging as more authentic, natural, and eternal—in marked contrast to the settlers' *historical* presence.[22]

This tortured logic has immediate, and devastating, material consequences. The foundational insight of settler-colonial studies—articulated by Patrick Wolfe in 1998—is that because "settler colonies were not primarily established to extract surplus value from indigenous labour," but rather for the purpose of "displacing indigenes from (or *re*placing them on) the land," they tend to the proliferation of legal, economic, social, and cultural strategies for making native peoples disappear.[23] These include ideological constructs like the "one-drop" rules that see indigeneity effaced by a single white ancestor; containment institutions like the Canadian residential school system or Australia's Stolen Generations, in which children were separated from their families and acculturated in (often) abusive state facilities or adoptive families; linguistic and religious assimilation; the legal denial of indigenous title and/or the translation of indigenous ownership into alienable freehold; and, of course, violence, including genocide. Wolfe's insight is that elimination is not a phase limited to the period of foundation, but a *structural logic,* immanent to settler society and persisting across time: "elimination is an organizing principle of settler-colonial society, rather than a one-off (and superseded) occurrence."[24]

The logic of elimination has at least two consequences for literary realism. First, it means that the foundational conflict of settler society is non-dialectical. Lukács saw literary realism as emerging from narratives, like Walter Scott's historical novels, that placed typified, representative characters in conflict, dramatizing social contradictions that could be resolved through synthesis.[25] But for a settler society, the posited future does not entail synthesis with the indigenous Other, but the native's (literal or discursive) annihilation. As Frantz Fanon observed of French Algeria, the settler-colonial world is "compartmentalized," divided between elements that "follow the dictates of mutual exclusion" and "confront each other, but *not in the service of a higher unity.*"[26] For this reason, literature of the settler frontier—including novels otherwise influenced by Scott's dialectical realism—tends to conclude with the narrative elimination of the native and the relegation of indigeneity to prehistory (examples of this pattern include James Fenimore Cooper's *The Last of the Mohicans* [1826] and William Satchell's *The Greenstone Door* [1914]). Second, and contradictorily, the *structural* dimension of settler-colonial elimination disrupts efforts to relegate indigeneity to the state of nature. Every Anglophone settler society today faces political, legal, and ideological challenges arising from the failure of prior efforts to eliminate indigeneity. Insofar as indigenous peoples have almost always survived the settler onslaught, the frontier can be understood as something that persists into the present as an ongoing structure of domination, if not as a literal borderlands territory. From this point of view, the settler polity is a place where the past is immanent to the present, and history tends to reemerge at unexpected moments to disrupt the perception of time as linear.

The third significant feature identified by settler-colonial studies concerns the most important cultural strategy by which settlers react to the contradictions of their ideology: indigenization. As we have seen, the settler contract establishes a binary between natives, who belong to the discursive realm of nature, and settlers, who are mobile yet carry sovereignty with them as an immanent possession, retroactively construct their appropriated territory as "home," and belong to the discursive realm of history.[27] This construction renders native peoples abject to the polity—making them targets for literal and/or symbolic "transfer" to the temporal-spatial exterior of the settler nation[28]—

and at the same time it establishes their indigeneity as a permanent obstacle to full settler identification with the colonized territory. For this reason, settler projects always entail efforts to appropriate an indigenous identity. Anna Johnston and Alan Lawson observe that settler cultural activities—including literature—have been shaped by this imperative to indigenize the settler:

> It is in the translation from experience to its textual representation that the settler subject can be seen working out a complicated politics of representation, working through the settler's anxieties and obsessions in textual form. Increasingly, the white settlers referred to themselves and their culture as indigenous; they cultivated native attributes and skills . . . , and in this way cemented their legitimacy, their own increasingly secure sense of moral, spiritual, and cultural belonging in the place they commonly (and revealingly) described as "new." They also began to tell stories and devise images that emphasized the disappearance of native peoples; the last of his tribe . . . , the dying race, even tales of genocide.[29]

As this passage implies, settler indigenization has been conjoined with the rhetoric of realism, understood as a search for expressive forms capable of representing the material and spiritual attributes of the appropriated territory. Yet as Veracini points out, indigenization must remain incomplete, because full identification with the native would undo the historical logic of the settler contract:

> Indigenisation . . . despite recurring fantasies of ultimate supersession, is never complete, and a settler society is always, in Derridean terms, a society "to come," characterised by the *promise* rather than the practice of a truly 'settled' lifestyle. Indigenisation . . . could then be seen as . . . asindotic . . . : the line separating settler and indigenous must be approached but is never finally crossed, . . . where sameness should be emphasised but difference is a necessary prerequisite of the absolute need to at once distinguish between settler self and indigenous and exogenous Others.[30]

The ideological paradoxes of settler colonialism are thereby encoded in narrative form. The indigenization project captures realism within its discursive gravity, transforming it into an aesthetic correlate of full belonging and locating the possibility of "accurate" representation in an impossible future state of "completed" settlement.

Tropology of Settler Realism I: Metamorphosis

Settler-colonial theory therefore suggests that the prominence of realism in frontier communities marks a cultural response to the ideological and material contradictions of an entirely *modern* social system—a system for which stadialist historical descriptions, and the rhetoric of belatedness they entail, are inappropriate. If we turn to literary examples, we can identify patterns that attest to the pressures placed on realism by this context. The remainder of this chapter explores two tropes that recur in settler writing: "metamorphosis" and "revelation." The following discussion is limited to examples drawn mostly from Australia and the Anglophone settler colonies of Africa. To be clear, I am not suggesting that settler literature is *simply* an aesthetic expression of settler-colonial ideology, and I am definitely *not* claiming that frontier literature plays an exclusively mystifying role. On the contrary, I see each text as an individual expressive work in which settler colonialism is one factor among many. While some novels naturalize frontier relations and reify the logic of elimination, others engage with them critically, de-naturalizing settler ideology and foregrounding the ongoing political salience of the frontier.

"Metamorphosis" describes the tropological outcome of attempts to narrativize the impossible: settler indigenization. Veracini observes that "settlers of all origins routinely transubstantiate as they enter the settler locale,"[31] and novels often depict this process. But the temporality of settler change makes for a twisted story. The founding of the settlement marks the beginning of a sovereignty that is supposedly eternal; the settler is a subject whose past involves *arriving* in a place *already* constituted as home. Identity is thus forged in the contradiction of movement in the service of rootedness. The tropological expression of this recursive logic is best described as *metamorphosis*. Metamorphosis entails a sudden, instantaneous ontological transformation that results in radical newness—but a newness that was immanent, latent, or unrealized within the pre-transformation subject. It is a kind of change that occurs only via the intervention of a catalytic extra- or nonhuman force. In the original model for this trope—Ovid's ancient epic—the mediating role is played by the gods; in settler fiction, it is usually a function of the colonized land itself.

An exemplary case of the metamorphic pattern is Tim Winton's *Cloudstreet* (1991), one of the most beloved works of Australian fiction. Tracing the lives of two families who share a house in Perth—rivals eventually united in marriage—*Cloudstreet* belongs to the tradition of national epic originating with Scott's sagas of historical unification. But as befits its positionality as a settler-colonial narrative, *Cloudstreet* is organized not by the dialectical temporality of metropolitan nationalism but the contingent—*metamorphic*—temporality of chance. The pattern is established at the outset, when each of the two families is transformed by unexpected luck mediated by the natural environment. First, Sam Pickles loses the fingers of his right hand in a fishing accident, and is then bequeathed ownership of the eponymous house by his cousin, who bought it with gambling proceeds and then died unexpectedly.[32] The Lamb family is likewise transformed when the younger son, "Fish," suffers a brain injury after almost drowning (32). Fish becomes the novel's narrator, and his disabling encounter with the water establishes a magical connection with the landscape. Despite its formal similarities to the national epic, *Cloudstreet* thus presents a social unit in which the division between families is not the driving force of change. On the contrary, human characters are fixed in their identities until they are subjected to the sublime agency of the natural world.[33]

Winton's novel attests to the ongoing salience of settler-colonial dynamics. The "great continent of a house" (43) is transparently a metaphor for Australia,[34] within which settler-colonial history is inscribed by the theme of haunting. Its original owner was a white woman who committed herself to "missionary purpose" and turned the house into an institution for Aboriginal girls, who were forcibly separated from their families and targeted for acculturation (36). After one inmate drinks poison, the white owner also dies, leaving the central room haunted by ghosts visible only to Fish (35–6). Frontier symbolism is reinforced when Sam, having gambled his money away, decides to lease half of the house, physically dividing it with a fence and declaring the communal areas to be "no man's land" (50). This divided space, marked by a frontier and haunted by the intangible presence of Aboriginal people, frames a narrative of white alienation. Fish's parents express the existential plight that they lack the cultural tools to resolve:

> You think maybe we don't belong here, like we're out of our depth, out of our country?
> We don't belong anywhere. When I was a girl I had this strong feeling that I didn't belong anywhere, not in my body, not on the land. It was in my head, what I thought and dreamt, what I believed, Lester, that's where I belonged, that was my country....
> Oriel put a blunt finger to her temple: This is the country, and it's confused. It doesn't know what to believe in either. You can't replace your mind country with a Nation, Lest. (256)

Such passages recapitulate a key claim of the Australian cultural tradition: that the repressed fact of indigenous presence blocks settler occupation and renders the dream of national belonging unobtainable. *Cloudstreet*'s constitutive splitting—of its disabled central character, rendered "incomplete" by his chance encounter with the water, and of its setting, the house divided between families, the living and the dead, the past and the present—thus parallels what Fanon describes as the social logic of the settler colony: it is "compartmentalized," and its opposing sectors are not resolvable through synthesis.

On the contrary, *Cloudstreet*'s resolution occurs through a fantasy of transcendence that enacts the logic of elimination symbolically while unifying the white subject with nature. Resolution begins when Rose and Quick, adult children from opposite sides of the familial divide, have sex in the haunted room. When Quick hesitates, Rose reassures him that their connection means "We're gonna be something else altogether" (347), a metamorphosis that will turn "that dead room" into "a new dwellingplace" (348). They are observed by the ghosts of the Aboriginal girl and her white persecutor, who, "torn by their halfness," are displaced by the affirmative act of the living (348). The exorcism is completed by the birth of Rose and Quick's baby, who comes into the world with "his fingers crossed," signifying the persistence of the temporality of chance into the next generation (425). Symbolically uniting the settler nation as "a new tribe" (464), this birth sees the family take undisturbed possession of the house now emptied of spectral inhabitants: "The spirits on the wall are fading, fading, finally being forced on their way to oblivion, free of the house, freeing the house, leaving a warm, clean sweet space among the living, among the good and hopeful" (425). This eliminatory resolution is paralleled at the individual level when Fish heals his spiritual division, drowning himself in the river and thus completing the metamorphosis that started with his abortive initial encounter with the natural world:

> I'm a man for that long. I feel my manhood, I recognize myself whole and human, know my story for just that long, long enough to see how we've come, how we've all battled in the same corridor that time makes for us, and I'm Fish Lamb for those seconds it takes to die, as long as it takes to drink the river, as long as it took to tell you all this, and then my walls are tipping and I burst into the moon, sun and stars of who I really am. (469–70)

Cloudstreet is thus a case study of the metamorphic narrative, reflecting the settler desire for indigenization along with the obstacles to achieving it. Numerous works attest to this longing for admittance to the realm of nature. Richard Flanagan's *Gould's Book of Fish* (2001), which depicts the establishment of the British penal colony in Van Diemen's Land in the 1820s, literalizes *Cloudstreet*'s metaphor by having its main characters metamorphose into actual fish.[35] Similarly, Dorothy Johnson's "A Man Called Horse" (1968) features a bored inhabitant of metropolitan New England who, taken prisoner by Native Americans, relinquishes his humanity and adopts the persona of a horse, achieving moral regeneration.[36] Albert Camus's "The Adulterous Wife" (1957) stages the same transformation in colonized Algeria, where a metaphorical sexual encounter with the Sahara gives the protagonist an experience of "recovering her roots, and the sap [rising] anew in her body."[37] Isak Dinesen's memoir *Out of Africa* (1937) similarly presents the colonized landscape as a sublime catalyst for the transformation of the white settler: "He had taken in the country, and in his eyes and his mind it had been changed, marked by his own individuality and made part of him. Now Africa received him, and would change him, and make him one with herself."[38]

Dinesen's passage foregrounds a key facet of the metamorphic trope: the land's role in mediating the settler's ontological transformation stands in for the function played by a socio-political antagonist in dialectical historical realism. Settlers might be changed by "Africa," but Africa is really a synecdoche for its indigenous peoples:

> The Natives were Africa in flesh and blood. . . . We ourselves, in boots, and in our constant great hurry, often jar with the landscape. The Natives are in accordance with it, and when the tall, slim, dark, and dark-eyed people travel . . . or work the soil, or herd their cattle, or hold their big dances, or tell you a tale, it is Africa wandering, dancing and entertaining you.[39]

Lukács writes that in the nineteenth-century novel, historical consciousness is "a process full of contradictions, the driving force and material basis of which is the living contradiction between conflicting historical forces, the antagonisms of classes and nations."[40] The settler-colonial frontier, however, is not organized by this Hegelian progressivism but the logic of elimination. The settler contract banishes the indigenous subject from history, rendering it continuous with the state of nature and abject to the settler polity. This ideological-legal operation is aestheticized by settler realism of metamorphosis: deprived of the human antagonist of metropolitan realism, the settler's encounter is with a nonhuman, natural Other, which possesses a non-historical temporality rendered as the sublime.

The logic of the settler contract is such that indigenization can never be complete, a fact reflected in many metamorphic narratives. "As 'being indigenous' by definition excludes ever *having become* indigenous, settlers can never 'be indigenous.' It is a paradox of the settler condition that can never be satisfactorily avoided—there is a reason why logics [sic] is shaped by universal laws, and even the sovereign in this case cannot decide on the exception."[41] Camus's "adulteress" reverts to her previous life as soon as her husband returns; Dinesen goes bankrupt and leaves Kenya; *Gould's Book* is a case of magical realism in which the redemptive metamorphosis is rendered ironic by a frame narrative, and so on. The openness of frontier realism—a form often shaped around acts of narrative failure—reflects the contradictions of this logic.

If we want to explore abortive metamorphosis in more depth, a good place to look is the Southern African farm novel, of which two examples stand out: Doris Lessing's *The Grass Is Singing* (1950), set in Southern Rhodesia, and Nadine Gordimer's *The Conservationist* (1974), from South Africa. Both center on white characters who relocate from urban to rural environments, seeking an encounter with the landscape that might enable a more authentic state of being. Lessing's protagonists, Dick and Mary Turner, derive a romanticized ideal of rural life from the settler fiction that posits their proper home to be the veld.[42] "Getting close to nature," in Mary's phrase, "was sanctioned . . . by the pleasing sentimentality of the sort of books" she read, "a reassuring abstraction" (51) with little connection to reality. Gordimer is similarly ironic about the agricultural fantasies of urban capitalists, for whom tax benefits complement the feeling of "having remained fully human" that is endowed by owning land.[43] According to J. M. Coetzee, the archetypal farm novel turns on a metamorphosis in which the settler's agricultural labor exceeds the minimal requirements of Lockean possession, becoming a metaphysical act justified in spiritual terms. "The final test that the bond between [white settler] and [African landscape] is supramaterial will be passed when a mystic communion of interpenetration takes place between them, when farmer becomes *vergroeid* (intergrown, interfused) with farm."[44] Gordimer's protagonist, Mehring, fantasizes of just such a union. In one scene, he drinks under the stars on a "miraculous" Christmas night, imagining that he will be joined by one of his Black workers, Jacobus, who will freely recognize him as a companion rather than employer or oppressor (204–9). Lessing also presents settler indigenization as a fantasy of symbolic union. But for Mary, her husband's partial metamorphosis provokes disgust rather than desire:

> Why, he seemed to be growing into a native himself, she thought uneasily. He would blow his nose on his fingers into a bush, the way they did; he seemed, standing beside them, to be one of them; even his color was not so different, for he was burned a rich brown, and he seemed to hold himself the same way. (158)

Both novels thereby present metamorphosis as an object of critical irony, predicated on the white characters' denial of the exploitative nature of their relationship with actual African workers.

The Grass Is Singing and *The Conservationist* make clear that settler metamorphosis *cannot* occur because it is predicated on a primary relationship—between settler and land—that is disrupted by a disavowed third factor. The indigenous population is synecdochally associated by settler ideology with the state of nature, meaning that it straddles the conceptual divide between human (settler) subject and natural object, rendering the binary aporetic. *The Conservationist* concludes with a scene in which Mehring suddenly realizes that a woman he has picked up for sex is not white but "Coloured" (meaning he is in violation of apartheid South Africa's anti-miscegenation laws), and might be planning to rob him. "They can have it, the whole four hundred acres," he exclaims, ceding his farm with an ease that proves he had never become *vergroeid* at all (264). Similarly, *The Grass Is Singing* culminates with Mary's murder by a Black worker she once whipped and then developed a sexual attraction to, and who ends up as her surrogate parent when she can no longer care for herself. These moments attest to the failure of metamorphosis, locating its cause in the settlers' inability to forge a coherent relationship with the indigenous subjects they have disavowed but cannot live without.

The fact that failure is inevitable is, to some extent, already a part of settler consciousness is hinted at by the opening chapter of *The Grass Is Singing*, which depicts the reaction of Dick and Mary's white neighbors to news of her death:

> The people in "the district" who knew the Turners ... did not discuss the murder; that was the most extraordinary thing about it. It was as if they had a sixth sense which told them everything there was to be known, although the three people in a position to explain the facts said nothing. (1–2)

This passage frames the narrative as a *typical* account of the settler dynamic: the events of the story need not be discussed because they can be inferred from what is already known about the society, as the manifestation of a general, structural logic. If Lessing thus proffers her novel as an adaptation of classical literary realism (which, as Lukács argued, uses representative characters to exemplify social roles)[45] it also transposes the issue of settler belonging into a problem of *knowledge*. Mary's death is met "as if some belief had been confirmed, as if something had happened which could only have been expected" (1). *The Grass Is Singing* thereby highlights another side to settler-colonial ideology: its *epistemological* dimension, its status as a matter of understanding, belief, and perception. In the shift from the ontological question of settler *being* to the epistemological issue of settler *knowledge*, we see a corresponding shift to a new narrative structure. Instead of metamorphosis, we find novels shaped by the trope of *revelation*, in which space is textualized and colonial possession becomes a matter of learning to read, interpret, and understand, rather than simply *be*.

Tropology of Settler Realism II: Revelation

"Revelation" names the aesthetic response to the contradictions of settler-colonial ideology at the level of epistemology. This is not to suggest that there is a strict division between ontology and epistemology in settler discourse; they are entangled, with the latter more likely to be foregrounded in contexts where the legitimacy of the colonial state has been brought into question by native activism, revisionist history, or efforts to publicize the suffering of indigenous peoples. In Australia and South Africa, as elsewhere, the period since the 1980s has seen a sustained challenge to the settler community's self-knowledge. The former has witnessed "history wars" over competing narratives about frontier history,[46] while the latter's efforts to democratize its national narrative found institutional expression in the Truth and Reconciliation Commission.[47] In these circumstances, narratives proliferate that hinge on moments of discovery, in which settlers troubled by inauthenticity are enlightened about the "true" history of the colonized territory. Revelation typically involves the acquisition of knowledge from or about indigenous peoples, and it can initiate change in the frontier dynamic. In many cases, however, the trope replicates the structural pattern of settler ideology, presenting discovery as a catalyst for the settler's redemptive transformation and acquisition of full belonging. In such instances, revelation mimics the narrative logic of metamorphosis, enacting the settler's indigenization and the native's elimination via an epistemological rather than ontological transformation.

As with the prior trope, revelation can be understood as an element of traditional realism re-contextualized in settler-colonial space. Lukács theorized nineteenth-century realism as an expression of the enlightenment project of universal historical understanding—an attempt to overcome the obfuscating effects of commodification by grasping the world system as an historically evolving totality.[48] This epistemological endeavor—which subsequent critics have associated with contemporaneous imperial exploration through the concept of cognitive mapping[49]—constitutes part of "the eidaesthetic project of the literary,"[50] a type of sociohistorical knowledge constructed through the conjunction of form and content in the realist novel. Lukács believed that this knowledge was necessarily circumscribed by a text's position within the social totality,[51] a principle that leads us to expect novels from settler-colonial contexts to reflect the interpretive limitations of their conditions of production. Thus, we can see "revelation" as a narrative response to the difficulties of cognitive mapping for settler subjects whose social position—predicated on the elimination of indigenous peoples whose identity they wish to appropriate—entails a degree of unavoidable bad faith.[52] Eli Park Sorensen argues that realism's totalizing project injects a proleptic or "utopian" temporality into its narrative form,[53] so it is unsurprising that many settler-colonial texts depend heavily on a trope derived from the Christian belief that individuals may be redeemed through the acquisition of sacred knowledge. Just as with the pre-Christian trope of metamorphosis, however, settler-colonial revelation tends to be mediated not by the divine but by colonized land, or else by the indigenous peoples who are its symbolic extension. As such, the "utopian-interpretive trajectory"[54] of frontier realism is rendered problematic by the internal contradictions of settler-colonial ideology.

The most canonical Australian example of a novel organized by the trope of revelation is Patrick White's *Voss* (1957).[55] Addressing an iconic theme of the frontier imaginary, White's protagonist is modeled on the German explorer Ludwig Leichhardt, who in 1848 disappeared while attempting to map a route through the interior of Australia. Voss's expedition is bankrolled by investors wanting new lands for colonization. The mystic explorer, however, sees his journey as a spiritual quest to unlock immanent knowledge through an encounter with inhuman, sublime space. "In this disturbing country," he explains, "it is possible more easily to discard the inessential and to attempt the infinite. You will be burnt up most likely, you will have the flesh torn from your bones, you will be tortured probably in many horrible and primitive ways, but you will realize that genius of which you sometimes suspect you are possessed" (29). Pain and death are the vectors of transformative discovery for Voss; in the novel's most famous passage, "true knowledge only comes of death by torture in the country of the mind" (437). Voss mocks the stupidity of settler culture, seeing in its imitation of British mores a denial of the spiritual truths encoded in the Australian landscape (107). As his expedition enters the continent's arid heart, Voss comes to "know" the land in a sexualized way that draws on both meanings of the archaic double entendre: "His soul must experience first, as by some spiritual *droit de seigneur*, the excruciating passage into its interior. Nobody here ... had known his own mind to the extent that would enable him to bear such experience" (130). *Voss* thus conjoins knowledge with male eroticization of the feminized continent. It draws a contrast between the inauthentic, materialistic settlement of the capitalist colonies, and the fertile—but annihilating—state of belonging that occurs when truth is revealed to a man who, in his own mind, becomes a ruler: "In the light of his own conquest, he expanded, until he possessed the whole firmament. Then it was true; all his doubts were dissolved" (352). In a move that reflects the contradictory nature of settler discourse, *Voss* presents its hero's insight as incommunicable. Voss's spiritual double, Laura Trevelyan, with whom he telepathically shares his discoveries, concludes by presenting him as an exemplar of what Australians will become—in the future—if they ever learn to understand the continent they have seized (437).

As we would expect, Voss's revelatory encounter involves contact with the indigenous people who are part of the landscape. The novel insistently describes Aboriginal characters as "trees" or "lizards" (184, 197, 198, 310, 334), asserting their status as "nature" in contradistinction to the civil society of the coasts. In a key episode, the expedition shelters in a cave decorated with Aboriginal rock art. For Voss, the images represent the romantic ideal of unmediated communication, a perfect alignment of signifier and signified which would allow direct access to noumenal reality—if they could be understood (267). In attributing to the indigenous subject a mediating role in the settler's encounter with the land, revelation thus differs slightly from the tropological structure of metamorphosis. In many examples analogous to *Voss*, the settler's acquisition of knowledge is sparked by an encounter with indigenous subjects, who are assumed to possess the understanding the settler needs. In Alex Miller's *Journey to the Stone Country* (2002), the white protagonist learns of her ancestor's role in a frontier massacre from an Aboriginal woman, information that reveals the problematic nature of her relationship to Australian history.[56] Similarly, Andrew McGahan's *The White Earth* (2007) turns on its protagonist's discovery of human remains on his family's farm, evidence of the genocidal basis of settlement that unlocks a deeper understanding of the country.[57] Alternatively, some novels turn on moments in which white characters discover their own Aboriginal ancestry, a repressed genealogical connection to indigeneity that allows them to transcend the paradoxes of the settler contract.[58]

This latter theme is central to Zoe Wicomb's *Playing in the Light* (2006).[59] Set just after the 1994 elections in South Africa, where the Truth and Reconciliation Commission has made the connection between knowledge and democratic belonging explicit, Wicomb's novel tells of a woman who discovers that her parents were "play-whites"—Coloured descendants of the Cape Colony's indigenous people who passed as white to evade apartheid. Prior to this revelation, Marion is uninterested in the past and alienated from society, hostile to personal and collective historical inquiry and thus unable to form deep personal relationships (3). When she discovers her indigenous roots, she is disturbed. Like a numb limb aching as sensation returns, her recovered historical sensibility not only causes psychological pain but also allows her to reevaluate her dissociation from her community:

> Now that she had a past, a family, no matter how distant, something like loneliness has crept in.... The history of the country, too, has slid from the textbook into the very streets of the city, so that these landmarks that constitute her world—Robben Island, Table Mountain—are no longer the bright images of the tourist brochures. Nothing is the same. (177)

Her father's mimicry of settler ideology—"We Boere can't mos survive without land, even if it's just a little bit of earth like a basin of dough in which to knead our fists" (181)—becomes ironic, as the knowledge that renders his pretended whiteness false now opens the possibility of a different, truer, but complicated, relationship to place.

The central revelation of *Playing in the Light* leads the narrative back to the archive of settler-colonial fiction, which Marion now reads with eyes attuned to the ambivalence of its representations. She travels to London, "shocked to find herself a stranger, so very different from the natives" (189), and reexamines South Africa as a textual—epistemological—object, reading novels by J. M. Coetzee and Nadine Gordimer "to get to know those dark decades when [her family was] playing in the light" (191). The concluding scene of *The Conservationist* is especially disturbing, as she discovers in Mehring's encounter with the Coloured woman a problematic representation of her own identity:

> Is the girl not, at some level, a version of herself? Of her mother? Marion is not sure of the story, of what happens at the end, but it is undoubtedly the scene with the girl that drives Mehring away; it is the encounter with the play-white that winds things up. (190)

In a parallel to the irony of her father's assumed Afrikaner-ness, Marion finds herself betwixt the compartmentalized identities of the frontier, unsure on which side she belongs. "With no desire for crossing boundaries, or none that she knows of, she is a traveler who has stumbled into another country" (201). If *Voss*'s revelations presented White's settlers with the prospect of an authentic but *future* state of belonging, Marion's creates a similarly proleptic but uncertain possibility. Her new knowledge opens the prospect that the (putatively, imitatively) white subject might resolve the contradictions encoded in the settler contract, but this actual resolution is deferred. It cannot yet arrive, because the frontier persists insofar as the structural logic of settler domination remains. *Playing in the Light* ends with Marion angrily terminating her relationship with a Black author who expresses a desire to write the story of Marion's family (218). She is not yet ready to relinquish narrative authority to another.

This sketch of settler-colonial fiction attests to the ongoing salience of realism for the modern novel. Notwithstanding sallies into the supernatural or anti-mimetic, the texts I have discussed are structured by questions of representational efficacy and the aesthetic correspondence to colonial reality that, in the rhetoric of cultural nationalism and the theorization of the novel, have tended to result in the discourse of belatedness. Settler-colonial studies provides us with the interpretive language to grasp the frontier as a socio-cultural space that is integral to the consolidation of the modern world system. Settler frontiers are not, after all, peripheral to modernity; they are its leading edge, the place where the multiplicity of indigenous lifeworlds is swept aside and primitive accumulation drives the extension of imperial networks. The realist novel is transformed in this context. Narratives of ontological and epistemological change—novels constructed under the signs of metamorphosis and revelation—attest to the paradoxical, recursive logic of settler ideology, its effort to square the circles of sovereign repetition and newness, movement and stability, nomadism and indigeneity. "We're gonna be something else altogether" (*Cloudstreet*, 347), declares Rose Pickles, Winton's putative Australian of the future. If only it were that simple.

Notes

1. Debjani Ganguly, "Introduction," in *The Cambridge History of World Literature*, ed. Debjani Ganguly (Cambridge: Cambridge University Press, 2021), 26–31.
2. James Belich, *Replenishing the Earth: The Settler Revolution and the Rise of the Anglo-World, 1783–1939* (Oxford: Oxford University Press, 2009).
3. Simon During, "Pacific Colonialism and the Formation of Literary Culture," in *Voyages and Beaches: Pacific Encounters, 1769–1840*, ed. Alex Calder, Jonathan Lamb, and Bridget Orr (Honolulu: University of Hawai'i Press, 1999), 292.
4. Tadhg Foley, "'An Unknown and Feeble Body': How Settler Colonialism Was Theorized in the Nineteenth Century," in *Studies in Settler Colonialism: Politics, Identity and Culture*, ed. Fiona Bateman and Lionel Pilkington (Basingstoke: Palgrave Macmillan, 2011), 10.
5. Cynthia Conchita Sugars, *Canadian Gothic: Literature, History, and the Spectre of Self-Invention* (Cardiff: University of Wales Press, 2014), 4.
6. Lawrence Jones, *Picking up the Traces: The Making of a New Zealand Literary Culture, 1932–1945* (Wellington: Victoria University Press, 2003), 83.
7. Bill Pearson, "Fretful Sleepers," *Public Address*, Accessed June 26, 2019, https://publicaddress.net/great-new-zealand-argument/fretful-sleepers/.
8. Allen Curnow, *A Book of New Zealand Verse, 1923–1945*, revised (Christchurch: Caxton Press, 1951), 29–30.
9. Franco Moretti, *Modern Epic: The World System from Goethe to García Márquez* (London: Verso, 1996), 195; original emphasis.
10. Pascale Casanova, *The World Republic of Letters* (Cambridge, MA: Harvard University Press, 2004).
11. See Neil Lazarus, *The Postcolonial Unconscious* (Cambridge: Cambridge University Press, 2011).
12. John Locke, *Two Treatises of Government: And a Letter Concerning Toleration*, ed. Ian Shapiro (New Haven, CT: Yale University Press, 2003), 121.
13. Belich, *Replenishing the Earth*, 147.
14. Edward Gibbon Wakefield, *A Letter from Sydney, the Principal Town of Australasia: And Other Writings* (London and Toronto: J.M. Dent and Sons, 1929), 68.
15. Belich, *Replenishing the Earth*, 164; Philip Steer, *Settler Colonialism in Victorian Literature: Economics and Political Identity in the Networks of Empire* (Cambridge: Cambridge University Press, 2020), 126, 141.
16. Louis Hartz, *The Founding of New Societies: Studies in the History of the United States, Latin America, South Africa, Canada, and Australia* (New York: Harcourt, Brace & World, Inc., 1964).
17. Ibid., 3.

18. Georg Lukács, *The Historical Novel*, trans. Hannah Mitchell and Stanley Mitchell (Lincoln: University of Nebraska Press, 1962), 64.
19. Carole Pateman, "The Settler Contract," in *Contract and Domination*, ed. Carole Pateman and Charles W. Mills (Cambridge: Polity, 2007), 56; original emphasis.
20. Lorenzo Veracini, *Settler Colonialism: A Theoretical Overview* (Basingstoke: Palgrave Macmillan, 2010), 53–55.
21. Pateman, "Settler Contract," 39.
22. Veracini, "Indigenes and Settlers," in *A Companion to Global Historical Thought*, ed. Prasenjit Duara, Viren Murthy, and Andrew Sartori (Somerset: John Wiley & Sons, 2014), 458.
23. Patrick Wolfe, *Settler Colonialism and the Transformation of Anthropology: The Politics and Poetics of an Ethnographic Event* (London: Continuum, 1998), 1.
24. Patrick Wolfe, "Structure and Event: Settler Colonialism, Time, and the Question of Genocide," in *Empire, Colony, Genocide*, ed. A. Dirk Moses (New York: Berghahn Books, 2010), 103.
25. Lukács, *The Historical Novel*, 36.
26. Frantz Fanon, *The Wretched of the Earth*, trans. Richard Philcox (New York: Grove Press, 2004), 3–4; emphasis added.
27. Pateman, "Settler Contract," 54–55.
28. Veracini, *Settler Colonialism*, 34–52.
29. Anna Johnston and Alan Lawson, "Settler Colonies," in *A Companion to Postcolonial Studies* (Malden, MA: Blackwell, 2000), 363.
30. Veracini, *Settler Colonialism*, 23; original emphasis.
31. Lorenzo Veracini, "Israel-Palestine Through a Settler-Colonial Studies Lens," *Interventions* 21, no. 4 (2018): 5.
32. Tim Winton, *Cloudstreet* (New York: Picador, 1991), 12, 21. Subsequent references in parentheses.
33. Salhia Ben-Messahel, "An Interview with Tim Winton," *Antipodes* 26, no. 1 (June 6, 2012): 12.
34. Peter Mathews, "Who Is My Neighbour?: Tim Winton's 'Aquifer' and the Ghosts of *Cloudstreet*," *Australian Literary Studies* 32, no. 1 (January 2017): 1.
35. Richard Flanagan, *Gould's Book of Fish* (Sydney: Picador, 2001). Subsequent references in parentheses.
36. Dorothy Johnson, "A Man Called Horse," in *Indian Country* (New York: Ballantine Books, 1968).
37. Albert Camus, *Exile and the Kingdom*, trans. Carol Cosman (New York: Vintage International, 2006), 25.
38. Isak Dinesen, *Out of Africa and Shadows on the Grass* (New York: Vintage, 1989), 342.

39 Ibid., 20.
40 Lukács, *The Historical Novel*, 53.
41 Lorenzo Veracini, "Decolonizing Settler Colonialism: Kill the Settler in Him and Save the Man," *American Indian Culture and Research Journal* 41, no. 1 (2017): 12; original emphasis.
42 Doris Lessing, *The Grass Is Singing* (New York: Harper Perennial Modern Classics, 2008), 66. Subsequent references in parentheses.
43 Nadine Gordimer, *The Conservationist* (London: Jonathan Cape, 1974), 22. Subsequent references in parentheses.
44 J. M. Coetzee, *White Writing: On the Culture of Letters in South Africa* (New Haven, CT: Yale University Press, 1988), 86.
45 Lukács, *The Historical Novel*, 35.
46 Stuart Macintyre and Anna Clark, *The History Wars* (Melbourne: Melbourne University Publishing, 2004).
47 Lisa Propst, "Reconciliation and the 'Self-in-Community' in Post-Transitional South African Fiction," *The Journal of Commonwealth Literature* 52, no. 1 (March 1, 2017): 84–98.
48 Georg Lukács, *Writer and Critic: And Other Essays*, trans. Arthur D. Kahn (New York: Grosset & Dunlap, 1970), 118.
49 Edward W. Said, *Culture and Imperialism* (Vintage: New York, 1994), 77; Lazarus, *Postcolonial Unconscious*, 108; see Fredric Jameson, "Third-World Literature in the Era of Multinational Capitalism," *Social Text* 15 (1986): 65–88.
50 Eli Park Sorensen, *Postcolonial Studies and the Literary: Theory, Interpretation and the Novel* (Basingstoke and New York: Palgrave Macmillan, 2010), 57.
51 Georg Lukács, *History and Class Consciousness: Studies in Marxist Dialectics*, trans. Rodney Livingstone (Cambridge, MA: The MIT Press, 1971), 164–171.
52 Hamish Dalley, "The Meaning of Settler Realism: (De)Mystifying Frontiers in the Postcolonial Historical Novel," *NOVEL: A Forum on Fiction* 51, no. 3 (November 2018): 463.
53 Sorensen, *Postcolonial Studies and the Literary*, 66.
54 Ibid., 53.
55 Patrick White, *Voss* (Harmondsworth, Middlesex: Penguin, 1960). Subsequent references in parentheses.
56 Alex Miller, *Journey to the Stone Country* (Sydney: Allen & Unwin, 2002).
57 Andrew McGahan, *The White Earth* (New York: Soho, 2007).
58 Peter Carey, *A Long Way from Home* (New York: Alfred A. Knopf, 2017).
59 Zoe Wicomb, *Playing in the Light* (New York and London: The New Press, 2006). Subsequent references in parentheses.

CONTRIBUTORS

Nasrin Babakhani received her PhD in North American Studies from University of Goettingen, Germany. Her thesis is called "Cultural Realism: Reconsidering Magical Realism in the Works of Contemporary American Women Writers" and is currently being turned into a book. Her research interests include postcolonialism, magical realism, questions of diversity and equality in literature, feminism, and political identities.

Barbara Bausch has written her doctoral dissertation on Ror Wolf's poetics of disruption at the Friedrich Schlegel Graduate School of Literary Studies, Freie Universität Berlin. Her research interests include German literature of the twentieth and twenty-first centuries, poetics and theory of prose, avant-garde movements and experimental literature, and literary activism/political art. She also works as editor and translator of literary works, most recently of Vítězslav Nezval's, *Akrobat* for the series *MAGMA. Osteuropäische Avantgarden* (2021).

Nadine Böhm-Schnitker works as a stand-in-professor of English literature and literary theory at Konstanz University and serves as a *Privatdozentin* in English Studies: Literature and Culture at Friedrich-Alexander-University Erlangen-Nürnberg, Germany. She specializes in Victorian and Neo-Victorian Studies and has recently completed the manuscript for a monograph entitled "Senses and Sensations: Towards an Aisth-ethics of the Victorian Novel." Her current projects deal with the cultural legacy of the Opium Wars, neo-Victorian negotiations of class and inheritance as well as comparative practices in the long eighteenth century.

Hamish Dalley is an associate professor of English at Daemen College in Amherst, New York, where he is responsible for teaching world and postcolonial literatures, writing, and English Studies. He received his PhD from the Australian National University, Australia, and is the author of *The Postcolonial Historical Novel* (2014). His research explores the intersection between literary form and the historical imagination, realism, and the world novel, and has appeared in *Research in African Literatures, NOVEL:*

A Forum on Fiction, The Journal of Postcolonial Writing. He is currently working on a book manuscript focused on realism and the novel in settler-colonial contexts.

Jens Elze is assistant professor of English literature and cultural studies at University of Goettingen, Germany. His research and teaching areas include the history and theory of the novel, literature and infrastructure, postcolonial literature and theory, and early modern drama. He is the author of *Postcolonial Modernism and the Picaresque Novel: Literatures of Precarity* (2017) and editor of *The Enigma of the Picaresque* (2017). He has just finished a manuscript entitled "The Legitimacy and Illegitimacy of the Modern Age: Shakespeare and the Politics of Immanence."

Nidesh Lawtoo is Assistant Professor of Philosophy and English at KU Leuven, as well as PI of the ERC project, *Homo Mimeticus*. He is the editor of *Conrad's* Heart of Darkness *and Contemporary Thought* (2012), and the author of *The Phantom of the Ego: Modernism and the Mimetic Unconscious* (2013), *Conrad's Shadow: Catastrophe, Mimesis, Theory* (2016; Adam Gillon Award 2018), and *(New) Fascism: Contagion, Community, Myth* (2019). His next books are titled, *Violence and the Oedipal Unconscious vol. 1, Violence and the Mimetic Unconscious, vol. 2* (under contract), and he is currently working on a manuscript titled, *Homo Mimeticus*.

Caroline Levine is David and Kathleen Ryan professor of the Humanities at Cornell University and the author of three books: *The Serious Pleasures of Suspense: Victorian Realism and Narrative Doubt* (2003), *Provoking Democracy: Why We Need the Arts* (2007), and *Forms: Whole, Rhythm, Hierarchy, Network* (2015). She is the nineteenth-century editor of the *Norton Anthology of World Literature* and is finishing a book on the humanities and climate change.

Andreas Mahler teaches English literature and literary systematics at Freie Universität Berlin. His main areas of research are early modern literature, the shift from realism to modernism, textual poetics, and literary theory (semiotics, intermediality, literary anthropology, and aesthetics). Among his most recent publications is an edited volume on the form of the early modern essay.

André Otto is currently working in a research project on the poetics of in-between spaces at Freie Universität Berlin. He received his PhD in English literature from Ludwig-Maximilians-Universität in Munich for a book on the poetry of John Donne: *Undertakings. Fluchtlinien der Exklusivierung in John Donnes Liebeslyrik* (2013). He has taught Spanish literature in

Munich and English literature at the Freie Universität Berlin and was visiting professor for English literature at Humboldt-Universität Berlin. His main research areas are early modern poetry, contemporary poetry of place and British "experimental" prose of the second half of the twentieth century.

Maren Scheurer is a researcher and lecturer at the Department for Comparative Literature at Goethe University Frankfurt. She is the author of *Transferences: The Aesthetics and Poetics of the Therapeutic Relationship* and co-editor of essay collections on subjects such as therapeutic encounters, serial fragments, and amputation in literature and film. She has published essays on psychoanalysis, literature, and other media as well as the late-nineteenth-century transformations of realism in a wide range of journals and edited volumes. With Aimee Pozorski, she serves as executive co-editor of *Philip Roth Studies*.

Eli Park Sorensen is an assistant professor in the Department of English at the Chinese University of Hong Kong. He specializes in comparative literature, postcolonialism, literary theory, science fiction, crime fiction, and adoption studies. He is the author of *Postcolonial Studies and the Literary: Theory, Interpretation and the Novel* (2010), *Science Fiction Film* (2021), *Postcolonial Realism* (2021), *East-West Dialogues* (edited collection, 2020), and has published in journals such as *NOVEL: A Forum on Fiction*, *Journal of Narrative Theory*, *Paragraph*, *Modern Drama*, *Research in African Literatures*, *Partial Answers*, *Forum for Modern Language Studies*, and *Studies in Canadian Literature*.

Kai Wiegandt is professor of literature at the Barenboim-Said Akademie in Berlin. His interests include postcolonial and world literature, migration literature, early modern literature, literary anthropology, and the intersections of philosophy and literature. He is the author of *Crowd and Rumour in Shakespeare* (2012) and *J. M. Coetzee's Revisions of the Human: Posthumanism and Narrative Form* (2019), and he edited a special issue of the *European Journal of English Studies* on *J. M. Coetzee and the Non-English Literary Traditions* (2016, with Maria-Jesús Lopez) and *The Transnational in Literary Studies: Potential and Limitations of a Concept* (2020).

Dirk Wiemann is professor of English literature at the University of Potsdam. His research areas include postcolonial theory with a focus on South Asia; genre transformations in world-literary space; and minor cosmopolitan politics and aesthetics. His monographs include *Genres of Modernity: Contemporary Indian Novels in English* (2008) and, co-authored with three colleagues from the University of Potsdam, *Postcolonial Literatures in English: An Introduction* (2019). He has co-edited a special issue of *Thesis Eleven* on *Postcolonial World Literature* (2021) as well as *European Contexts for English Republicanism* (2013) and *Perspectives on English Revolutionary Republicanism* (2014).

INDEX

1832 Reform Act 49

abjection 141, 142, 144, 147, 149
Abrams, M. H. 85
abstraction 12, 14, 20, 48, 66, 184, 211, 219, 222, 223
actor-network theory (ANT) 2, 7, 8, 213, 218
Adam Bede (Eliot) 5, 15, 41, 43–8, 52
Adichie, Chimamanda Ngozi 20, 200–3
Adorno, Theodor W. 118, 205, 222
"The Adulterous Wife" (Camus) 257
adventure of writing 107–10
adventure-time 113–16
aesthetic(s) 2, 19, 44, 48, 52, 70, 73, 138, 149, 213
   challenges 192, 193
   impressionistic 7
   modernist mimetic 85
   political 2–6, 14
   realist 20, 162, 229
   reflection 84, 85
   Western 7, 81, 83, 84
affect 6–8, 10, 16, 43, 49, 87, 91, 92, 94, 97, 98, 210
Africa 252, 255, 258
aisth-ethics 15, 43–5, 47–9, 52
Akakichi No Eleven (1970–1) 204
Alaimo, Stacy 43
Albert Angelo (Johnson) 136
Ali, Monica 178
Allen, Paula Gunn 160, 161
Allende, Isabel 156
alternative modernities/modernization 13

America. *See* United States
Americanah (Adichie) 20, 200–1, 203
Americanization 216
Améry, Jean 174
Anglophone literary criticism 216
Anglophone settler colonies 255
Anglo-world 249
Angry Young Men 132
Anjaria, Ulka 5
Anthropocene 10, 20, 82, 88, 96, 99, 203
anthropocentrism 10, 87
Antinomies of Realism (Jameson) 7, 126 n.12
anti-realism 2, 4, 9, 12, 18, 71, 93, 228, 245
apophenia 220–2
Appadurai, Arjun 13
Aren't You Rather Young to Be Writing Your Memoirs? (Johnson) 136
Aristotle 81, 154, 172, 213
art(s) 73, 85
   autonomy of 4
   conceptual 32, 33
   definitions of 195
   mimetic 84
   realist 60
   representative 3
   and science 64, 66, 71
   Western 32
assemblage 6–14, 204, 211
Assmann, Jan 160
Attridge, Derek 192
Atwood, Margaret 185
Auerbach, Erich 3, 31, 81, 83
Austen, Jane 6, 219

Australasia 252
Australia 21, 255, 256, 261, 262
authenticity 45, 46, 123, 141, 252, 259, 264
autobiography 139
avant-garde 110, 121, 130 n.59, 132, 196

Bakhtin, Mikhail 5, 110, 113, 114, 116, 175, 179
Balsamo, Anne 211
Balzac, Honoré de 4, 9, 61, 62
Banville, Théodore de 30–2
Barad, Karen 15, 43
Barak, Julie 162
Barchester Towers (Trollope) 198
Barthes, Roland 5, 33, 155, 187 n.38
Bataille, Georges 95
Bateson, Gregory 92
Baudelaire, Charles 88
Bautista, Susana 211
Beecroft, Alexander 217
belatedness, rhetoric of 249–51
Belich, James 249
Belsey, Catherine 35, 155
Benjamin, Walter 81, 150 n.24
Bennett, Jane 6, 8, 92
Ben-Yishai, Ayelet 229
Bernard, Claude 62–6, 70, 71, 75
Beyond Good and Evil (Nietzsche) 96
Bildungsroman 43
Blackwood, John 48
Bleak House (Dickens) 11, 20, 197
Blumenberg, Hans 110, 122, 123, 135, 148
Bock, Martin 88
Bohr, Niels 43
Bolsonaro, Jair 192
Boltanski, Luc 212, 213, 216, 217, 220
Bone Clocks, The (Mitchell) 222
"Bonjour, Monsieur Courbet" (Banville) 31
Bonjour Monsieur Courbet. See La Rencontre, The Meeting (Courbet, painting)
Booth, Wayne C. 34

Borges, Jorge Luis 36, 156
Braidotti, Rosi 220
Bridle, James 217, 220, 221
Brown, Allison E. 160
Brown, Marshall 133, 144
Bruyas, Alfred 29

Caldwell, Janis 62
Call the Midwife (2012–) 20, 202–3
Camus, Albert 257, 258
Canada 250
Canavan, Gerry 191
Canterbury Tales (Chaucer) 185
capitalist globalization 2, 12, 13
Capitalist Realism: Is There No Alternative? (Fisher) 210
Caracciolo, Marco 177
Carpentier, Alejo 156, 157
Cartesian subjectivity 157
Casanova, Pascale 250, 251
Cassirer, Ernst 49
Castells, Manuel 217, 220
Champfleury (Jules François Felix Fleury-Husson) 30
Chanady, Amaryll Beatrice 157
characters/characterization 3, 6, 10, 11, 15, 18–20, 36, 42–5, 47–53, 62, 63, 70, 71, 75, 108, 109, 112, 120–2, 127, 134, 154, 160, 162, 174, 177–81, 183, 184, 202, 205, 220–2, 231, 234, 236, 239, 240, 242, 253, 256–60, 262, 263
Charon, Rita 64
Chaucer, Geoffrey 185
Chavkin, Allan 165
Chavkin, Nancy Feyl 165
Cheah, Pheng 12, 13
Chiapello, Ève 212, 216, 217, 220
Christian belief 261
chronotope 17, 110, 123, 220
cinema 138
civil society 252
climate catastrophe 192–4, 201
climate change 2, 10–11, 19, 99, 193, 200
Cloud Atlas (Mitchell) 9, 20, 222
Cloudstreet (Winton) 255–7

Coetzee, J. M.   18, 19, 169, 173, 175–8, 185, 259, 263
cognitive mapping   9, 221, 222, 261
collective memory   159–61, 183
collectivity   21, 165, 166, 231, 240, 242
colonialism   156, 249
colonization   159, 160, 230, 262
communal ethics   96, 97
community   16, 95–6, 99
composite soul   94–9
"The Concept of Reality and the Possibility of the Novel" (Blumenberg)   110
Confessiones (St. Augustine)   184
Connolly, William E.   93
Conrad, Joseph   6, 7, 16, 82–99, 156
  "Duel, The"   82
  Heart of Darkness   82, 83, 85, 91, 98, 156
  Nigger of the "Narcissus", The   82
  Secret Agent, The   82
  "Secret Sharer, The"   82, 90
  Shadow-Line: A Confession, The   16, 82, 85, 87–99
  Typhoon   82
Conservationist, The (Gordimer)   258, 259, 264
contingency   17, 108–12, 115, 117, 118, 122–4, 137, 222
Cooper, James Fenimore   253
Courbet, Gustave   15, 21, 29–31
Covid-19 pandemic   83, 86, 90
Critique of Pure Reason (Kant)   175
cross-culturalism   153
cultural belatedness   249
cultural difference   13, 14, 157
cultural heterogenization   13
cultural nationalism   249, 250, 264
cultural traditions   157, 158
Curnow, Allen   250
Cusk, Rachel   19, 21, 169, 178, 179, 183–5
  Kudos   19, 169, 178–85
  Outline   19, 169, 178–85
  Transit   19, 169, 178–85

Daniel Deronda (Eliot)   43, 52–3
Darwin, Charles   71
Das Kapital (Marx)   212
Das Parfüm (Süskind)   156
Das Schloß (Kafka)   156
De Anima (Aristotle)   172
Deckard, Sharae   215
decolonization   12, 165, 230
Déjerine, Jules   71
Derrida, Jacques   185
Descartes, René   154, 172, 174
description   3, 5, 8, 10, 17, 34, 35, 42, 46, 108, 113, 116–20, 122, 134, 159, 173, 255
dialectics   6, 8–14, 21, 210, 213, 221, 232, 233, 240, 242, 250, 251, 255
Diamond, Cora   173, 175
Dickens, Charles   4, 9, 20, 197, 198, 200
diegesis   109, 111, 112, 117, 120, 122, 123, 240
diegetic levels   31, 32, 47, 108, 122
diegetic world   45, 47, 49, 53, 119
Die Verwandlung (Kafka)   157
Dinesen, Isak   257, 258
distributed network   211
Doctor Pascal (*Le docteur Pascal*, Zola)   15, 62, 63, 66, 71
"the dominant"   214
Dostoevsky, Fyodor   5, 175, 176
Dublin   138
"Duel, The" (Conrad)   82
"Du Réalisme" (1855)   15, 30
During, Simon   249
Durix, Jean-Pierre   155

Early Life (Hardy)   61
ecocriticism   194
Ehrlich, Paul   64
electricity flow   200–1
Eliot, George and realism   4, 5, 41–53, 62, 68, 197, 198
  Adam Bede   5, 15, 41, 43–8, 52
  Daniel Deronda   43, 52–3
  Middlemarch   15, 43, 48–53, 196
  "The Natural History of German Life"   47

"Notes on Form in Art" 51
Elizabeth Costello (Coetzee) 18, 169–79, 185
embeddedness 15, 19, 173–8
embodiedness 19, 143, 170, 172–8
embodiment 19, 49, 71, 89, 146, 163, 171, 177, 179
emotion 4, 7, 44, 45, 48, 51, 52, 65, 68, 96, 144, 146, 176, 196, 197
England 136
ens realissimum 222
epidemic(s) 85
  contagion 82–3
  patho-logies 90–4
  reality of 86–8
  surviving 94–100
epistemology 5, 18, 21, 43, 47, 51, 53, 63, 70, 132, 133, 136–8, 140–7, 150 n.24, 169, 175, 213, 228, 260, 261, 264
Erdrich, Louise 18, 154, 158, 159, 161, 162, 164–6
Esther Waters (Moore) 198–9
Esty, Jed 2, 8, 13, 215
ethnic groups 157, 158
Europe 63, 88, 250, 251
European culture 157
European ethnocentrism 156
evidence-based medicine 63
experientiality 176, 177
experimental medicine 62, 70, 75
Experimental Novel, The (*Le roman expérimental*, Zola) 62, 70, 73
experimental poetry 191
Exposition Universelle, Paris 29–30
Eyeshield 21 (2002–9) 204

Fame (1980) 204, 205
Family Matters (Mistry) 20, 21, 229–44
Fanon, Frantz 253, 256
Faris, Wendy B. 159
Felski, Rita 196, 213
fiction 15, 31, 42, 61, 65–8, 74, 82, 88, 123, 133, 137–9, 177, 221
Fincham, Tony 61
Fine Balance, A (Mistry) 231, 234, 236, 240, 241, 244

Fisher, Mark 210–13
Flanagan, Richard 257
Flaubert, Gustave 4, 9, 33, 36, 62, 182
Fleming, Alexander 64
Fleury, Maurice de 71
Fludernik, Monika 177, 183
focalization 10, 183, 242
folklore 158
form-content dichotomy 209, 210
Forster, E. M. 217
Fraiman, Susan 199
French Algeria 253
Freud, Sigmund 160
Friday Night Lights (2006–11) 204
frontier cultures 251–4
Fuentes, Carlos 156
Furst, Lilian 61–3

Galton, Francis 71
Gandhi, Indira 231
García Márquez, Gabriel 154, 156
Gemeinschaft 97
genre(s) 3, 18, 34, 42, 43, 47, 119, 133, 136, 138, 185
  adventure 110, 113–15, 121, 123
  literary 178, 184
  literary-philosophical 176
  oral 179
  realist 231
Ghosh, Amitav 9, 11, 191
Ghostwritten (Mitchell) 222
Gibson, William 217, 220–2
Girard, René 86, 91, 94
Glee (2009–15) 204
Glissant, Edouard 192
global capitalism 12, 13, 19–21, 215, 236
globalization 12–14, 19, 20, 153, 216, 217, 248
globalization plot 217, 219
global modernity 248, 249
global network society 217
Goldmann, Lucien 8, 220
Gombrich, Ernst 32
Goodlad, Lauren 12, 215
Gordimer, Nadine 258, 259, 263

Gould's Book of Fish
    (Flanagan)   257, 258
"*grand miroir*"   88–90
Grass Is Singing, The
    (Lessing)   258–60
Great Debaters, The (2007)   204
Great Derangement, The (Ghosh)   11
"Great Stink" (1848)   11
Great War   88
Greek revolution   32
Greenstone Door, The (Satchell)   253
Grimm, Jacob   119
Gun Island (Ghosh)   9, 11
Gutenberg Galaxy   41

Hadjiafxendi, Kyriaki   44
Haeckel, Ernst   71
Halberstam, Jack   192
Handmaid's Tale, The (Atwood)   185
Haraway, Donna   215
Hardt, Michael   213
Hardy, Thomas   15, 16, 61–3,
    66–71, 75
Hart, Patricia   156
Hartz, Louis   251
Hassam, Andrew   139
Hazlitt, William   85
Heart of Darkness (Conrad)   82, 83,
    85, 91, 98, 156
Heidegger, Martin   12
Hempfer, Klaus   31
Herman, David   176, 177
hermeneutics   8, 9, 14, 44, 50, 51, 53,
    86, 211
heterotopy   140, 145
Hindu Shiv Sena party   231, 232, 242
historical consciousness   210, 258
historical defamiliarization   202–3
historical materialism   6, 10, 14
historicity   137, 240, 242
HIV   86
Hodgins, Jack   154
Holocene   10
homo duplex   82, 86
homoiosis   84
homo mimeticus   81, 82, 85
hooks, bell   160
Horkheimer, Max   205

horror   113, 115
humanism   93, 222, 228. *See also*
    posthumanism
humanity   72, 75, 100, 170–2,
    218, 222
humor   108, 118, 124
hybridization   13, 248

idealism   33, 135
ideology   2, 4, 5, 21, 62, 155, 191,
    205, 212, 228, 248, 249, 252–4
  Cold-War   215
  political   6, 7
  settler-colonial   21, 255, 259–61,
    263, 264
illusion   32, 33, 36, 67, 84, 109, 115,
    116, 121, 144, 199, 228, 237
India   231
indigenization   13, 21, 252–5, 257–9
indigenous people   252–4, 258,
    259, 261–3
Indo-Pakistani war (1971)   231, 232
intra-activity   43–4, 53
Introduction to the Study of
    Experimental Medicine
    (*Introduction à l'étude de*
    la médicine expérimentale,
    Bernard)   62, 70
invention   5, 108, 209, 213, 214, 250
Iqbal (2005)   204
Irwin, T. H.   44

Jakobson, Roman   1, 60, 61, 134, 214
James, Henry   62
Jameson, Fredric   7–9, 210, 211, 213,
    215, 217, 221
Jane Austen, Virginia Woolf and
    Worldly Realism (Morris)   6
Johnson, Bryan Stanley   17–18,
    132–3, 136, 137, 139, 143–5,
    147, 149, 150 n.24
  Albert Angelo   136
  Aren't You Rather Young to Be
    Writing Your Memoirs?   136
  Trawl   18, 138–49, 151 n.38
Johnson, Dorothy   257
Johnston, Anna   254
Jones, Lawrence   250

Journal of Narrative Theory 228
Journey to the Stone Country
 (Miller) 263
Joyce, James 17, 137
Jung, Carl Gustav 160

Kafka, Franz 156, 157, 171–3
Kant, Immanuel 175, 222
Keller, Lynn 191
Kimpton, Virginia 139
Klinkert, Thomas 73
Knausgård, Karl Ove 179
Knowles, Owen 88
Kohl, Stephan 35, 40 n.25
Köhler, Wolfgang 171
Kraniauskas, John 209, 214
Kristeva, Julia 142, 144
Kudos (Cusk) 19, 169, 178–85

La Berge, Leigh Claire 209
Lacoue-Labarthe, Philippe 85
language 1, 4, 5, 7, 17, 42, 43, 46, 51, 66, 70, 108–9, 123, 135, 136, 138, 140, 161, 173, 176, 241, 264
La Rencontre, *The Meeting* (Courbet, painting) 29–31
Larkin, Brian 14
Last of the Mohicans, The
 (Cooper) 253
Latin America 157
Latour, Bruno 8, 213, 218
Lawson, Alan 254
Lawtoo, Nidesh 6
Lazarus, Neil 215, 230
Lee, Allison 155
Leichhardt, Ludwig 262
LeMenager, Stephanie 191
Lessing, Doris 258–60
Levine, Caroline 5, 11, 42, 45, 47, 217
Levine, George 1, 5, 17, 135, 136
literary critics 191, 196, 203
literary studies 2, 19, 81, 82, 191, 192, 195, 216
literary texts 17, 20, 108, 117, 124, 133

literature 15–20, 33–5, 41, 62, 64, 66, 71, 73–5
Literature and the Anthropocene
 (Vermeulen) 10
Locke, John 154, 250
London Review of Books 178
lo real maravilloso 156, 157
Love Medicine (Erdrich) 18, 158–65
Lucas, Prosper 71
Lukács, Georg 8, 9, 11, 21, 23 n.42, 155, 210, 223, 251, 253, 258, 260, 261
Lye, Coleen 13, 14

McGahan, Andrew 263
McHale, Brian 134
Macherey, Pierre 210
Mackay, Robert William 49
magical/magic realism 5, 18, 153–9, 258
 anthropological 156, 157
 metaphysical 156
 ontological 156
Makropoulos, Michael 109
malaria 82, 87, 90
"A Man Called Horse"
 (Johnson) 257
Manzanas, Ana M^a 162
Marx, Karl 222
Marxism 213, 217
Marxist literary criticism 9, 210
Marxist theory 213
Marxist tradition 213
mass culture 205
materialism. *See* historical materialism; new materialism
matter 3, 4, 6, 8, 15, 33, 43, 52, 53, 61, 71, 73, 108, 111, 113, 119–21, 136, 142, 144, 147, 148, 201, 218, 219, 221, 222, 239
Maudsley, Henry 63, 65, 66
media-historical approach 138
mediality 33, 42, 43, 45, 46, 137, 138
mediation 5, 84–5, 87, 91, 115, 123
medical discourse 61, 62
medical practice 64, 69, 78 n.53

medicine   16, 61, 62, 64, 65, 67, 70, 71
memory   111, 113, 133, 142, 143, 147, 160, 161, 165, 166
metafiction   19, 111, 119, 132, 133, 138–40, 143
metamorphosis   21, 254–60
metaphor(s)   83, 86, 138, 143, 145–6, 148, 160, 216, 237, 256
  mirror   32
  moon/halo   83–6
  musical   53
  political   89
  scientific   50
  web   51
metaphysics   68–70, 75, 84, 156
Mezey, Jason   222
Middlemarch (Eliot)   15, 43, 48–53, 196
Miller, Alex   263
Miller, John Hillis   46, 47, 51, 83
mimesis   3, 4, 7, 12, 16, 32–3, 36, 81, 82, 84, 85, 154, 213, 220
  modernist   7, 16, 83–86
Mimesis: The Representation of Reality in Western Literature (Auerbach)   3, 31, 81
mimetic ecology   92
mimetic illusion   132, 134
mimetic poetics   83–5, 87–93, 95, 97
mimetic principles   83, 84, 86
mimetic theory   6, 82, 84, 85, 86
mimetic turn   81–2, 87
Mirror and the Lamp, The (Abrams)   85
Mistry, Rohinton   20, 229–34, 236, 237, 239–42, 244, 245
  Family Matters   20, 21, 229–44
  Fine Balance, A   231, 234, 236, 240, 241, 244
  Such a Long Journey   231, 234, 236, 237, 240, 241, 244
Mitchell, David   9, 20, 221, 222
"mode of the maybe"   109–12, 122, 124
Modern Epic (Moretti)   250
modernism   6, 62, 136, 196

modernist mimesis   83–8
modernist poetics   83, 85
modernity   11, 21, 32, 122, 150 n.24, 163, 179, 222, 264
Modern Language Quarterly   228
montage sequence   204–5
Moore, George   198, 199
Moore, Jason   220
moral norms   41
moral sentiment   44, 45, 55 n.25
Moretti, Franco   194, 210, 250
Morris, Pam   6, 134, 135, 219
Morrison, Toni   154
mortality   172, 174
Morton, Timothy   192
Moten, Fred   192
Mouffe, Chantal   230
Musée Fabre, Montpellier   29
museum-as-network   211–12
My Struggle (Knausgård)   179
myths   158, 163

Nadar (Tournachon, Gaspard-Félix)   32
Nagel, Thomas   176
Nancy, Jean-Luc   95
Narrative Medicine (Charon)   64
narrative/narration   3, 5, 18, 32, 33, 36, 46, 64, 83, 111, 114, 117, 123, 140, 142, 166, 175, 177, 261
  closure   198–9
  conversational   182, 183, 185
  (im)possibilities of   117–22
  institutionalized oral   183–5
  metamorphic   257, 258
  mimetic   93, 98
  patterns   3, 7, 16, 17, 115, 123
  of personal experience   181
  realistic   19, 176
  as realistic thinking   169–85
  self-reflexive   15, 17, 41, 108, 110, 132
  of struggling team   203–6
  written   182, 185
narratology   36, 176, 177, 183
National Health Service   202

nation-state 86, 248
Native American culture 158, 162, 163, 165, 166
Native Americans 158–61
Natural Causes and Supernatural Seemings (Maudsley) 65
"The Natural History of German Life" (Eliot) 47
naturalism 8, 15, 61, 62, 75
natural magic 67
Negri, Antonio 213
Nelson, Brian 134
neo-avant-garde movement 108
neoliberal culture 204
neoliberal economy 216
neoliberalism 194
network realism 20, 209–23
networked structure 220
New Historicism 217, 218
new materialism 2, 6–10, 14, 44, 218
New Yorker 178
New York Times 178
New Zealand 250
Nietzsche, Friedrich 96, 97
Nigeria 200, 201
Nigger of the "Narcissus", The (Conrad) 82
Nixon, Robert 10
nominalism 33
nonhuman forces 8, 11, 87, 89, 90
nonhumanity 218
non-realistic prose 109
"Notes on Form in Art" (Eliot) 51
Novel: A Forum on Fiction 229
novelism 216
novel(s) 34, 215
  contemporary 138, 216, 221
  form of 137, 139, 141
  global 9, 210, 216
  historical 10, 21, 32, 242, 244, 253
  realist 5, 20, 154, 182, 198, 213, 230, 236, 242, 244, 264
  world 9–10, 20, 216, 217, 219–21

oikos. *See* web of life
Okri, Ben 154
one-drop rules 252–3

ontology 5, 7, 10, 18, 42, 43, 84, 95, 156, 163, 169, 175, 212, 255, 258, 260, 261, 264
orality 179, 181, 184, 185
otherness 42, 44
Our Mutual Friend (Dickens) 11
Outline (Cusk) 19, 169, 178–85
Out of Africa (Dinesen) 257–8
outsider 32
  perspective of 200–2
Overcomer (2019) 204
Ovid 255

paranoia 9, 217, 220, 221
Parry, Benita 215
Pateman, Carol 252
Pattern Recognition (Gibson) 220
Paul, Jean 124
Pearson, Bill 250
perception 44–52, 70, 111, 113, 123, 141, 158, 175, 192, 197, 198
phallogocentrism 185
photography 32, 33
Pilzer und Pelzer (Wolf) 108–24
plague 86
Plato 35, 81, 83, 84, 155, 184
Platonic tradition 84
Playing in the Light (Wicomb) 263, 264
plot 9, 11, 17, 42, 45, 50, 51, 53, 71, 109, 110, 119, 134, 139, 154, 159, 198, 199, 201, 204, 205, 209, 211, 217, 232, 239, 242–4
poetics 136, 142, 144, 176, 213
poiein 221
poiesis 213
poietic 220, 222
political (con)texts 88–90
Political Unconscious, The (Jameson) 8
polyphony 5
postcolonialism 12, 153, 155, 156, 232, 242
postcolonial studies 11, 12, 20, 228–30
postcolonial world literature 11–13
posthumanism 6, 8, 10, 87, 220

postmodernism 153, 210–12
Potolsky, Matthew 156
Pouchet, Georges 71
power 1, 19, 36, 49, 73, 89, 90, 92, 97, 98, 161–6, 210, 217, 219, 220, 230, 240, 241
Power, Susan 154
precarity 14, 192–4, 199
Problems of Dostoevsky's Poetics (Bakhtin) 175
Progress of the Intellect, The (Mackay) 49
Prussian Academy of Sciences 171
pseudo-orality 19, 182, 184
psychosoterica 222
public infrastructures 201, 203
Puchner, Martin 178

qualia 176–7

racial stereotypes 165
Radin, Paul 162
Ramanujan, Srinivasa 170
Rancière, Jacques 3, 4, 6
realism 1, 7, 14, 133, 149, 169, 179, 194, 196, 232
  aesth-ethical 45
  aesthetic 82
  agential 15, 43, 52, 53
  causality/causes and effects 235–6
  classical 31
  climate 10
  community/communal identities 232–3
  and constructivism 213
  cultural 5, 153–66
  definition of 154, 155, 174, 229
  dialectical 21, 253, 258
  dissensual 2, 14, 21
  Edwardian 137
  experimental 66
  expressive 35
  history of term 15, 33–5
  literary 12, 16, 20, 34, 61, 109, 134, 174, 175, 228, 229, 231, 244, 249, 253, 260
  magical 5, 18, 153–9, 258
  medical 62–6, 75

  mimetic 82
  modern 154
  moral/sympathetic/ethical 15, 41, 42, 44–8, 52
  novelistic 4, 10
  organic 42
  political dimension of 229
  postcolonial 20, 228–30, 244
  and private sphere 233–5, 244
  progressive/deviant/of estrangement 134
  psychological 42, 232, 245
  scientific 66
  sociological 42
  and space/spatiality 9, 11, 20, 42, 47, 85, 110, 111, 115–18, 122, 139, 140, 142, 145, 163, 175, 177, 202, 211, 220–2, 234, 235, 244, 252, 253, 260, 262
  of surprise 42
  for sustainability 191–206
  term in history 29–33
  and time/temporality 7–14, 20, 42, 45, 99, 110, 112, 115, 116, 118, 122, 134, 142, 143, 145, 175, 177, 202, 210, 211, 234, 235, 241, 243, 250, 252, 255, 257, 258, 261
  Victorian 132
  worlding 12
Realism (Morris) 134
Realism in the 20th Century Indian Novel (Anjaria) 5
Realismus: Theorie und Geschichte (Kohl) 35, 40 n.25
realist defamiliarization 5, 20, 194, 197, 198
realist fiction 42, 61, 135, 194
realistic prose 123
realistic techniques 107–10, 121
realist literature 14, 16, 17, 215
realist turn 1, 210, 215
reality 1–7, 9, 11, 15, 16, 19, 31, 32, 42, 45–7, 49, 60, 64, 66, 68, 69, 73, 75, 82, 85, 109, 110, 115, 118, 119, 141, 142, 144, 175, 176, 212, 237–9

concept of 122–4, 133–5, 137, 149, 229
  effect 19, 33, 47, 68, 121, 141, 179, 187 n.38, 212, 213
  fictional 119
  notion of 5, 133, 134, 138
  political 234
  as possibility 122–4
  social 8, 18, 19
  unmediated 17
  of words 240–2
reason 170–2, 174
Rebentisch, Juliane 121
religiosity 238
religious belief systems 72, 74
Remember the Titans (2000) 204
Renaissance 32
Report to an Academy (Kafka) 171–3
representation 3, 31–4, 42, 48, 60, 111, 123, 133, 138, 141, 144, 147, 213, 214
  aesthetic 81 (*see also* aesthetics)
  artistic 84
  context 132–6
  of history 161
  literary 11, 17, 47
  mimetic 109, 115, 134, 177, 210, 212, 220, 229
  realist 45, 46, 52, 124, 214
  reality of 111, 121
  techniques 134, 135, 140
  traditions of 134
Republic (Plato) 83–4
revelation 260–4
Revenge of the Nerds (1984) 204
Rhetoric of Fiction (Booth) 35
Ricardou, Jean 109
Richardson, Angelique 67
Ricoeur, Paul 213
Rise of the Novel, The (Watt) 154
rituals 164–6
Robinson Crusoe (Defoe) 39 n.21
Rody, Caroline 156
Rothfield, Lawrence 62
routine 195–8

St. Augustine 170, 184
Sánchez, Jesús Benito 162

Sandlot, The (1993) 204
Satchell, William 253
Say Salaam India (2007) 204
Schober, Rita 71, 72
Schoene, Berthold 222
Schultz, Lydia A. 163
science
  experimental 62
  and fiction 191, 203
  medical 62, 64, 74
  religion and 72, 73
  Western 157
science-fiction 191, 203
"The Science of Fiction" (Hardy) 66
scientific methodology 61
scientific models 61, 66
Scott, Walter 32, 253, 255
Searle, John 176
seasickness 141–3, 146
Second World War 142, 143
Secret Agent, The (Conrad) 82
"Secret Sharer, The" (Conrad) 82, 90
Seliski, Robert 221
semiotic systems 49, 134, 214
Sentimental Education (Flaubert) 36
settler-colonial fiction 263, 264
settler-colonial frontier 248–51, 258, 264
settler-colonial identity 21
settler colonialism 10, 21, 248–50, 252, 254, 256
settler-colonial literatures 248, 249
settler-colonial realism 21, 248–9
  metamorphosis 21, 254–60
  revelation 260–4
  rhetoric of belatedness 249–51
settler colonial studies 251–4
settler-colonial theory 249, 254
settler contract 252–4, 258, 264
Shadow-Line: A Confession, The (Conrad) 16, 82, 85, 87–99
Shaolin Soccer (2001) 204
Shapiro, Stephen 215
Shaw, Bernard 65
Shelley, Percy 192
Shklovsky, Victor 192, 195, 196, 198, 199
Siebers, Tobin 192

INDEX

Simal, Begoña 162
Siskin, Clifford 216
Smith, Jeanne Rosie 162
Smith, Zadie 17
social consciousness 136
social structure 9, 94–7
sociology 42, 54 n.13
Socrates 184
Sohn-Rethel, Alfred 220
solidarity 87, 91, 96, 98, 99, 134, 159, 164, 165
solipsism 94, 95, 138, 141, 145, 147
Solnit, Rebecca 185
Sorensen, Eli Park 9, 261
South Africa 21, 261, 263
sovereign communication 95, 99
sovereign subjectivity 89
Spanish Flu Pandemic (1918) 88
spatial movement 111
Spencer, Herbert 71
Spindler, William 156–7
Stadialist discourse 250, 251
Stand and Deliver (1988) 204
state of emergency (1975) 231, 232
state of nature 252
state violence 230
Stendhal 32, 33, 61
Stern, J. P. 229, 241
Stone Butch Blues (Feinberg) 199
storytelling 136–8, 149, 158, 165, 179, 181–3, 185, 237–9
Such a Long Journey (Mistry) 231, 234, 236, 237, 240, 241, 244
Sugars, Cynthia 250
Summer, Star J. 52
Süskind, Patrick 156
symbolic forms 48–52, 53
sympathy 44–8, 53, 55 n.25
S/Z (Barthes) 5, 155

Taylor, Charles 173
Taylor, Jenny Bourne 69
temporality 7–14, 20, 42, 45, 99, 110, 112, 115, 116, 118, 122, 134, 142, 143, 145, 175, 177, 202, 210, 211, 234, 235, 241, 243, 250, 252, 255, 257, 258, 261
textuality 31, 36, 132

therapeutic relationship 63, 64
Toronto, Canada 231
totalitarianism 228
totality 8, 9, 155, 210, 221, 222, 228
totalization 5, 7, 8, 11, 13, 14, 209, 222
trans-corporeality 43
transgender literature 199
Transit (Cusk) 19, 169, 178–85
transnational capitalism 212
transnationalism 216, 248
"transposition d'art" 31
Trawl (Johnson) 18, 138–49, 151 n.38
tricksters 18, 162–3, 165, 166
Trollope, Antony 198
Trump, Donald 192
Trump administration 192
truth 16, 32, 42, 43, 45, 46, 61, 65–6, 68, 69, 74, 75, 123, 133, 134, 136–8, 141, 147
  cathartic 145–9
  novelistic 145, 147
  realist 135, 137
Truth and Reconciliation Commission 261, 263
Turner, Victor 162
Typhoon (Conrad) 82
typographic shape 139, 144

Ulysses (Joyce) 137, 250
Umwelt 213
United States 200, 201, 203, 252

Velie, Alan 163
Veracini, Lorenzo 252, 254, 255
Vermeulen, Pieter 2, 10, 11
Victorian age 41
Victory (2013) 204
Virchow, Rudolf 71
vocabulary 141
Voss (White) 262–4

Wakefield, Edward Gibbon 251
Ward, Megan 68
Warwick Research Collective 215
Washington Post 179
Waste Land, The (Eliot) 250

Watt, Ian   87, 143, 154, 155
web of life   220
Weismann, August   71
Weltanschauung   24 n.42
Welthaftigkeit   110, 123, 124
Western culture   185
Western epistemological-
    representational models   229
What Is a World? (Cheah)   12
White, Patrick   262
White Earth, The (McGahan)   263
Whitman, Walt   205
Wicomb, Zoe   263
Winton, Tim   255, 256, 264
Wire, The (TV series)   209, 210, 214

Wolf, Ror   17, 108–10, 112, 113, 115, 117, 119, 121–4, 130 n.59
Wolfe, Patrick   252, 253
Wolfzettel, Friedrich   71
Woodlanders, The (Hardy)   15, 62–3, 66–70, 72
Woolf, Virginia   137
world literature   2, 11–14, 215, 216, 248, 251
World Republic of Letters, The (Casanova)   250

Zero History (Gibson)   220
Zola, Émile   15, 16, 61–4, 66, 70–5, 78 n.53

www.ingramcontent.com/pod-product-compliance
Lightning Source LLC
Chambersburg PA
CBHW052215300426
44115CB00011B/1690